AF478271

MICHAEL CAINE

PHOTOGRAPHED BY TERRY O'NEILL

THE DEFINITIVE COLLECTION

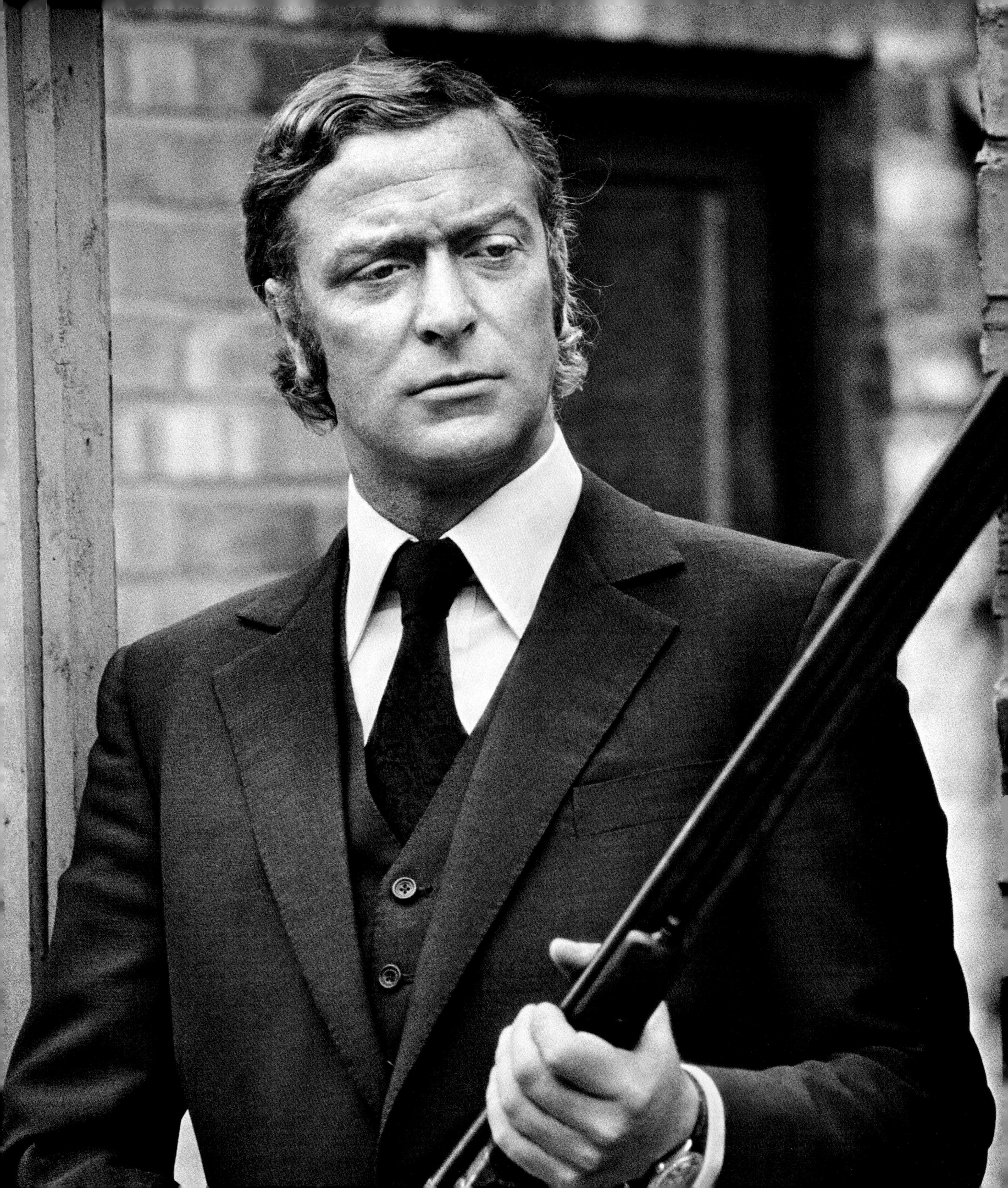

MICHAEL CAINE

PHOTOGRAPHED BY TERRY O'NEILL

THE DEFINITIVE COLLECTION

James Clarke

ACC ART BOOKS ICONIC IMAGES

CONTENTS

"Terry was a great friend. He was a member of our Mayfair Orphans club (a small band of friends who had lost their mothers) and we would meet for lunch with Doug Hayward (the celebrated tailor), and Philip Kingsley (noted trichologist) often. He was the most charming and cheeky photographer who got the best photographs by making everyone totally relaxed for his iconic shots. He knew and understood his subjects, he got the best photos by putting everyone at ease and made them trust him with humour.

Loved him dearly and miss him."

Sir Michael Caine

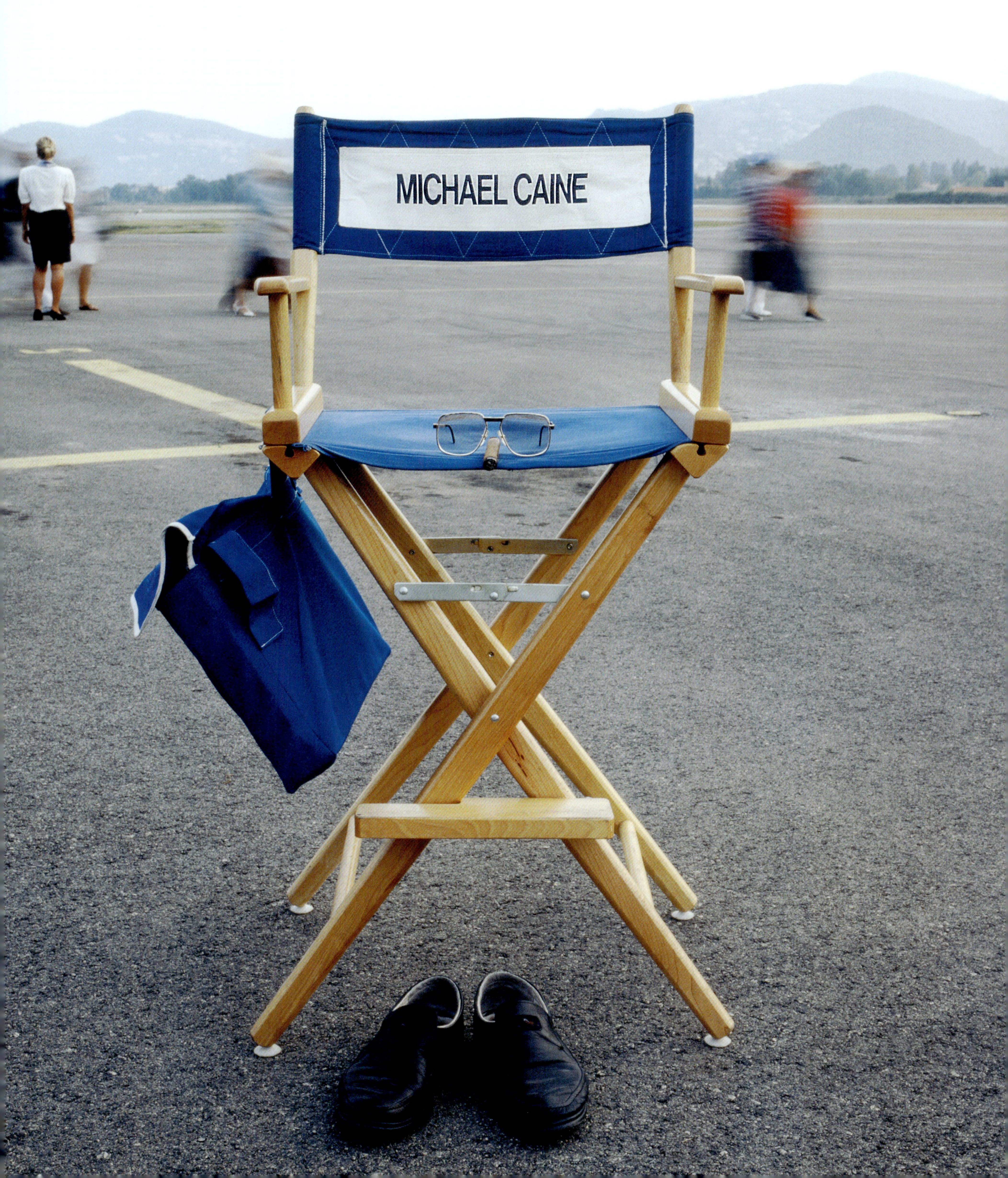
MICHAEL CAINE

Michael Caine
As Icon

In the rather miraculous fusion of being both 'themselves' and something more, movie stars can mean so much to so many. Movie stars have long held the position of aspirational dream figures and they certainly embodied that for this writer as a movie-obsessed child and teenager. It was a fascination shared by young Maurice Joseph Micklewhite Jr, born in 1933. As I grew up, my love of movies endured and I'm lucky to be able to incorporate that in my work as a writer. Young Maurice, however, grew up into the dream itself and became one of the world's biggest film stars: Sir Michael Caine. Starring across all movie genres, Caine's is an essential presence in film; his performances carefully calibrated, quietly pulling us into even the quietest moments on screen.

In his formative years, Caine attended drama class at a local youth club and, by all accounts, this is where Caine's fascination with acting was sparked. As a boy, Caine was mesmerised by cinema, enthusiastically reading biographies of famous actors. "...I had to be an actor. I wanted to be an actor. And of course, you have to remember with me, the alternative was a factory."[1] He was a movie fan who would become a movie star. His understanding of the allure of movie stars shaped his own screen image. In his memoirs he explains, "There's no one sure-fire trajectory to the movies, no one route to Hollywood. There's not one book to read, or one café to sit in. Your performance in all public arenas is part of the screen test."[2]

Whilst an actor might not necessarily set out to become famous and recognisable to all (they might want to just keep working), Michael Caine did find himself on a trajectory that took him from jobbing actor – starting in repertory theatre in London and Suffolk in the 1950s – and on towards film stardom. Caine's big-screen debut was in *A Hill in Korea* (1956). Despite his obvious talent, success was not guaranteed. Caine later observed: "There was no place allowed for the likes of me in the firmament of actors."[3]

But this wasn't true for long. The 1960s ushered in a fresh new era and with it came opportunities for young working-class men and women,

Opposite page: Caine, still wearing his trademark heavy-rimmed glasses

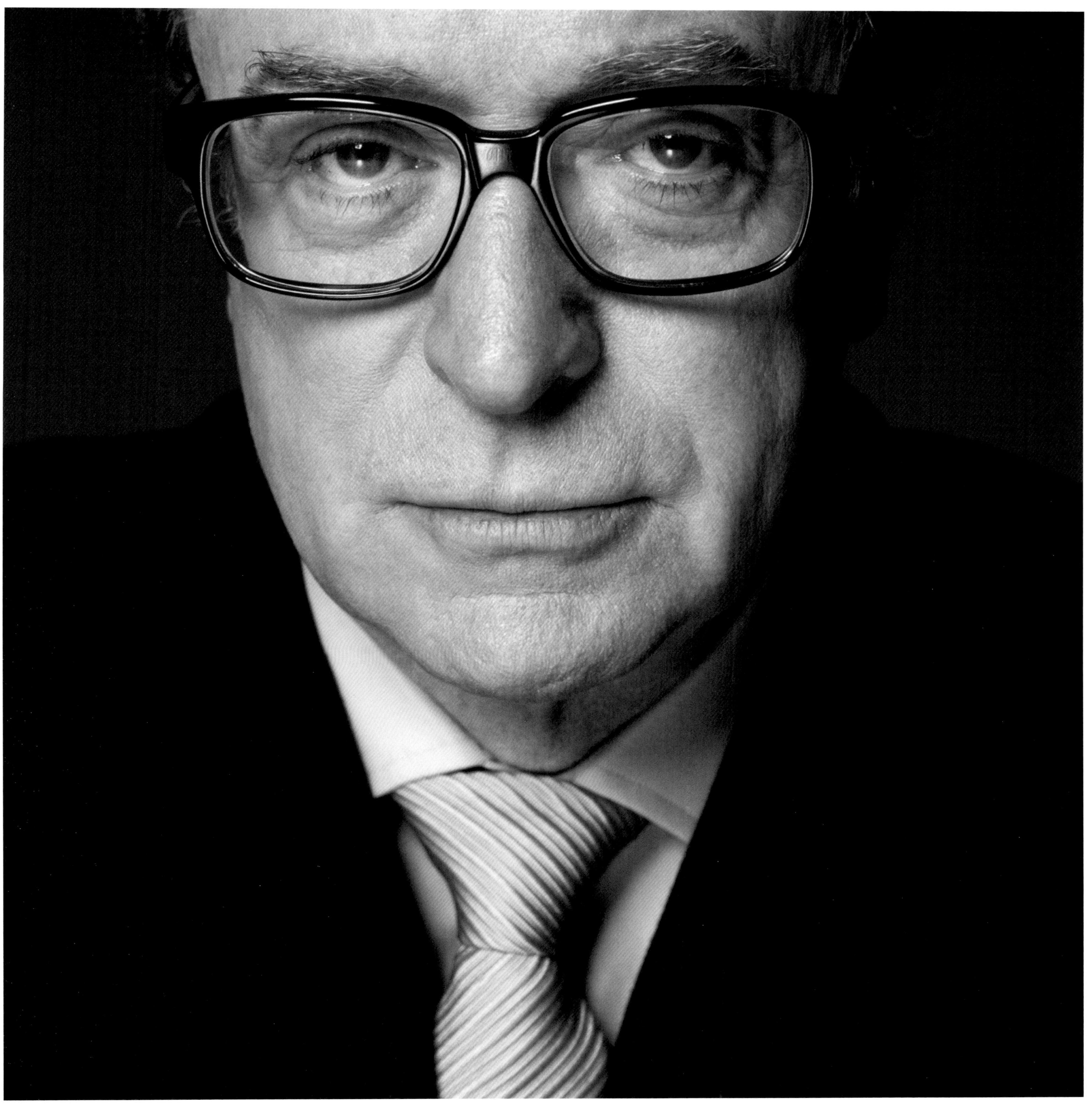

marking a seismic cultural shift. "Pop culture went bang, exploded and just kept going. Working class kids everywhere."[4] It was like something of the old world had fallen away as a result of World War II; a space had opened up and a number of Caine's generation of actors raced through the breach in the cultural defences. What they brought with them was grit, determination and authenticity. As Caine put it: "Behaving realistically and truthfully in front of a camera is an exacting craft, one that requires steadfast discipline and application."[5]

That sense of truth has sustained Caine's career and a number of the films included in this book have endured as essential Caine classics. His apparent 'ease' at expressing the truth of a character in terms of how they behave, act and react can be seen in his early work: *Zulu* (1964) being a notable entry with another being the title role in *Alfie* (1966), which centred on the swinging '60s life of a London womaniser.

Critically, Caine was considered a working-class hero who made it big in the movies and this was a watershed moment.

One of the appeals of Caine's performances lies in the way in which he can acutely get at the fragility of the male ego. Caine once said of portraying Harry Palmer – and similar characters – that "I've always played real people... Because I was a loser. Until I started playing losers, I never became a success."[6]

Certainly, with *The Ipcress File* (1965), Caine's screen image began to coalesce and something fundamental to Harry Palmer has been an undercurrent of so many Caine performances. Yes, he has portrayed a wide range of characters across so many genres, but the foundational work that he did during the 1960s has endured. As film historian David Parkinson puts it: "Demonstrating his knack for phlegmatic improvisation, Caine's first starring role also revealed an ease with cerebral complexities, acerbic wit and cool insubordination that would become his 1960s trademark."[7]

Talking about trademarks... The story goes that, having seen the rushes, the studio heads were nervous, demanding a more 'traditionally male' portrayal of Harry Palmer. But, as Robin Stummer wrote in his introduction to his conversation with Len Deighton (who created the literary character of Harry Palmer), *The Ipcress File* connected with a time and mood when "...London was in full swing. Like Harry Palmer – Michael Caine's sullen, cuisine-and-'girl'-addicted character – the British were feeling insubordinate, bolshie and confident. So, the heavy, black-rimmed glasses remained on Caine's deadpan, alabaster face, thereby making a 60s icon; his 'girl' left the kitchen work to the man; and Harry made a Spanish omelette."[8]

Those Curry & Paxton glasses (also seen in *The Italian Job)* became Caine's trademark item. In something of a testament to this association, even now the company espouses the connection on their website. There's another dynamic at work in all this talk of film fame and it's this: the longstanding relationship between movie stars and fashion. In the early phase of his career Caine established his fashion credentials and what could rightly be described as a 'cool Britannia' sensibility.

Opposite page: Caine in his early years as an emerging film star in *Funeral in Berlin.*

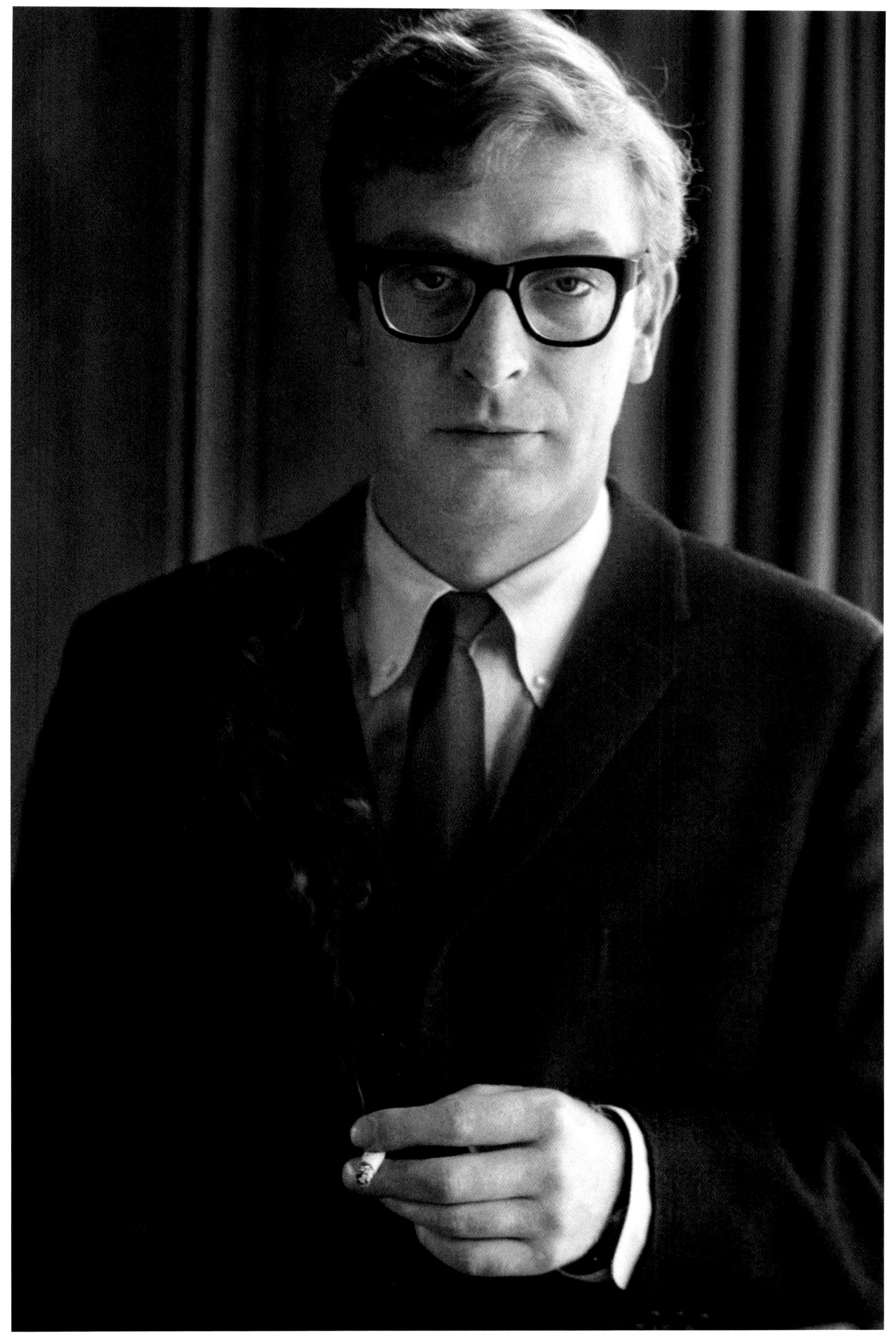

An article in GQ magazine recently noted: "Caine's approach to fashion is centred around the classics – double breasted suits, printed ties, pocket squares, polo necks – and the decade that kicked off the style he became known for was the 1960s. With Caine's consistently good tailoring, underlayers, overcoats and loafers (always leather, FYI), there's a bunch of lessons to learn from him during this period."[9] Staples of Caine's urbane sartorial elegance would be: the black turtleneck, cardigan, mac, leather jacket and double-breasted suit. Terry O'Neill's photographs offer plenty of images that capture this signature style.

Another Caine trademark is his oft-mimicked 'Cockney' accent. However, Caine grew up in The Elephant and Castle, a patch of London just south of the River Thames. Geography, therefore, dictates that he is not a Cockney at all. As Caine noted in his memoirs: "After all the years in the business, some people still think of me as a professional Cockney. As if people were paid for being Cockney. I'm actually from South London, not Bow, and any day of the week you will find 1.3 million Cockneys more authentic than me."[10]

For all his creative and commercial success, the span of an enduring career like Caine's has also known its moments of career uncertainty, doubt and wondering whether there might ever be any more satisfying and rewarding roles. One of the films included in this book, *Midnight in St. Petersburg*, proved to be, as Caine recalls it in his memoir, "...my worst professional experience ever.[11] However, even if it marked an end of sorts it therefore signalled a beginning, too. Soon after, he went to on to appear in *Blood and Wine* (1997) with Jack Nicholson and Caine found his energies and enthusiasm for the work renewed. Indeed, this turnaround bears out Caine's philosophy: "Use the difficulty."[12]

And use it he did: Caine is one of the highest grossing actors of all time. As of 2020, he has appeared in over 130 films,[13] has been Oscar-nominated six times and won twice – for his roles in *Hannah & Her Sisters* in 1987 and *The Cider House Rules* in 2000. From thrillers and spy dramas, including such totemic titles as *The Ipcress File, Get Carter* and *The Fourth Protocol*, to comedies – *Hannah And Her Sisters, Dirty Rotten Scoundrels* and *Educating Rita* – Caine has starred in a body of now-iconic movies. Then, too, there are the cult movies – less widely-known but cherished, nonetheless, by smaller and highly dedicated audiences; a film like *Deadfall* (featured in this book), for example.

Considering Caine's image, then: in the movies themselves and in the mass of promotional images that span six decades and that spin out of and surround those movies, Caine is a major figure, an iconic figure; not only on account of his affecting performances and film-star aura, but also because his career is a lens through which to view the ebb and flow of British, European and American cinema. At the time of writing, Caine's most recent movie, *Tenet* (2020), has been released and, as such, it places Caine right in front of a new generation of audiences and – like his other appearances in Christopher Nolan's films – assures him participation in another decade of movies. The '50s, '60s, '70s, '80s, '90s, '00s, '10s and, now, the '20s all have Michael Caine in them.

Opposite: Caine with his wife, Shakira. In his memoirs, Caine recalls thinking the first time he saw her: 'That girl is the most beautiful girl in the world.'

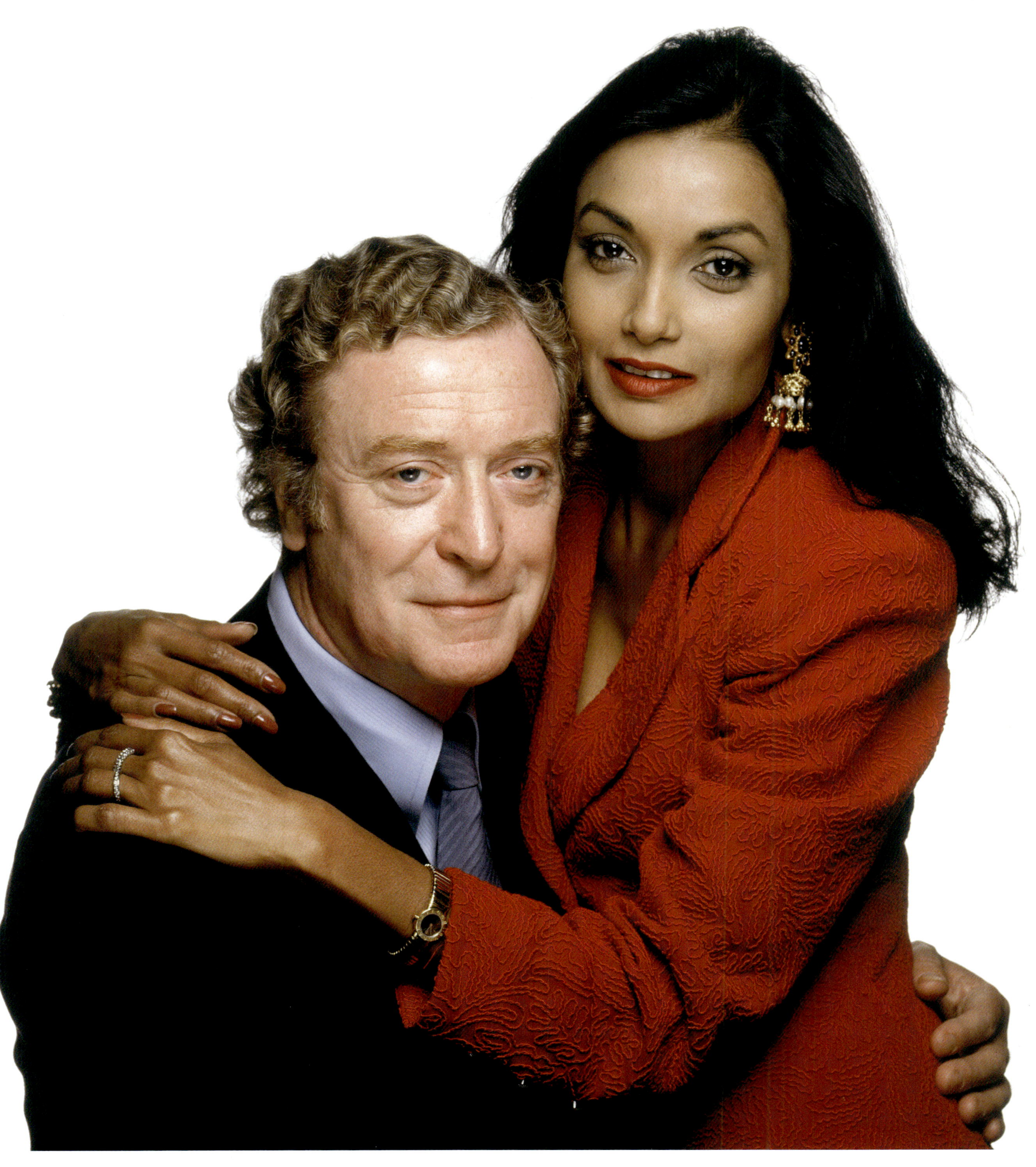

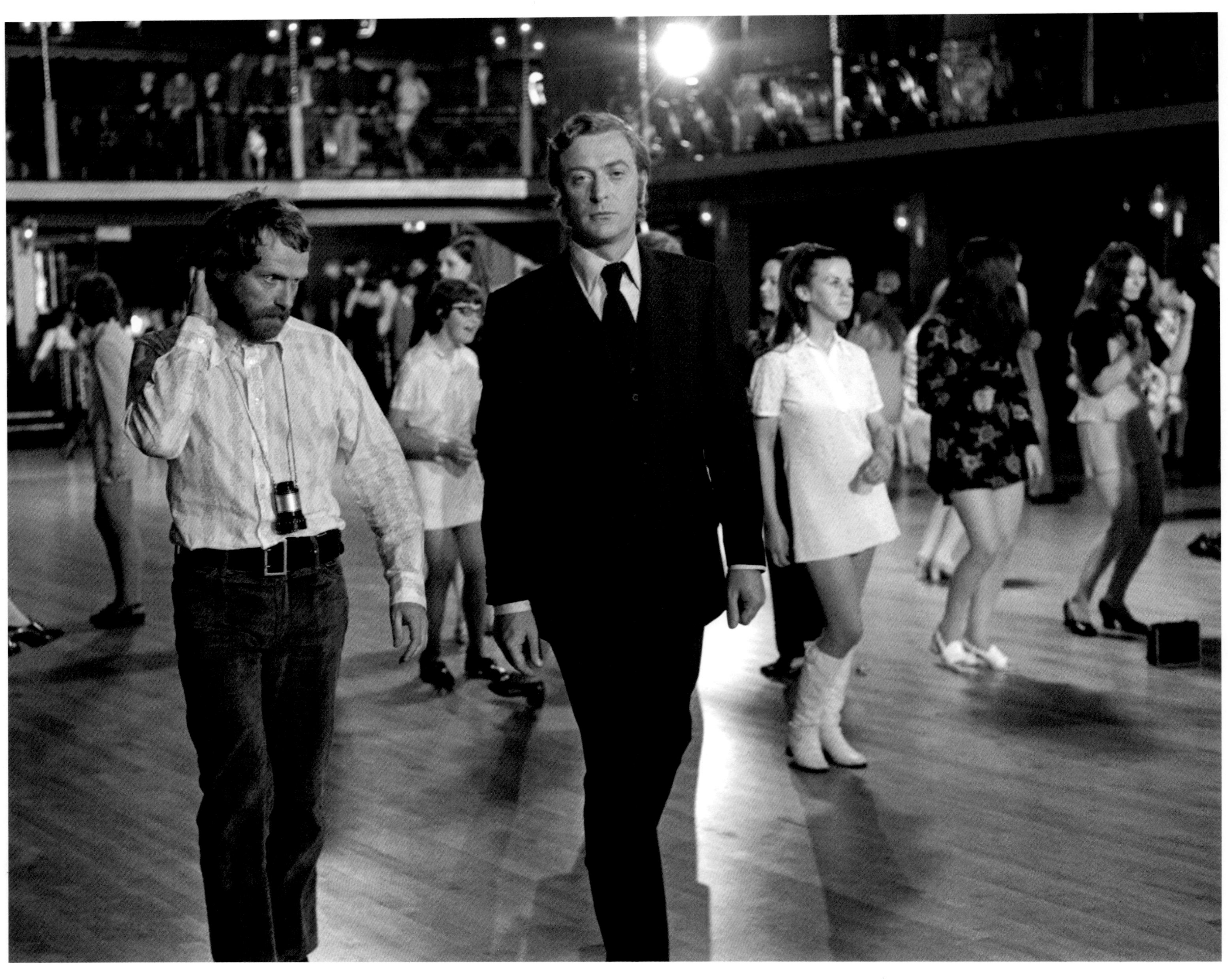

Above: On location for *Get Carter* as Caine and director Mike Hodges cross the floor of the Oxford Galleries, a famous dance venue in Newcastle upon Tyne.

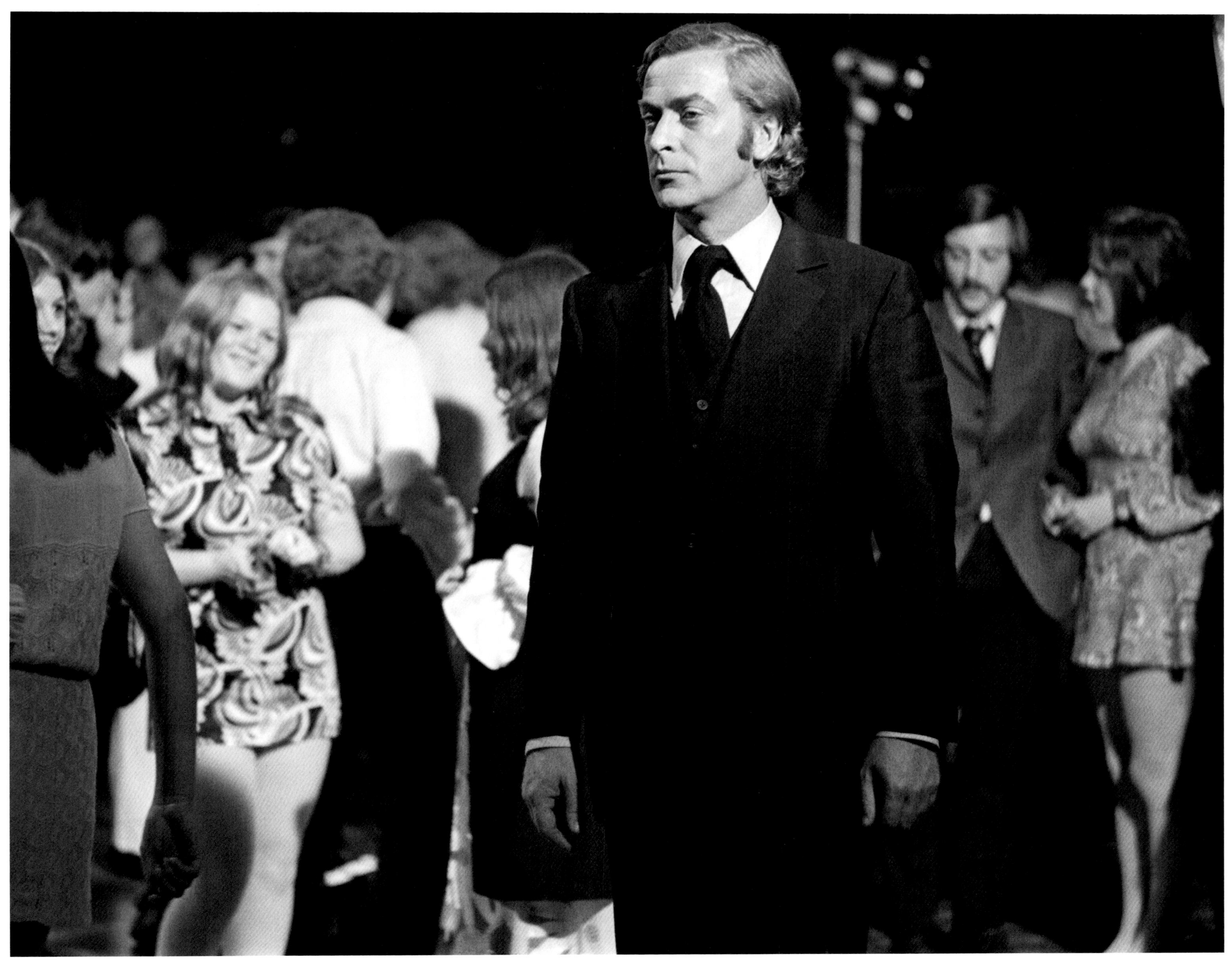

Above: In his Dormeuil Tonik® suit, Jack Carter (Michael Caine) exudes style.

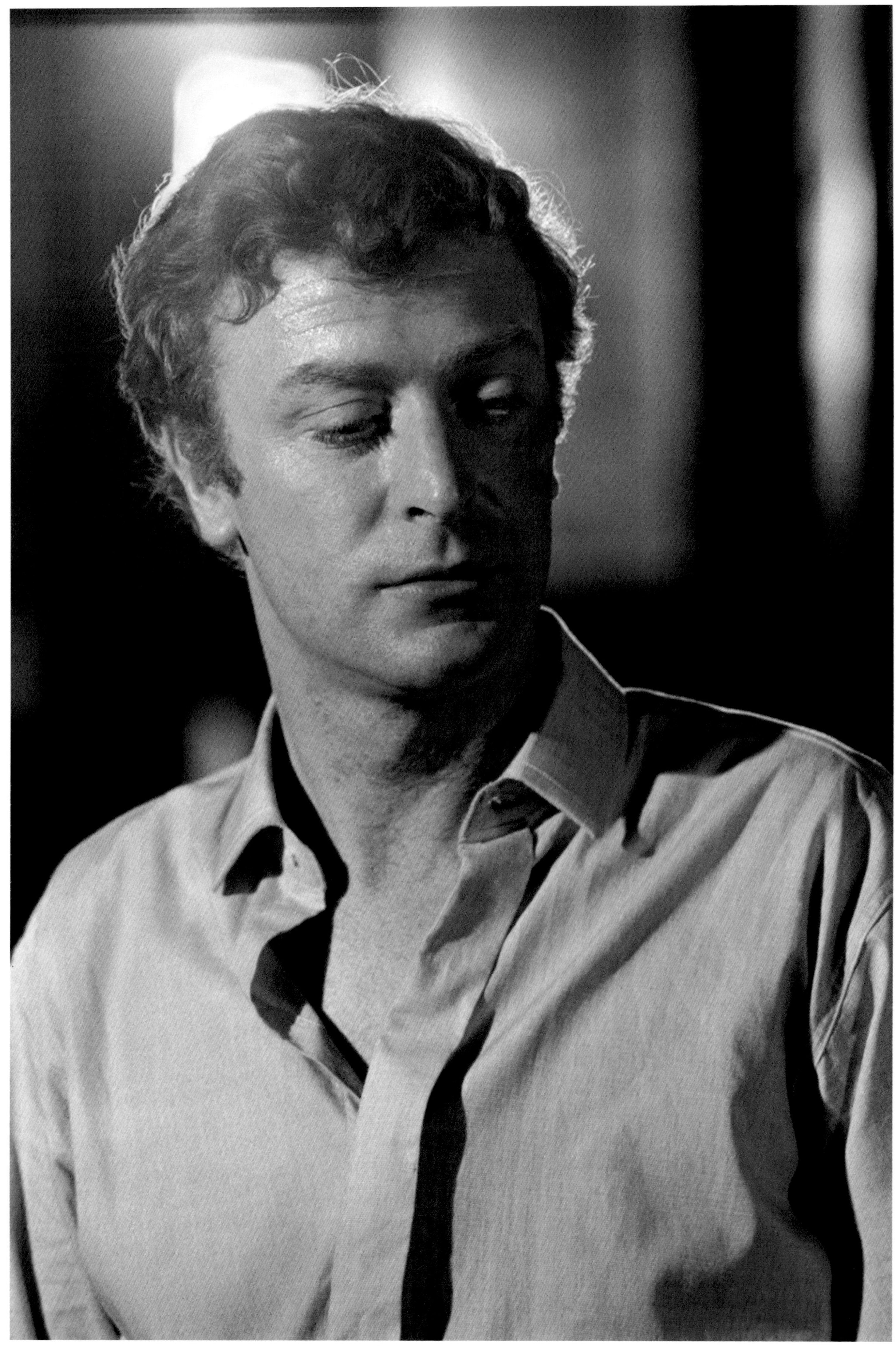

Michael really embodies the characters he plays. He's also one of the only actors who can take on a serious role one minute, a thriller the next and then follow up with a comedy. He's just incredibly gifted.

Terry O'Neill

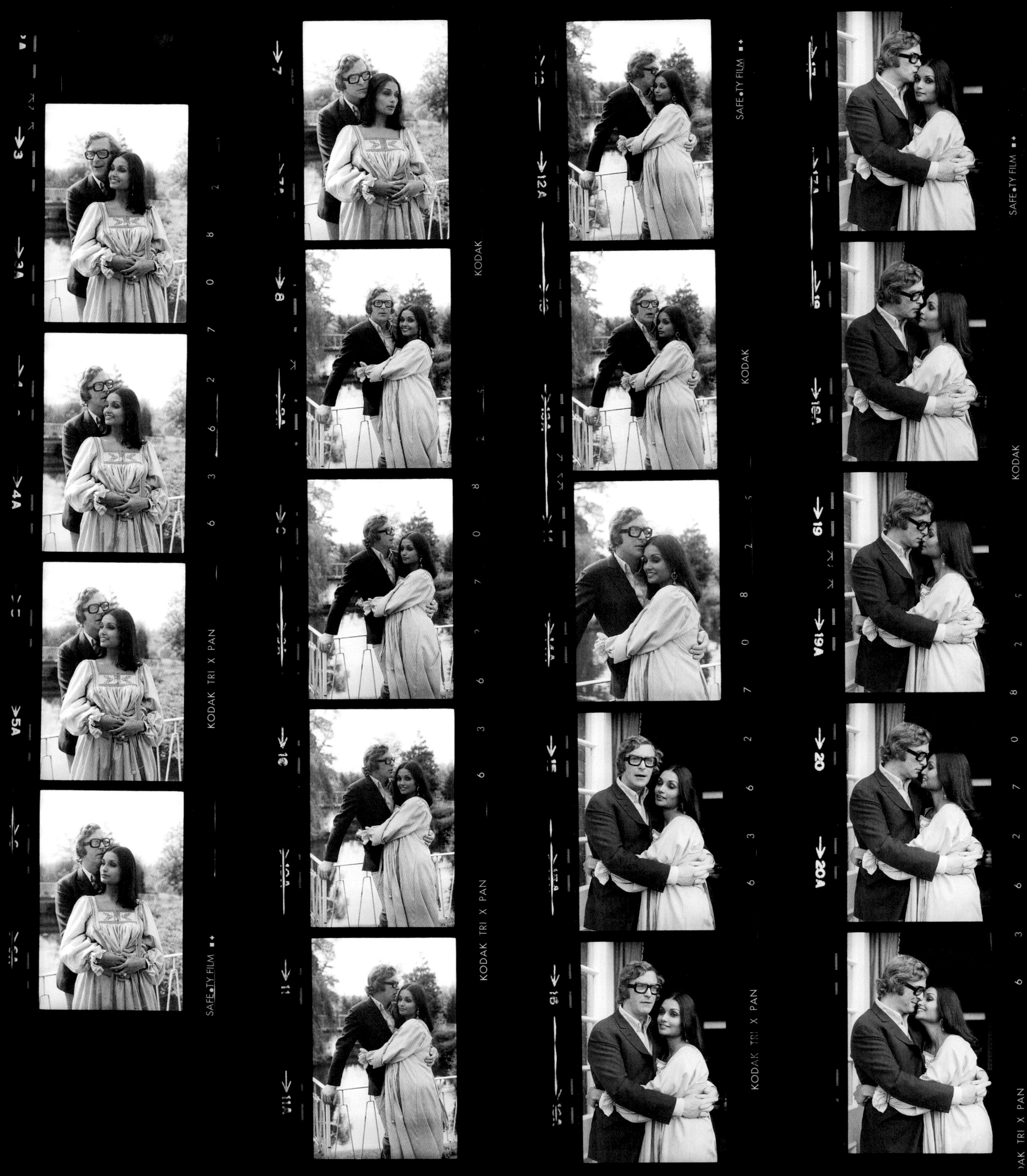
KODAK TRI X PAN
KODAK
SAFETY FILM

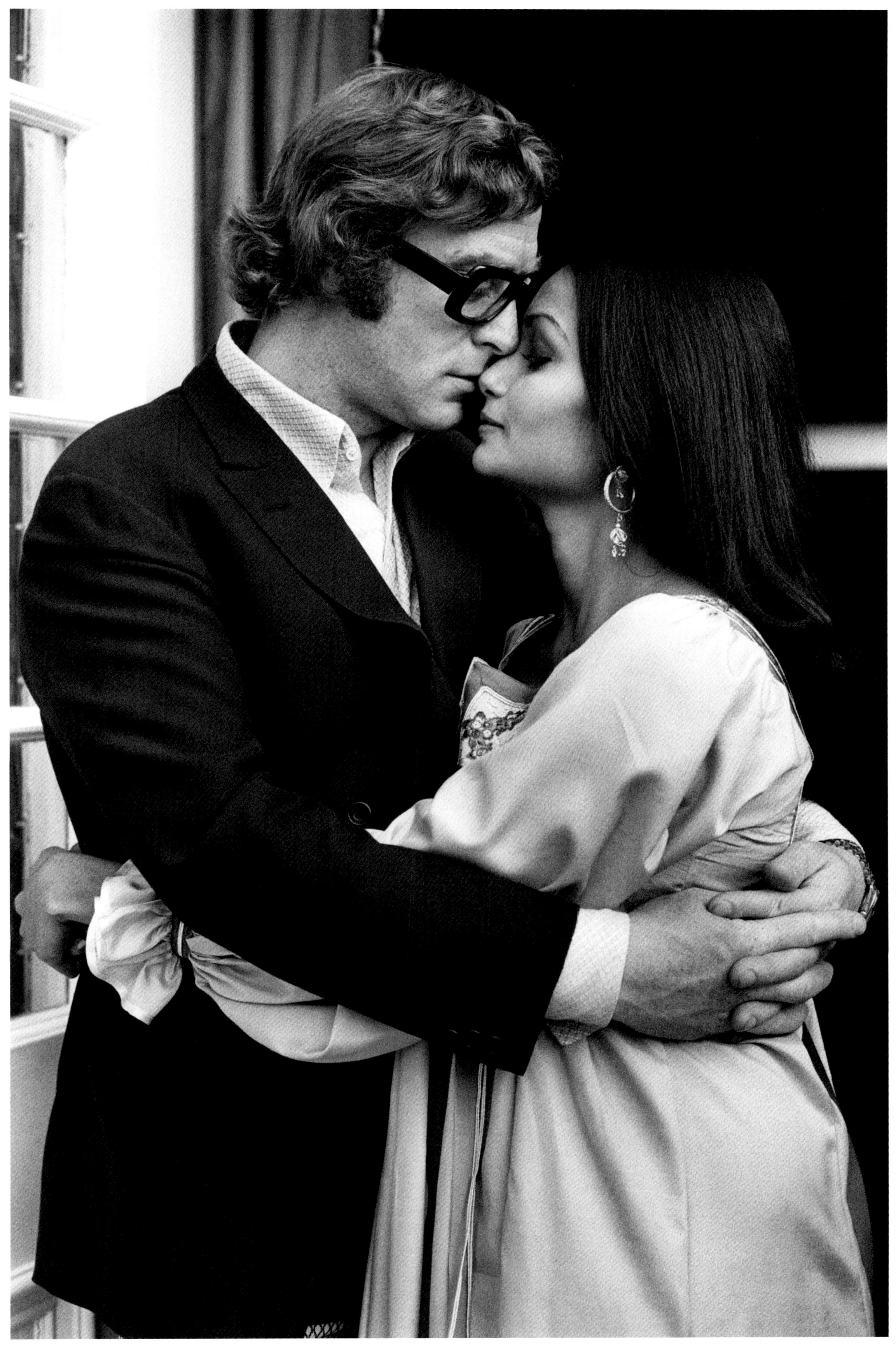

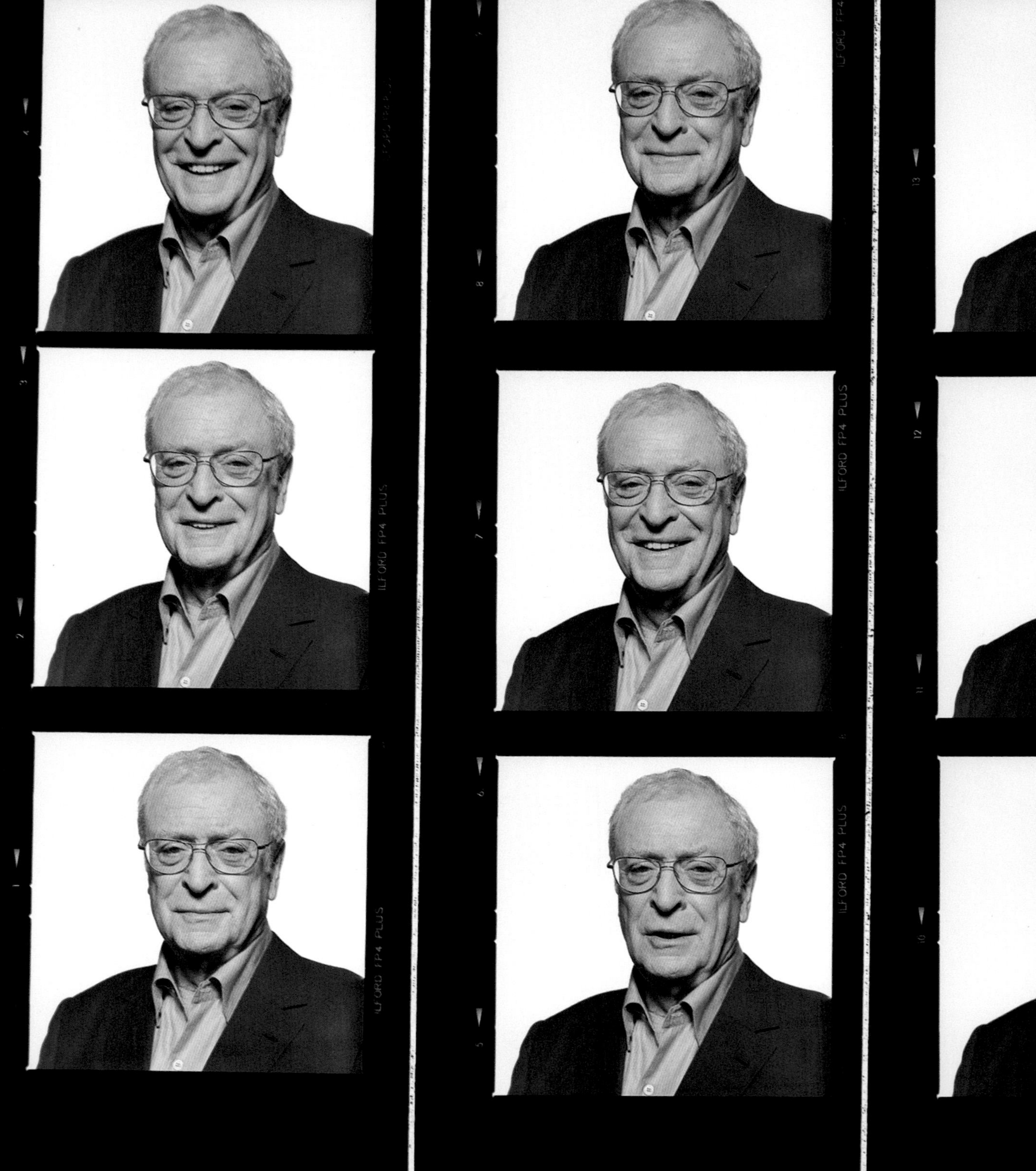

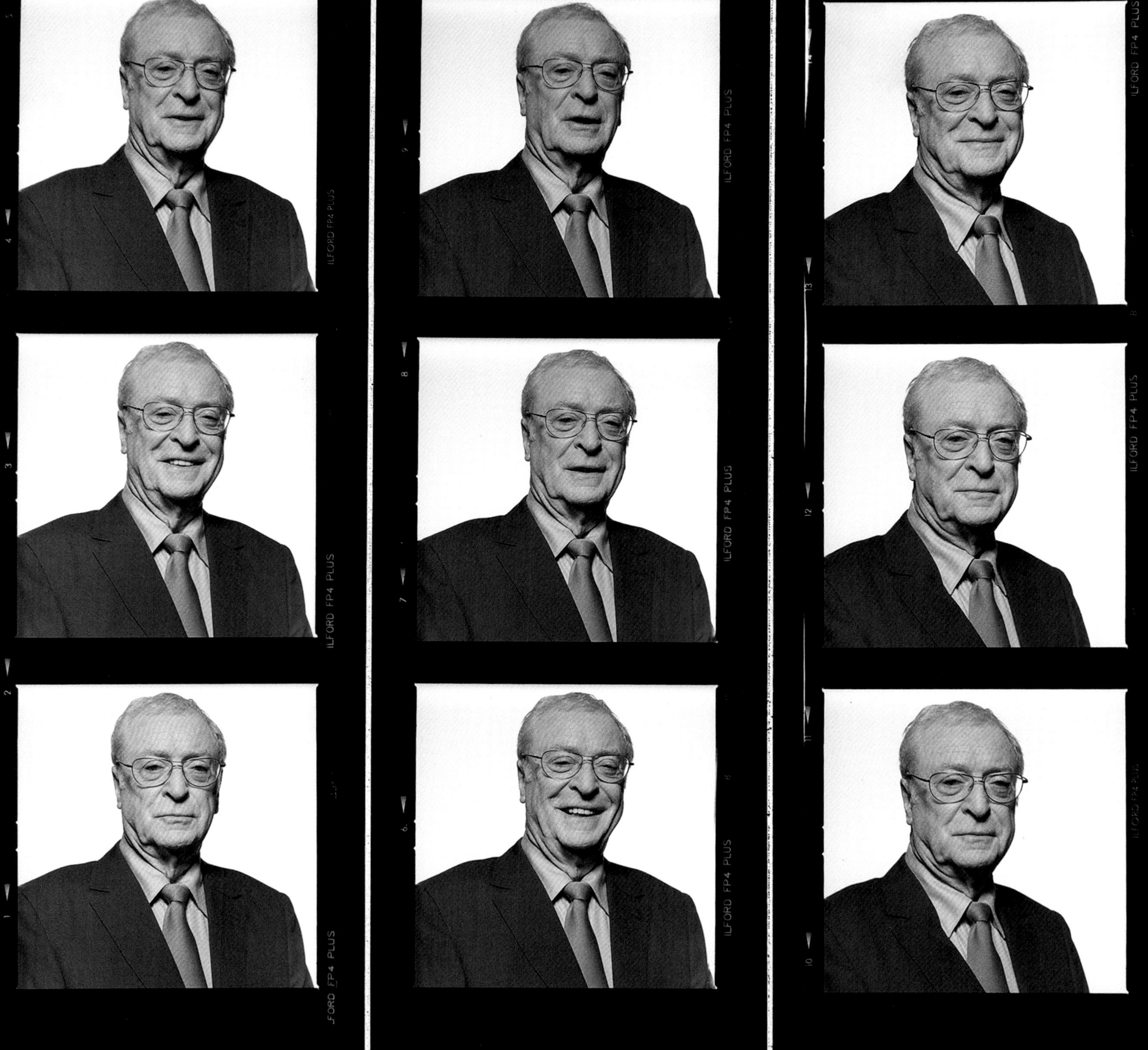

Terry O'Neill
Pop Culture Image Maker

On 17 November 2019 – a quiet, chilly morning – the world awoke to the news that Terry O'Neill had died. Immediately, print and online channels filled with heartfelt expressions of admiration for his work and his professionalism.

Firmly established as one of the major photographers of the 20th century, the story of how O'Neill got started in his career and, eventually, found himself venturing into the world of British and Hollywood film industries makes for an intriguing and charming read. It was certainly a long way from his earliest intention to train for the priesthood. As O'Neill once recalled: "I was told I had too many questions to be a priest. I loved jazz and my heart was set on being a jazz drummer."[1]

In the hopes of finding a job that would get him to New York (and its jazz clubs), O'Neill applied to work for BOAC (later British Airways) as an air steward. However, fate intervened and whilst the company didn't have any openings for an air steward, they did give him a job in the photographic unit at Heathrow airport. One day O'Neill took a candid photography of R.A. 'Rab' Butler, the then Home Secretary, taking a nap in the departure lounge at Heathrow. This was the moment that would change the direction of his career path. The image caught the interest of Fleet Street and O'Neill was given a job on a newspaper called the *Daily Sketch;* he was aged just twenty.

Of his developing approach to the art and craft of photography and the profession and how that proved to be a case of the right man in the right place at the right time, O'Neill has explained: "I was totally self-taught, and I didn't know what I was doing."[2] He admits: "(*The Daily Sketch*) took me on because I was a musician, and the editor had an inkling that pop music was going to be big in the '60s. They said: 'your first job is to go down to Abbey Road and photograph this new group called The Beatles' – and that was the start of my life."[3]

In an interview with *The Daily Telegraph*, O'Neill recalled that "I'd do five or six jobs a day, while the old timers wanted to do one and go back to the darkroom and play shove ha'penny." This ensured he fast became one

Opposite page: Terry O'Neill and his camera. Whether shooting documentary-style on a set or capturing an actor in or out of character, every image intrigues and invites you into the moment.

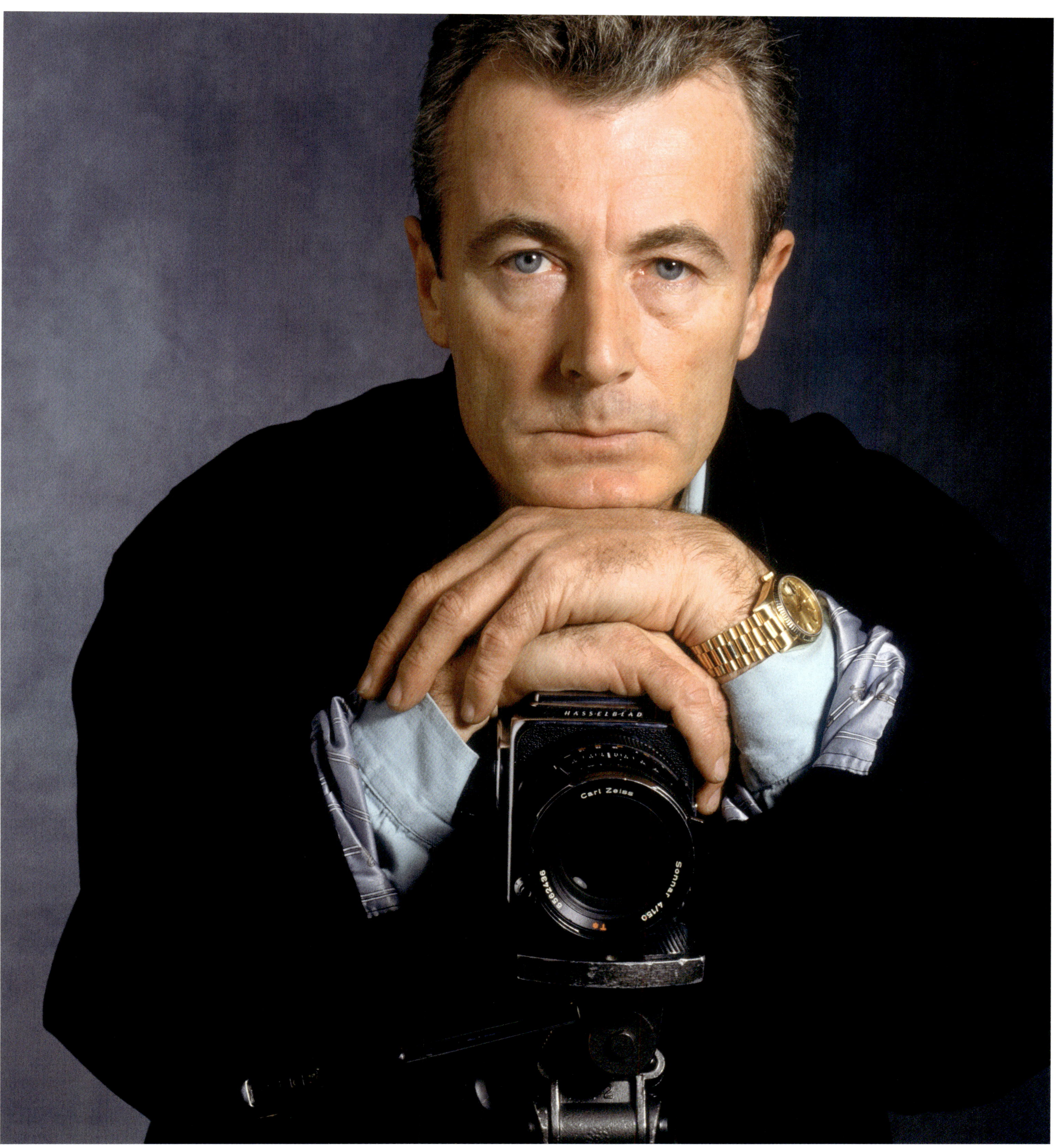
HASSELBLAD
Carl Zeiss
Sonnar 4/150

of the most published photographers of the Sixties. "Within two weeks I had photographed the Beatles and the Stones...nobody ever fazed me after that."[4]

O'Neill recognised that youth culture was becoming a major force to contend with during the early 1960s and that this game-changing moment was not confined to pop music and fashion but also included the movies. "I started to do film-set photography in the mid-1960s. Up until that point, I was mainly known for taking photos of musicians such as The Beatles, The Animals, The Dave Clark Five and The Rolling Stones. Don't get me wrong, I loved taking those photos. I wanted to be a musician myself, so music-based photography was a very natural fit. But I knew that if I was going to have a lasting career as a photographer, I needed to diversify."[5]

O'Neill's move into film stills photography offered just the right opportunity, as his exacting methods resulted in images that perfectly capture a film star's presence in and out of character. His images of film stars belong to a moment in time when other photographers such as David Bailey and Douglas Kirkland were capturing the allure of the film star and the worlds of fashion and style. O'Neill was notable for photographing actors and actresses in moments of candour, away from a more posed and designed set up. O'Neill would bring a journalistic aesthetic of immediacy to so many of his images. In turn, that immediacy captured the film star's essential allure and appeal.

In an interview with *The Daily Telegraph,* O'Neill described his technique as "...chasing what's known as 'the bull', as in bullseye – the centre spread of the Sketch's tabloid pages. I thought, I've got to get that spread, and it was always in me. I'd plan one image, down to the last detail and it all worked from there."[6]

O'Neill's newspaper experience informed his sense of how a photo might work best within a layout and O'Neill has explained how he would shoot with a newspaper or magazine spread in mind when composing his images. "So confident is O'Neill of his ability to recognize a picture or a picture sequence that he will have nothing to do with motorized cameras, even to the extent of insisting that he would not regard a frame selected from a burst fired off with such equipment as his picture at all, but something simply recorded by a cumbersome and over noisy machine."[7]

O'Neill's compelling body of work in the world of movies reminds us of the value that still photographs continue to have for studios in the promotion of their films. They can provide and tap into a sense of audience anticipation for that rather magical, first look at a movie before, even, a trailer is released.

O'Neill's photography proved that photos of leading men had value and his plentiful images of Caine were a part of this shift in pop culture.

For movie work, O'Neill typically used either a Nikon or a Leica M4 – getting the most out of its 50mm lens with Tri-X exposed at 1/125 sec at f/2.8. Of his trusty (near silent) Leica, which he used for rehearsals and takes, O'Neill explained: "The Leica was very important to me. It was a fabulous camera to use – quick

Opposite page: Caine in the mid-1980s; a time of commercial and creative success for Caine in Britain and the USA.

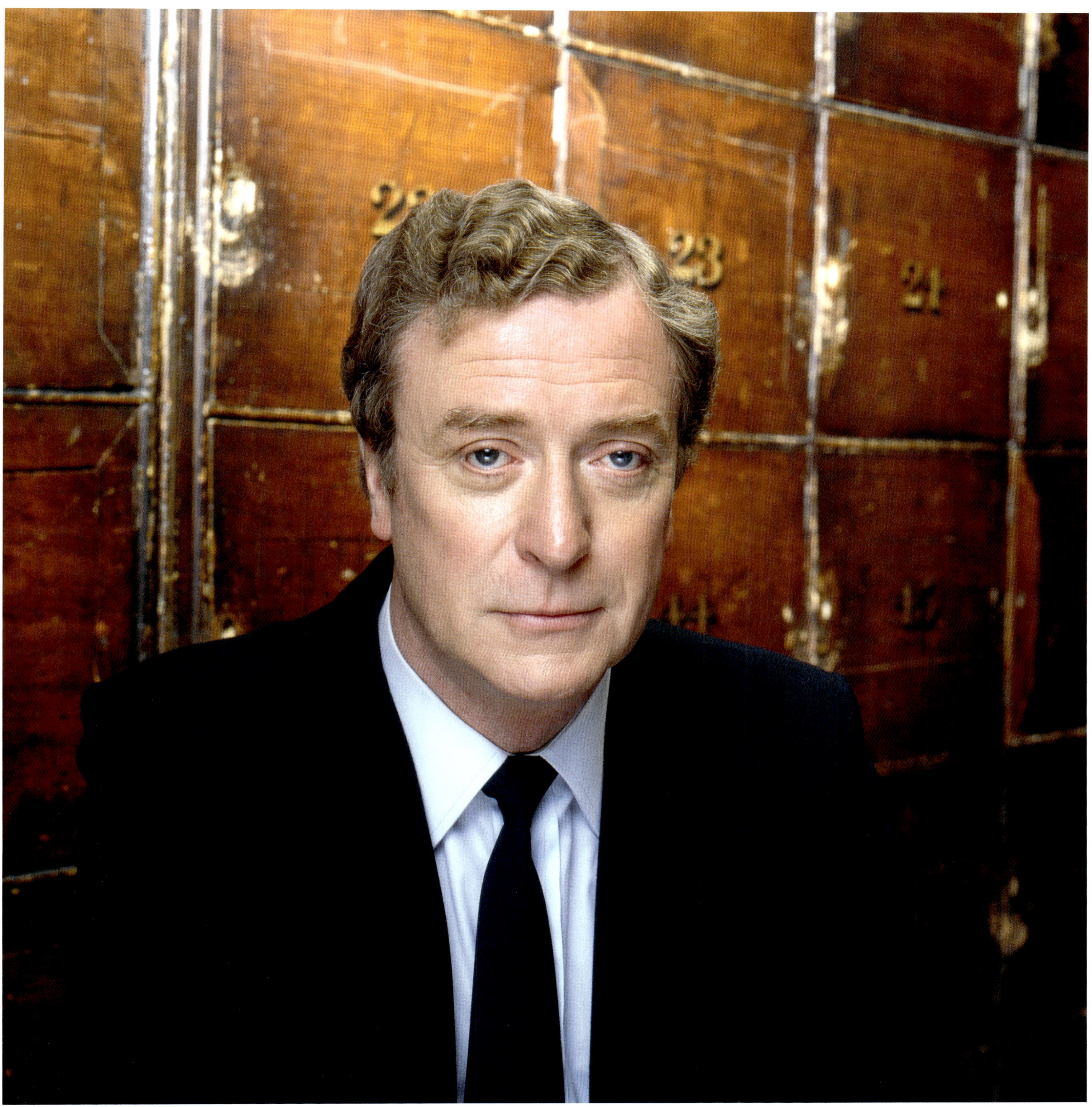

as a flash, anywhere, anytime..."[8] The Nikon was for the photographic portraits that he shot of actors in and out of character. In more controlled settings, he would turn to his trusty Hasselblad. O'Neill noted, "when I was doing portraits, like for *Dirty Rotten Scoundrels*, that's when I'd use the Hasselblad. I had time to set the scene."[9] O'Neill's photographs certainly attest to how film starts are a magical combination of both themselves and the characters they portray on screen.

At the time of his death, Terry O'Neill was internationally recognised as one of the greatest photographers of the 20th Century. Perhaps best known for his work with A-list music stars – The Beatles, The Rolling Stones, Elton John and Bowie – and portraits of icons such as Audrey Hepburn; he was also one of the most important figures in film stills photography of the 1960s to '90s. And his contribution to film and popular culture did not go unnoticed: in summer 2019, he was awarded the CBE in the Queen's Birthday Honours List, receiving his medal in October 2019 from the Duke of Cambridge in an investiture ceremony at Buckingham Palace. Of this career-capping recognition, O'Neill said with quiet pride: "It's a real recognition for the art of photography."[10]

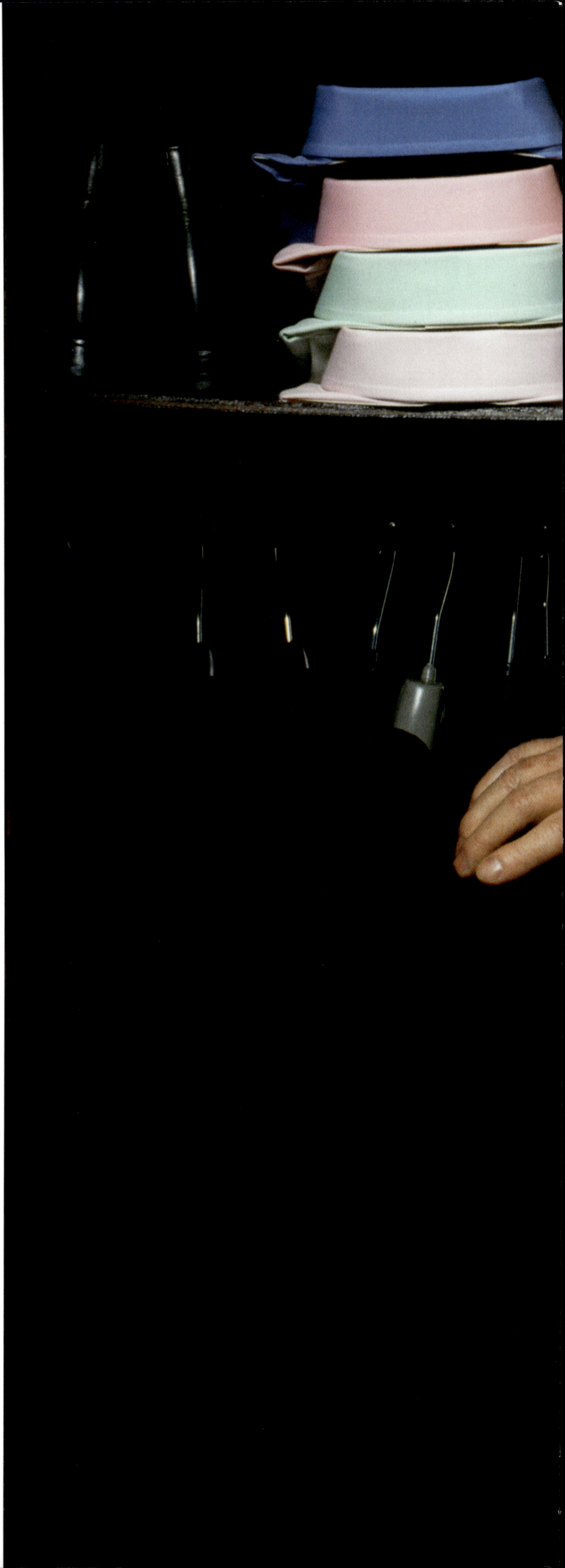

Caine has long been synonymous with good tailoring and sharp urban style.

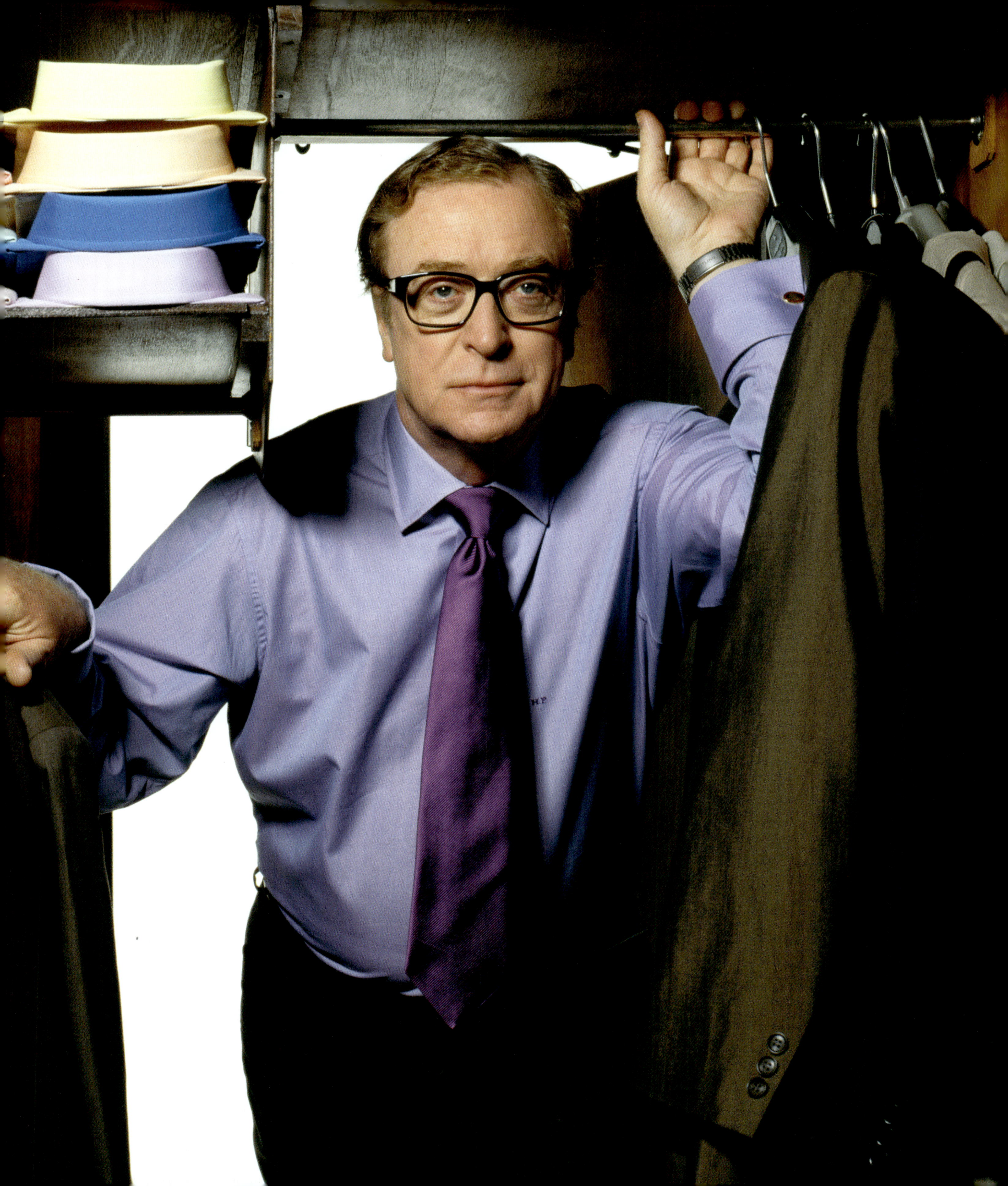

Michael and Terry
Collaborators and Friends

In his memoir, Caine recalls "I first met Terry O'Neill when he took my photograph. By the time we met he had already photographed the Queen in her palace at Sandringham and Frank Sinatra in his palace – the Fontainebleau Hotel in Miami, where he was surrounded by his version of palace guards – and we became firm friends."[1]

Terry O'Neill was not just a friend but also a fan: "Michael really embodies the characters he plays. He's one of the only actors who can take on a serious role one minute, a thriller the next and then follow up with a comedy. He's just incredibly gifted. Just look at what he did in the mid-sixties; he plays a serious detective the one minute, a sly comedy the next, and then back to the detective. I can't think of another actor that has so much versatility."[2]

O'Neill's photographs resound in their capacity to draw out the inner life of an actor or something of the character that they are portraying...elegantly composed portraits... candid on the fly pictures...his contribution to the visual pop culture starting in the early '60s found an ally in Michael Caine.

During a career that spanned six decades, O'Neill photographed almost every major film star, his innate discretion gaining him intimate access: "When working, I stayed anonymous. I never joined the entourage, I stayed in the shadows to get my photographs. But, of course, I got to know them privately and I got to know them as ordinary people who happened to have jobs as rock or film stars. That enabled me to capture the real personality behind the image being projected on stage or screen. And Caine, yeah, he's a great mate."[3]

O'Neill's photographs chart Caine's growth as a screen actor and a screen presence. There are images here that document an actor at work and others that suggest the rapport between photographer and subject. Certainly, the professional collaboration and friendship between Caine and O'Neill brings a real warmth to many of the images. Shot after shot, these photographs crystallise what Caine is about: that combination of craft and charisma.

This book, then, celebrates Michael Caine the actor, movie star and pop culture icon through the perceptive lens of Terry O'Neill.

Opposite page: Caine and O'Neill: collaborators and friends.

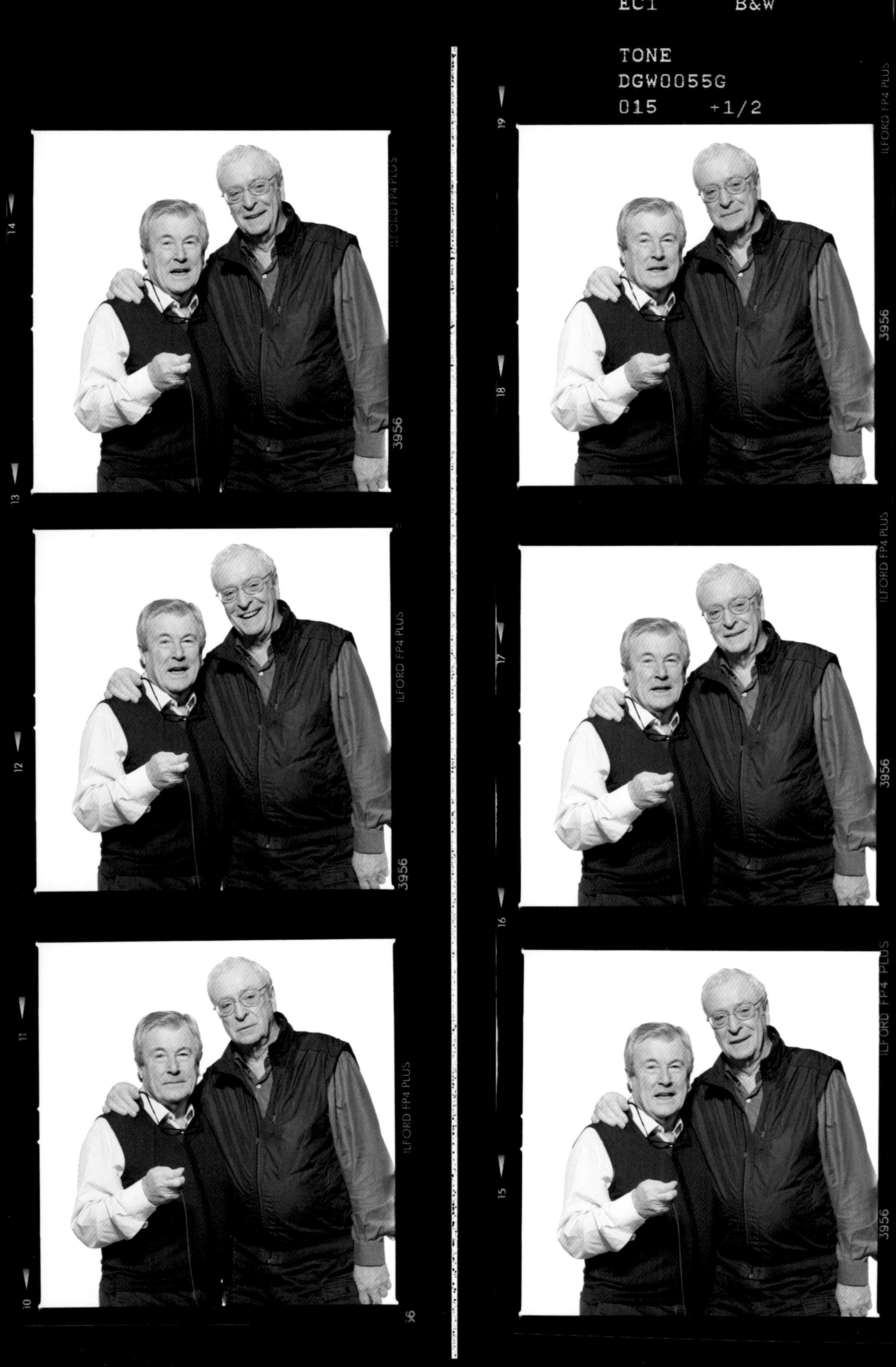

EC1 B&W
TONE
DGW0055G
015 +1/2
ILFORD FP4 PLUS
3956

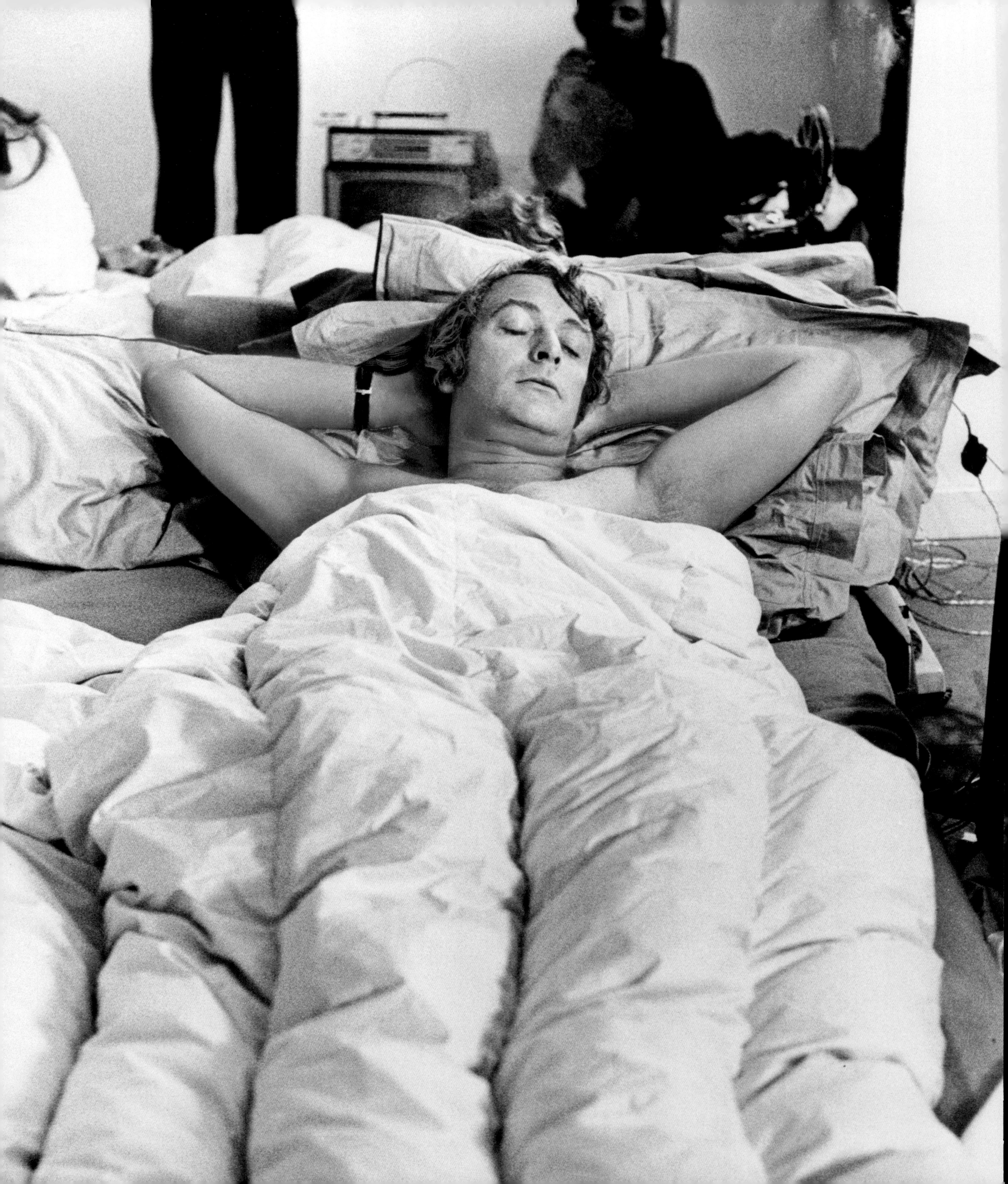

FUNERAL IN BERLIN

1966

"Funeral in Berlin is a key title among the 1960s British cycle of spy films, tapping as they did into the zeitgeist around the Cold War."

In this major title in his body of work in the thriller and espionage genres, Caine reprises the character of Harry Palmer from *The Ipcress File* (1965), his first proper starring role. Palmer was key to defining Caine's screen persona and lay the foundation for how the audience perceives Caine. But of course, as Caine points out in his autobiography, *The Elephant to Hollywood*, this is all part of the illusion, he is not like his characters: "Those are all people that I know, not people that I am."[1]

Funeral in Berlin is a key title among the 1960s British cycle of spy films, tapping as they did into the zeitgeist around the Cold War. In a promotional short film about the making of the movie, Caine comments about the Berlin Wall: "It's an awful thing, but somehow, it's fascinating. You find yourself walking around in a sort of atmosphere of ghosts... You get the feeling of violence at any time."[2]

Based on Len Deighton's third Harry Palmer novel, the film's premise sees Palmer given the job of going to Berlin to arrange for the defection of a Soviet spy. Sure enough, Palmer finds himself embroiled in a tangle of competing interests. Caine plays the role of Len Deighton's loner character with conviction, deftly employing his spectacles as a character aid – "I wore glasses naturally so I knew how to use glasses..." – despite the Studio's initial concern that they emasculated Palmer.[3]

Harry Saltzman, producer of *The Ipcress File*, saw Harry Palmer as the antithesis of James Bond and Saltzman more than anyone would surely be attuned to that contrast having co-produced the two earliest Bond movies *Dr No* (1962) and *From Russia With Love* (1963). To paraphrase film scholar Alan Burton, the Bond movies are spy-thrillers, whereas the Harry Palmer movies are espionage drama.[4]

Previous page: Caine takes a nap on the set of *Funeral in Berlin.*
Opposite page: On location at the Berlin Hilton for the restaurant scene in *Funeral in Berlin.*

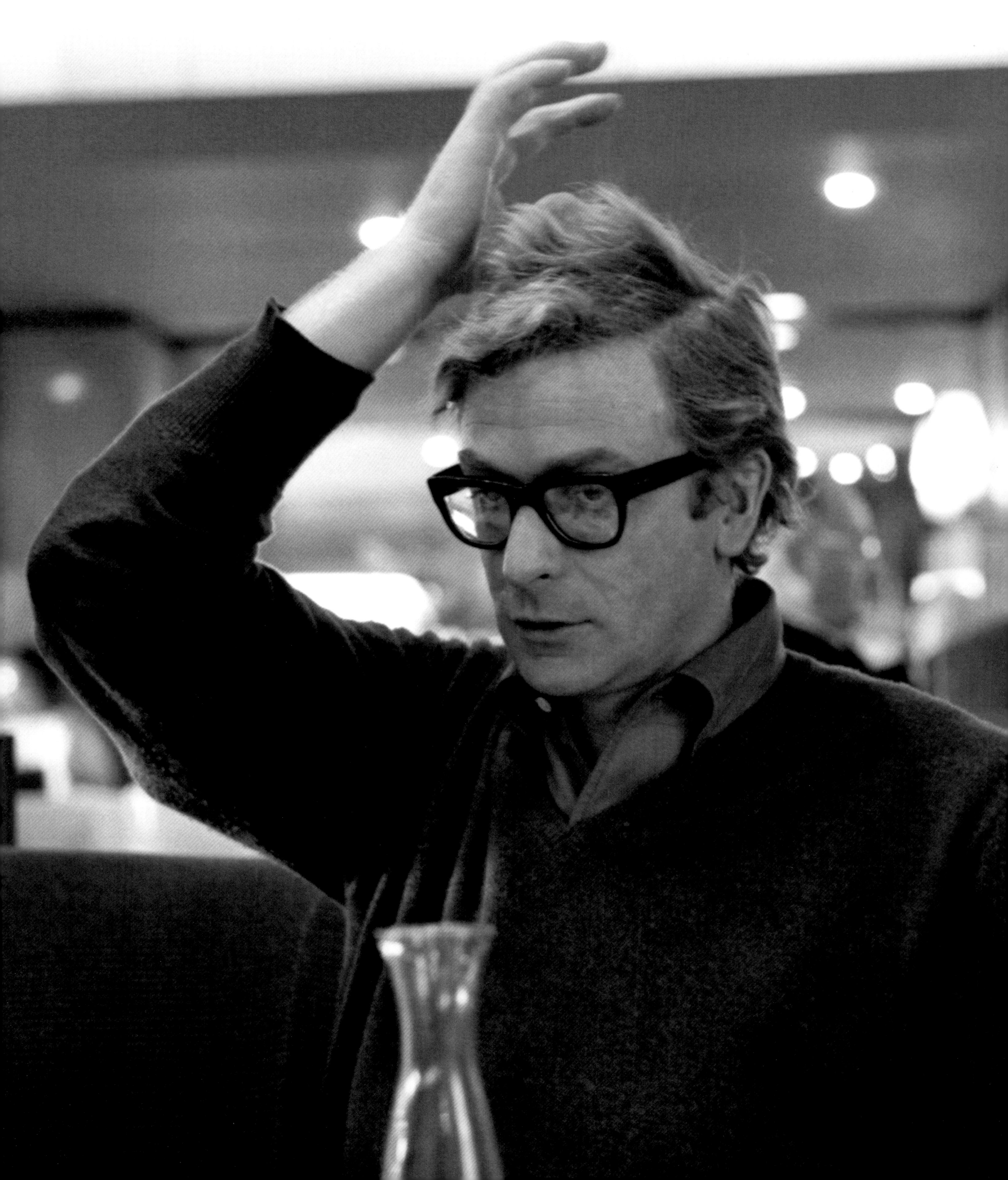

Essential to the film's documentary-eque style was the use of telephoto lenses so that Caine/Palmer could walk through the streets of Berlin without a camera in his immediate proximity. *Variety's* review observed that "*Funeral in Berlin* is the second presentation of the exploits of Harry Palmer, the soft-sell sleuth...excellent scripting, direction and performances...semi-documentary feel."[5] Caine himself was less sure of the resulting movie. Commenting on director Guy Hamilton, Caine noted in his memoir, "I'm not sure in retrospect he was quite the right man to give Harry Palmer the gritty edge he needed to differentiate him from James Bond."[6]

Whilst on location with Caine at the Hilton Berlin, O'Neill took a number of photographs of Caine having a meal with his girlfriend. At the time, her divorce was yet to be finalised from Robert Evans, Hollywood film producer and Head of Production at Paramount Pictures, which released the film in the US, in 1966.

Michael Caine and O'Neill's friendship had already sparked when Caine was at the very beginnings of his career. However, it was the filming of *Funeral in Berlin* in 1966 that brought O'Neill and Caine together for a sustained run of projects that ran through the 1970s and '80s, and with a handful of forays in the early 1990s.

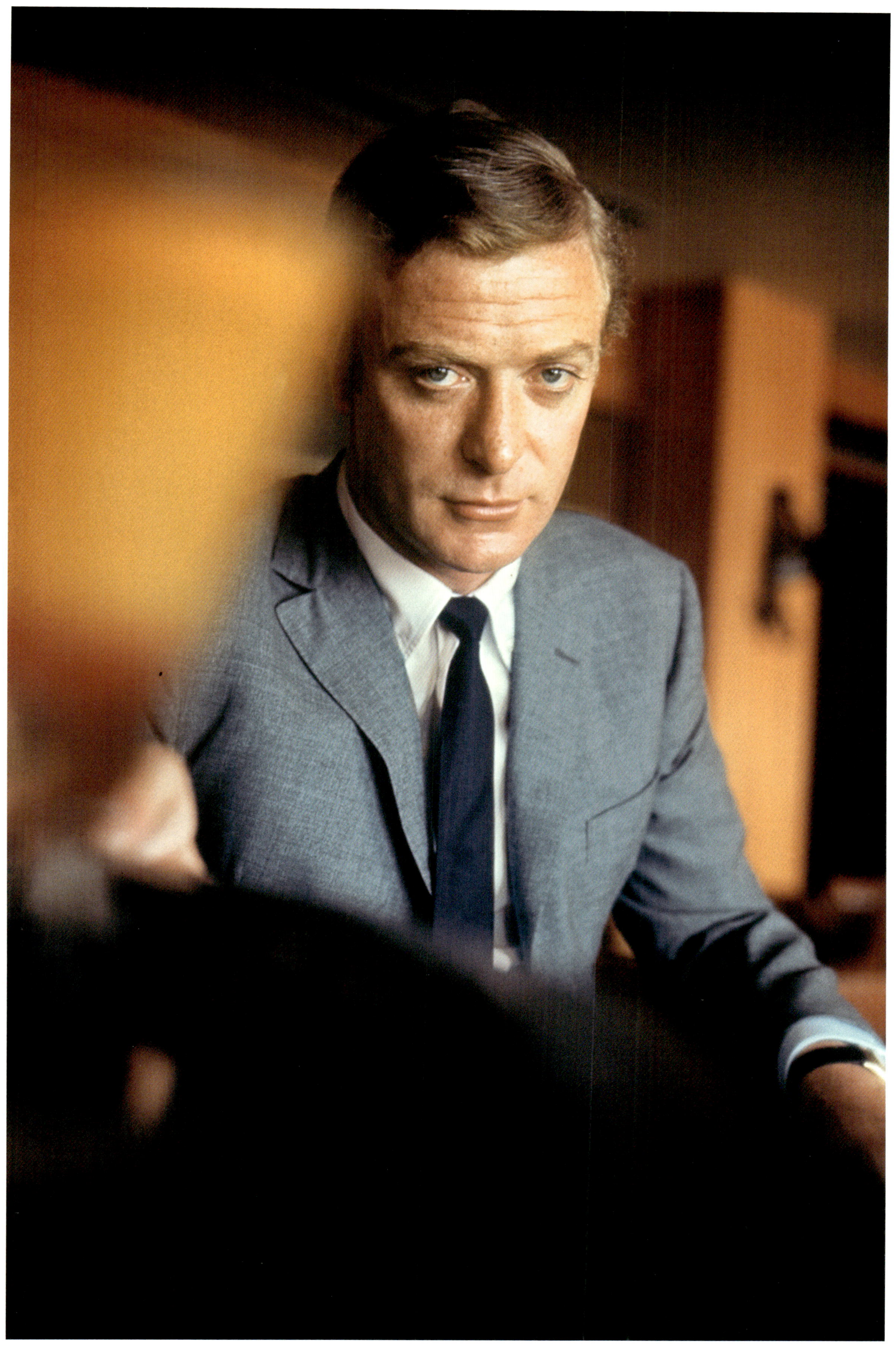

I wore glasses naturally so I knew how to use glasses…

Michael Caine

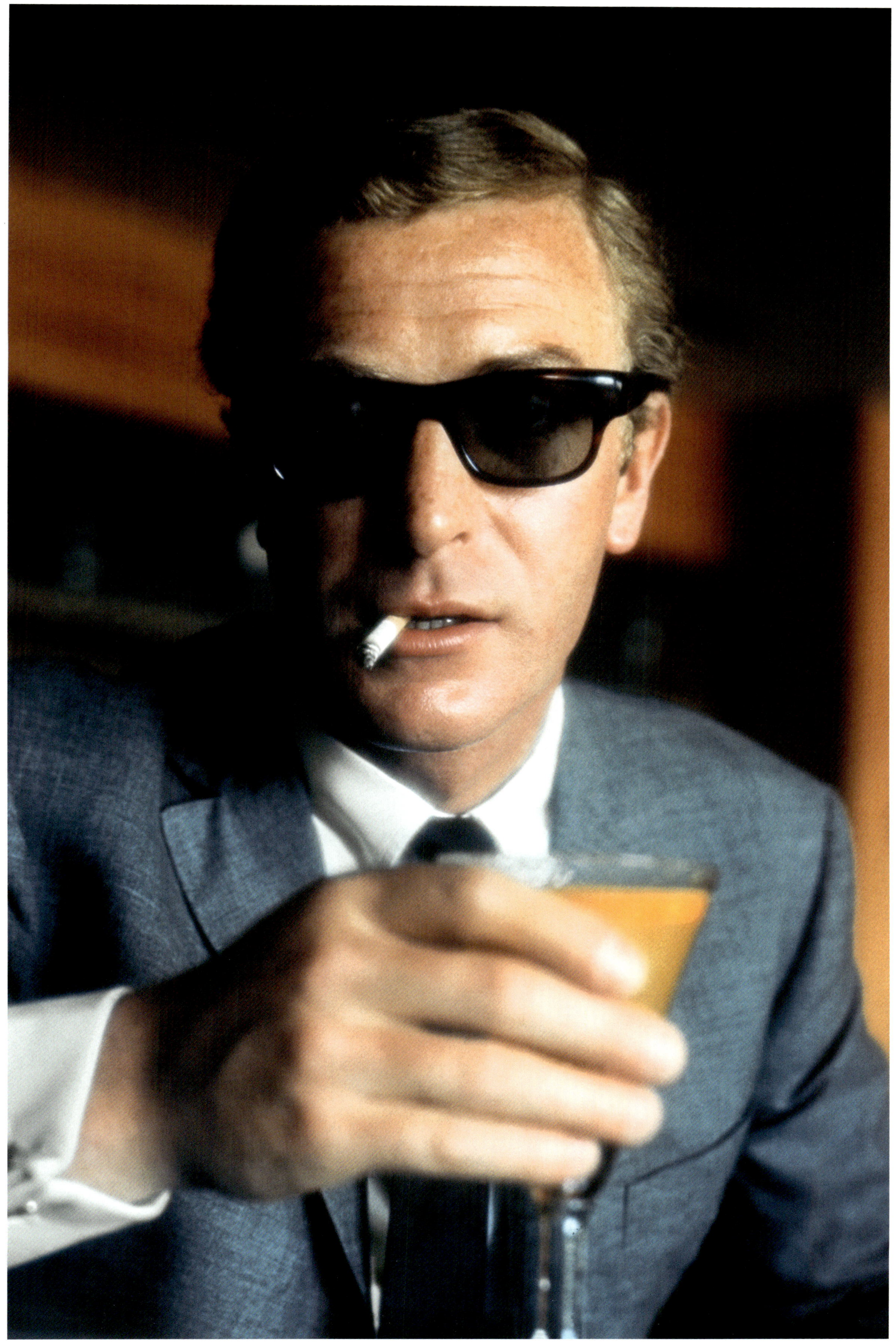

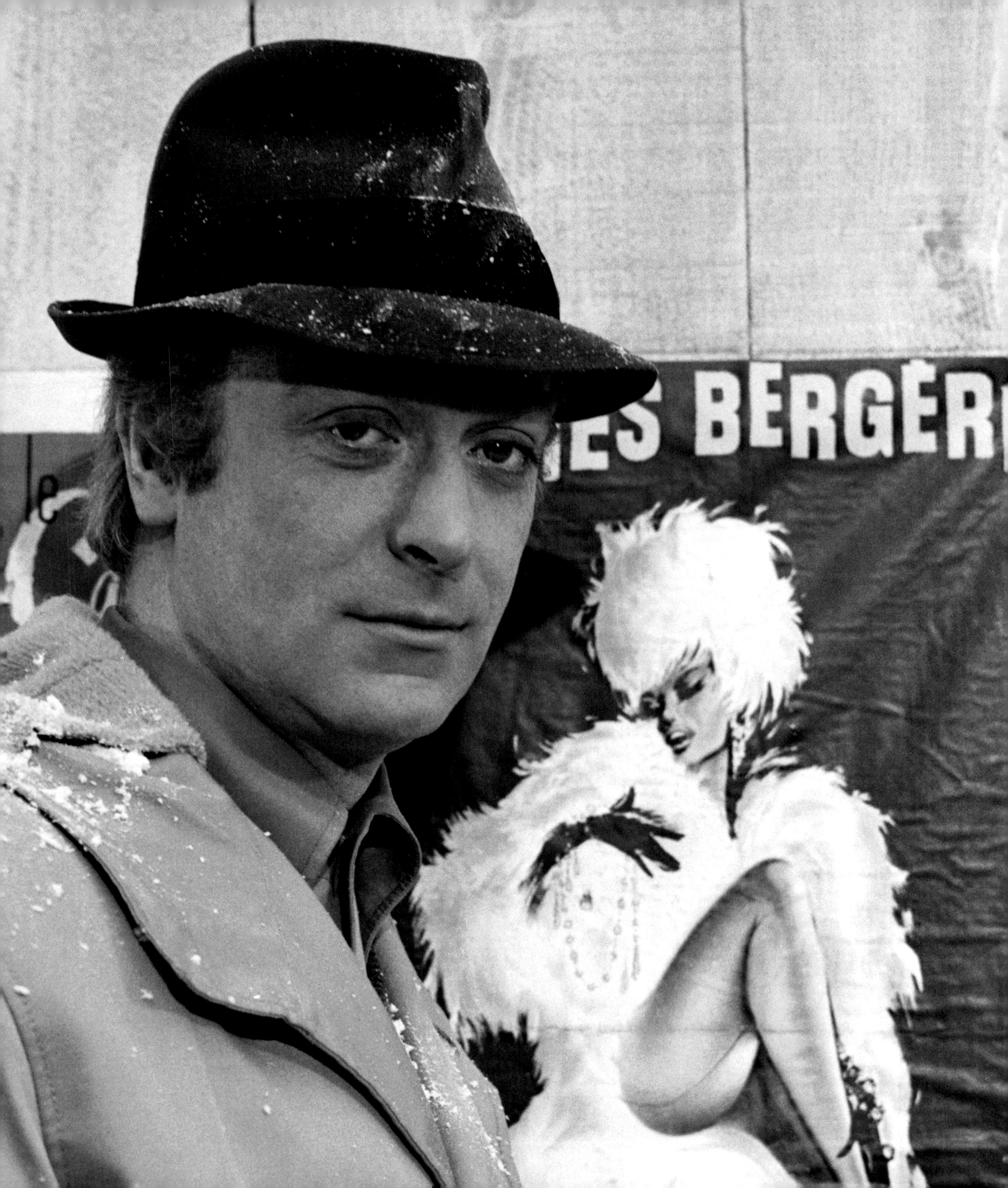

WOMAN TIMES SEVEN

1967

"O'Neill's images from the Paris location shoot capture the concentrated energy of the film and also the warmth of friendship between Caine and MacLaine as they work together."

"I shot off to Paris for a bit of fun. I had a bit part in Shirley MacLaine's new film, *Woman Times Seven*, and I was only too happy to do it in return for everything Shirley had done for me in Hollywood."[1] The gratitude that Caine expresses here refers to MacLaine having invited him to be cast alongside her in the crime caper *Gambit* (1966), introducing Caine to American audiences.

The film was directed by Vittorio De Sica, who had burned so brightly as an instigator of the Italian neorealist cinema in the immediate post-WWII years. De Sica directed an all-time classic in *The Bicycle Thieves* (1948); his filmography includes *Umberto D.* (1952), *Yesterday, Today and Tomorrow* (1963) *Marriage Italian Style* (1964) and *After the Fox* (1966).

Shot in Paris and notable for its glamorous aesthetic – Pierre Cardin gowns, Van Cleef & Arpels jewellery – *Woman Times Seven*, is very much in the European cinema mode, including the subject matter of adultery.

An anthology film, *Woman Times Seven* features MacLaine in different roles in each of the seven vignettes; MacLaine was nominated for a Golden Globe for her performance (losing out to Anne Bancroft for her role in *The Graduate*). The film's male cast includes Caine, Alan Arkin, Rossano Brazzi, Vittorio Gassman and Peter Sellers.

Previous page: Caine in Paris.
Opposite page: Caine has something of a cameo in the film, in the vignette entitled 'Snow'.

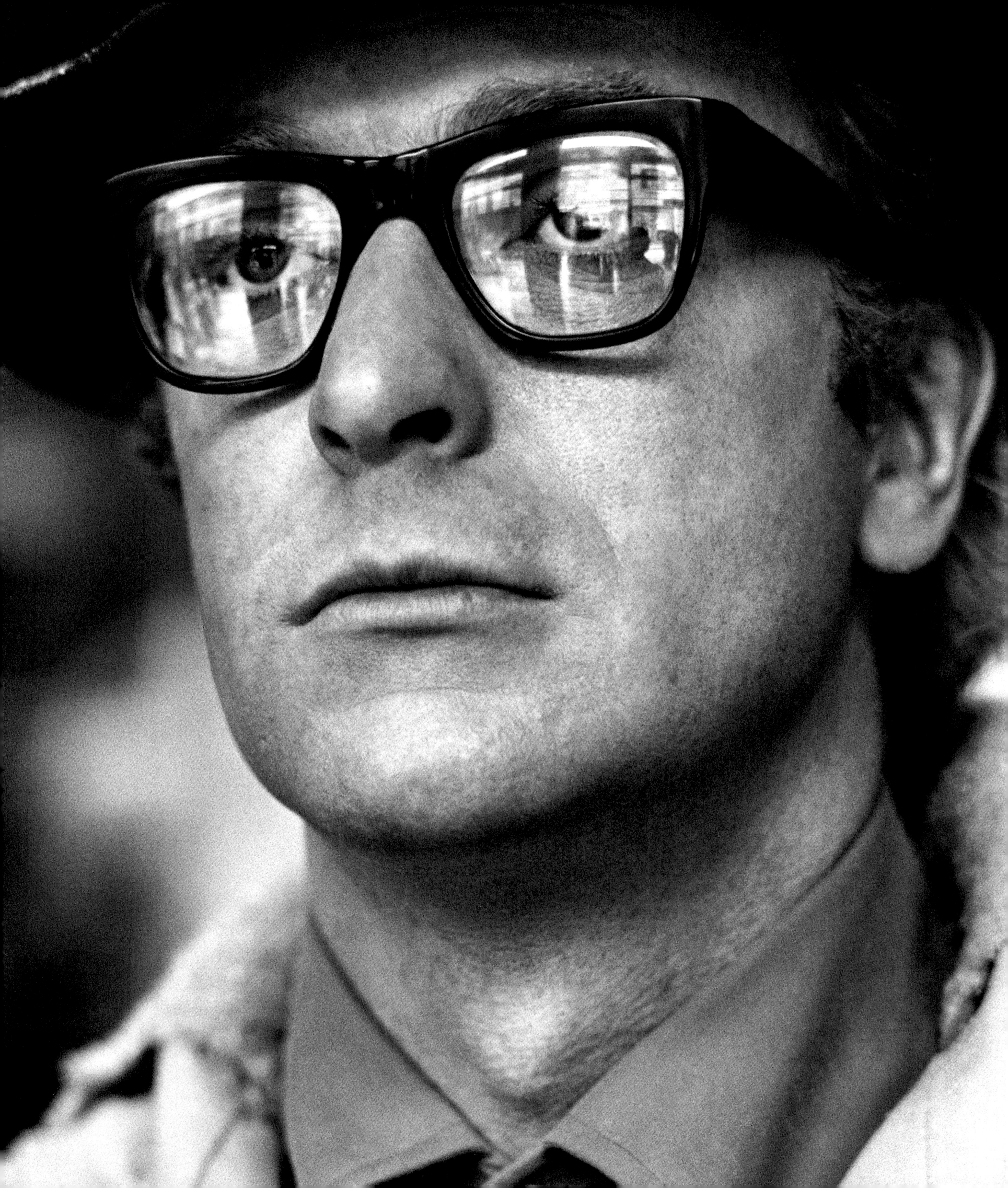

In the vignette entitled *Snow*, MacLaine's character, Jeanne, meets with her friend, Claudie (Anita Ekberg) at a restaurant for lunch. They notice that a handsome stranger (Caine) is watching them. They decide they will head off in separate directions and see who he follows; it is Jeanne. Just at this moment a snowstorm hits... Caine's unnamed character is, in fact, a private detective hired by Jeanne's husband to determine whether she is having an affair.

O'Neill's images from the Paris location shoot capture the concentrated energy of the film and also the warmth of friendship between Caine and MacLaine as they work together. The image of Caine amidst snowfall is quite poetic.

The melancholy that O'Neill sometimes captures echoes an insightful point that Caine made in his memoirs: "The modern film actor knows that real people in real life struggle not to show their feelings. It is more truthful, and more potent, to fight against the tears, only yielding after all those defence mechanisms are exhausted.... In other words, screen acting is much more a matter of 'being' than 'performing'."[2]

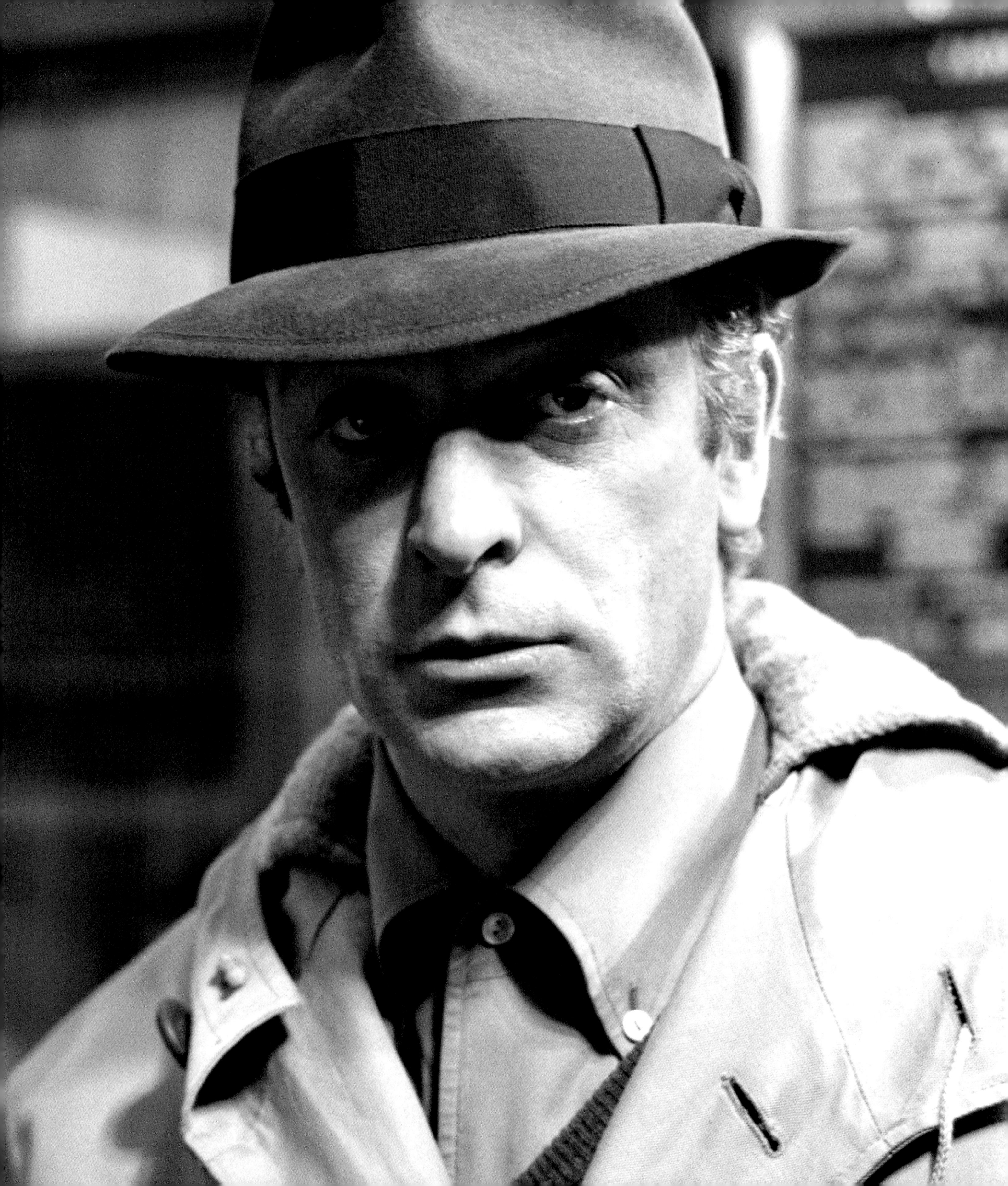

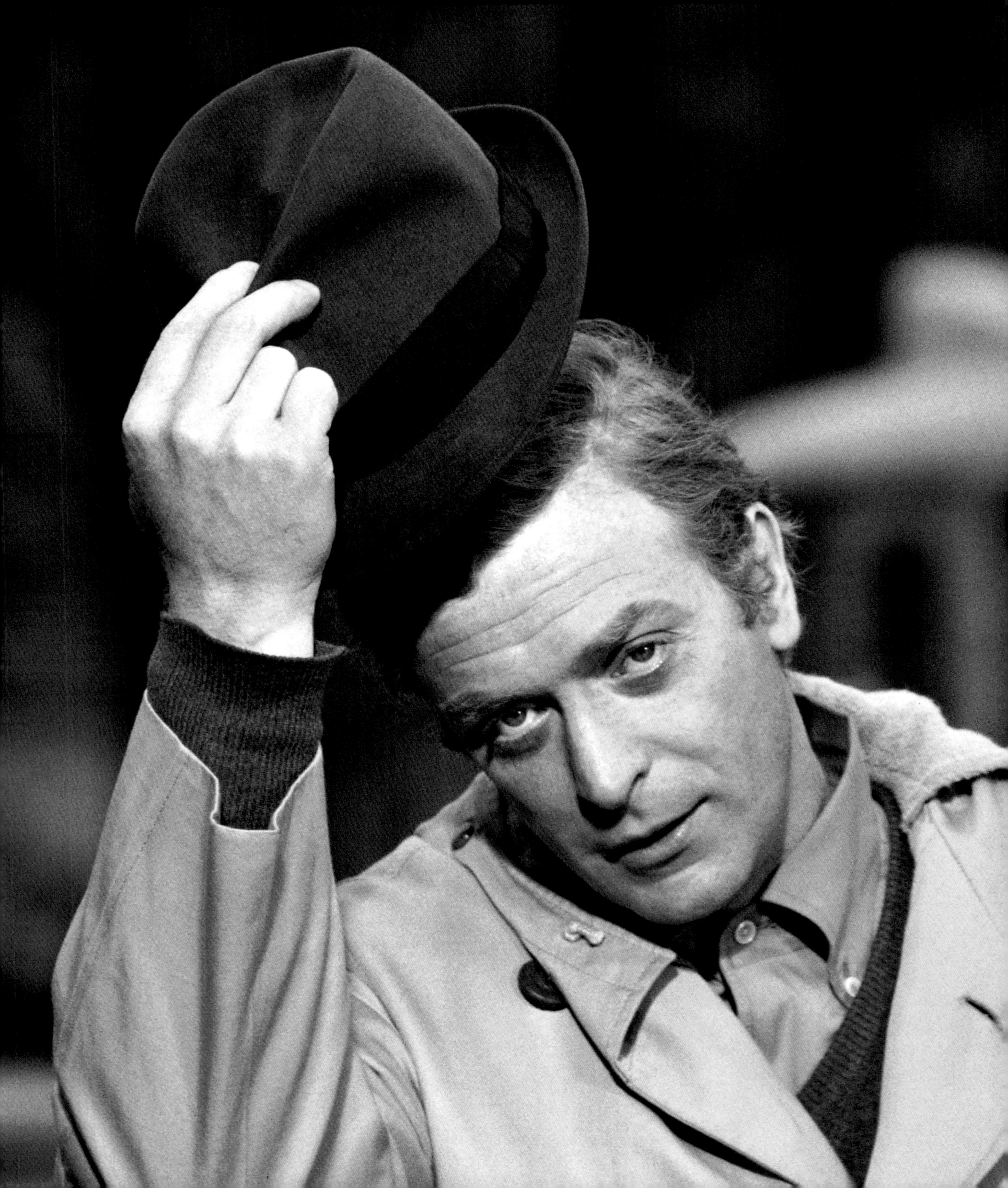

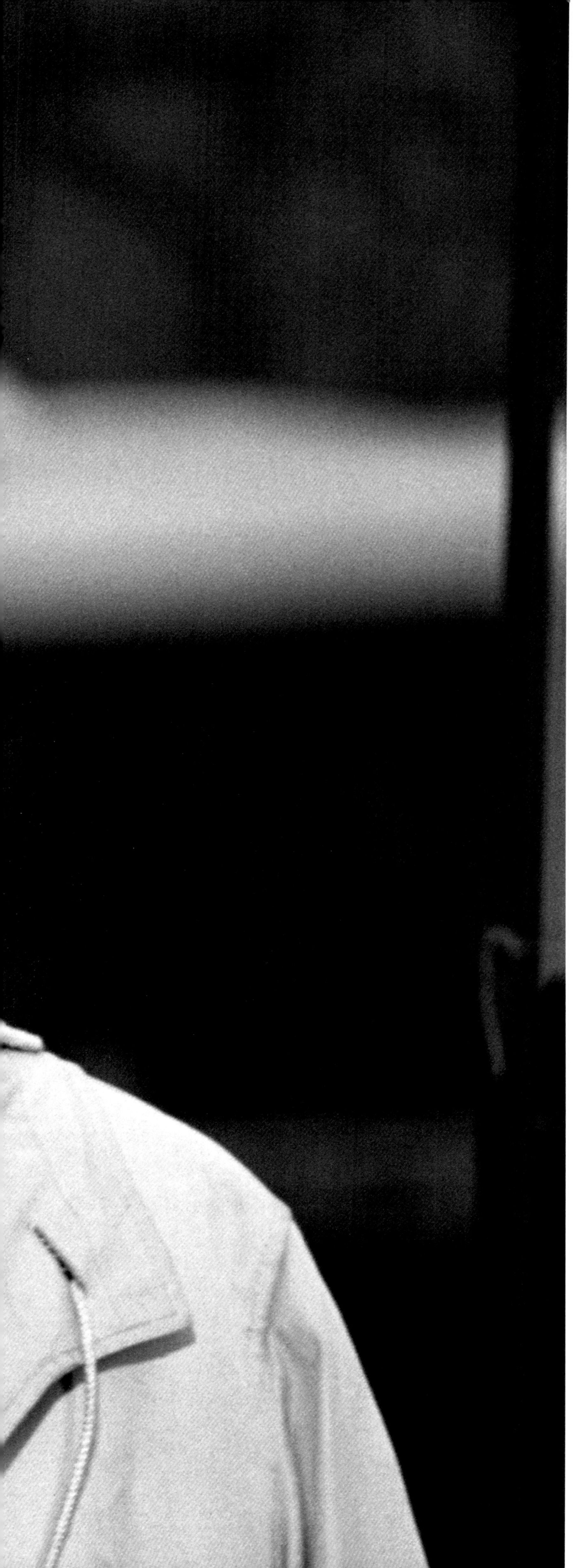

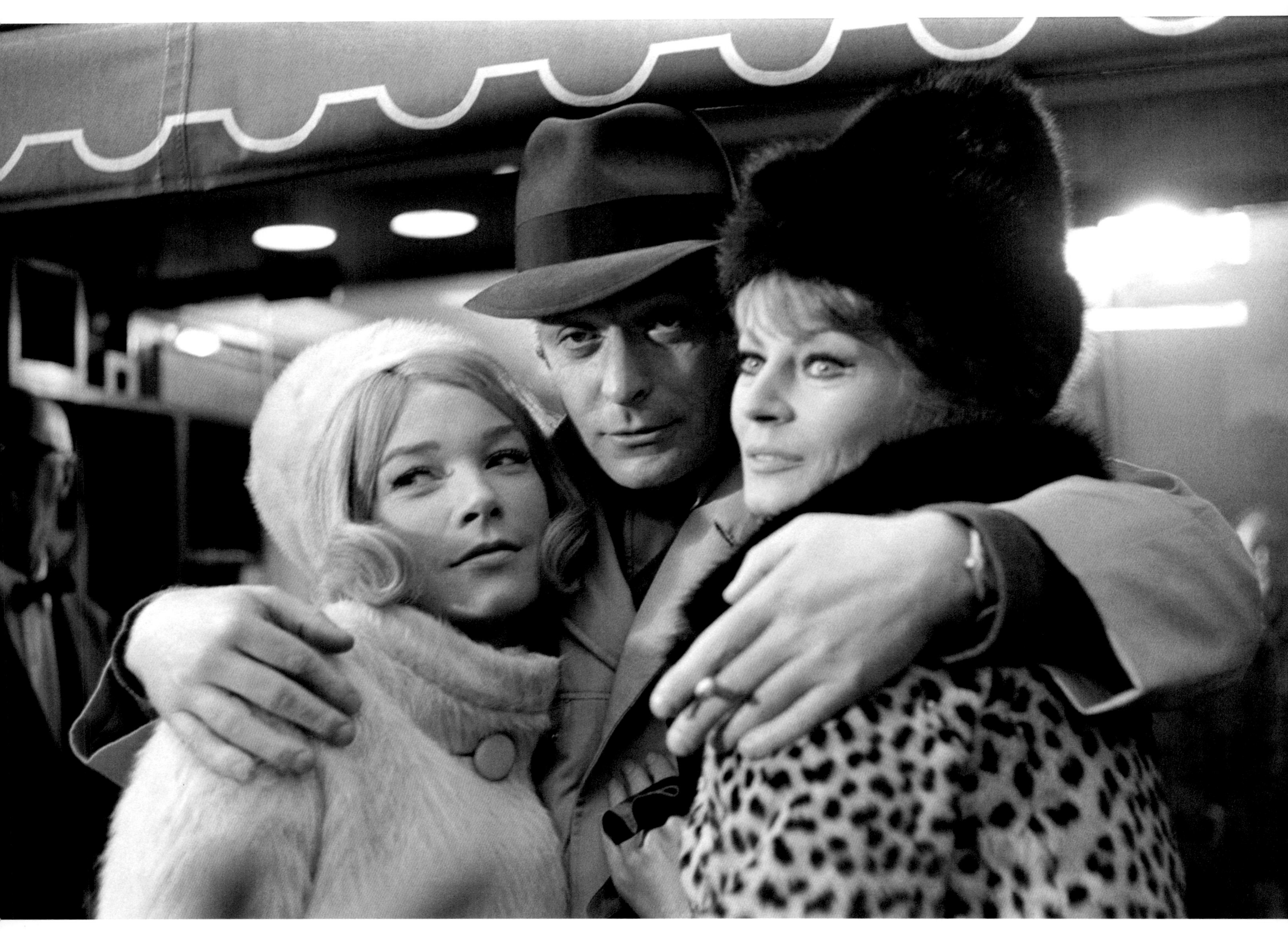

Above: Caine on location in Paris with Shirley MacLaine (Jeanne) and Anita Ekberg (Claudie).

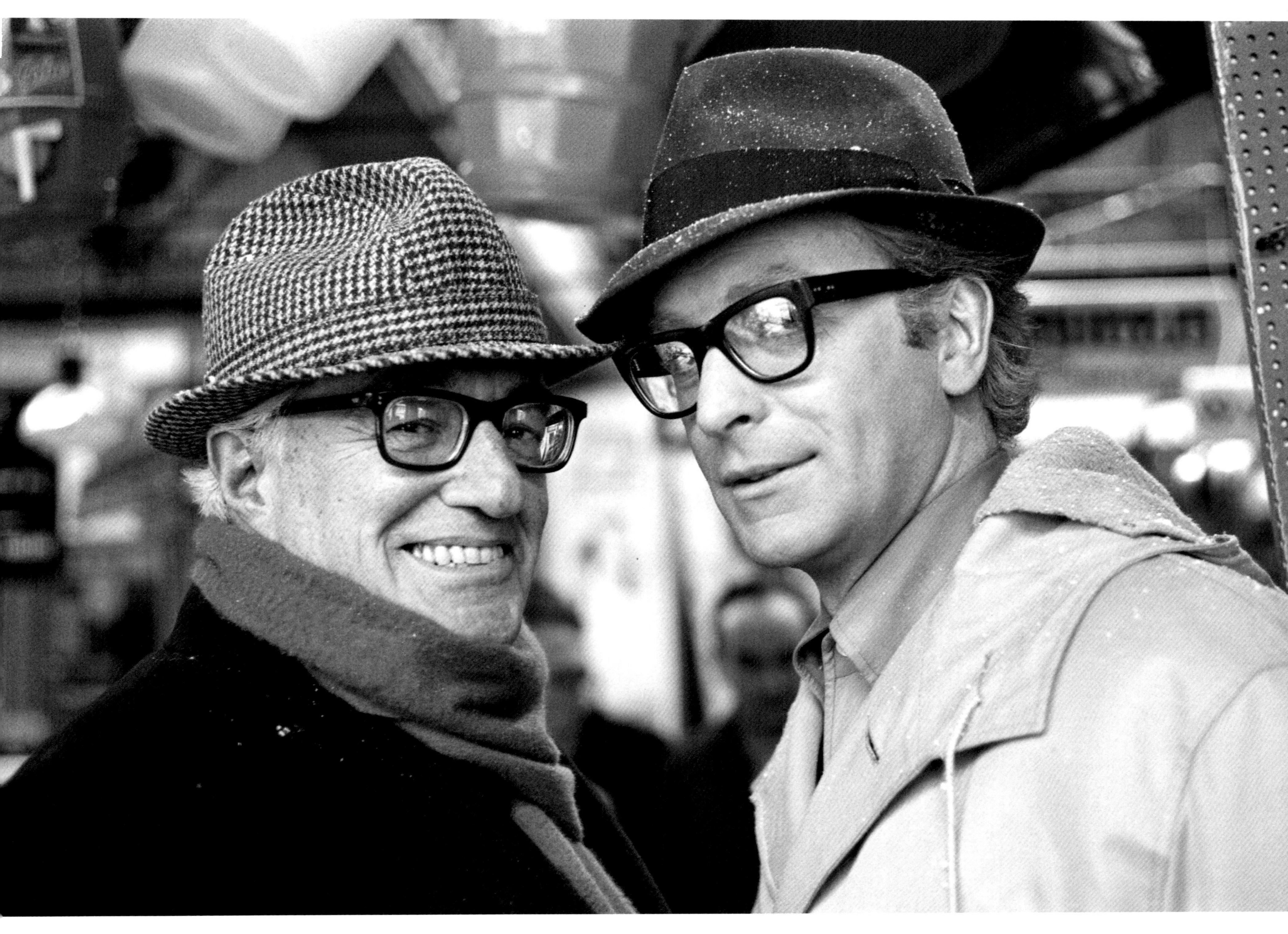

Above: Caine with *Woman Times Seven* director, Vittorio De Sica.

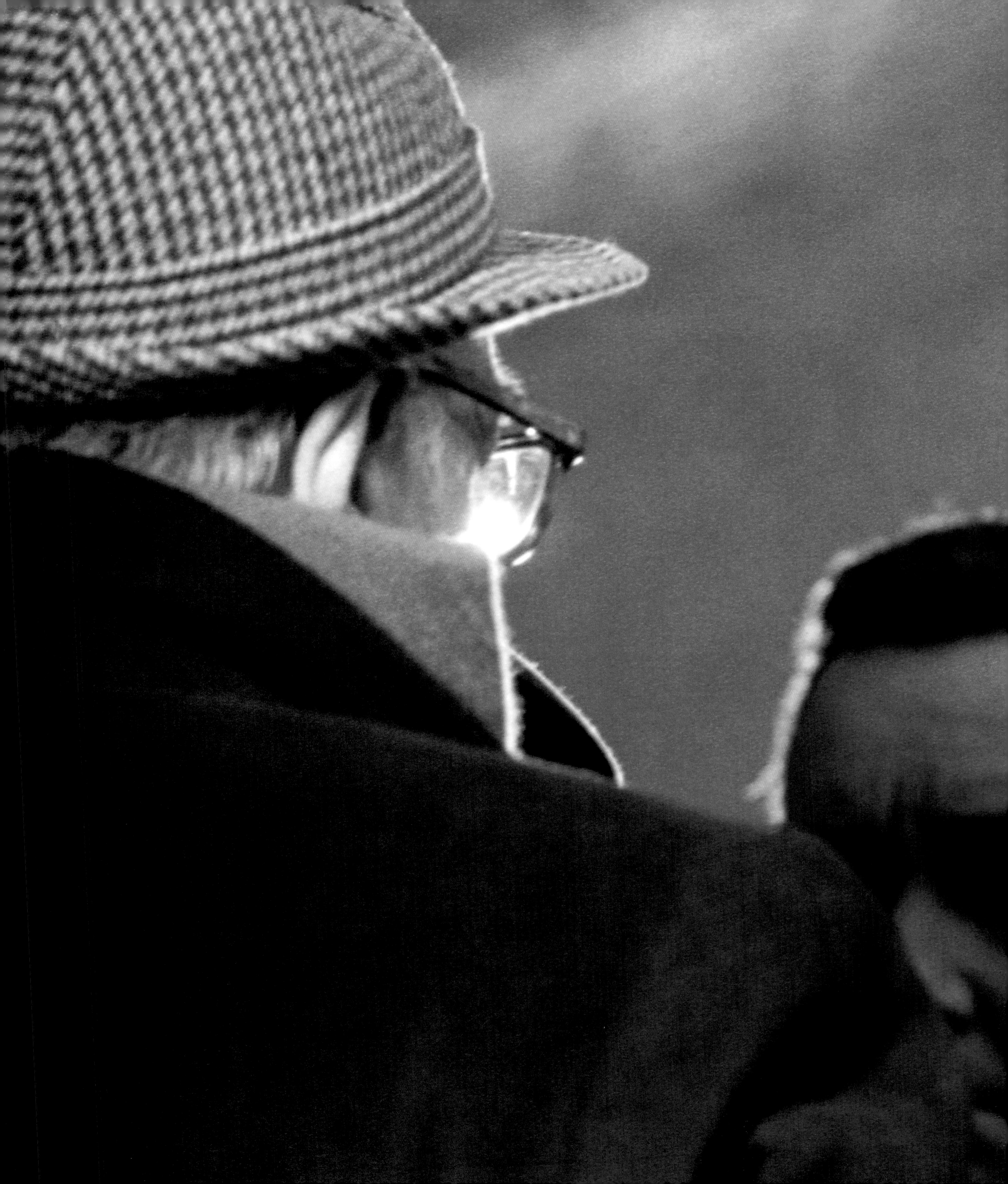

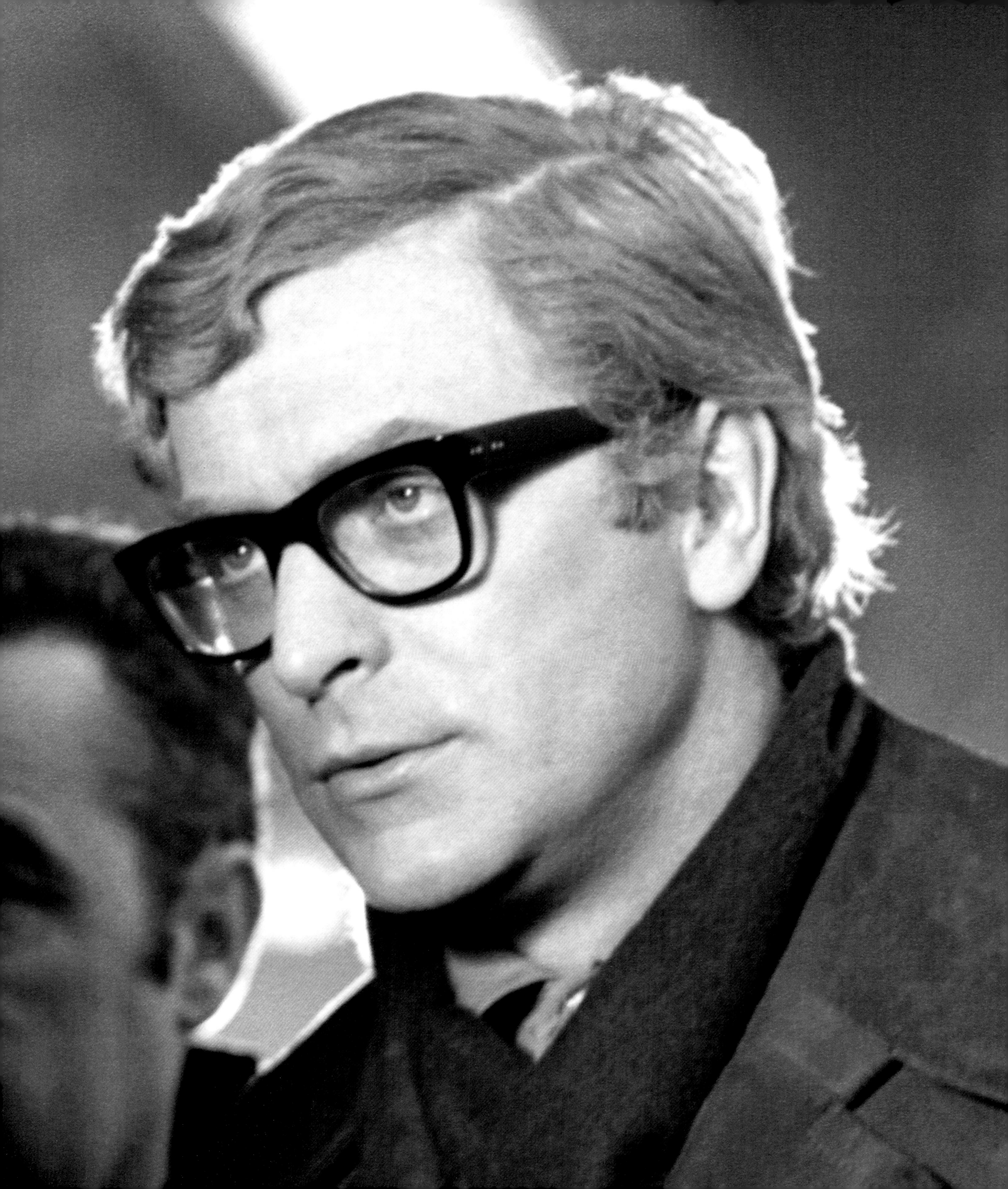

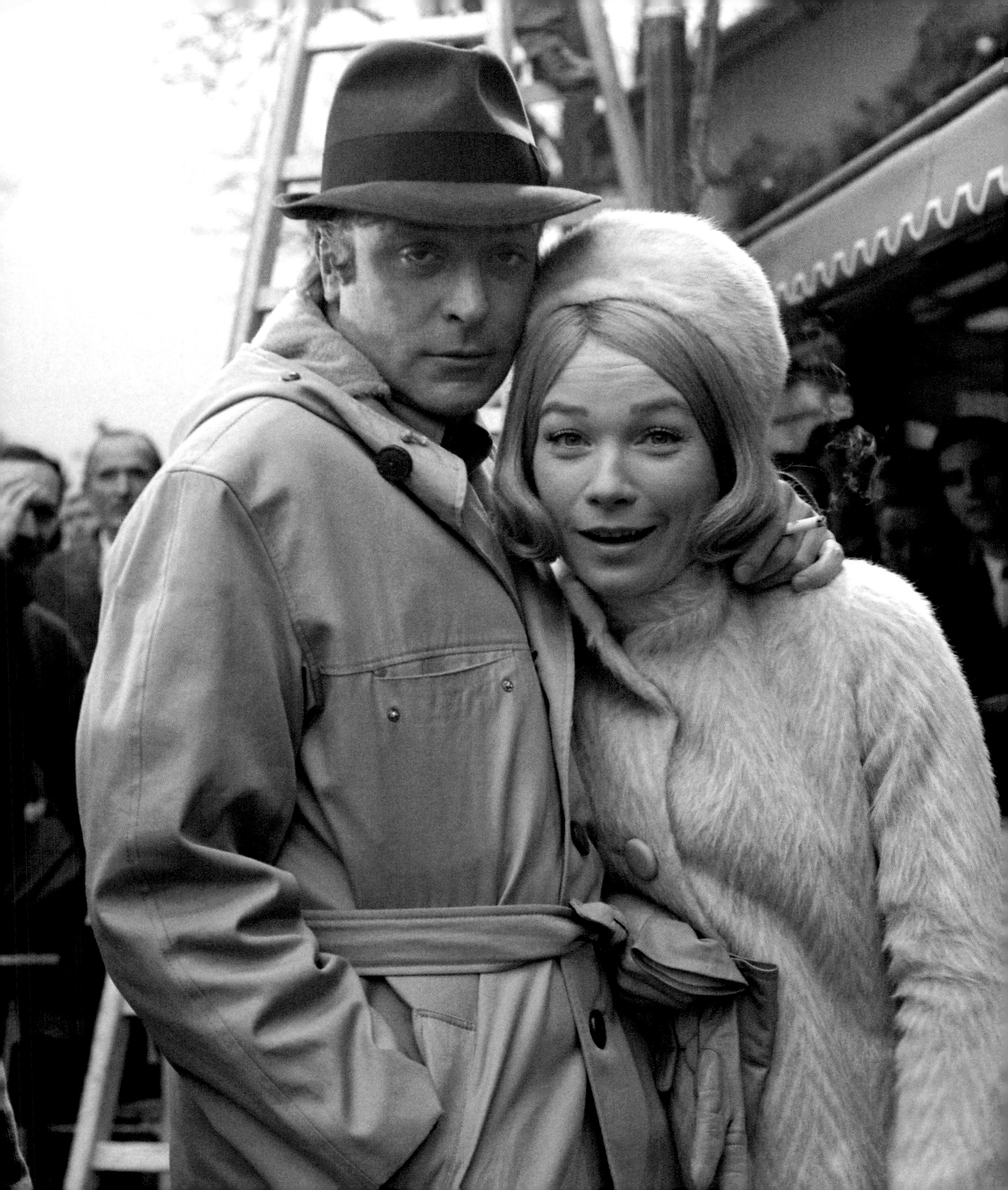

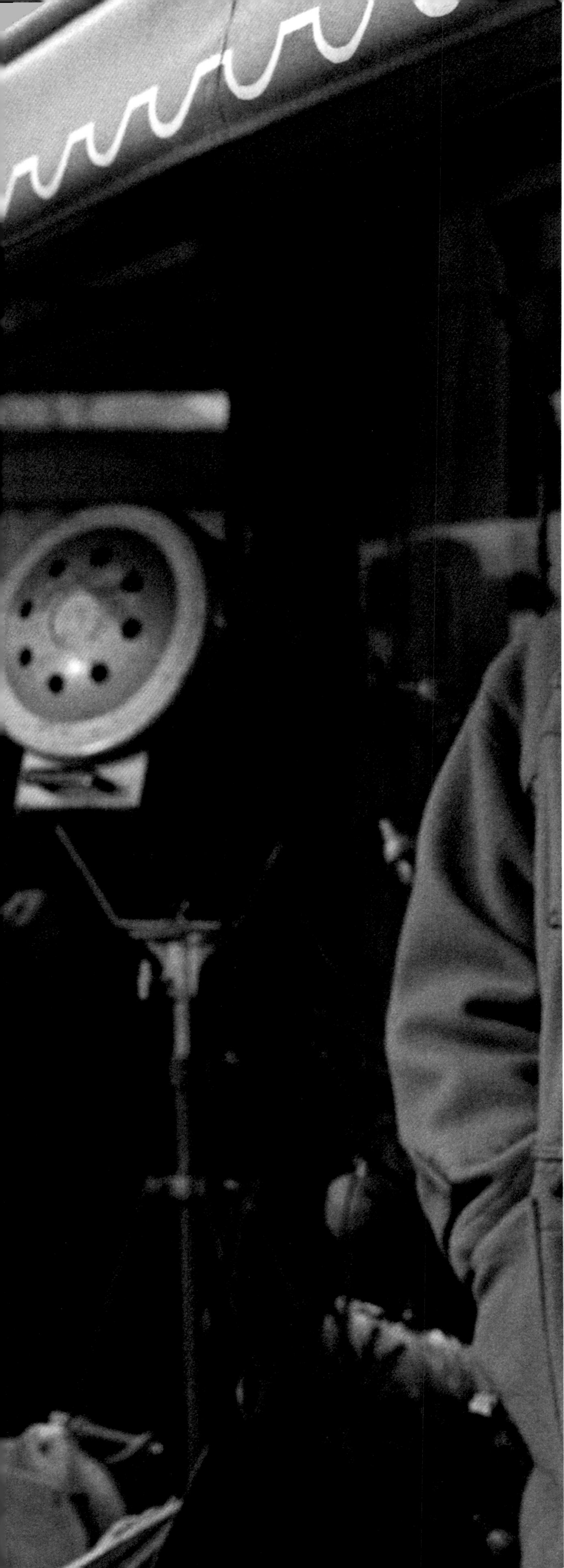

Left and following pages: Caine and MacLaine. Caine took the role in the film in the spirit of friendship with, and gratitude to, the film's star Shirley MacLaine for her role in his earlier career.
Pages 52 and 53: Anita Ekberg on location in Paris.

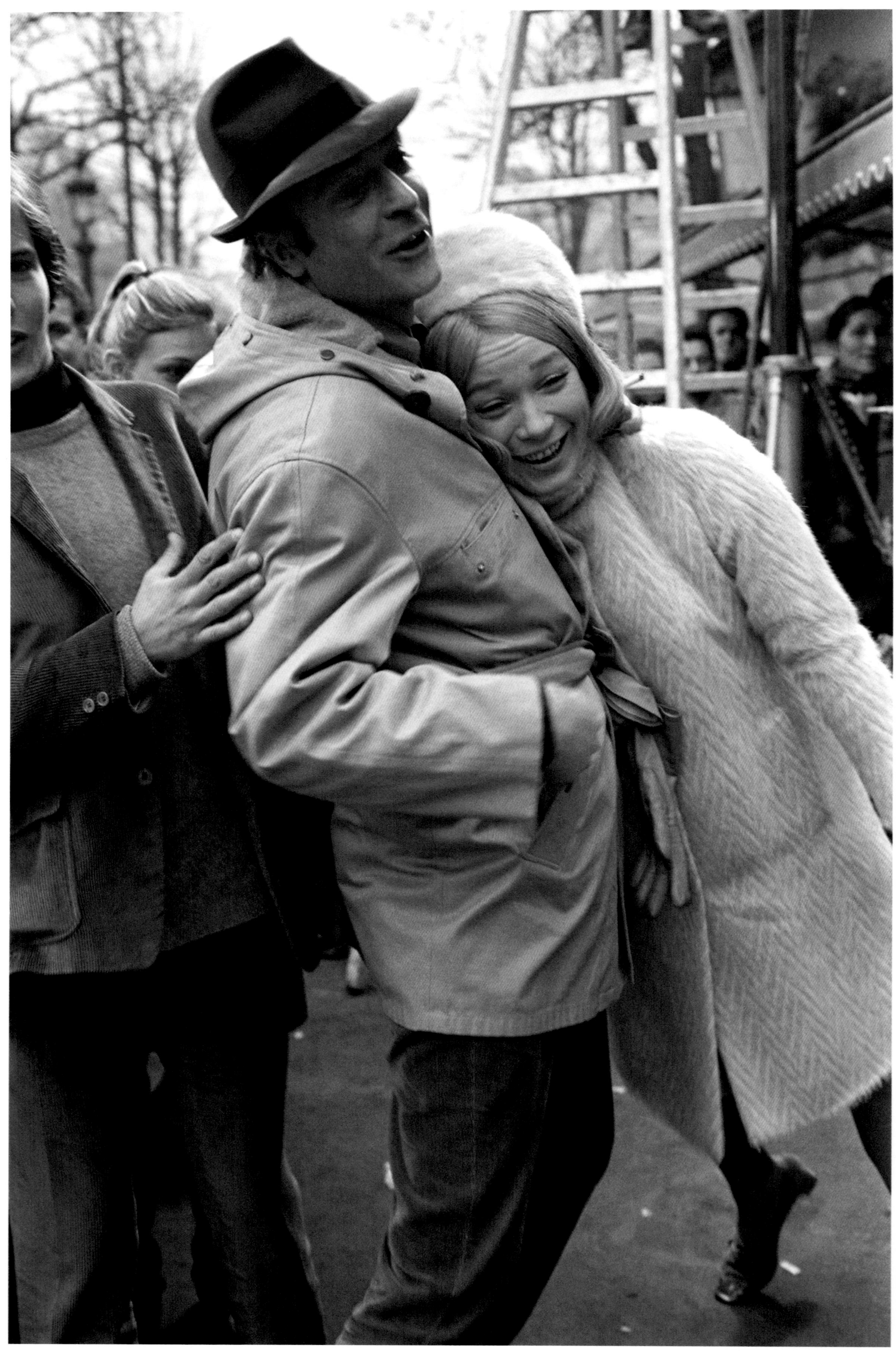

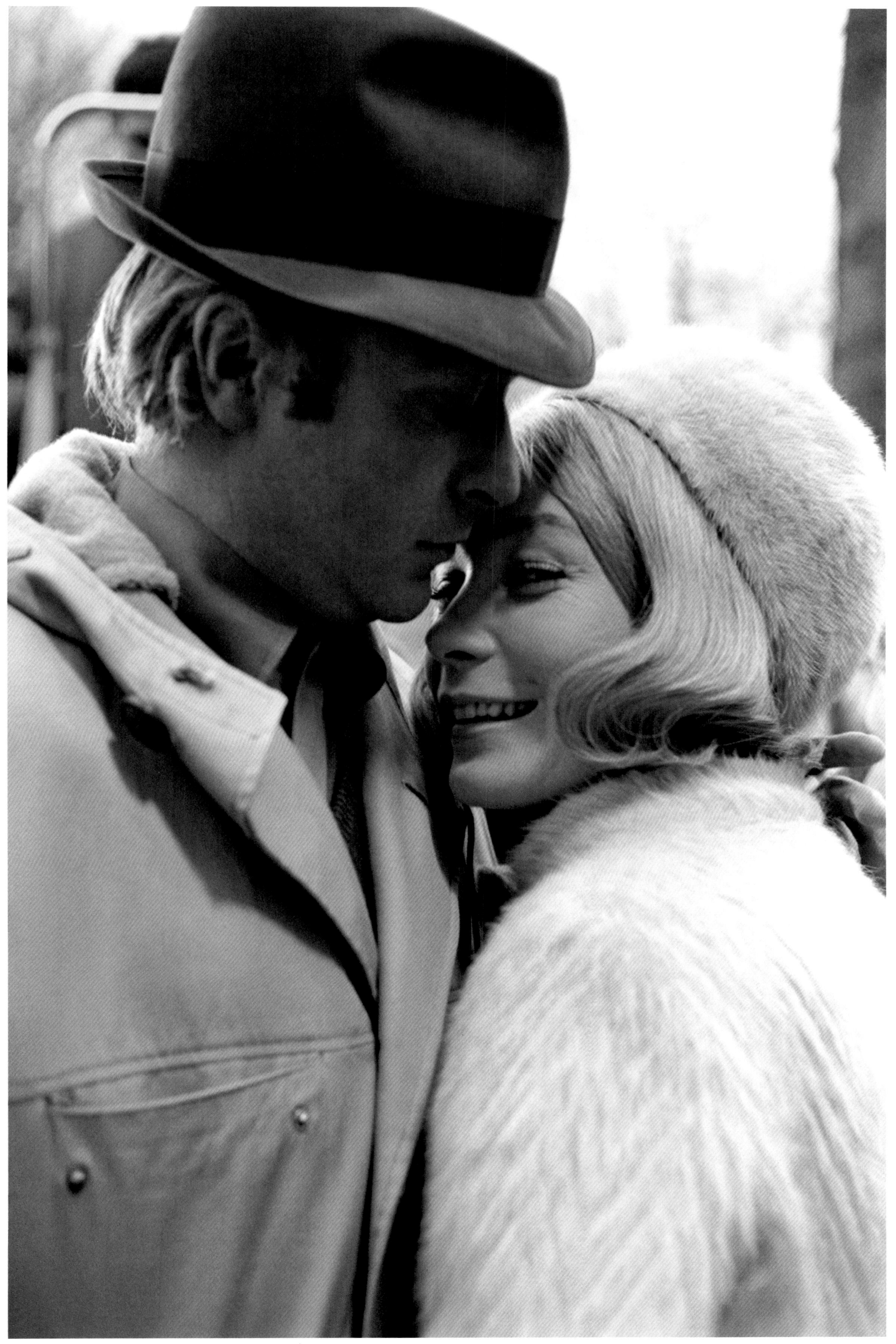

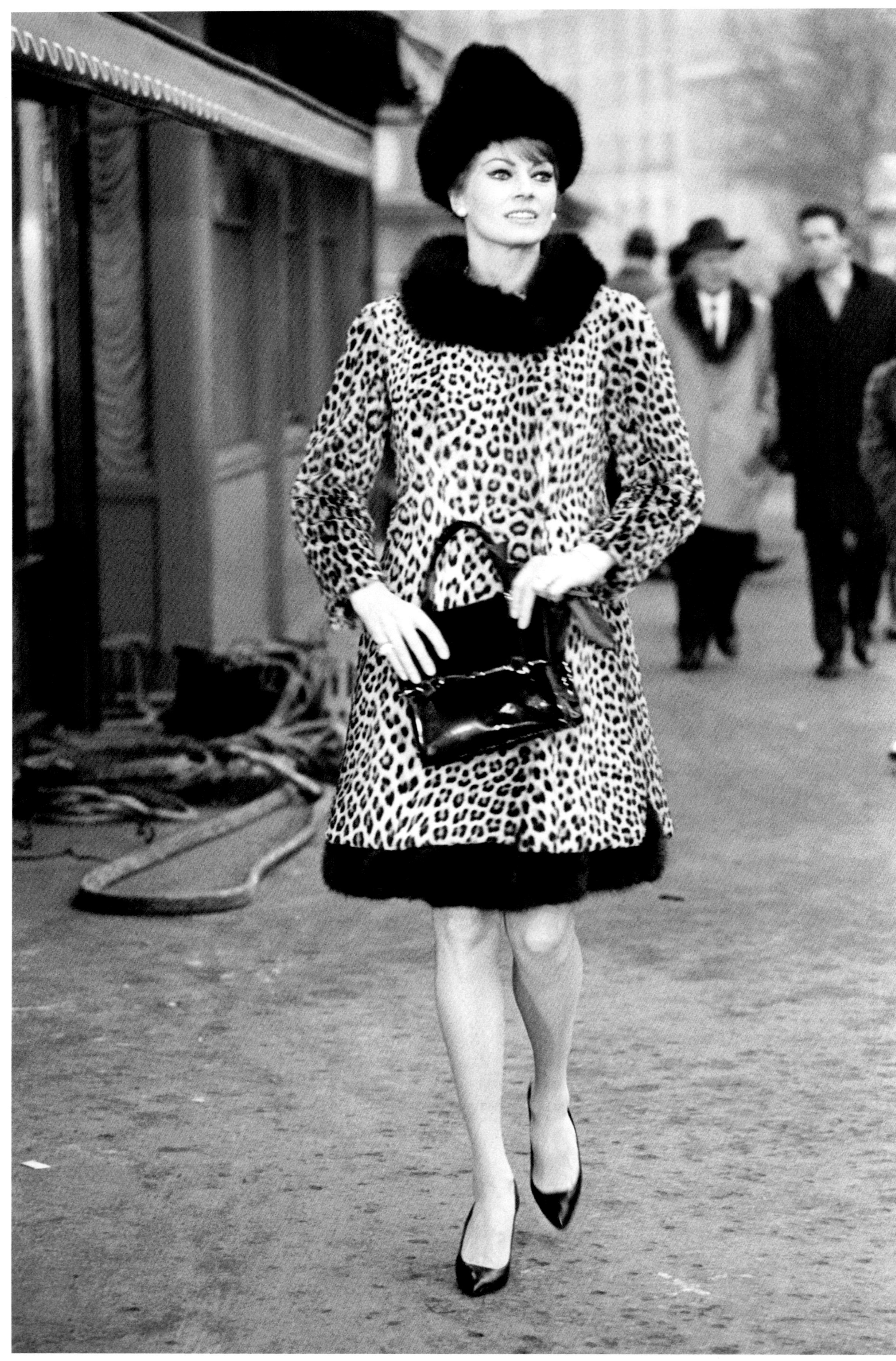

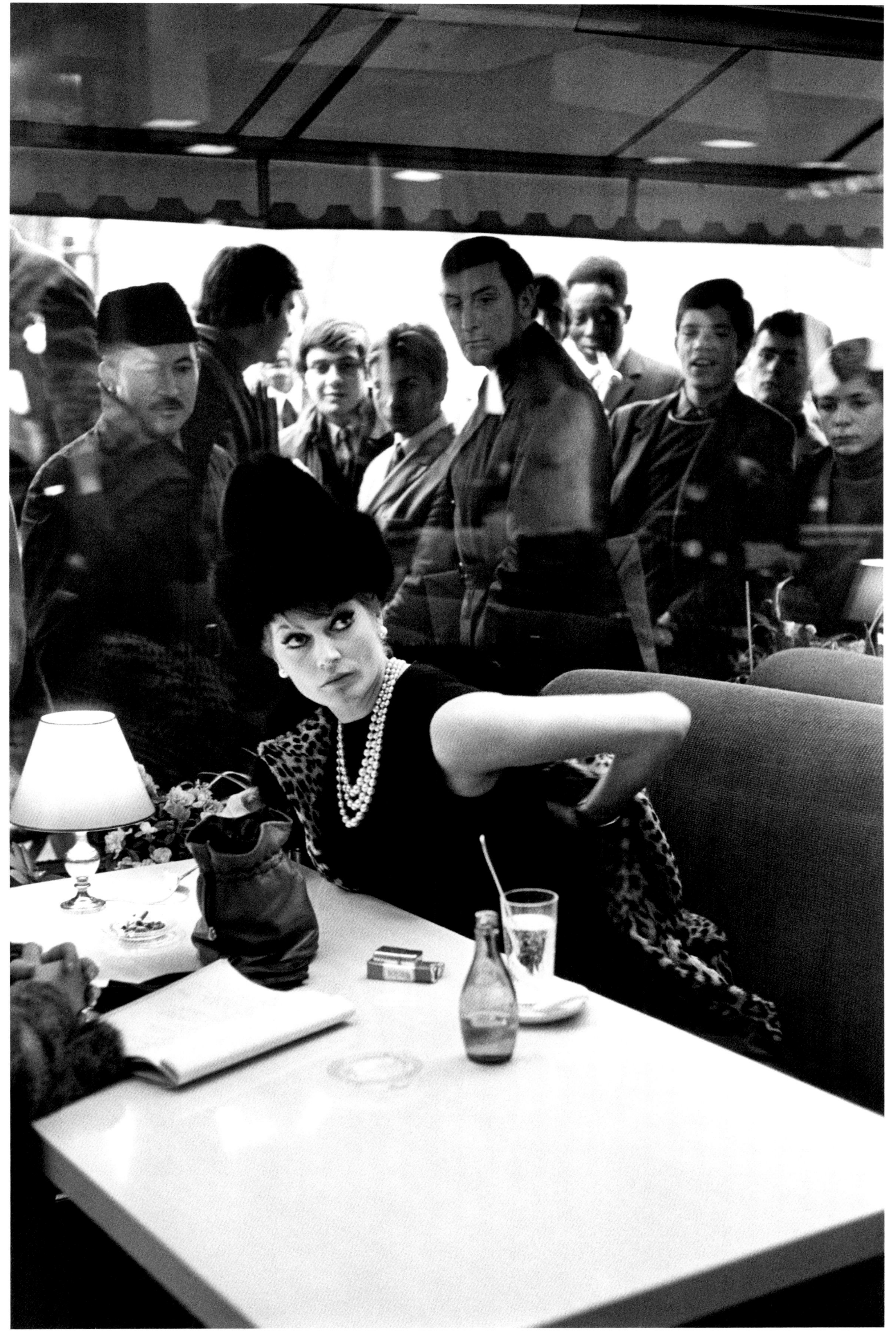

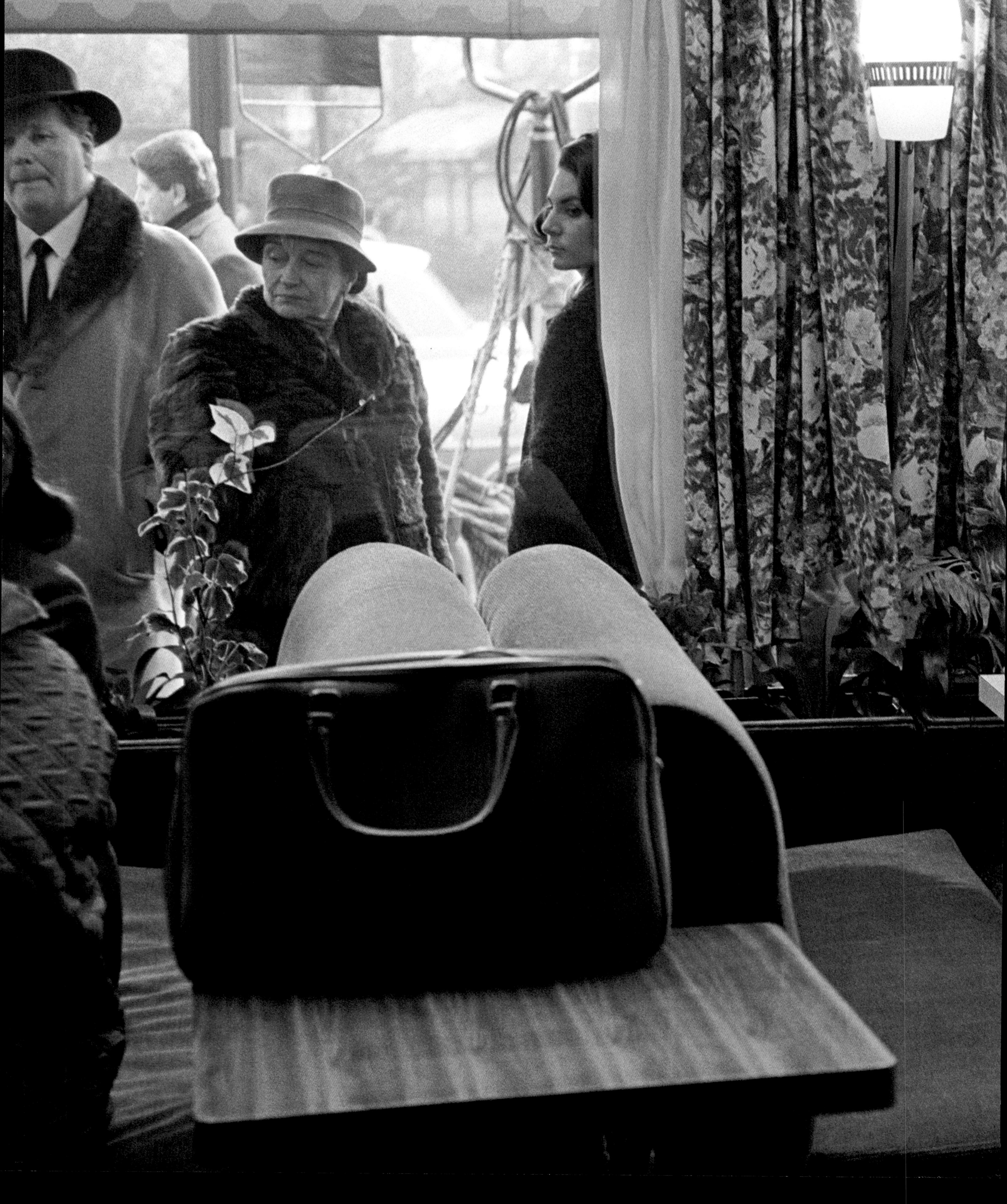

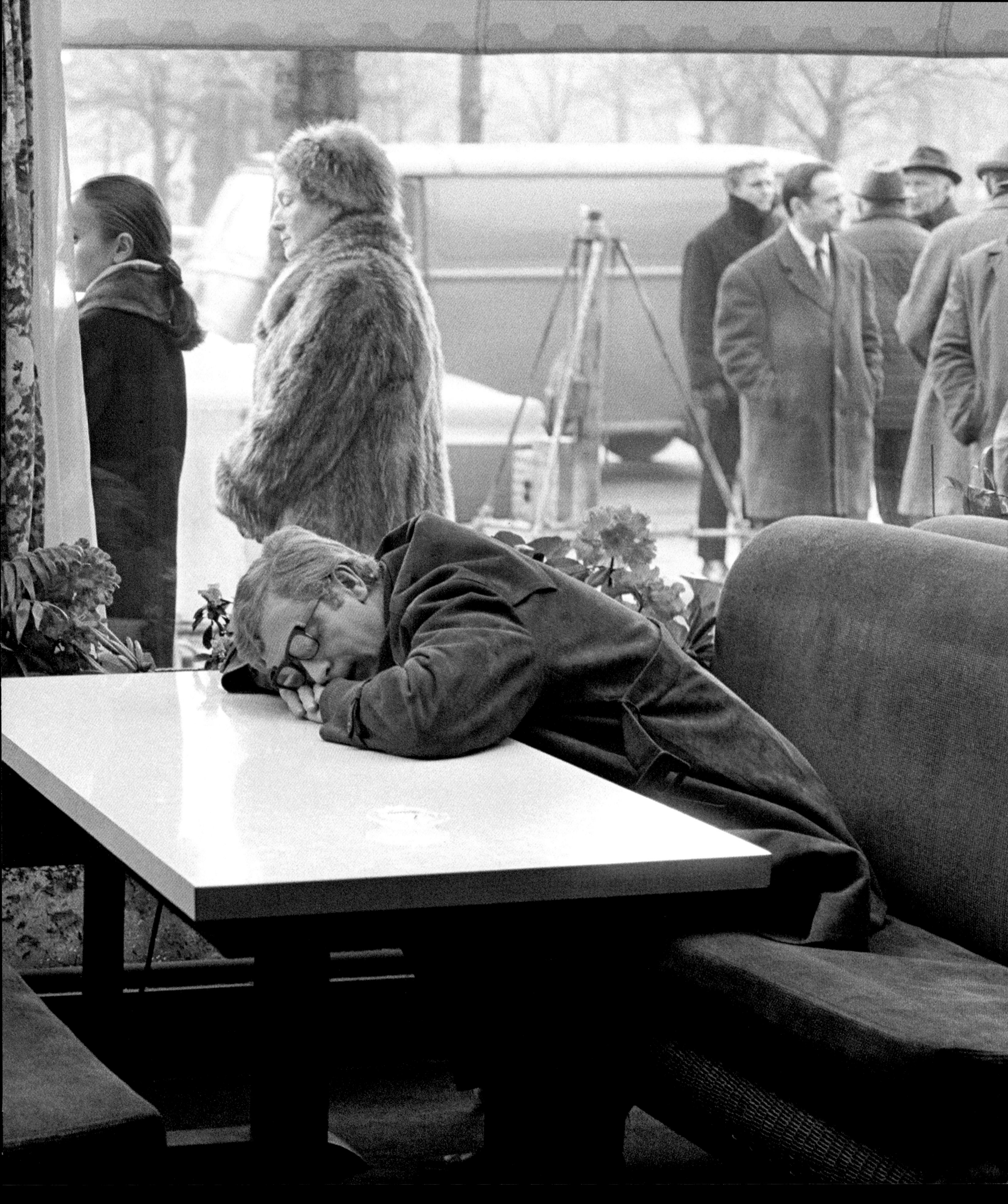

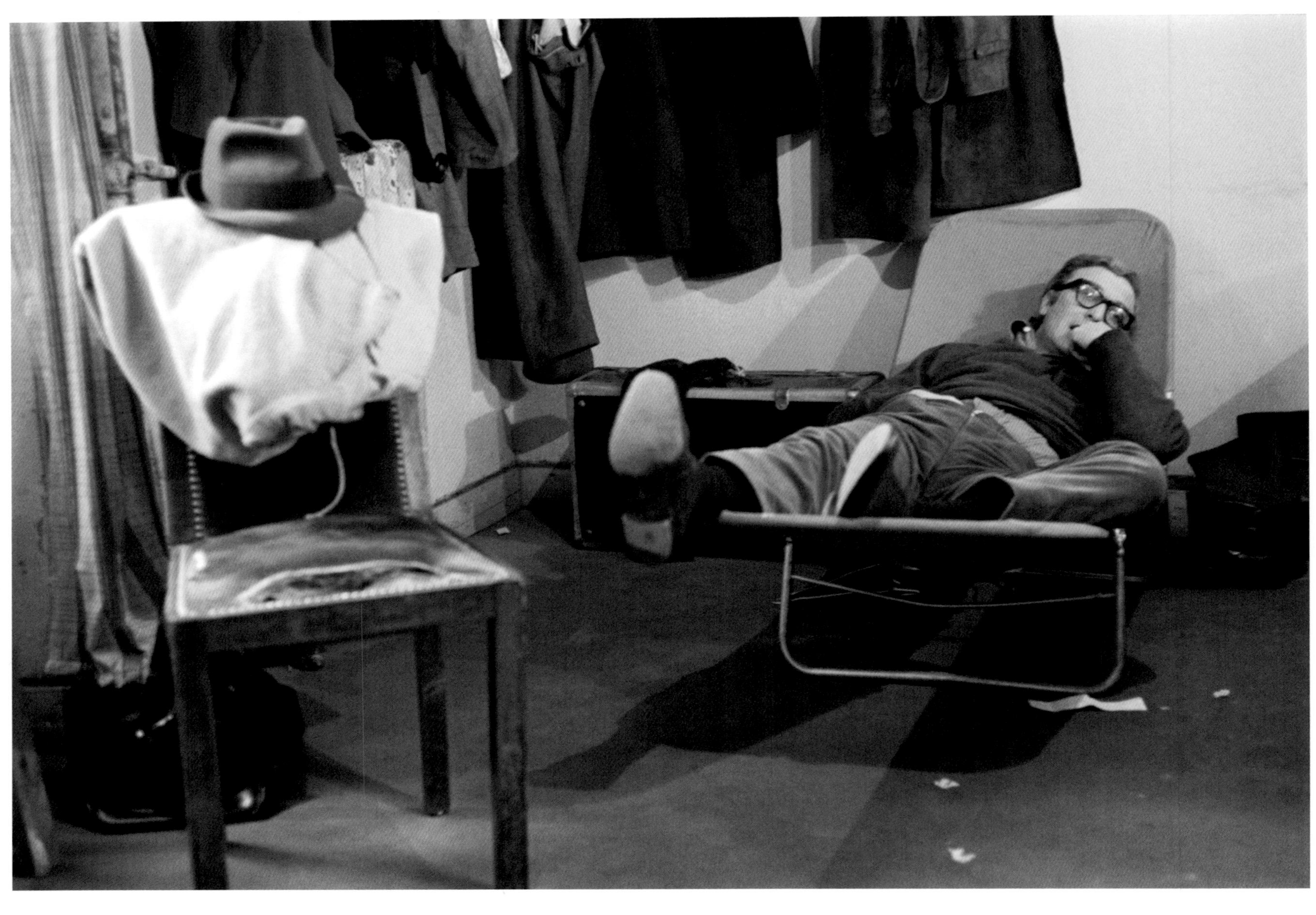

Caine is legendary for taking naps on set. "... whenever I was working with Michael Caine and there was any down time, I somehow always caught him nodding off, catching forty winks." Terry O'Neill

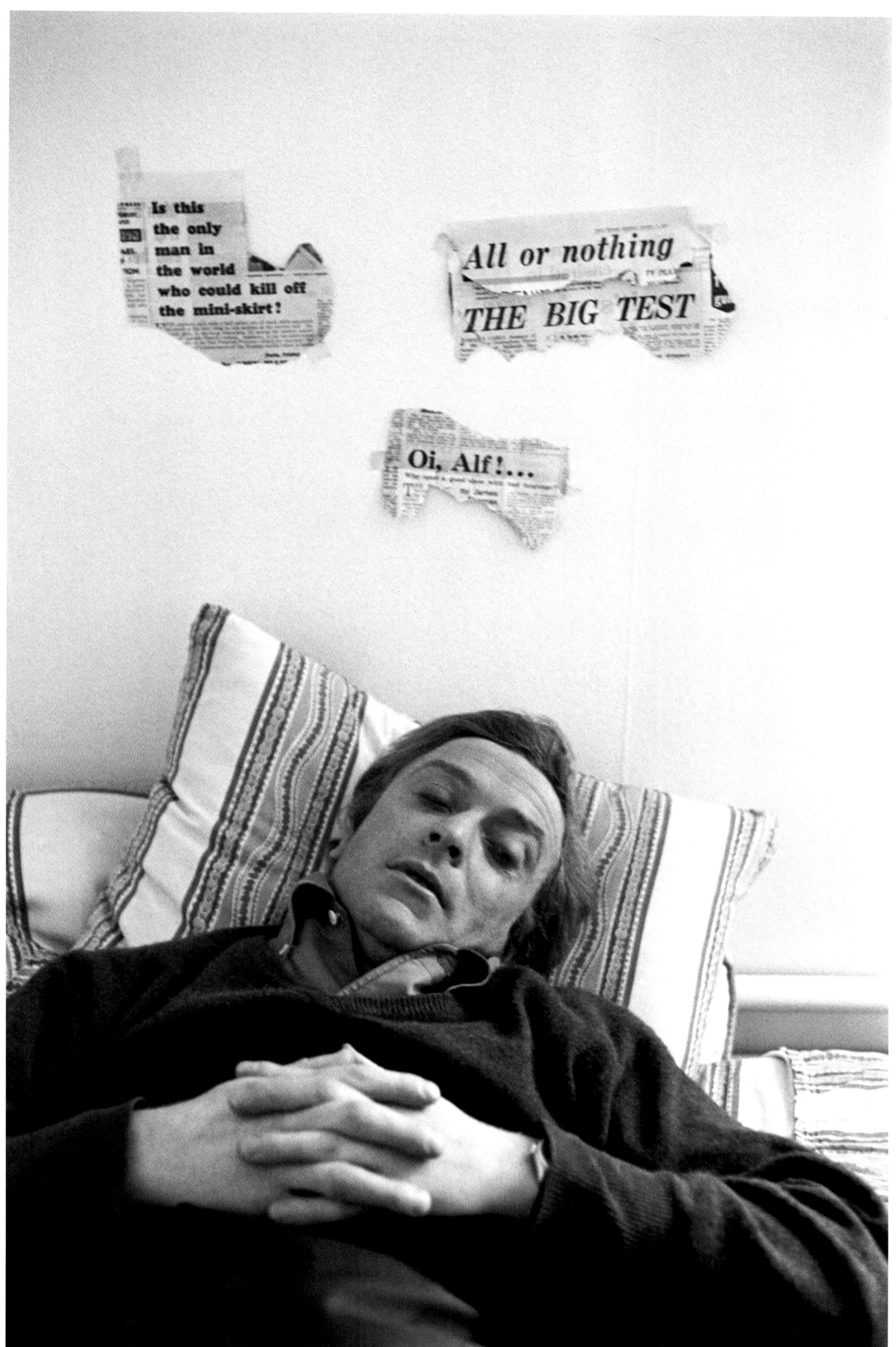
Is this
the only
man in
the world
who could kill off
the mini-skirt!
All or nothing
THE BIG TEST
Oi, Alf!...

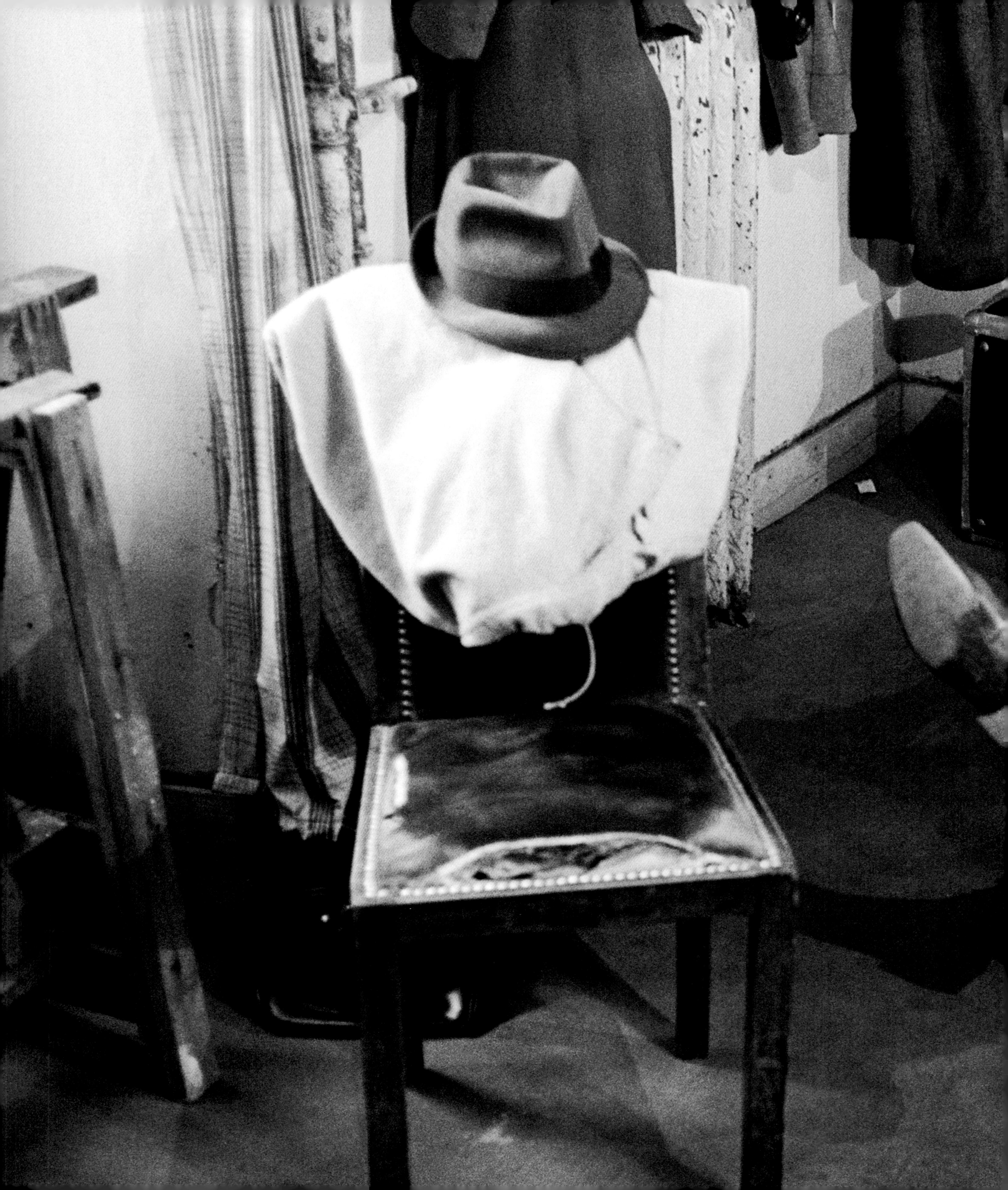

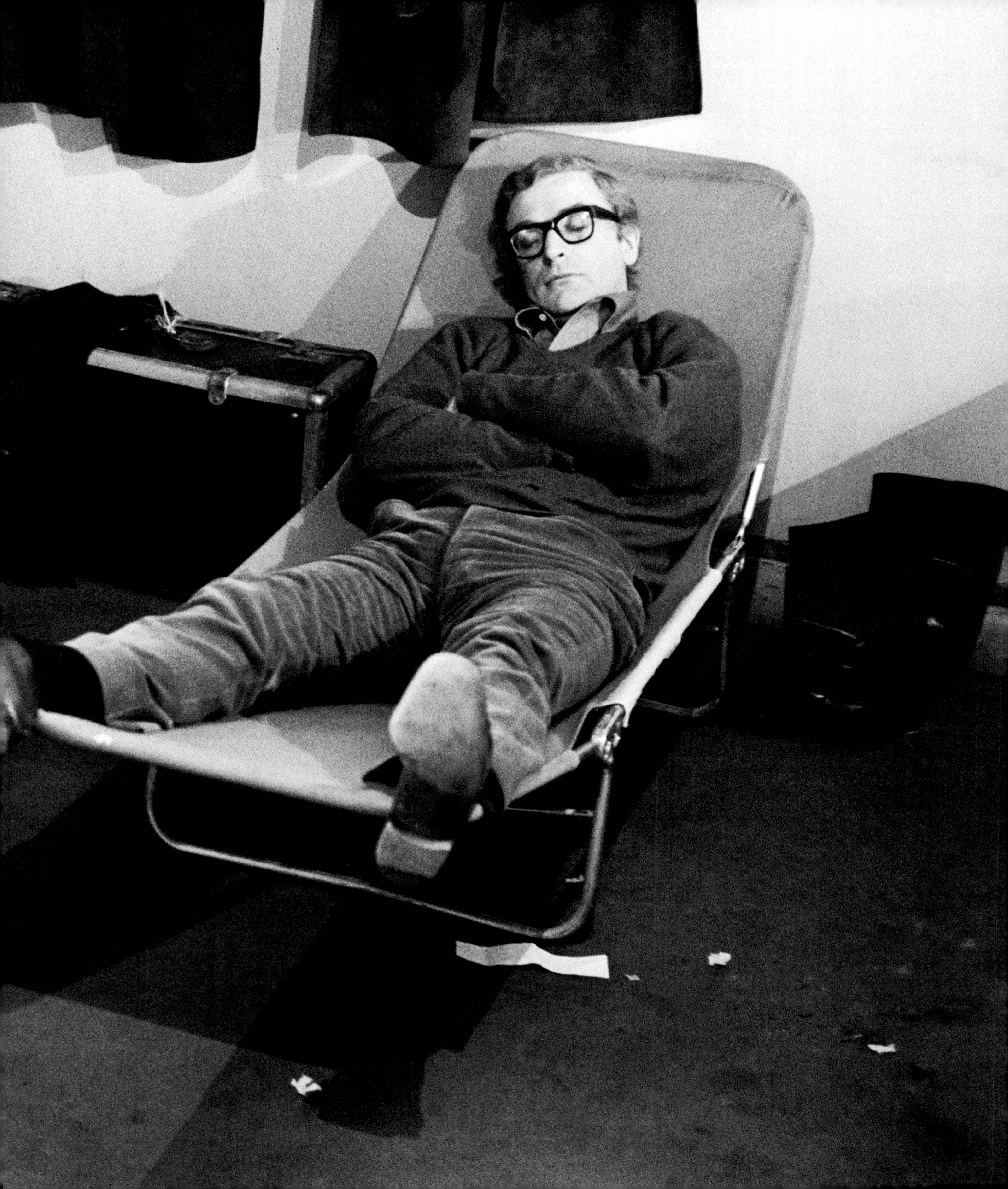

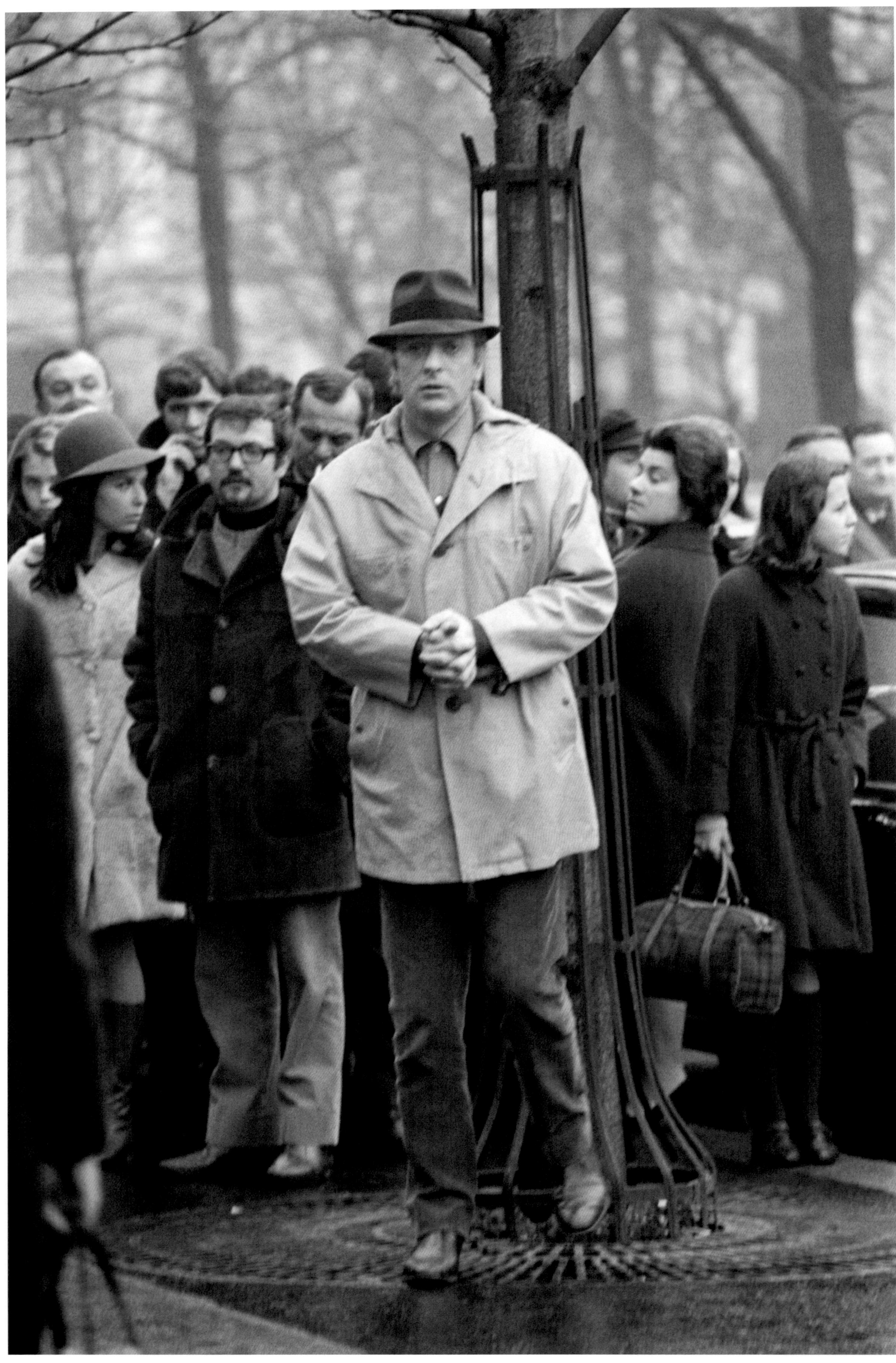

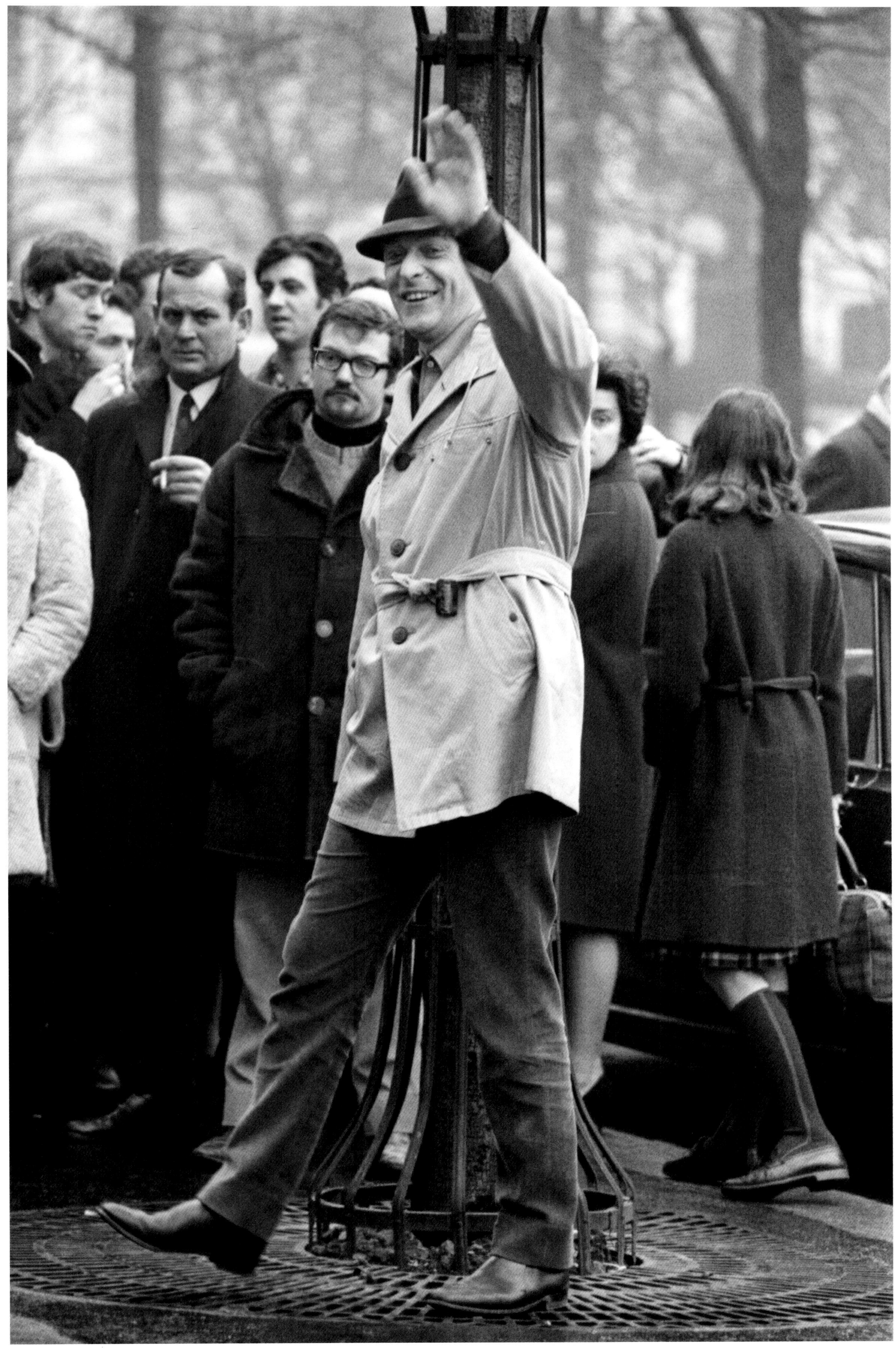

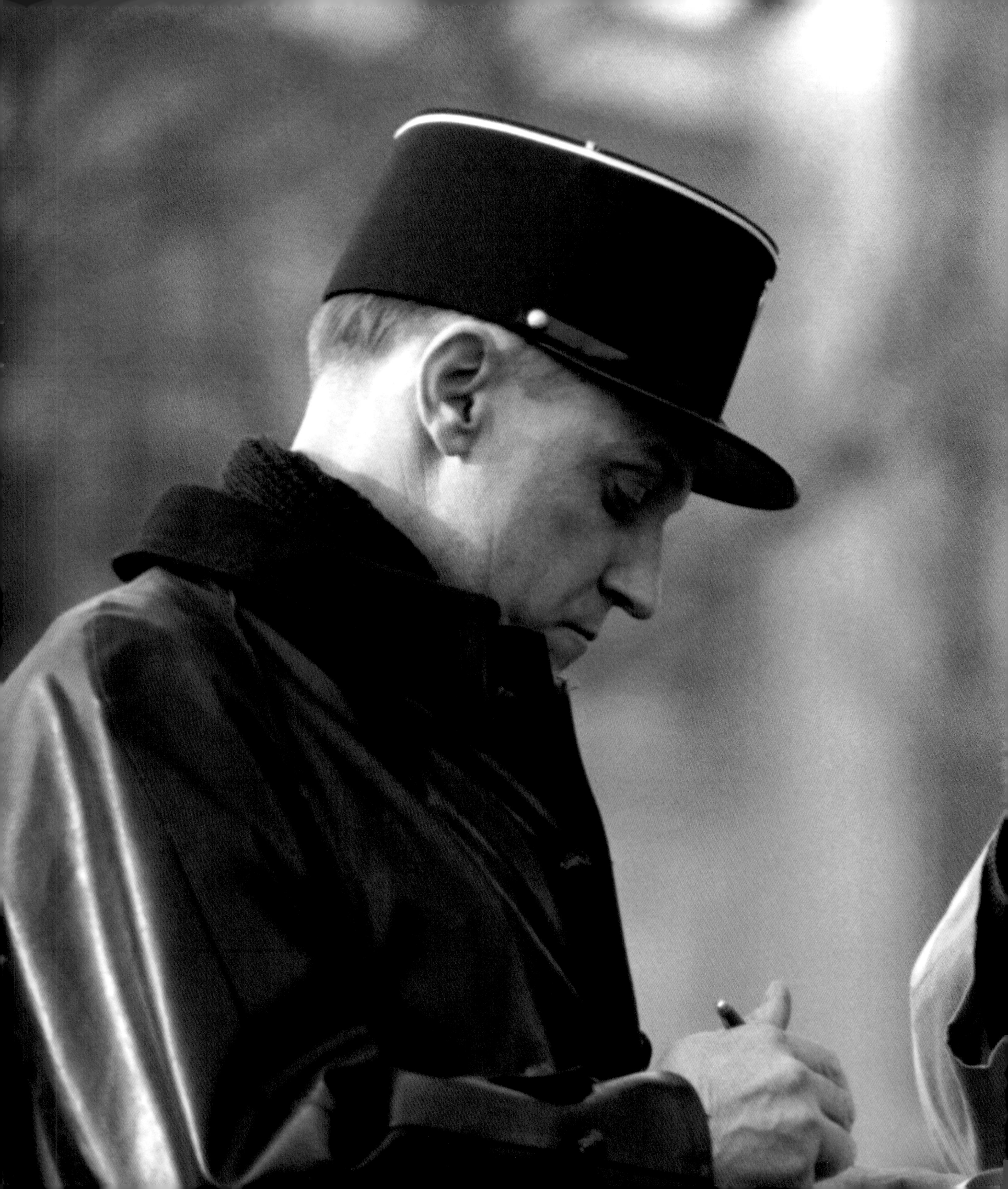

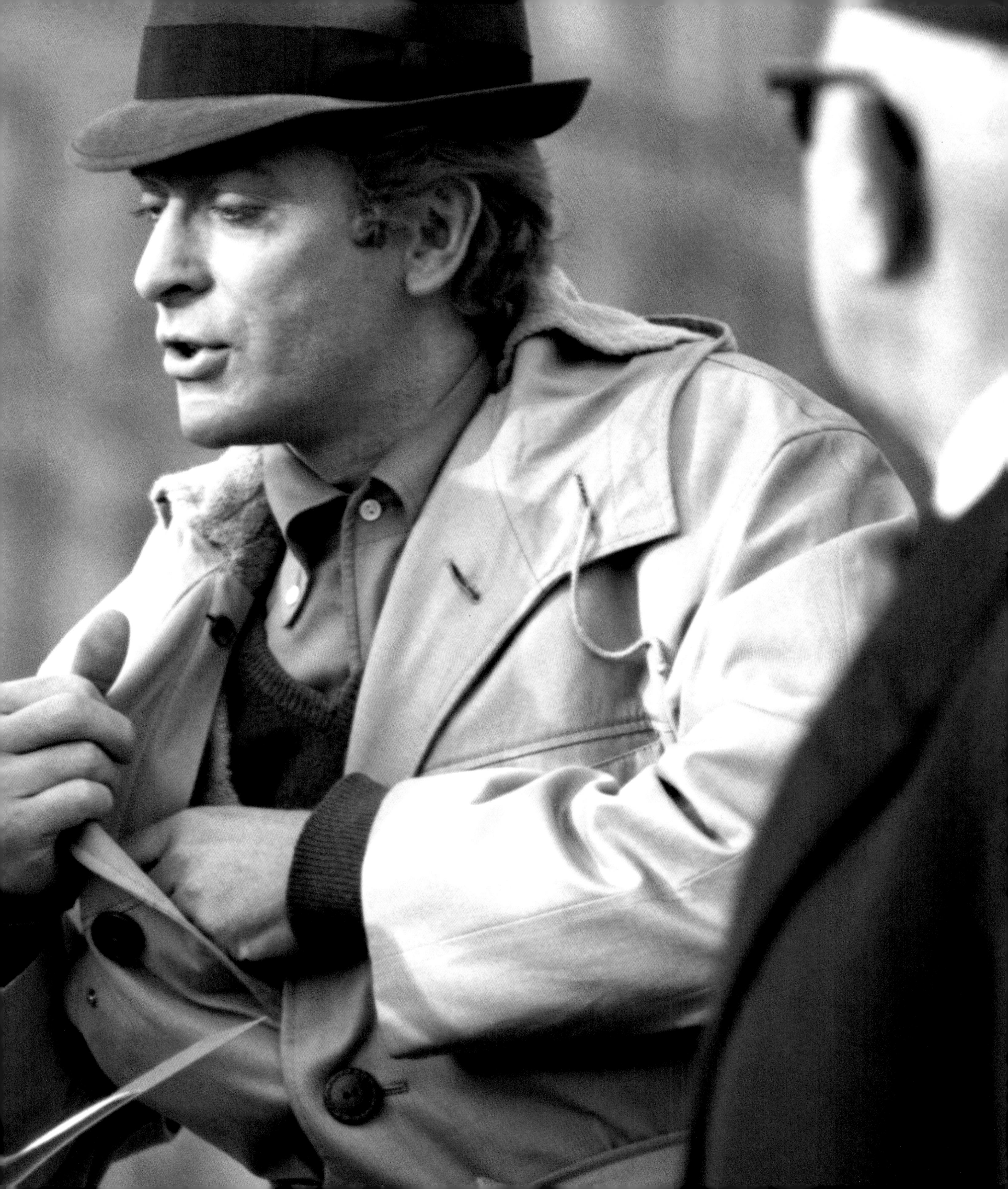

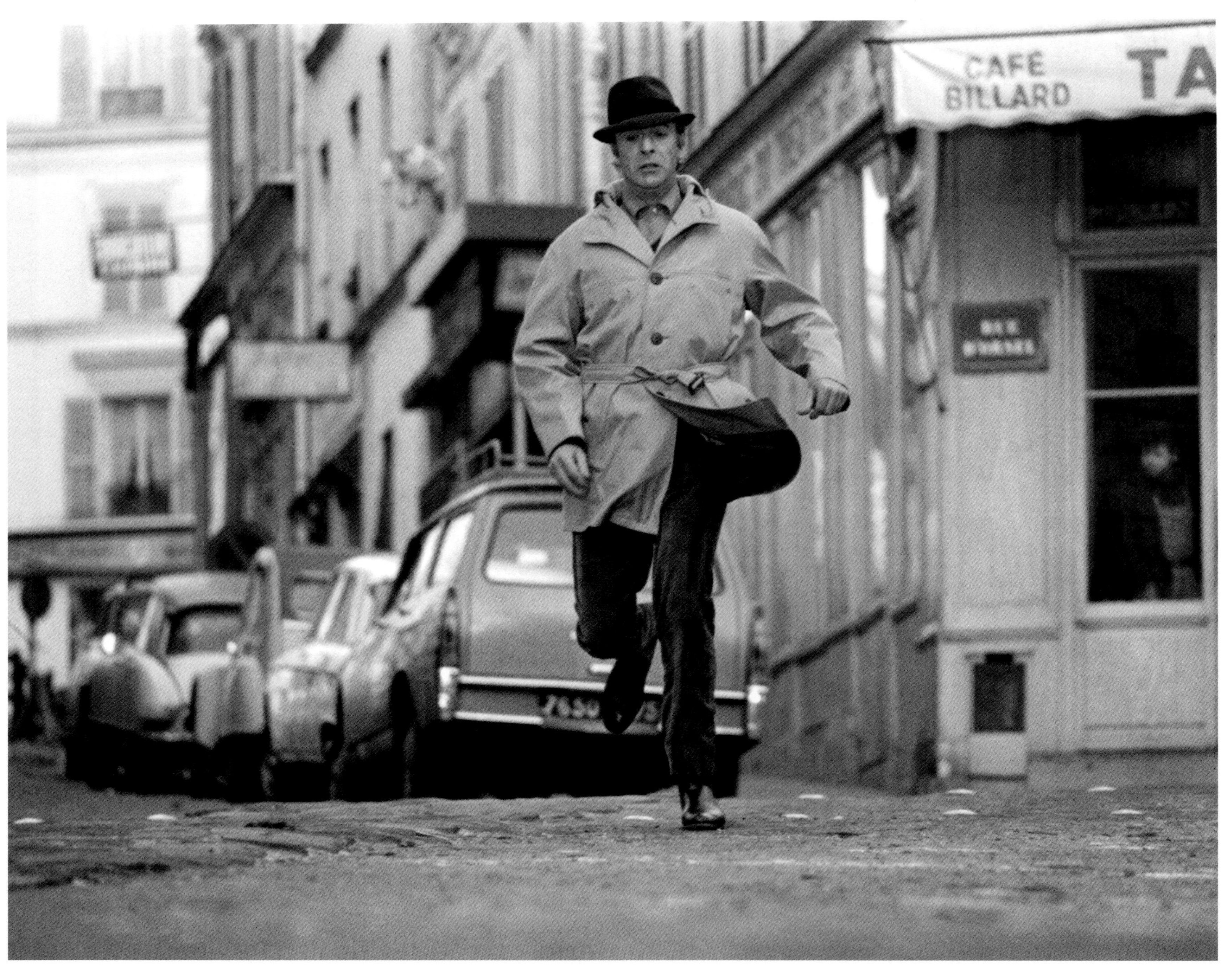

Above: Caine as the unnamed man, who is in fact a private detective hired by a jealous husband to follow his wife.
Previous page: Caine, out of character, with a gendarme on the streets of Paris during filming for the 'Snow' vignette of *Woman Times Seven*.

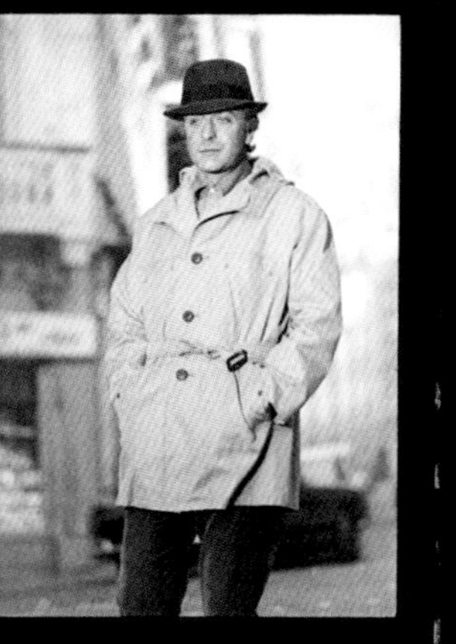
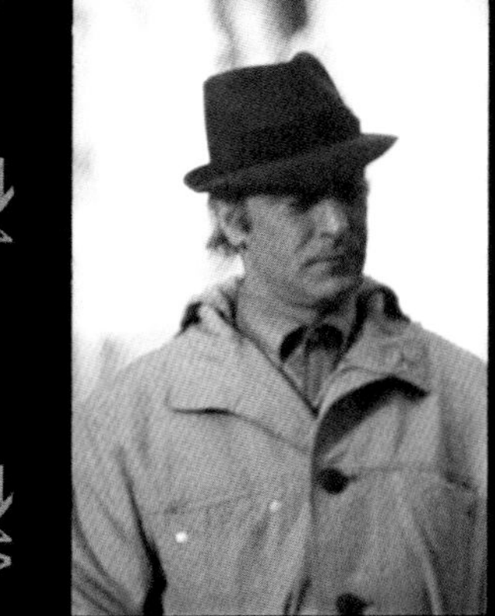
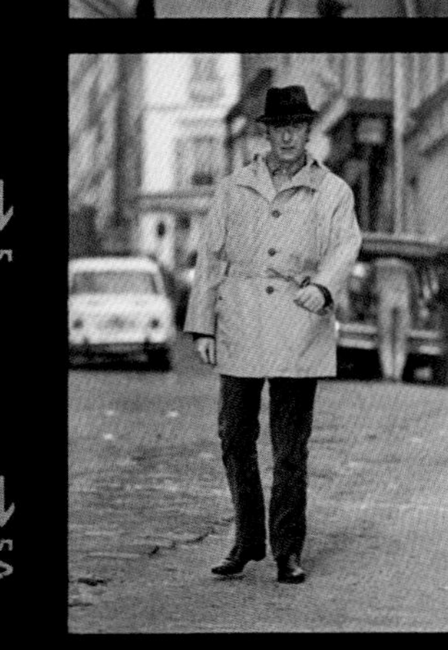
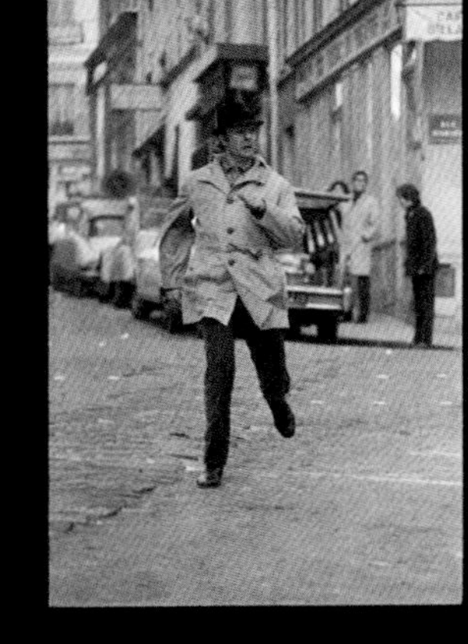
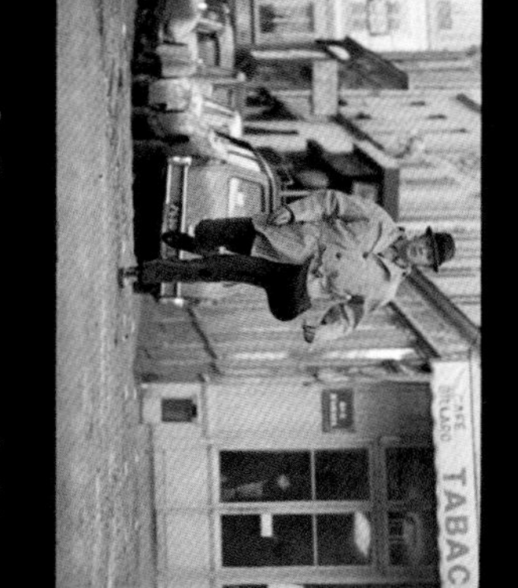
TABAC
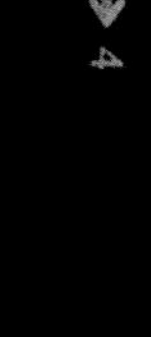
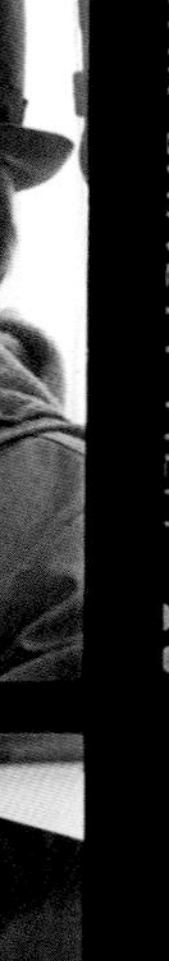
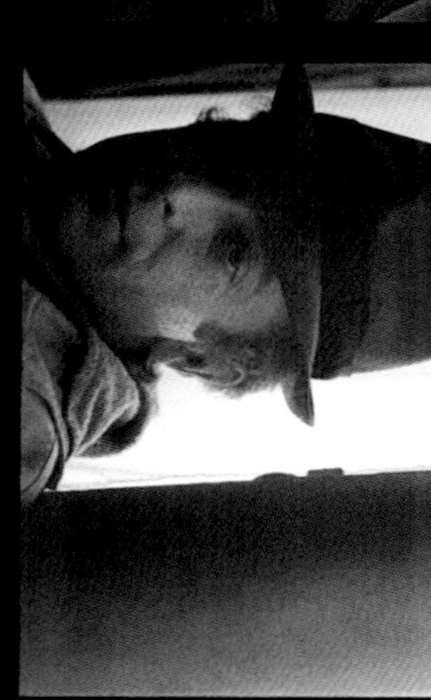
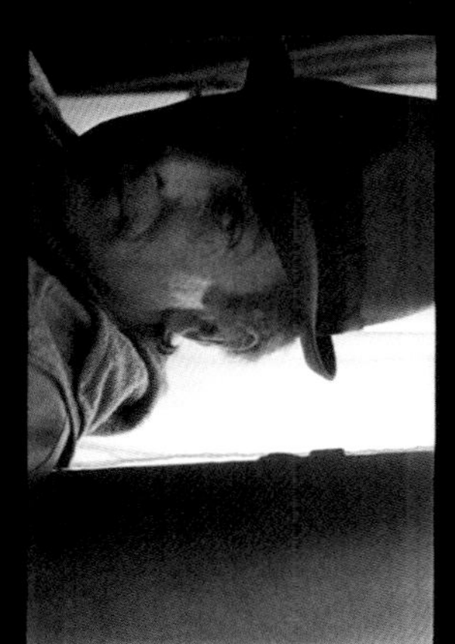
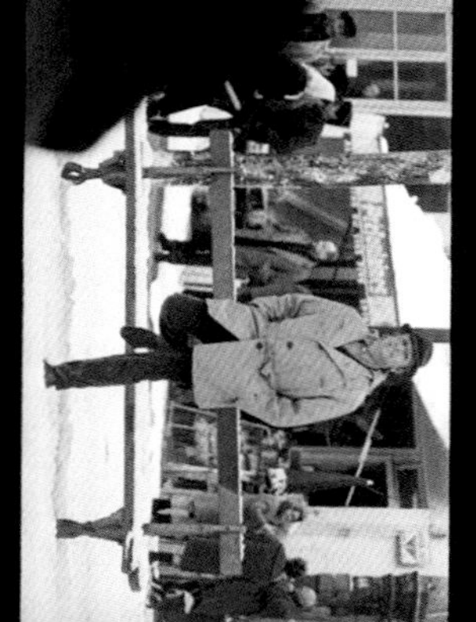
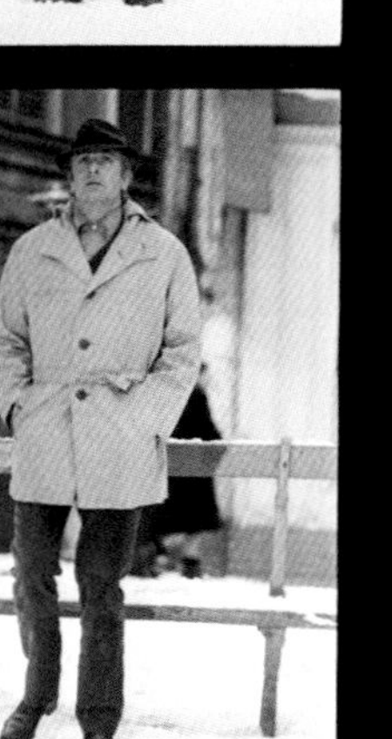
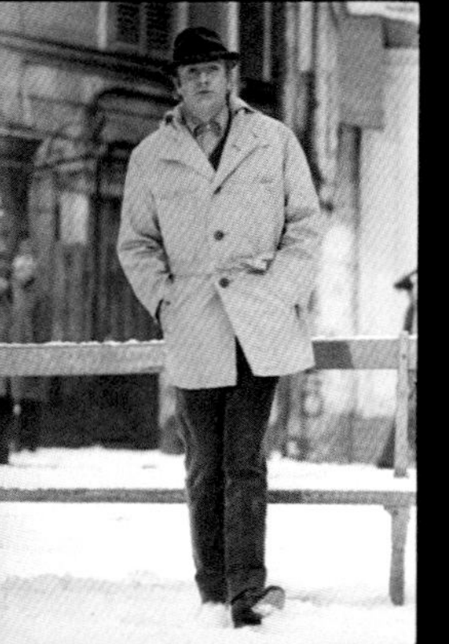
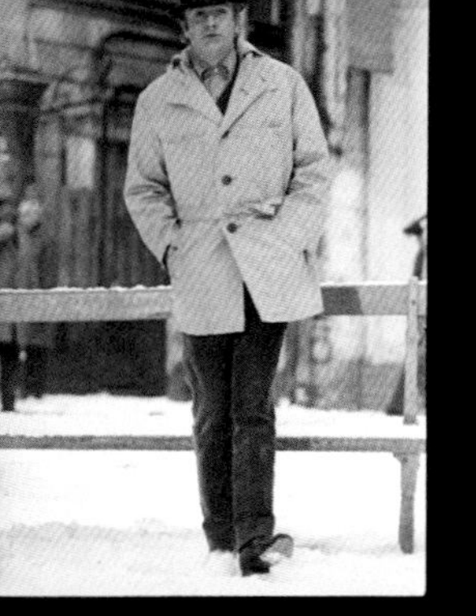
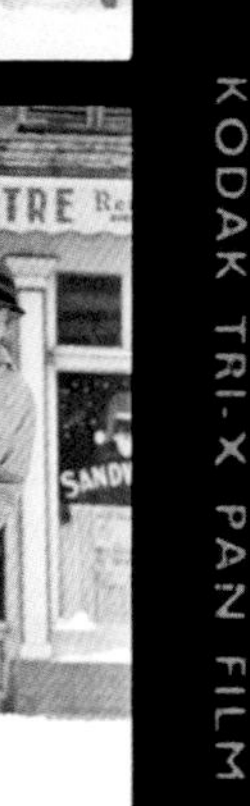
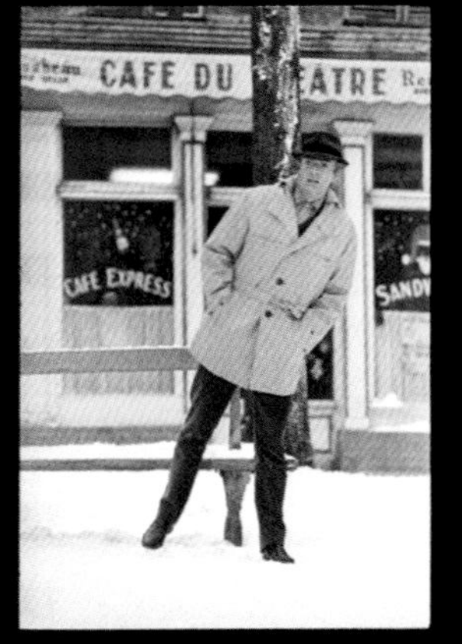
CAFE DU THEATRE
CAFE EXPRESS
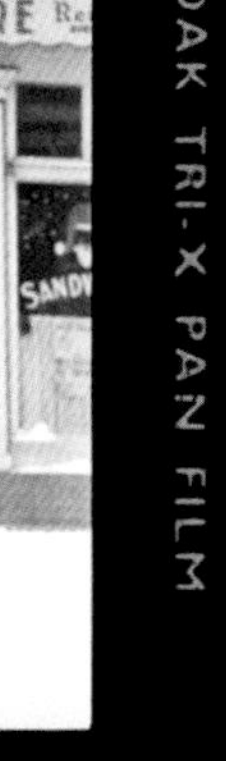
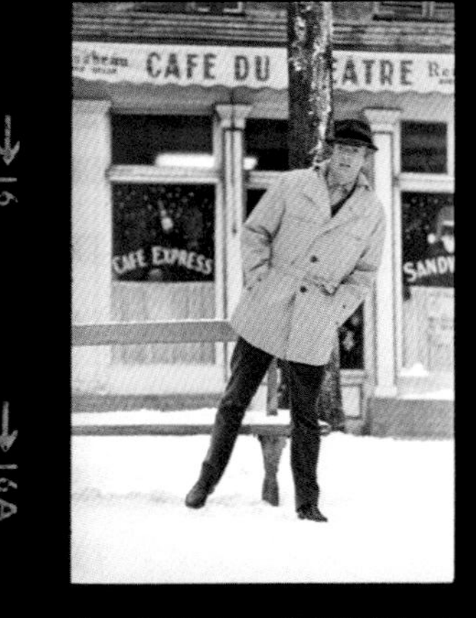
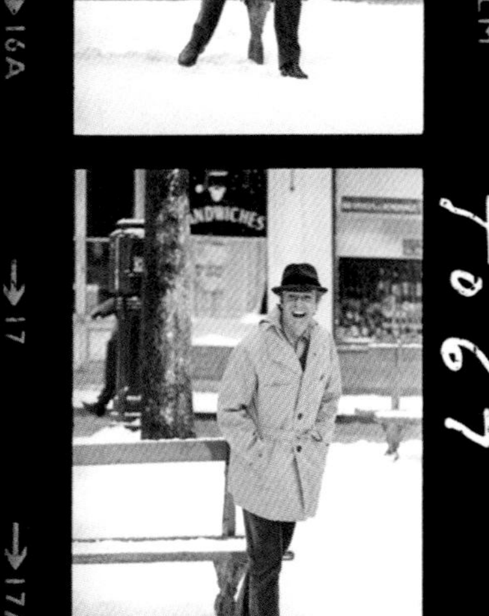
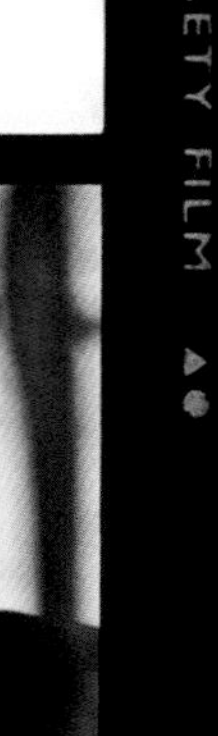
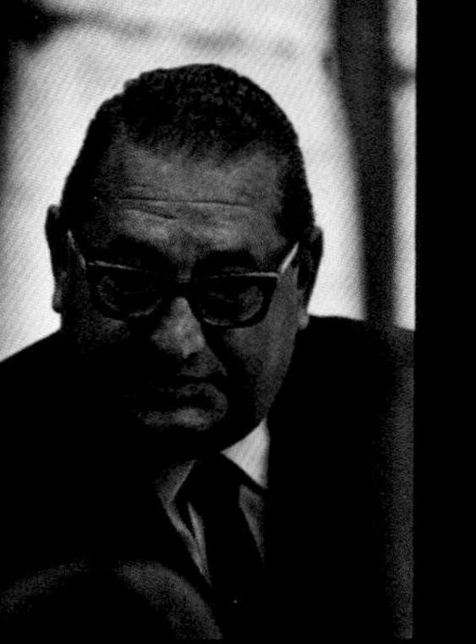
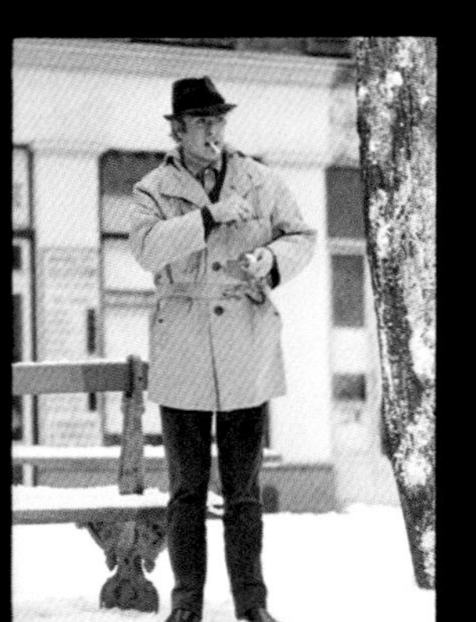
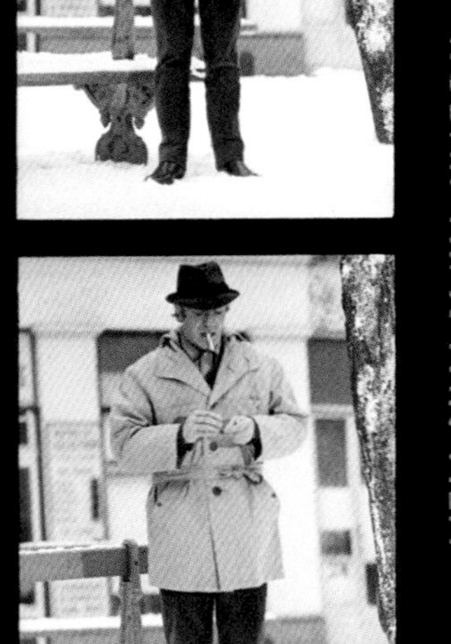
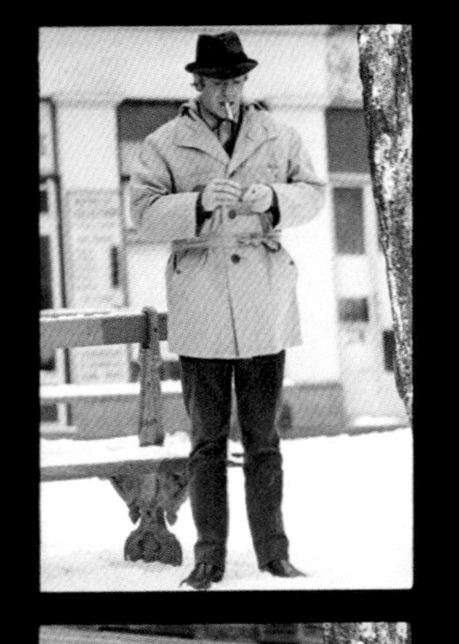
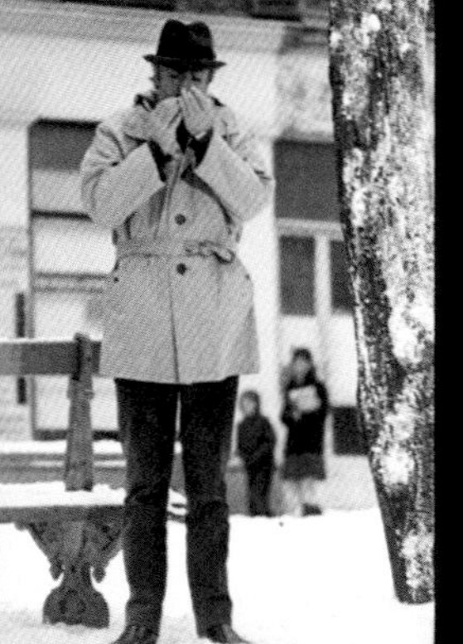
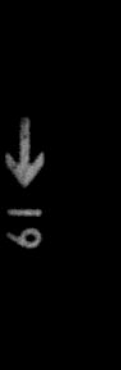
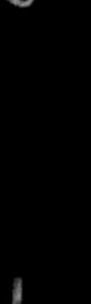
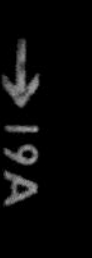
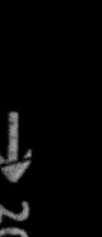
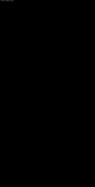
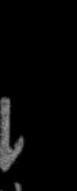
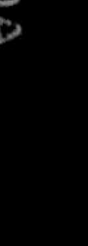

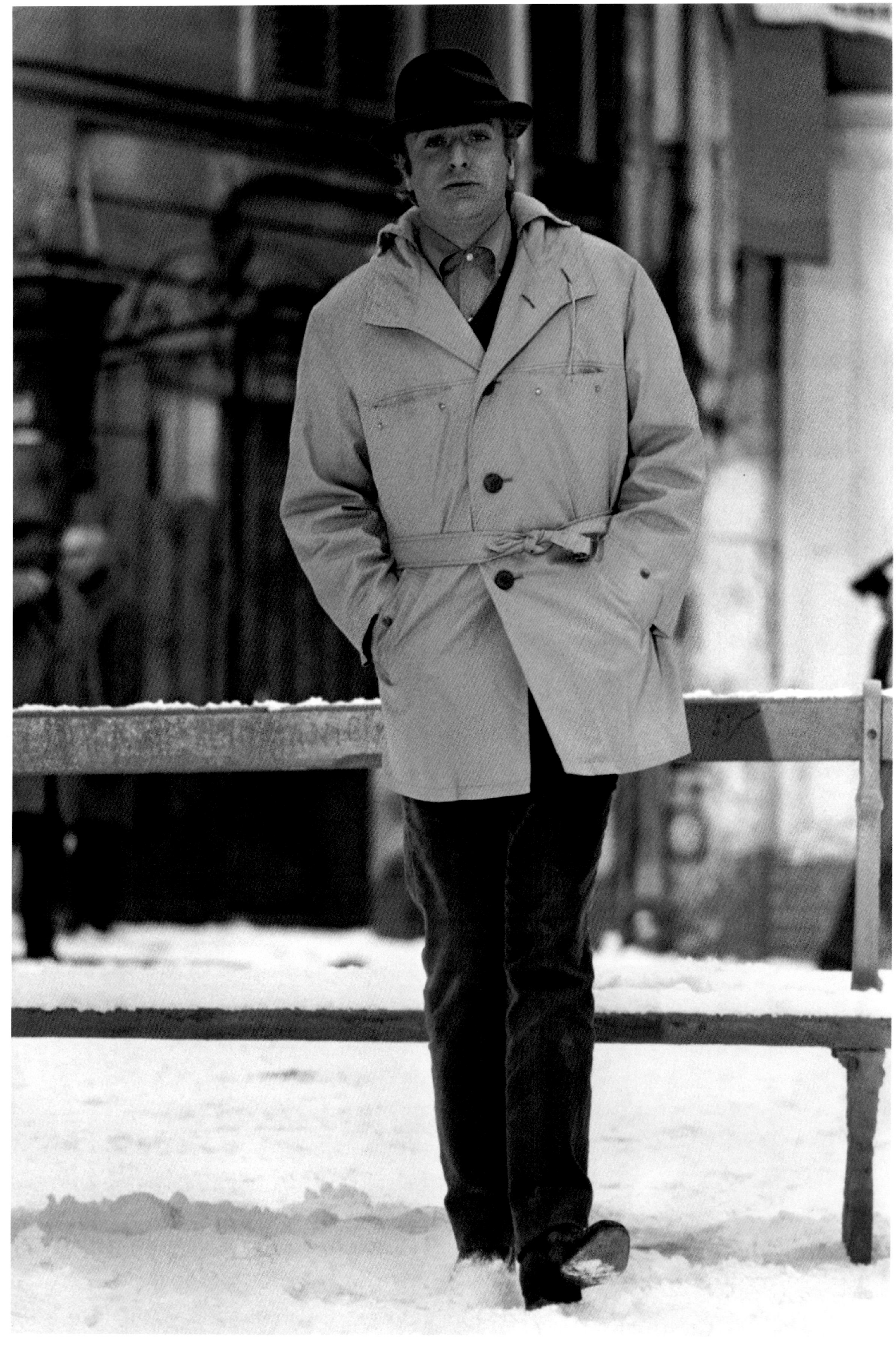

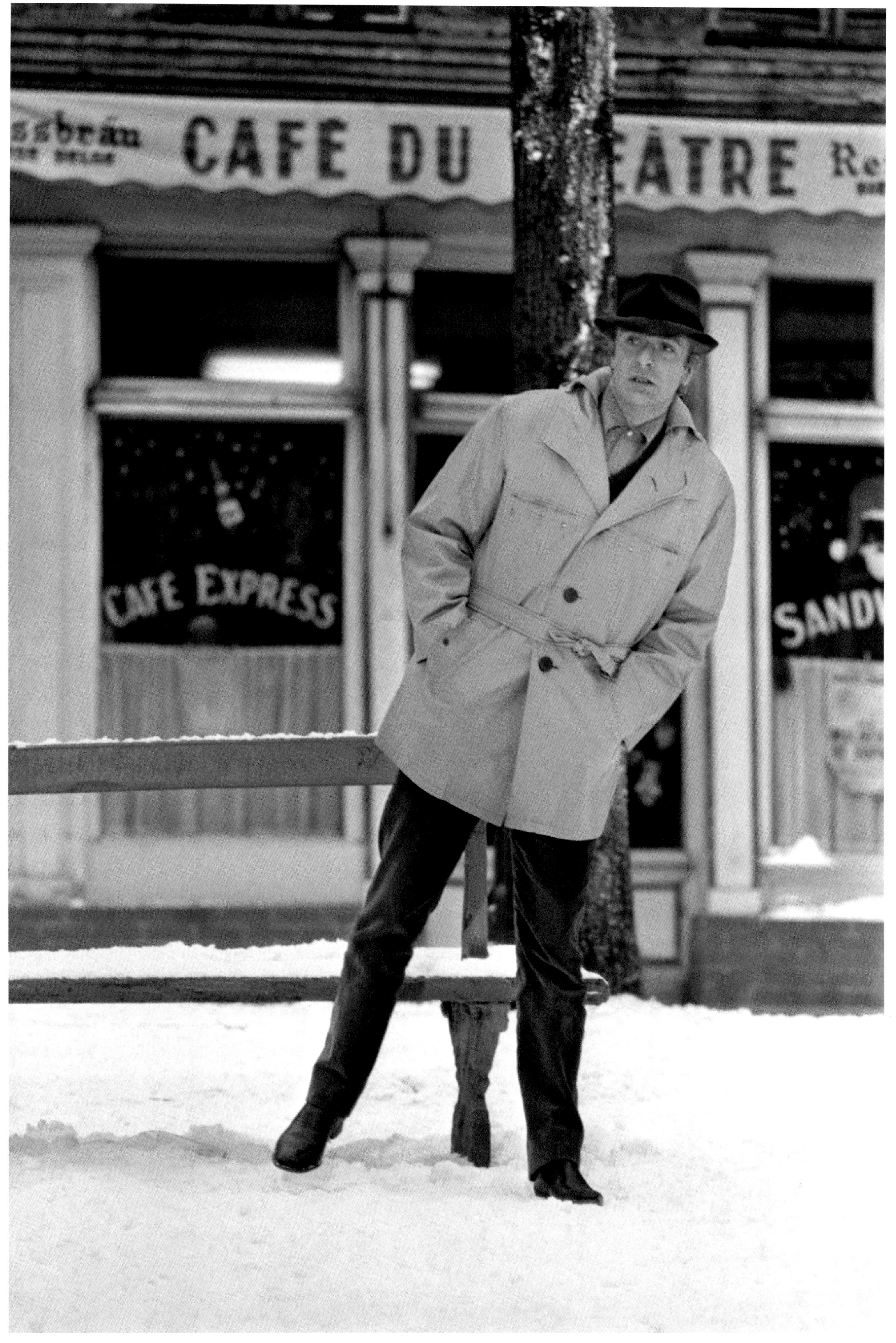
CAFE DU
CAFE EXPRESS

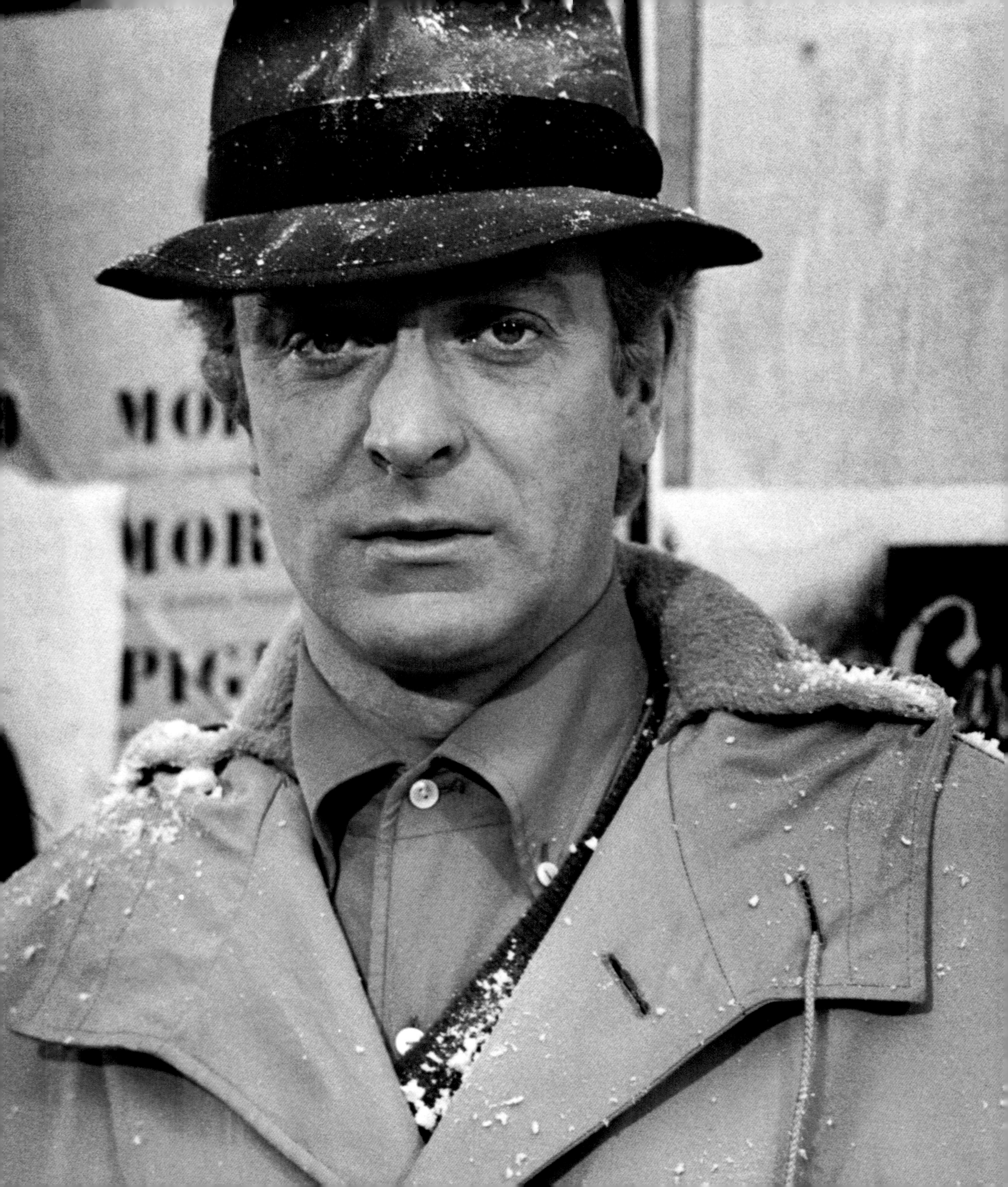

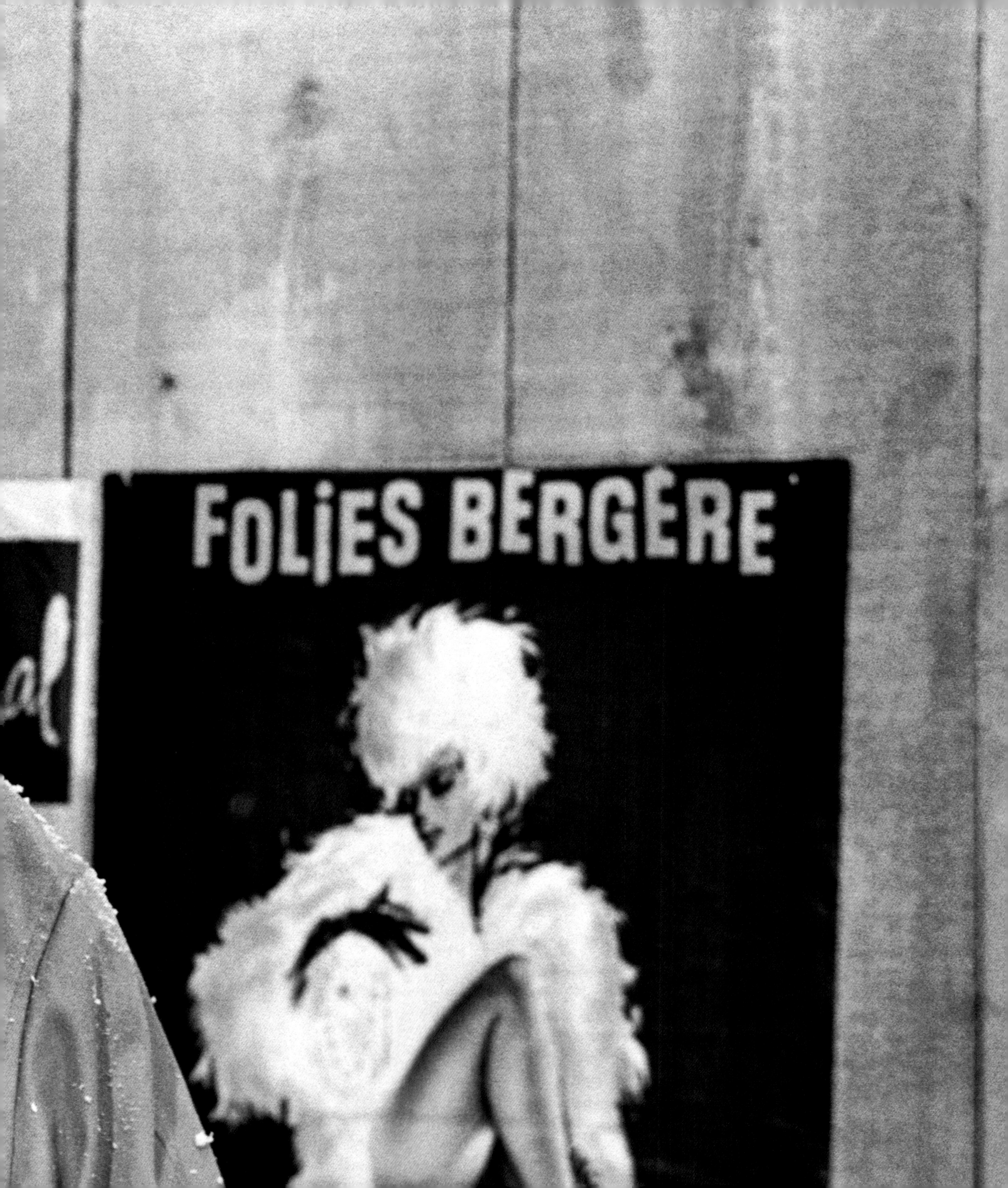

FOLIES BERGÈRE

... screen acting is much more a matter of 'being' than 'performing'.

Michael Caine

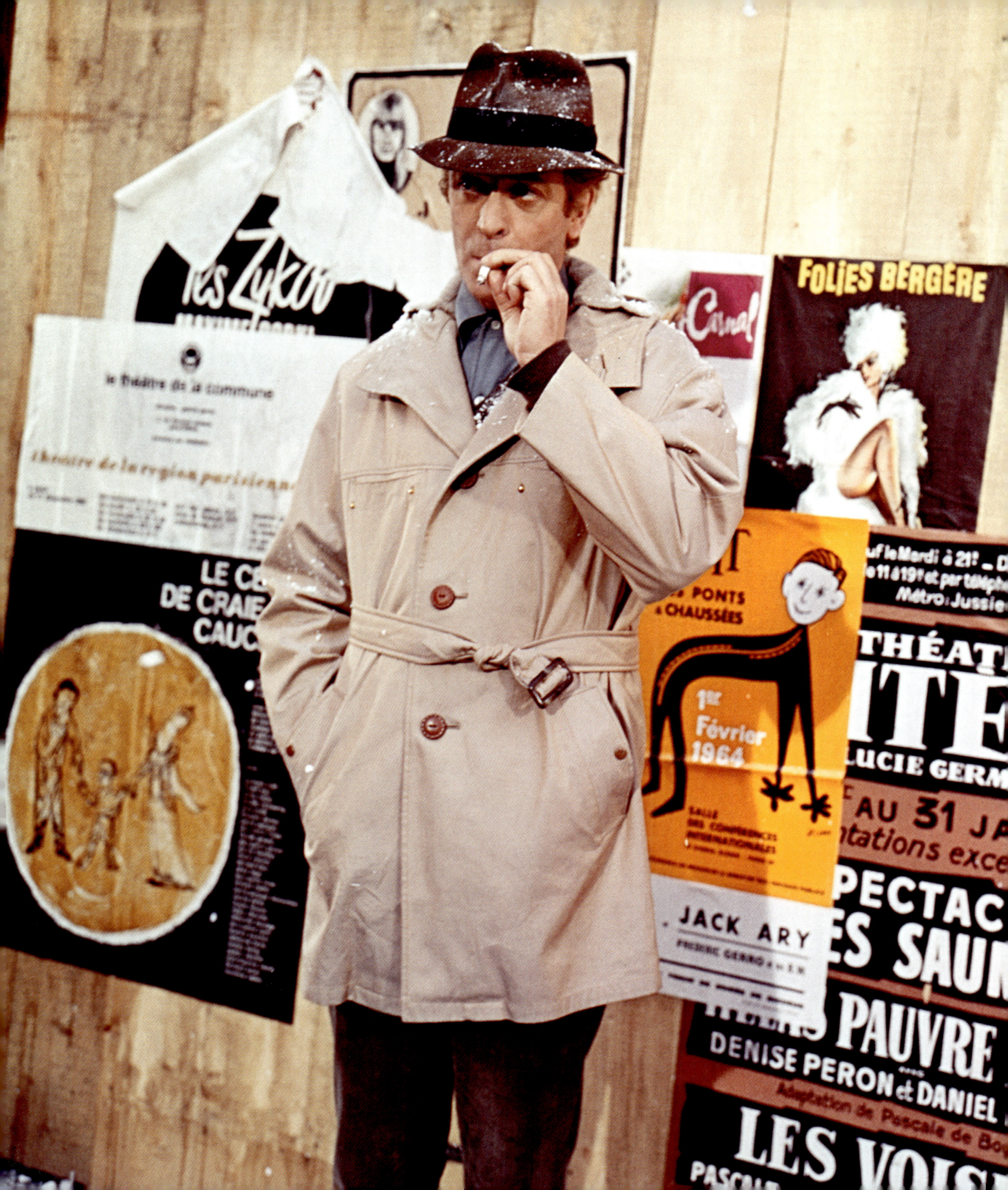
FOLIES BERGERE
PONTS
& CHAUSSÉES
1er
Février
1964
JACK ARY
PAUVRE
DENISE PERON et DANIEL

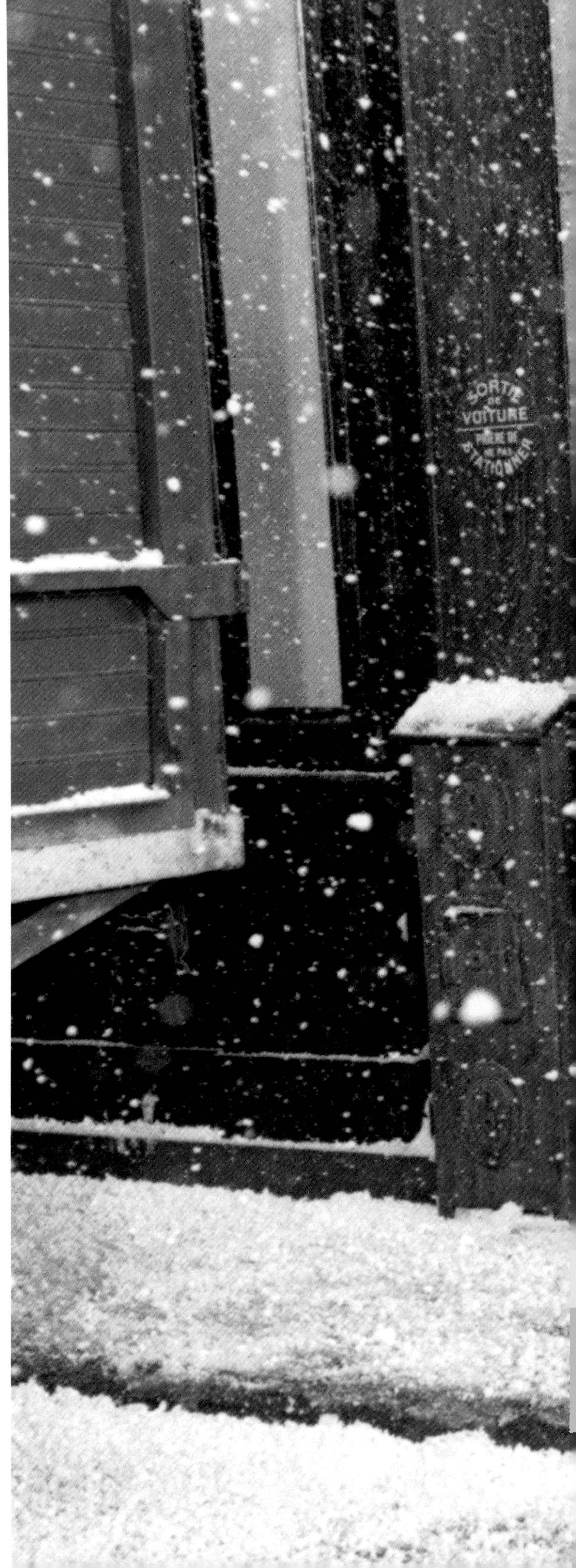
SORTIE DE VOITURE
STATIONNER

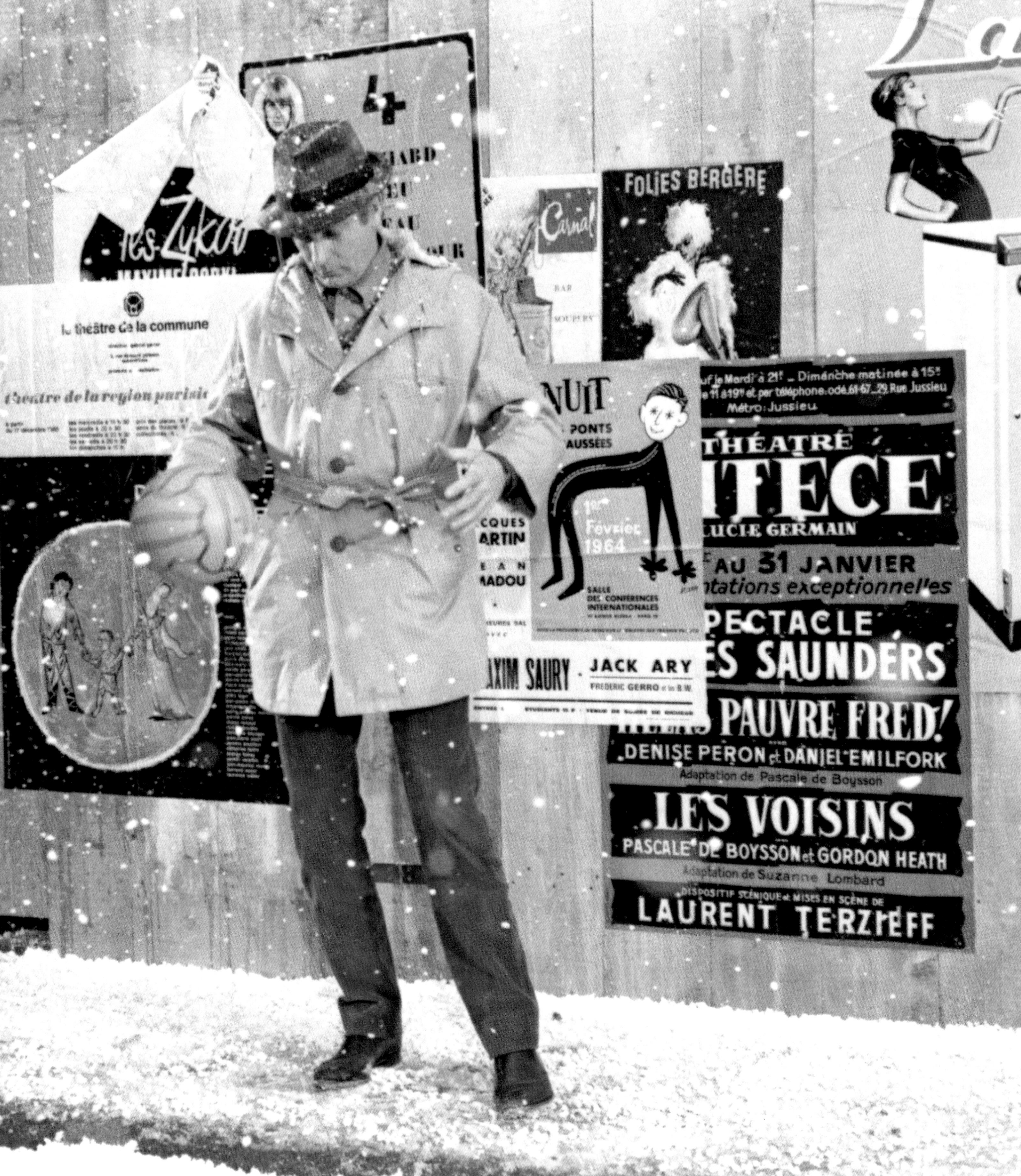

les Zykov
le théâtre de la commune
FOLIES BERGERE
Carnal
BAR
SOUPERS
Métro : Jussieu
THÉATRE
LUCIE GERMAIN
AU 31 JANVIER
NUIT
PONTS
1er Février 1964
SALLE DES CONFERENCES INTERNATIONALES
JACK ARY
FREDERIC GERRO et les B.W.
ES SAUNDERS
PAUVRE FRED!
DENISE PERON et DANIEL EMILFORK
Adaptation de Pascale de Boysson
LES VOISINS
PASCALE DE BOYSSON et GORDON HEATH
Adaptation de Suzanne Lombard
DISPOSITIF SCÉNIQUE et MISES EN SCÈNE DE
LAURENT TERZIEFF

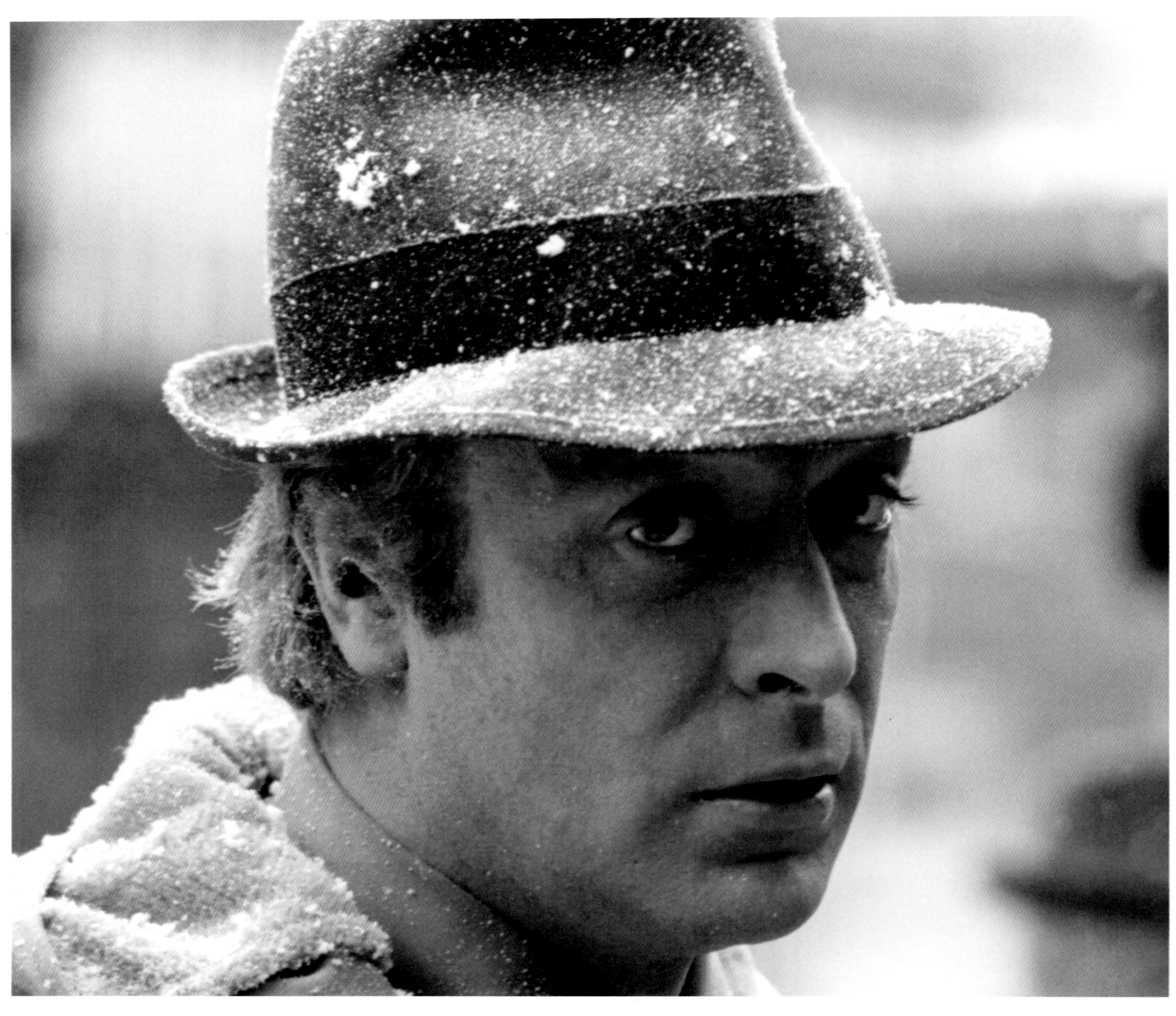

O'Neill's close-ups of Caine as the unnamed man in the 'Snow' segment of *Woman Times Seven*, remind us of Caine's facility for portraying characters that are reserved and low-key; that muted quality drawing us into a character's behaviour.

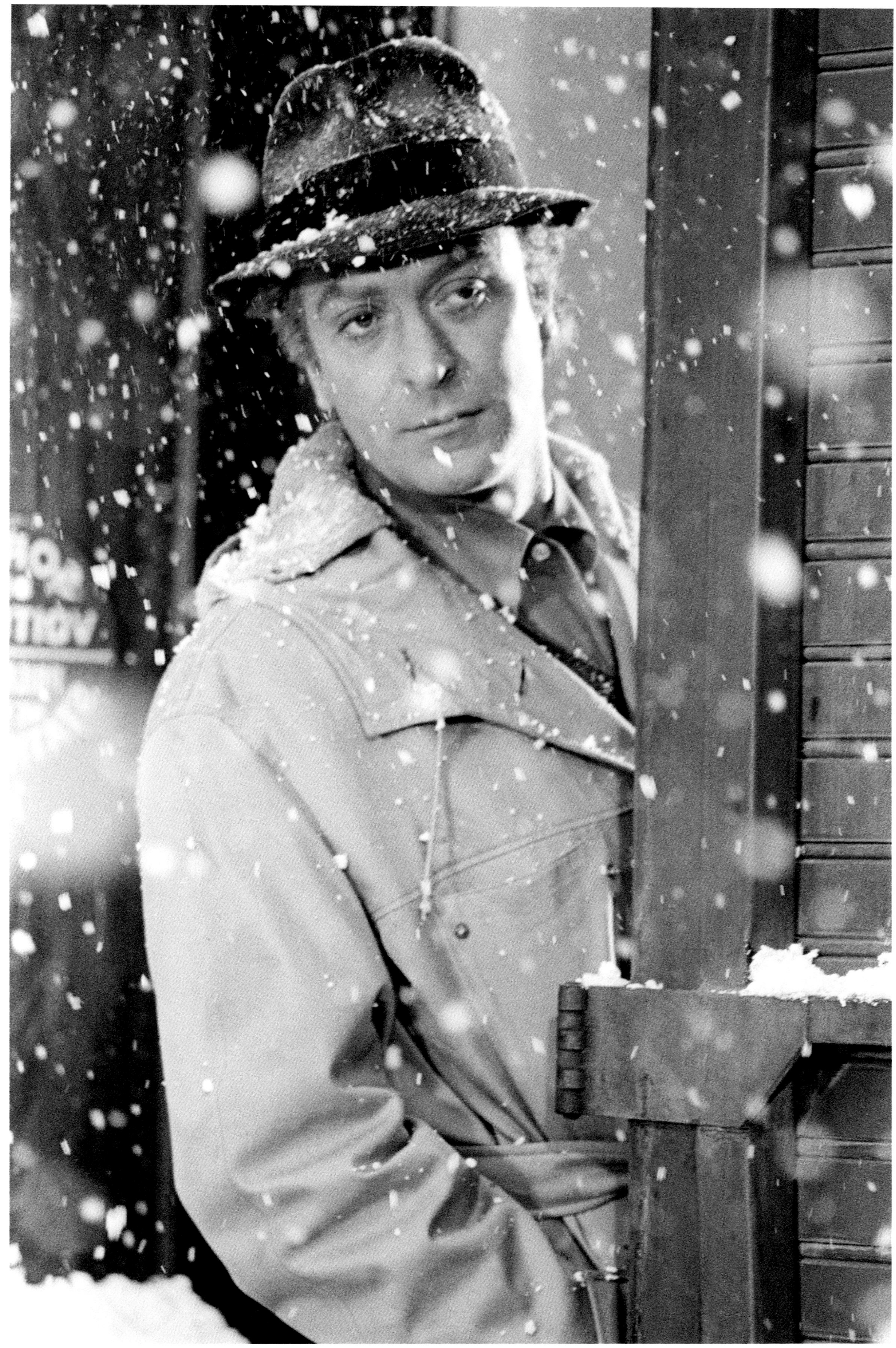

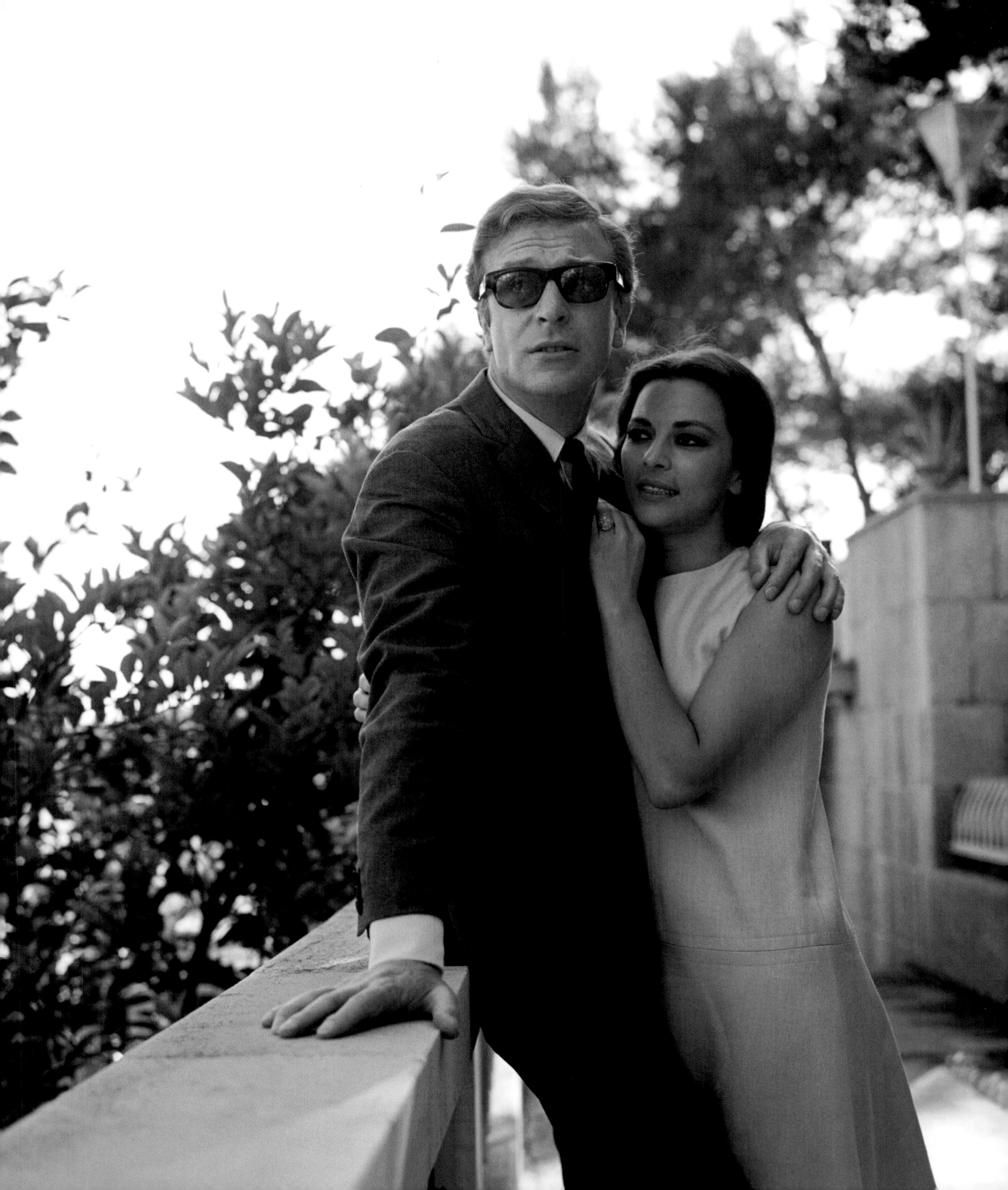

DEADFALL

1968

"The film's cult standing has enjoyed improving fortunes in the decades since its release; in particular, the twenty-minute heist sequence in the film is regarded as a deft example of Forbes's facility for shaping tension..."

During the same time period as working on *The Magus*, Caine also starred in Hollywood studio Twentieth Century Fox's *Deadfall*, an adaptation of Desmond Cory's heist/psychological thriller novel. It was directed by British filmmaker (and a friend of Caine's) Bryan Forbes, who had established himself as a major figure in the British film industry, having directed *Whistle Down the Wind* (1961), *The L-Shaped Room* (1962) and *Séance on a Wet Afternoon* (1964).

Deadfall centres on a burglar named Henry Clarke, who is trying to 'dry out' at a sanitorium. He is dragged back into his old life by Richard Moreau and his wife Fé, who plan to steal diamonds from a millionaire's chateau. Inevitably, Caine's character falls in love with Fé, played by Italian film star Giovanna Ralli; Richard, who already has a male lover encourages the couple, but there are more sexual secrets to be revealed...

Deadfall was shot at Pinewood Studios and on location in Madrid and Majorca, including at the Castillo De Bendinat and Marivent Palace. The film's cult standing has enjoyed improving fortunes in the decades since its release; in particular, the twenty-minute heist sequence in the film is regarded as a deft example of Forbes's facility for shaping tension, with the influence of legendary filmmaker Alfred Hitchcock felt quite vividly. Also of note, is John Barry's music, which Forbes used to the propel the action and heighten the mood by intercutting the robbery with a guitar concert performance.

O'Neill's location shoot captures a number of delightful images of Caine and Ralli. Caine recalls: "...although the movie didn't turn out as well as we'd hoped, it was a happy time."[1]

Previous page: Caine and his co-star Giovanna Ralli on location for *Deadfall*.
Opposite page: Caine and Ralli. On location at the Jardine de Alfabia in Majorca.

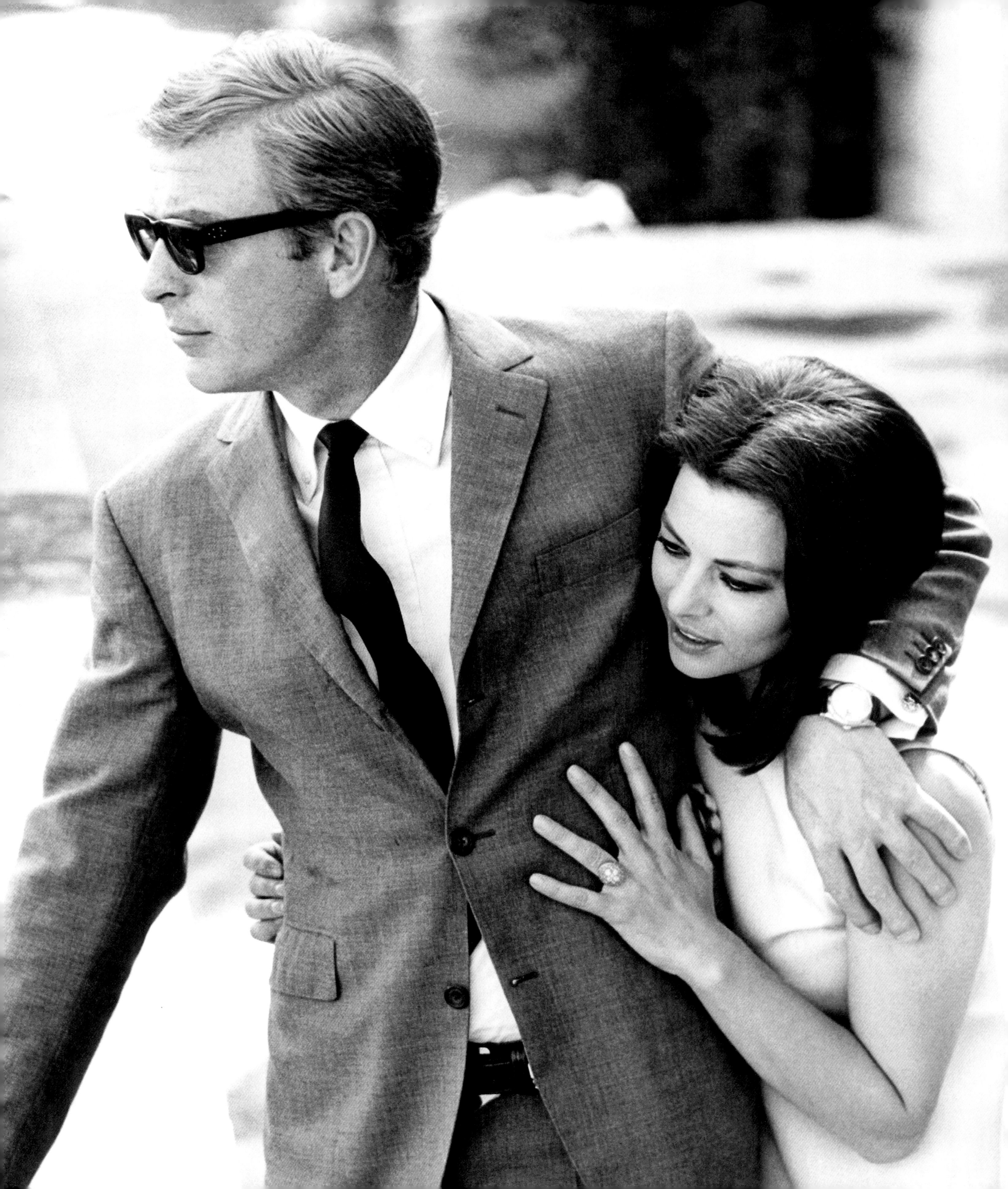

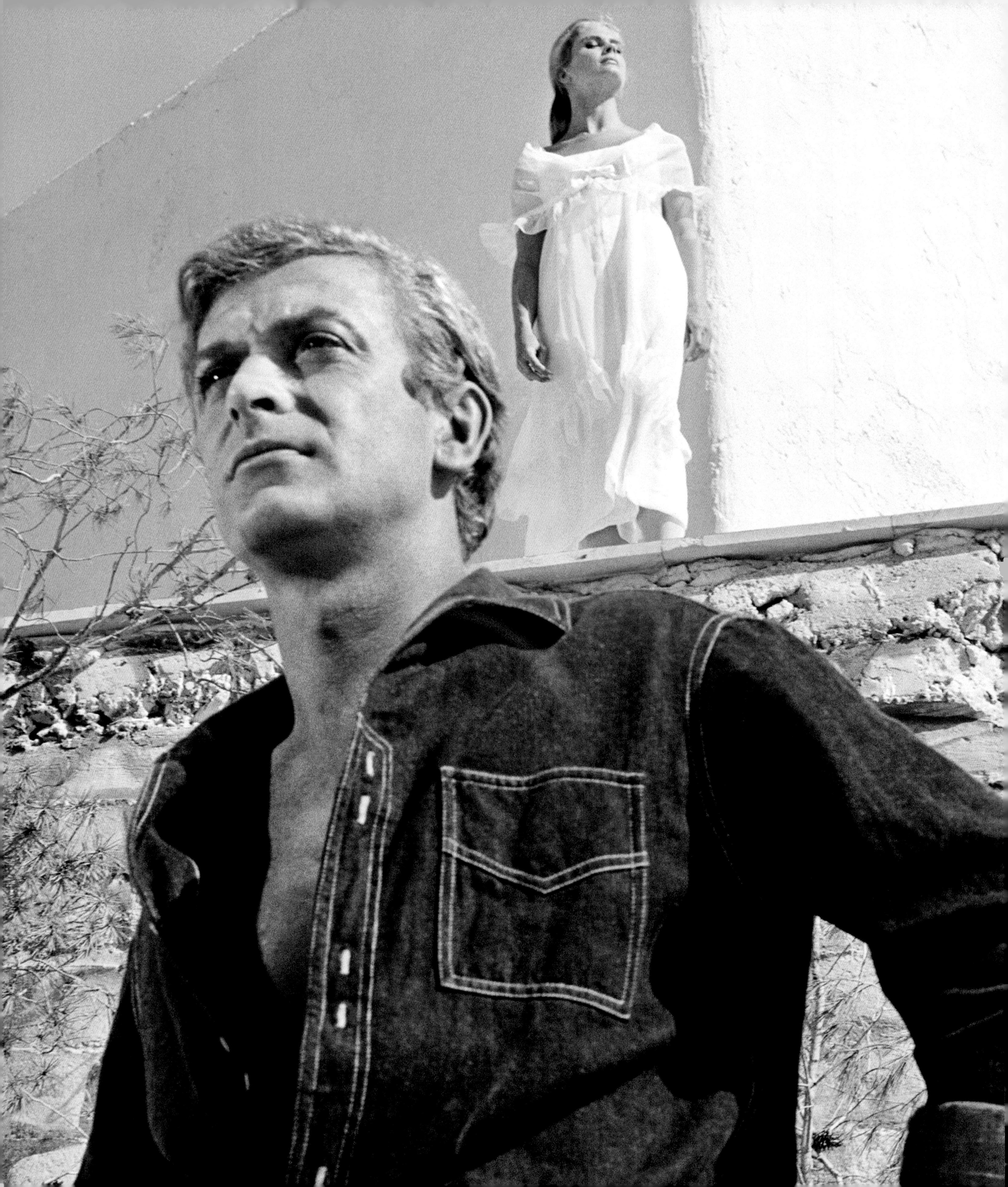

THE MAGUS

1968

"O'Neill's images from the film's production, largely in black and white, capture a sense of place and also the sense of ease between the lead actors."

Based on John Fowles's expansive – running to just shy of 700 pages – 1965 novel, the film was a critical flop. Caine himself comments " ...a terrible film of John Fowles's book *The Magus*, which none of us understood, and neither, it seemed, did the audience."[1]

Fowles wrote the screenplay for the film adaptation himself and perhaps that speaks to the film's core problem: novels and screenplays are fundamentally different beasts. The film attempts to *compress* rather than more actively *adapt* the novel and, perhaps, therein lies its lack of clarity.

All of that said, the film now has something of a cult status and not every review came down so hard on the film. *Variety* noted, "This near-miss is not without many notable virtues. Fowles's script sustains interest in its convolutions; direction is resourceful and sensitive; Caine is far more dynamic than usual and Quinn and the two femme stars register strongly."[2]

The New York Times review included particular comment about Caine's performance and, importantly, his screen presence: "Caine's special quality as an actor, the handsome, viable but essentially passive and bewildered hero, is just right for the kind of real unreal bargain he strikes with Conchis—never knowing whether he is part of a game, an experiment, a simple event, a madness or a fantasy, as the movie, like the novel, keeps inquiring of itself what its plot is going to be. The director, Guy Green, is remarkable in knowing what to show, what to drop, what to put in relief."[3]

Previous page: Candice Bergen and Michael Caine in character on the set of *The Magus*.
Opposite page: Caine as Nicholas Urfe.

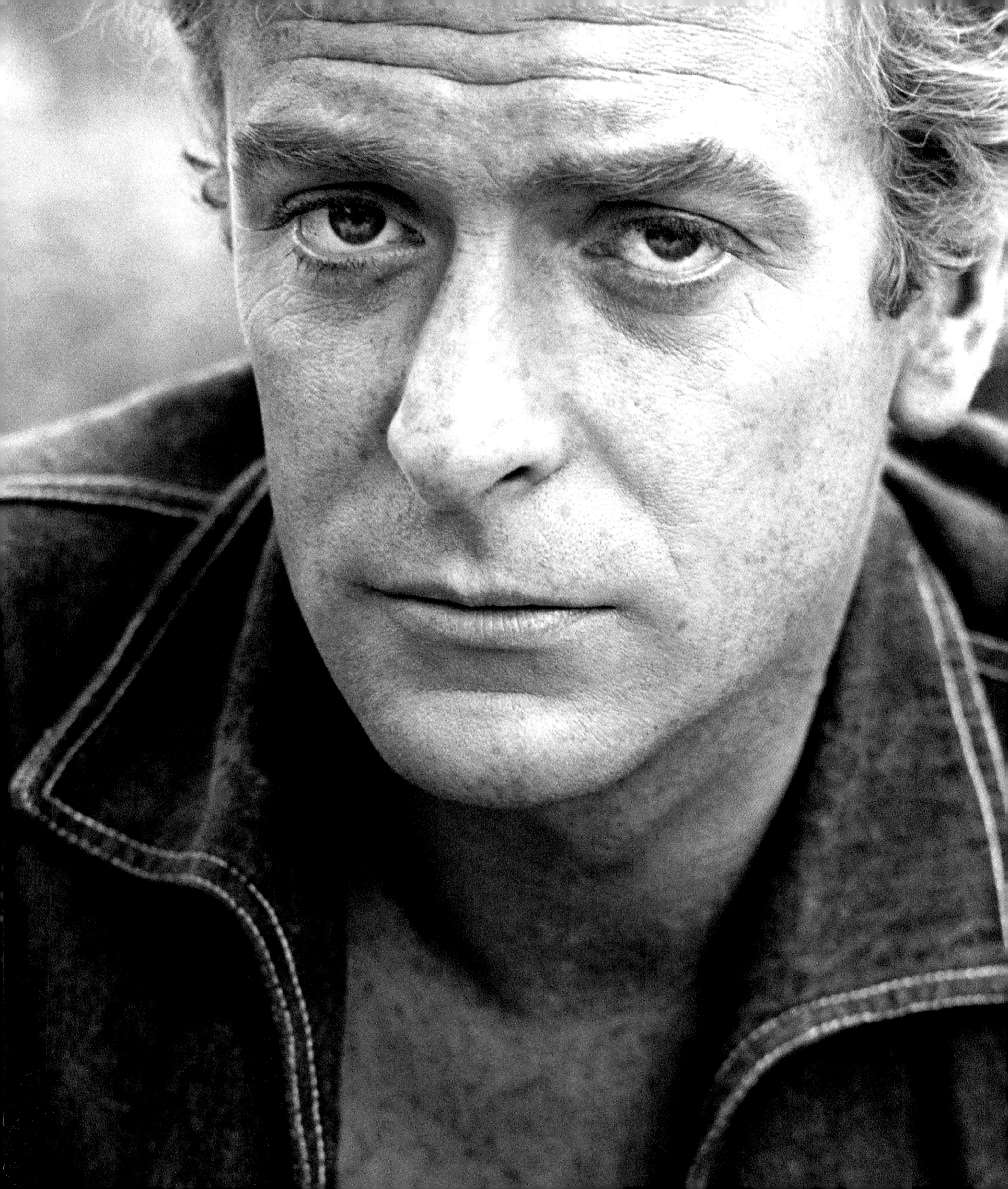

Caine portrays protagonist Nicholas Urfe, a schoolteacher who has travelled from the UK to the fictional Greek island of Phraxos (based on the real island of Spetses, where Fowles had taught at a boarding school 1951–52). Urfe comes to the island to replace a teacher who committed suicide in mysterious circumstances. To some extent, the story of *The Magus* concerns itself with the move from innocence to experience and with the tension between appearance and illusion; the film does go some way in engagingly dramatising this.

Anthony Quinn, a major international movie star at the time – *La Strada* (1954), *Lawrence of Arabia* (1962), *Zorba the Greek* (1964) – plays the film's title character, Conchis, the "resident eccentric millionaire".[4] He controls events on the island rather like a magician controls an illusion. O'Neill's images capture Quinn both in and out of character on set.

American actor, Candice Bergen, was cast in the role of Conchis's companion Lily. *The Magus* was a very early entry in Bergen's filmography and she would go on to star in such films as *Soldier Blue* (1970) and *Carnal Knowledge* (1971) and garner an Oscar nomination as Best Supporting Actress in *Starting Over* (1979).

The role of Anne (Alison in the novel) was played by Danish-French actor, Anna Karina. Instantly recognisable for European audiences, Karina had already established herself as a key presence in European cinema and the French New Wave, having starred in Jean-Luc Godard's effortlessly cool *Bande à part* (1964). Legend has it, Godard 'discovered' Karina having seen her in a Palmolive soap commercial.

O'Neill's images from the film's production, largely in black and white, capture a sense of place and also the sense of ease between the lead actors.

Opposite: Caine and co-star Anthony Quinn.

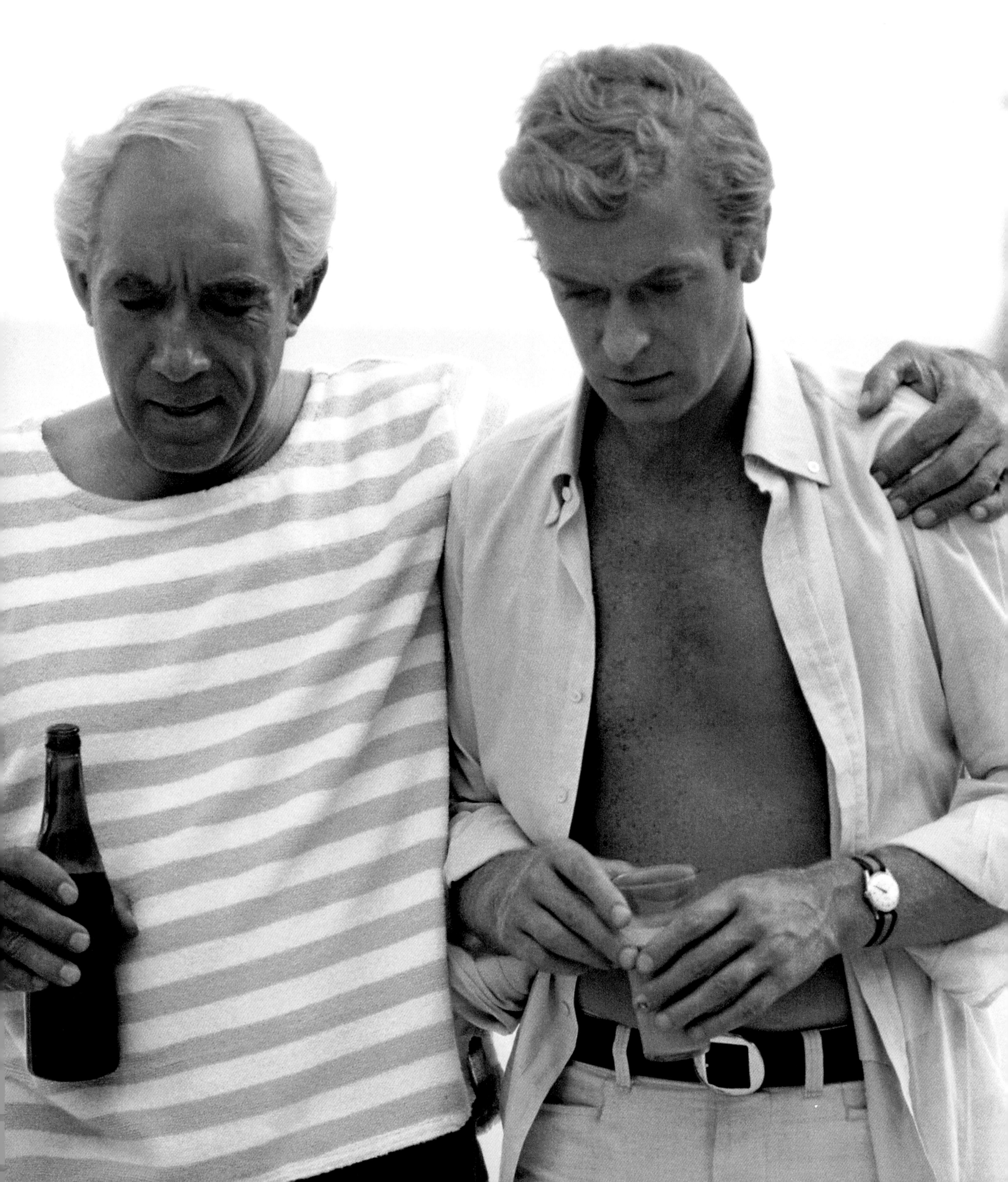

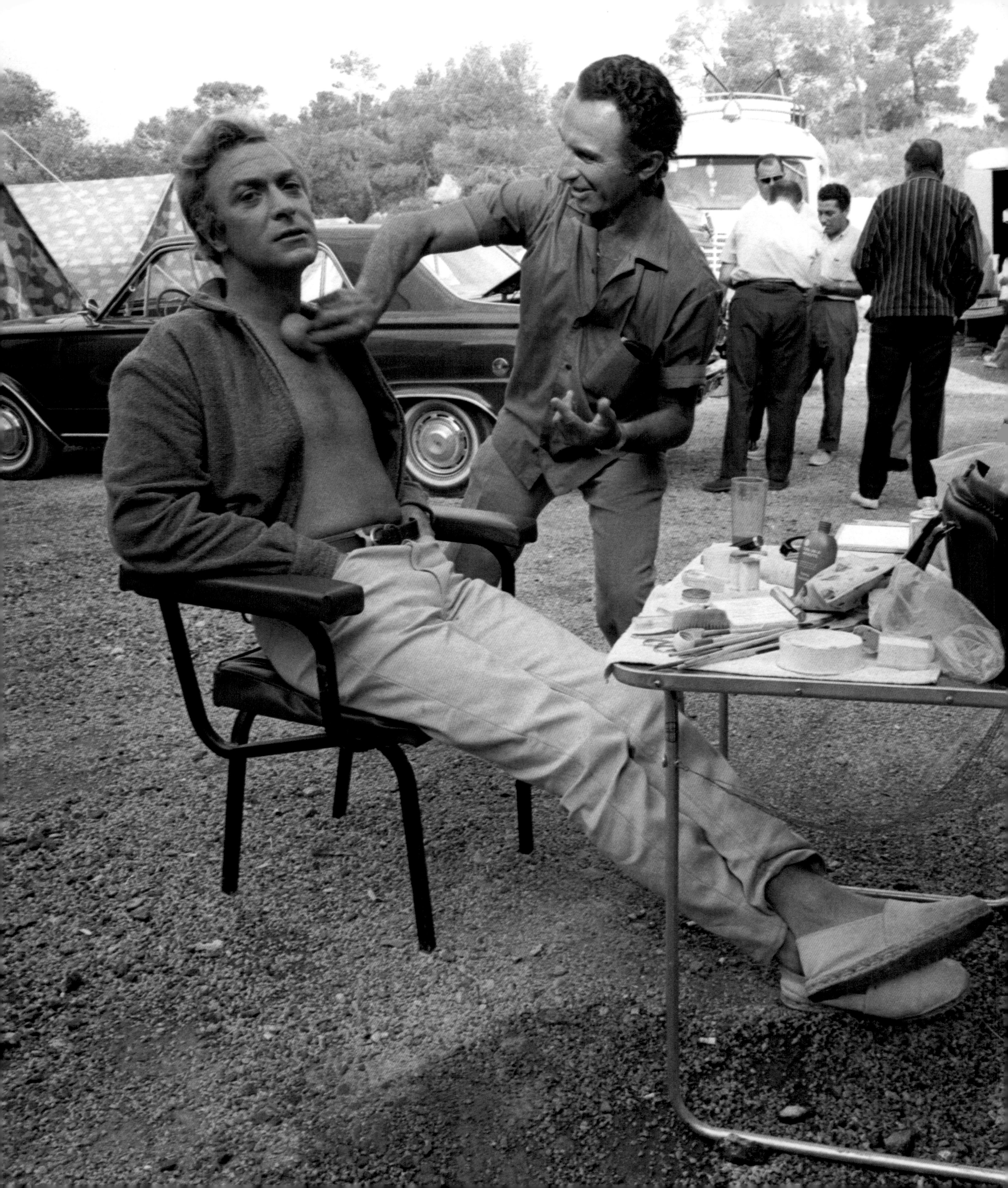

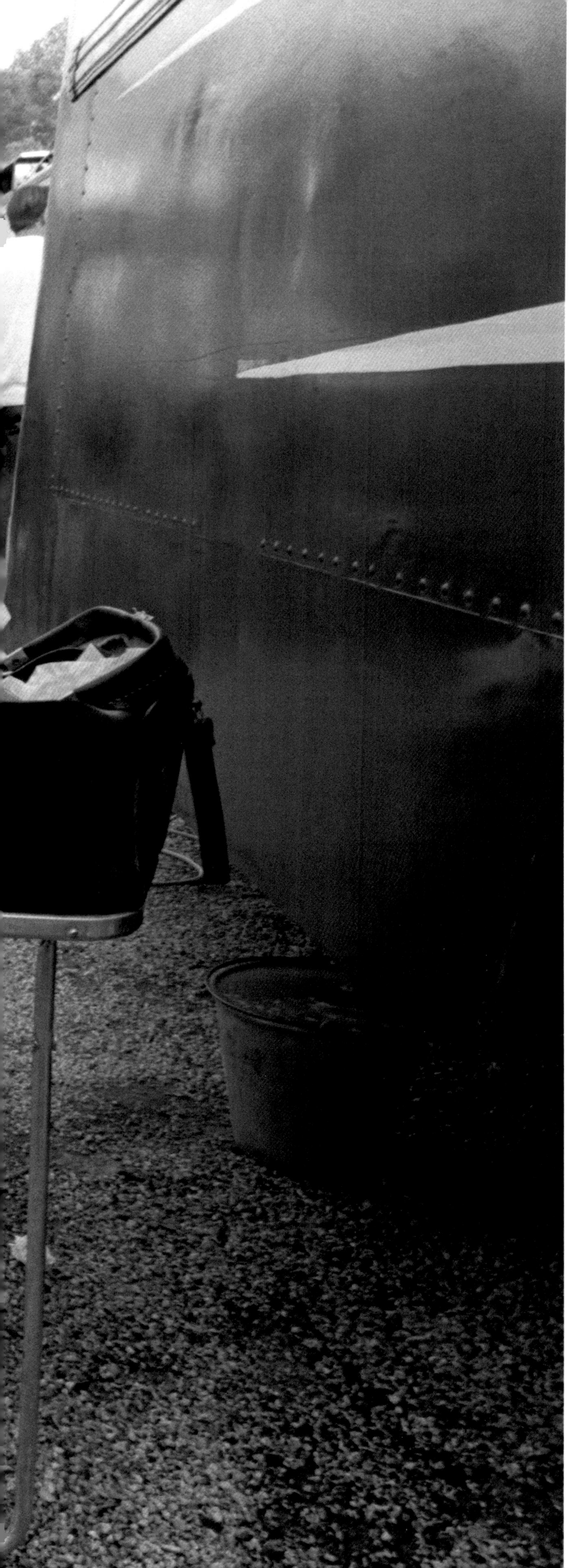

Left: In make-up.
Following page: O'Neill's archive is replete with candid images of the cast between takes. Caine, Bergen and Quinn.

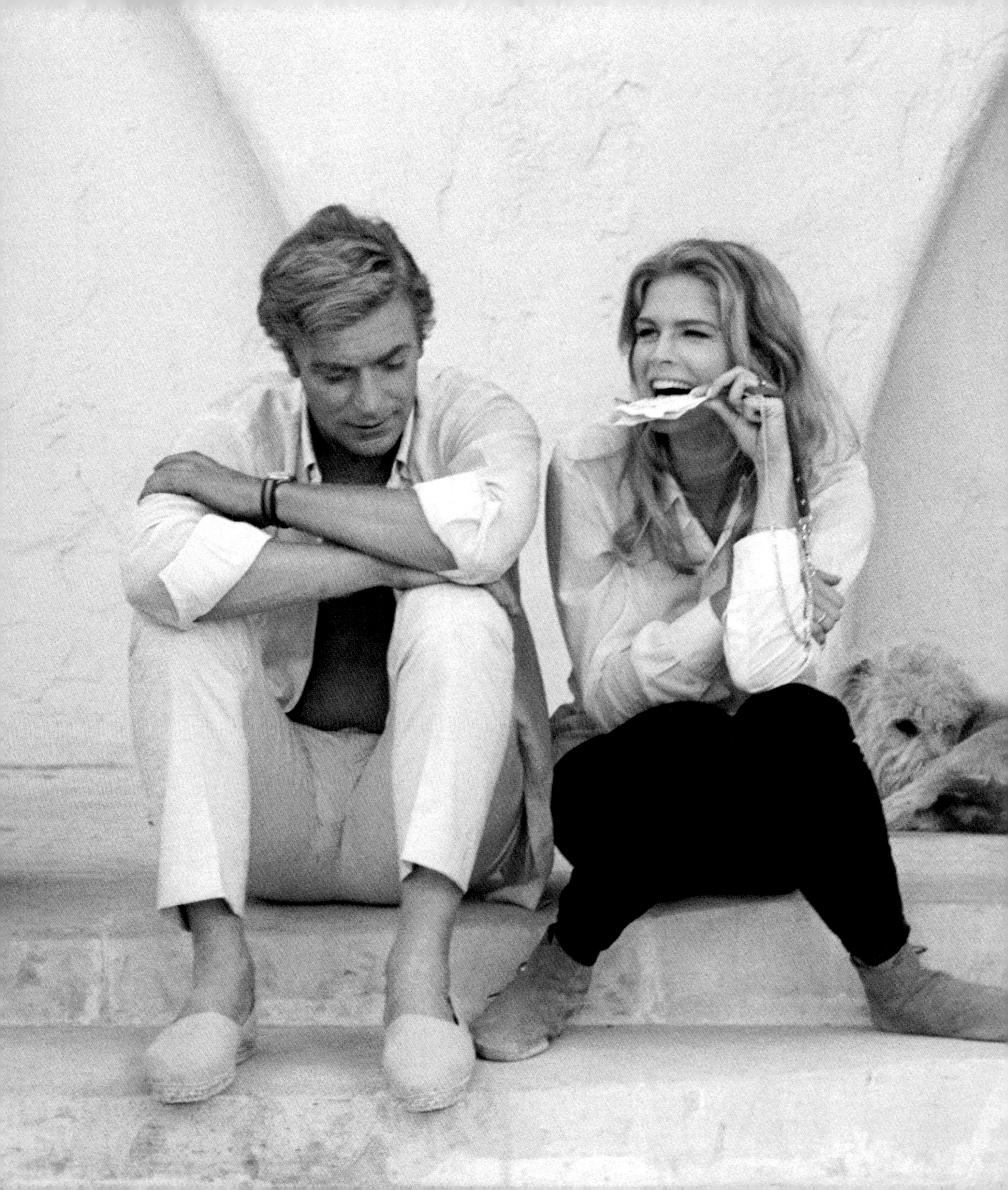

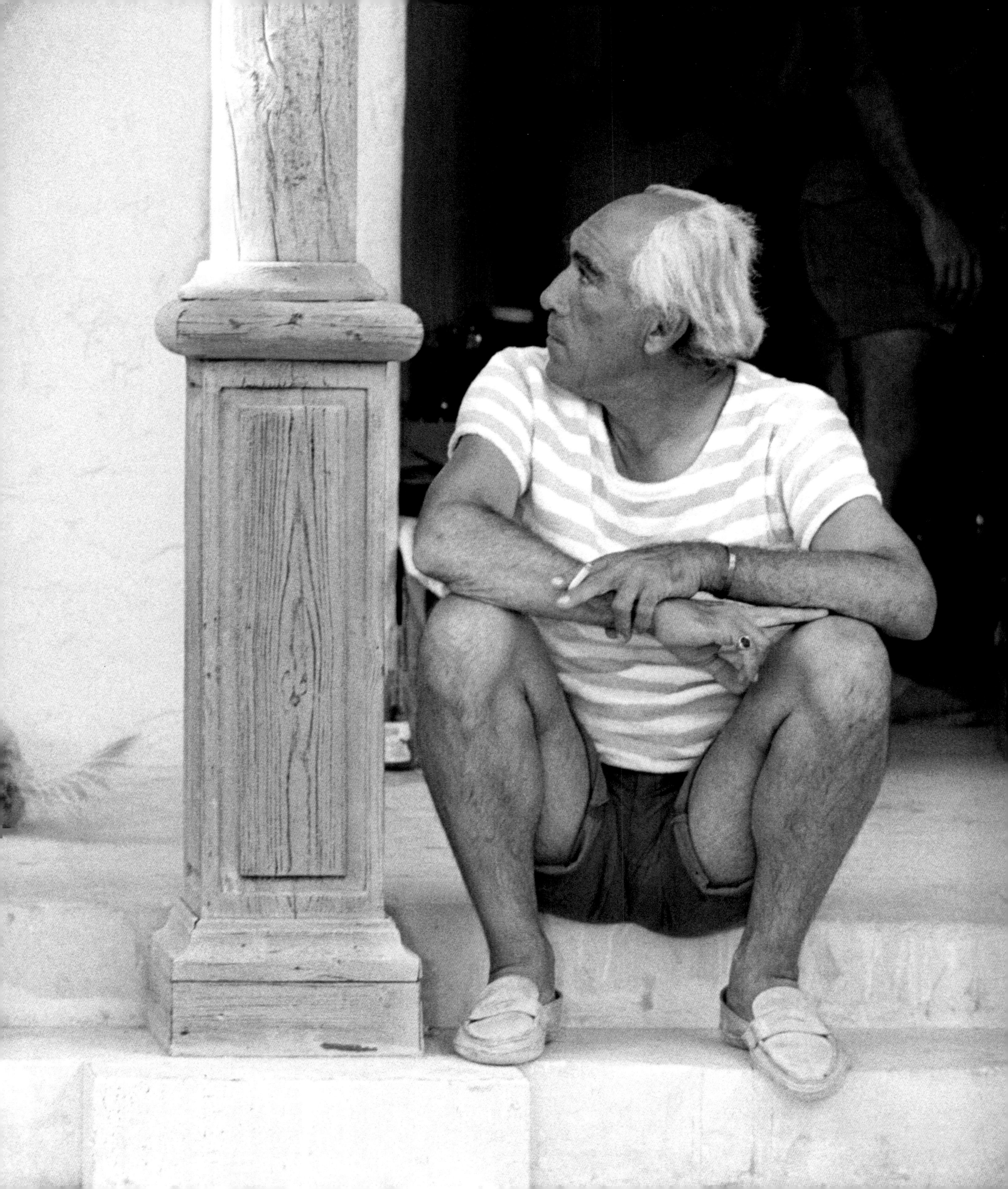

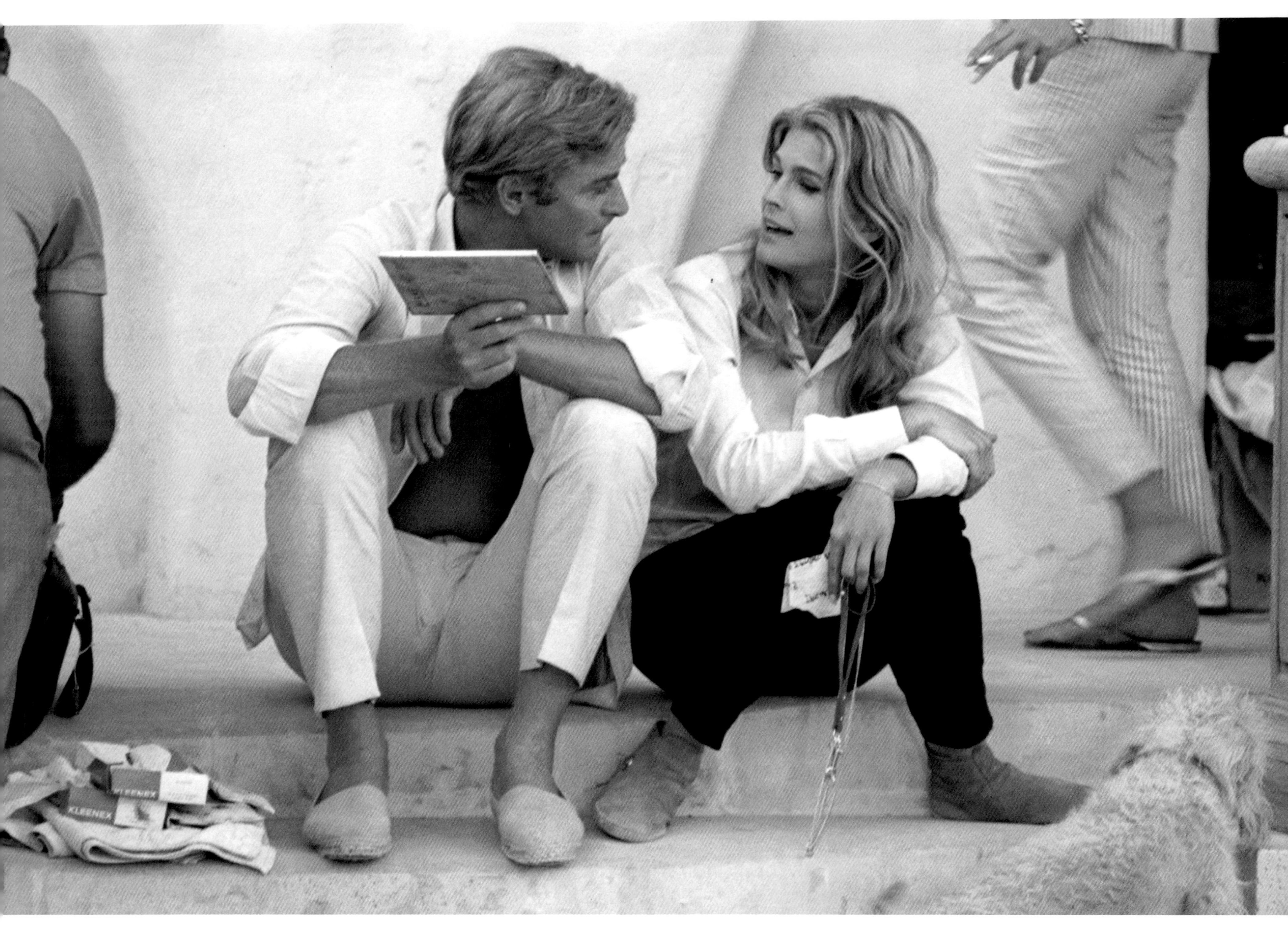

Above: Caine and Bergen. *The Magus* was one of Bergen's earliest film appearances.

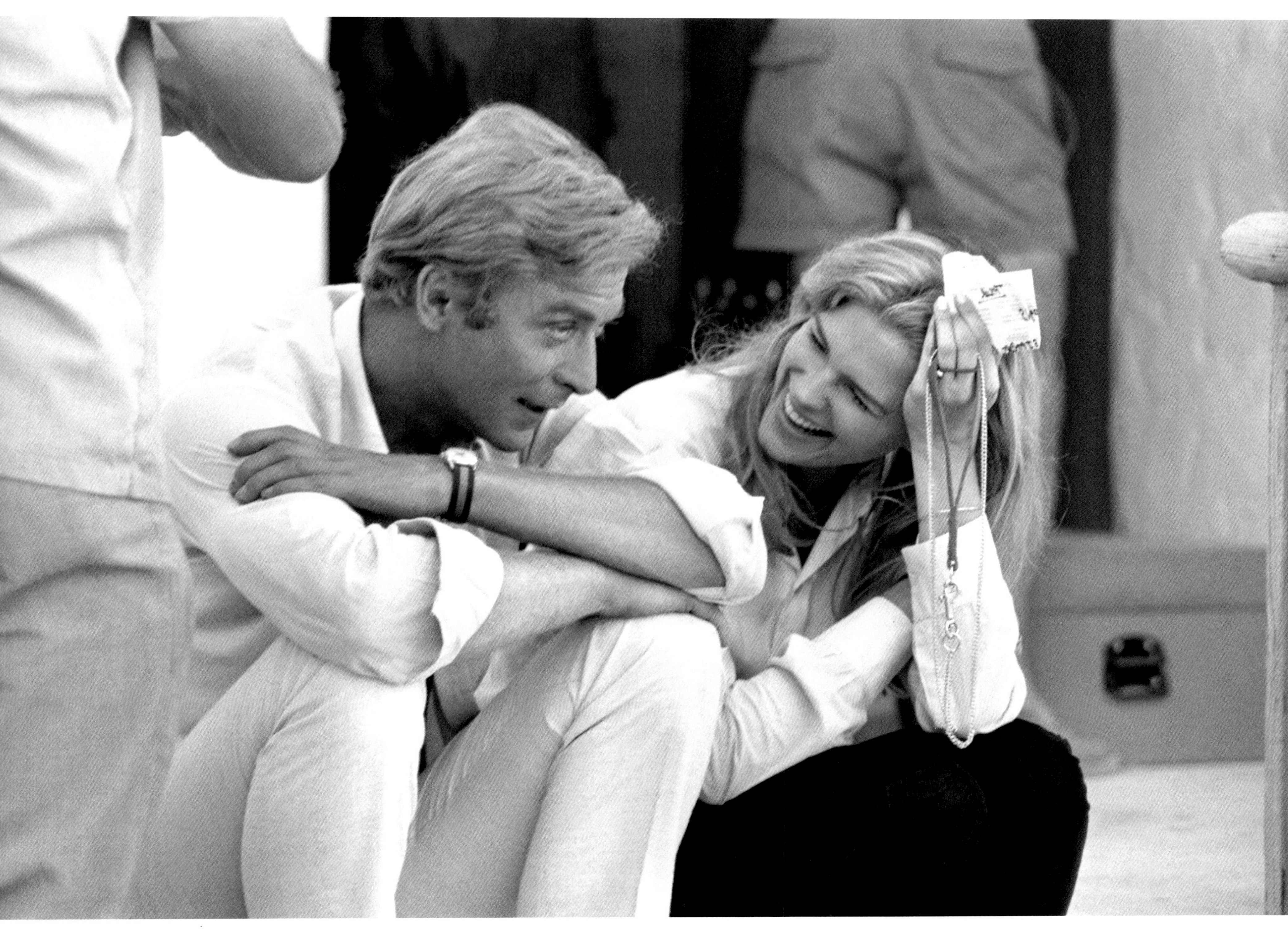

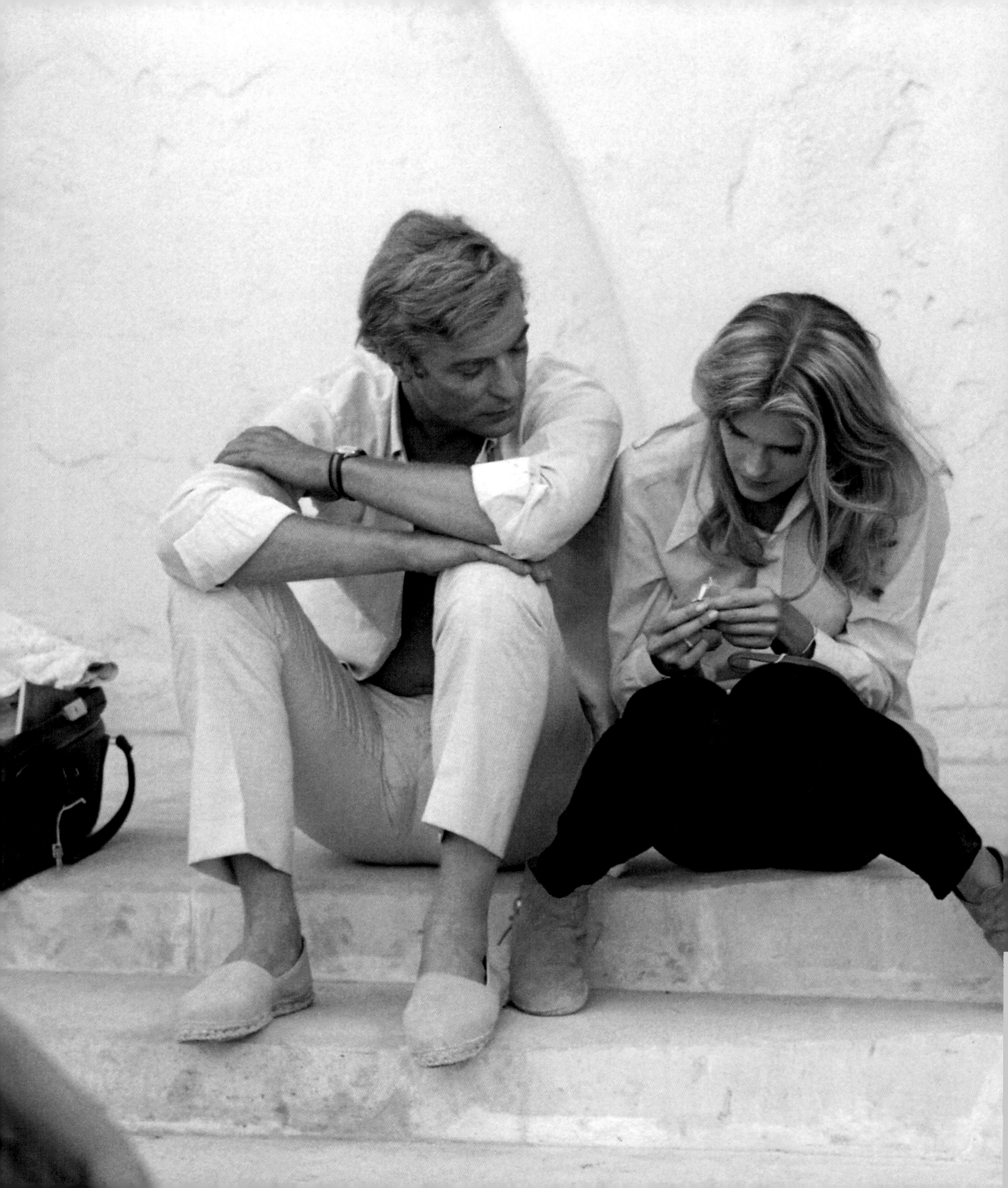

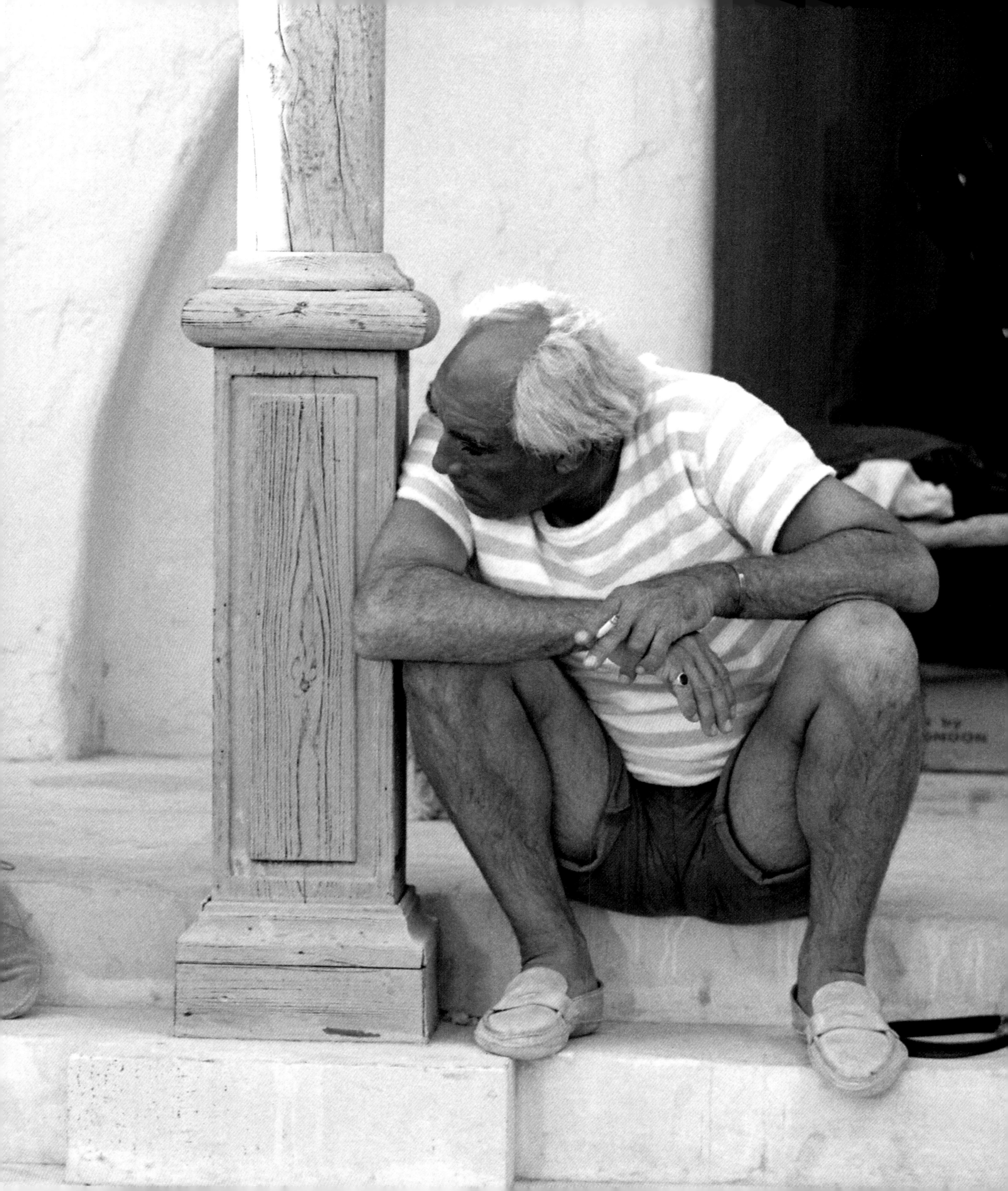

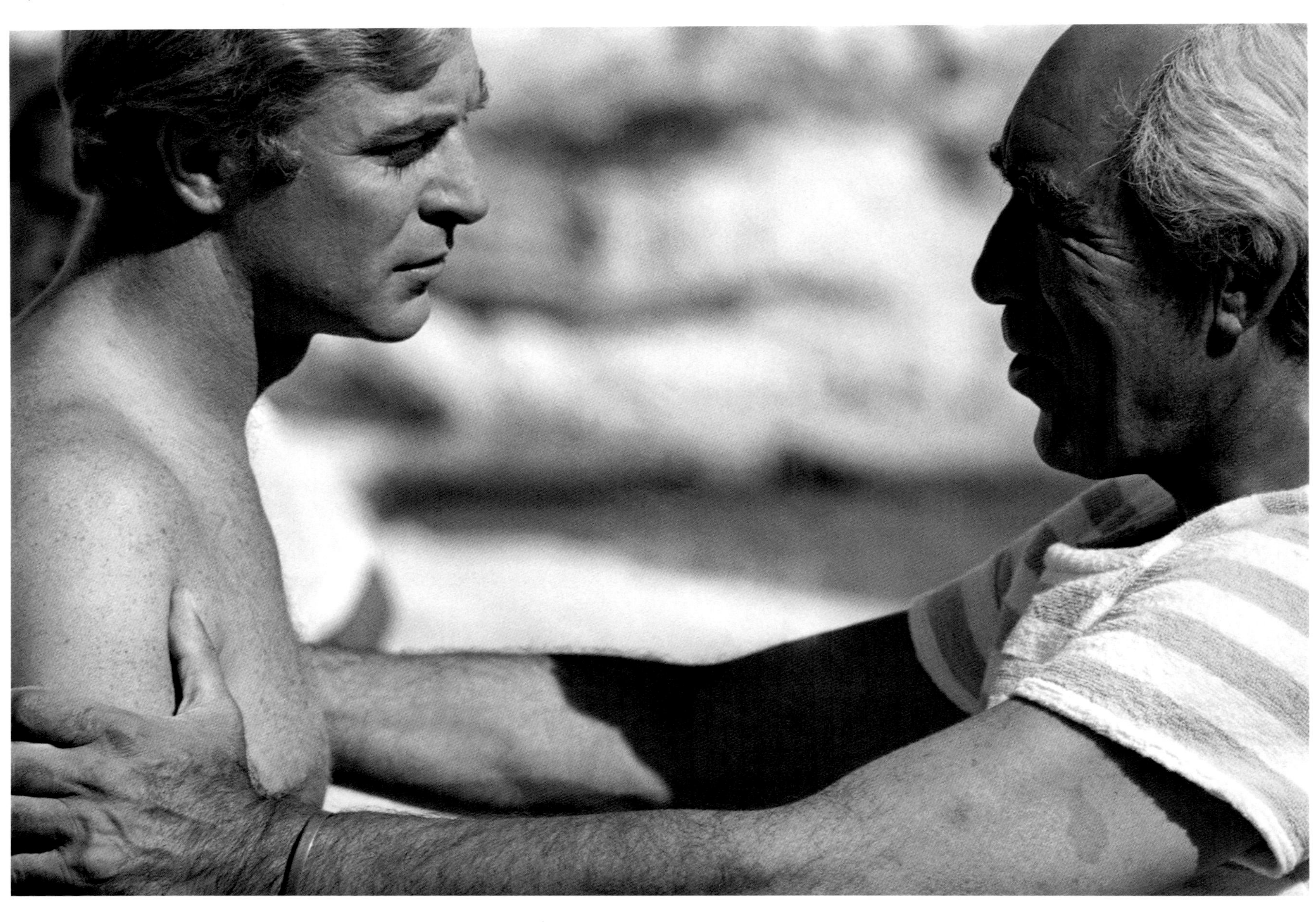

Above: Caine's character, Nicholas Urfe, finds himself manipulated by Conchis.

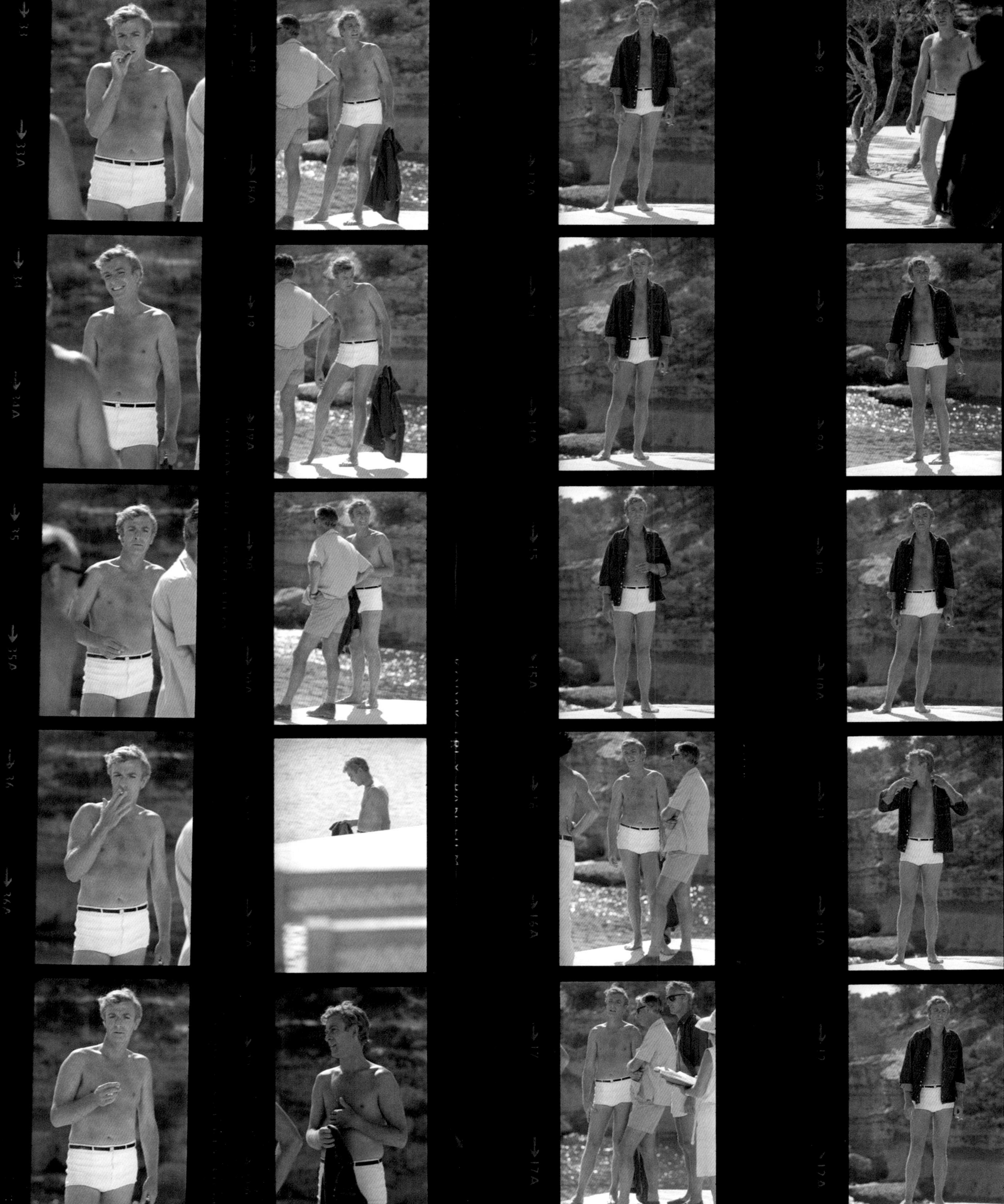

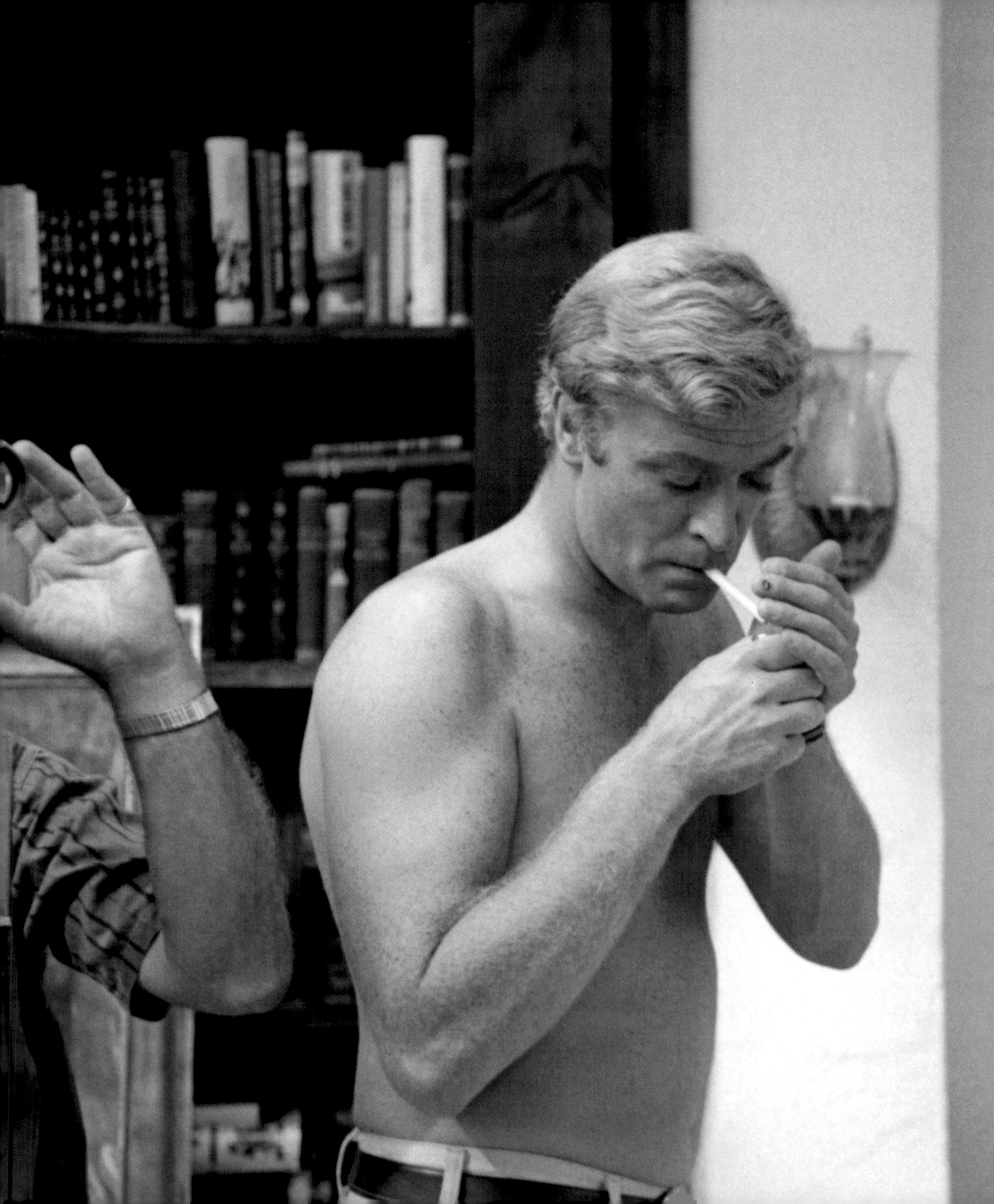

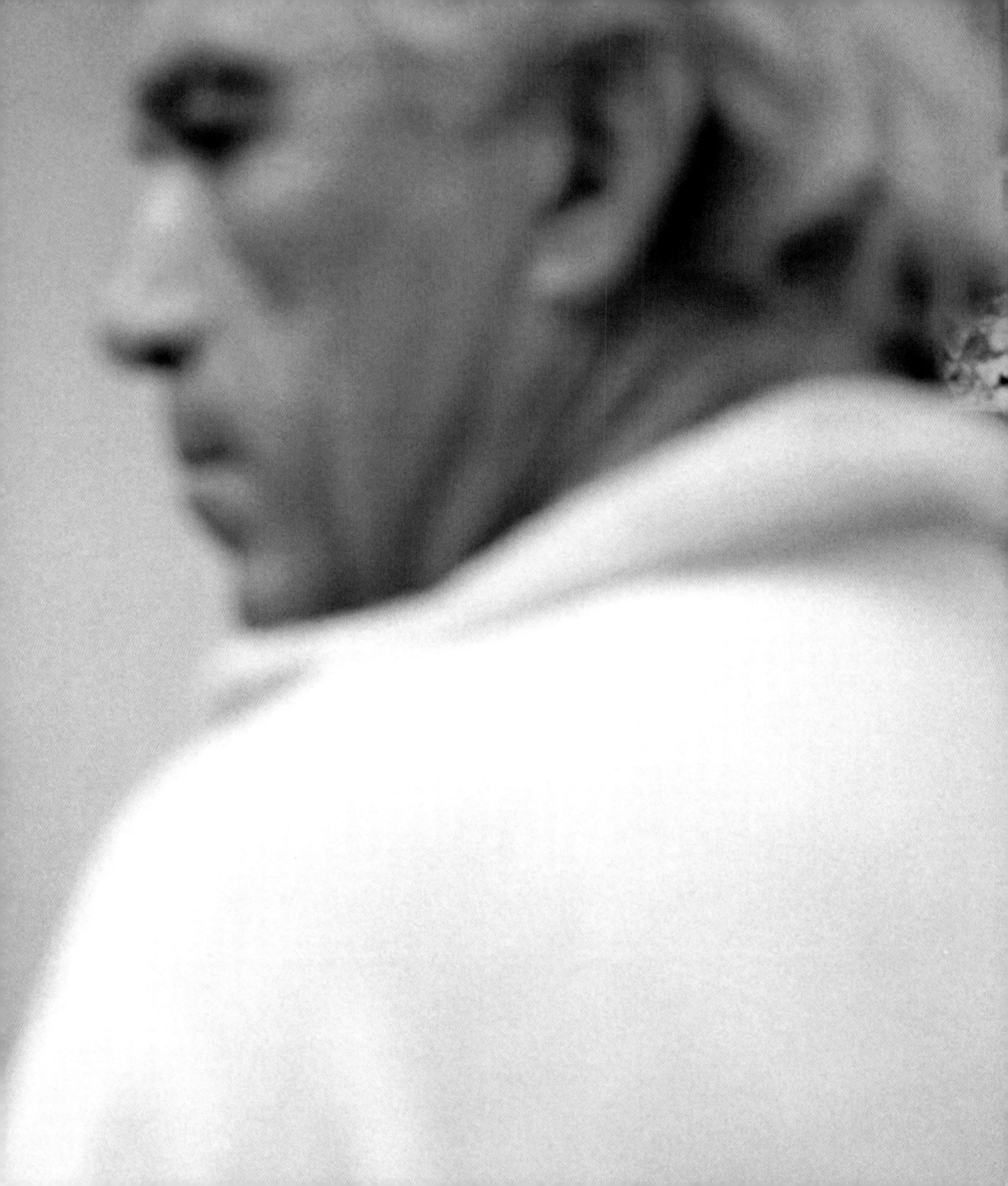

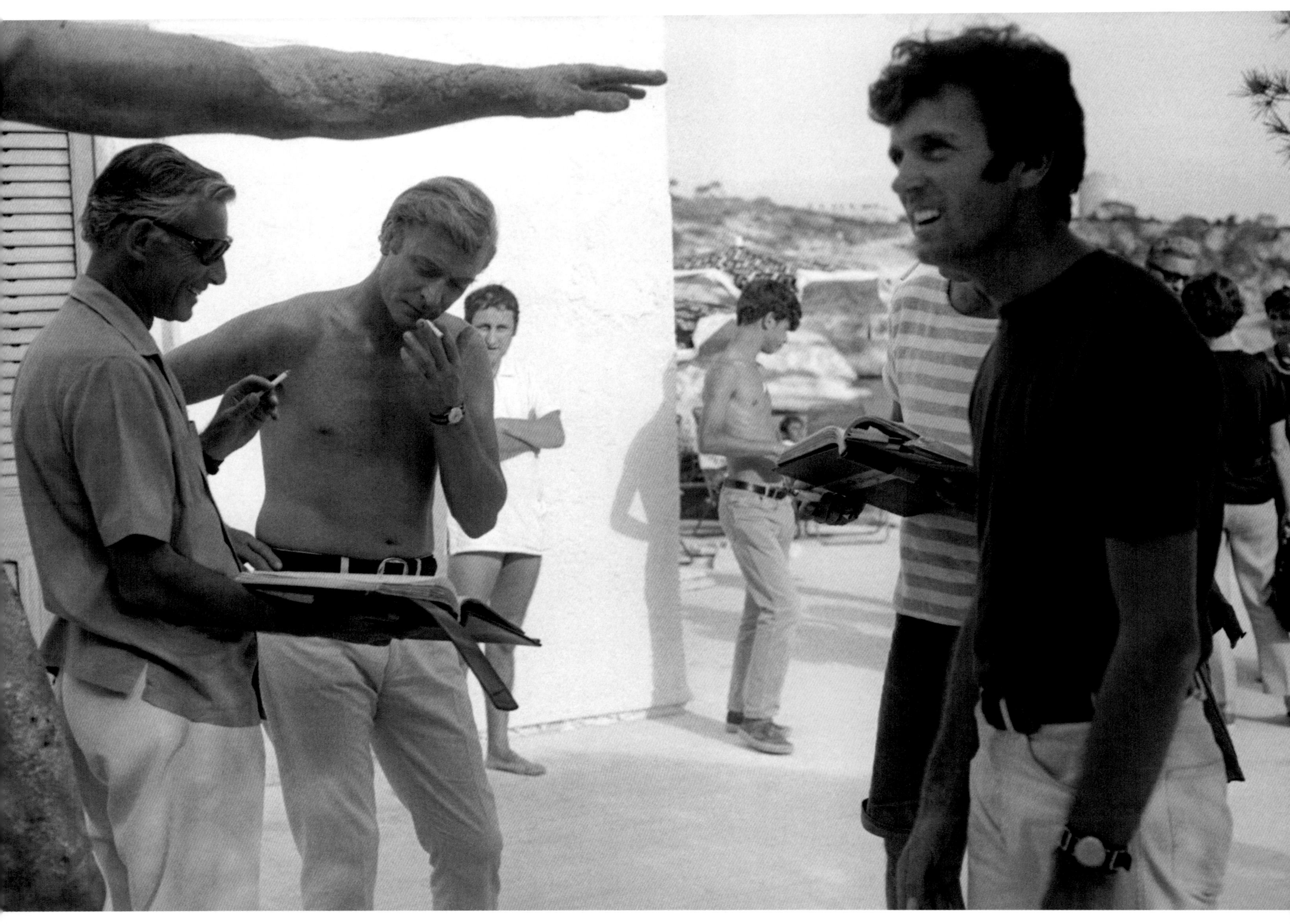

Above: Caine refers to the screenplay with the director, Guy Green.

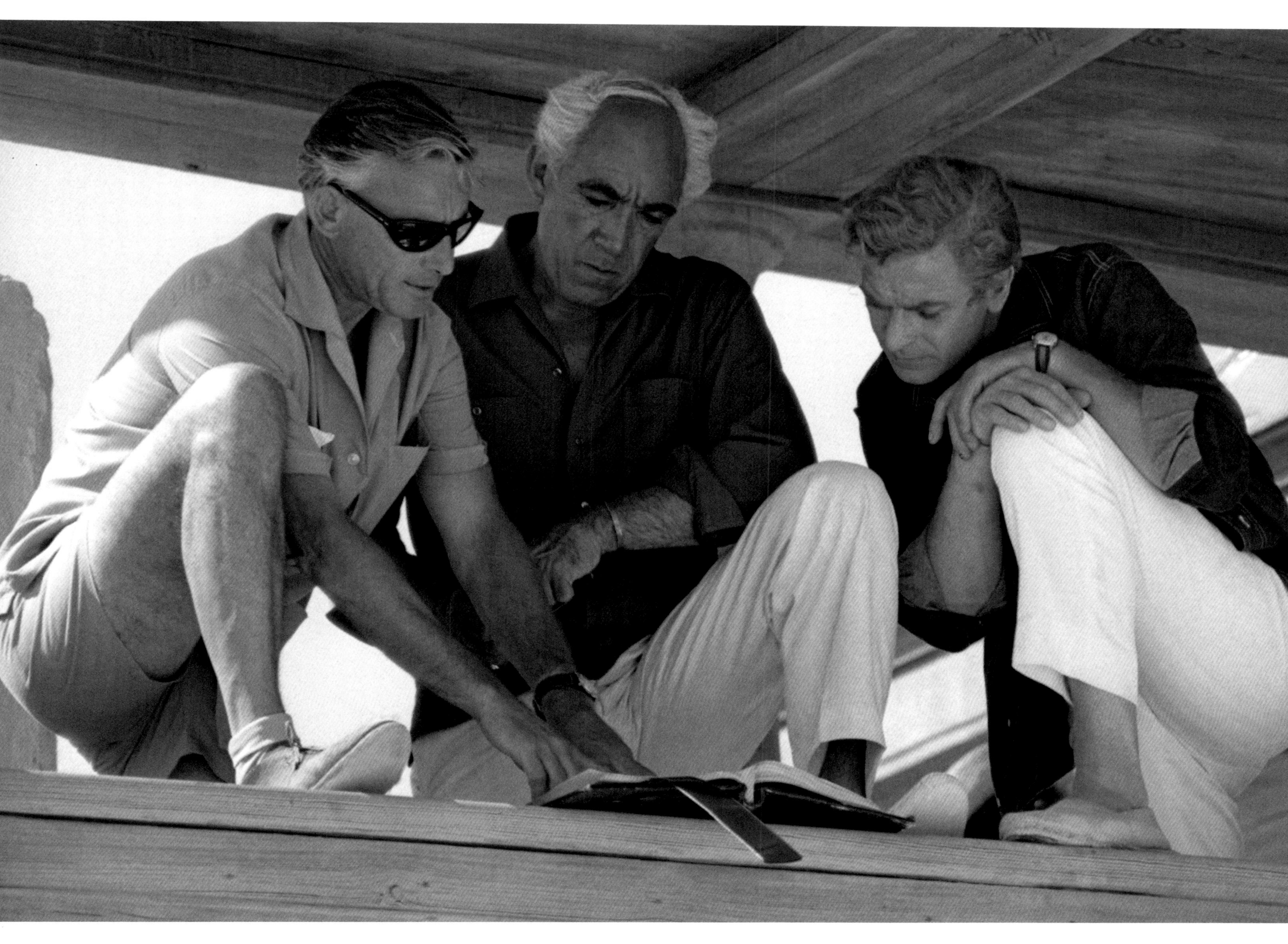

Above: Caine, Quinn and director Green prepare for a scene.
Following page: Caine takes a rest, as Quinn enjoys conversation between takes.

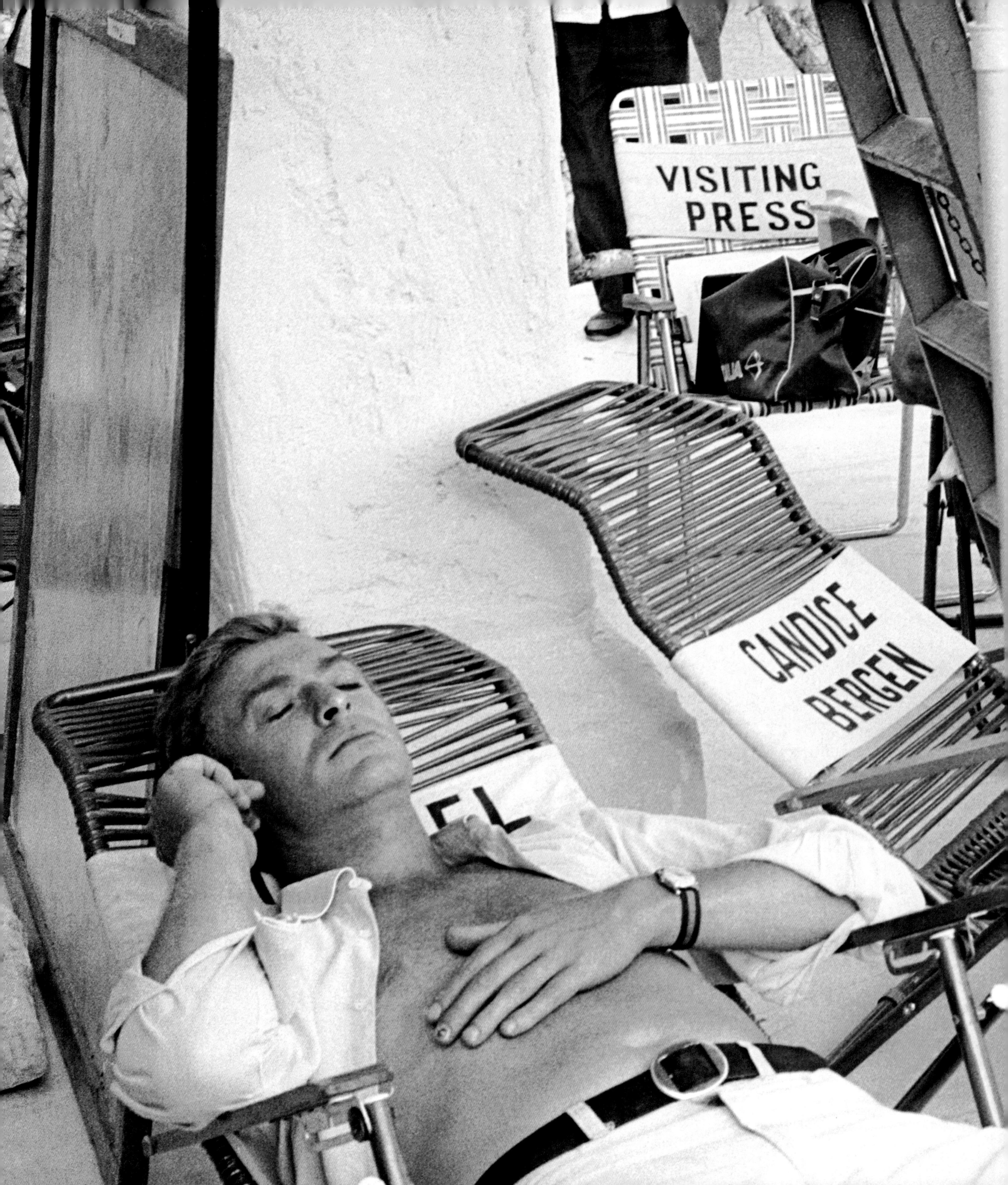
VISITING
PRESS
CANDICE
BERGEN

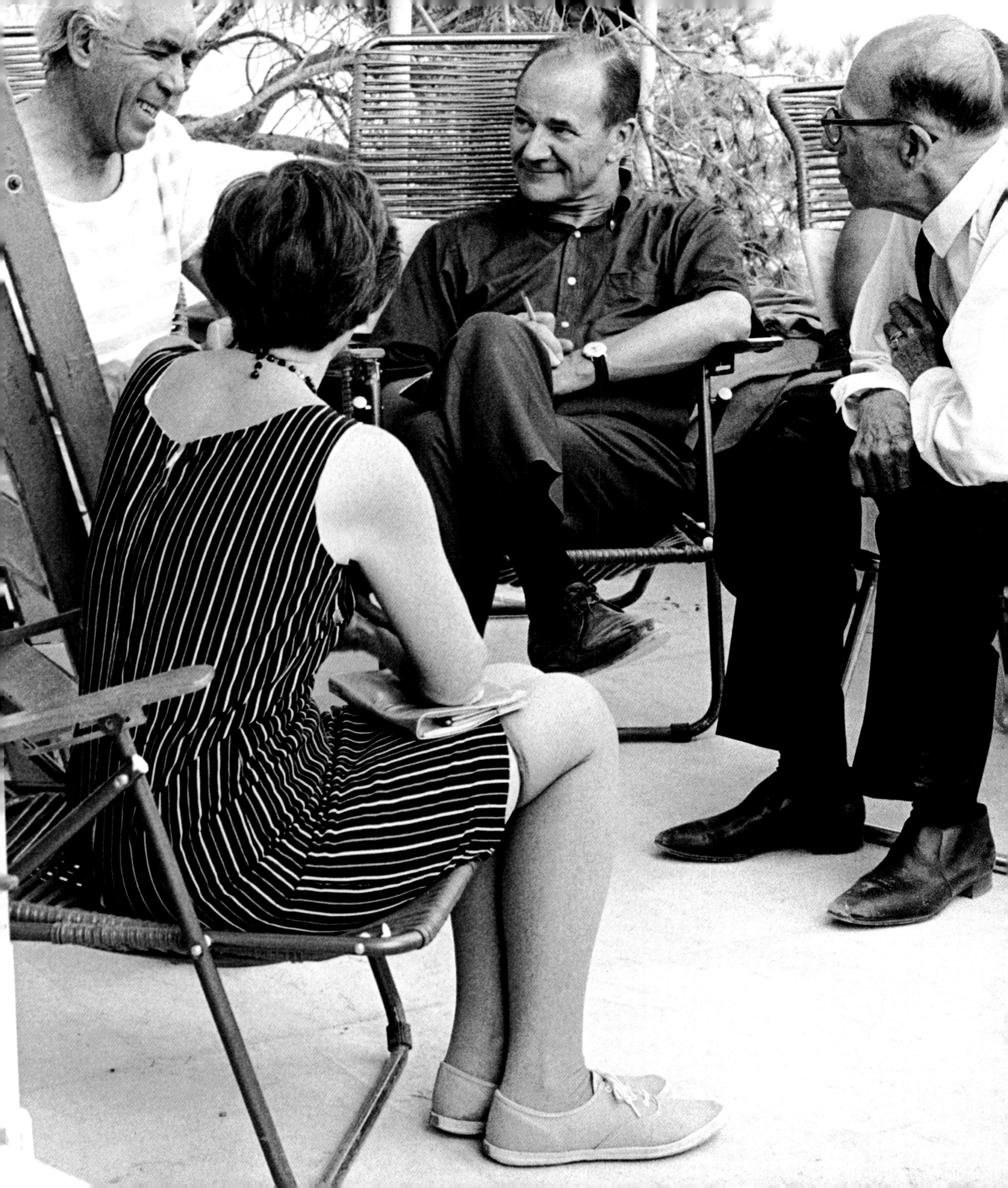

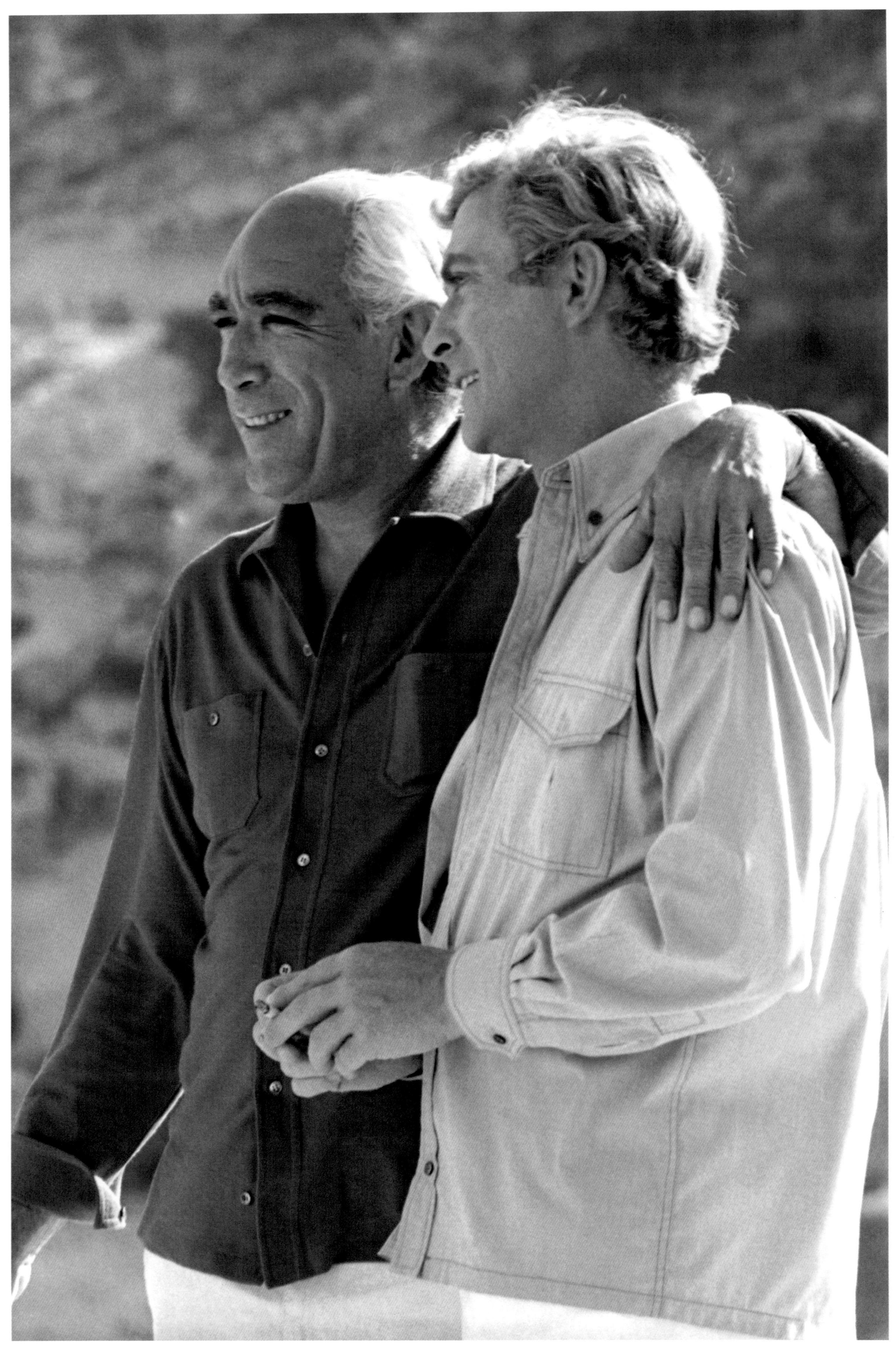

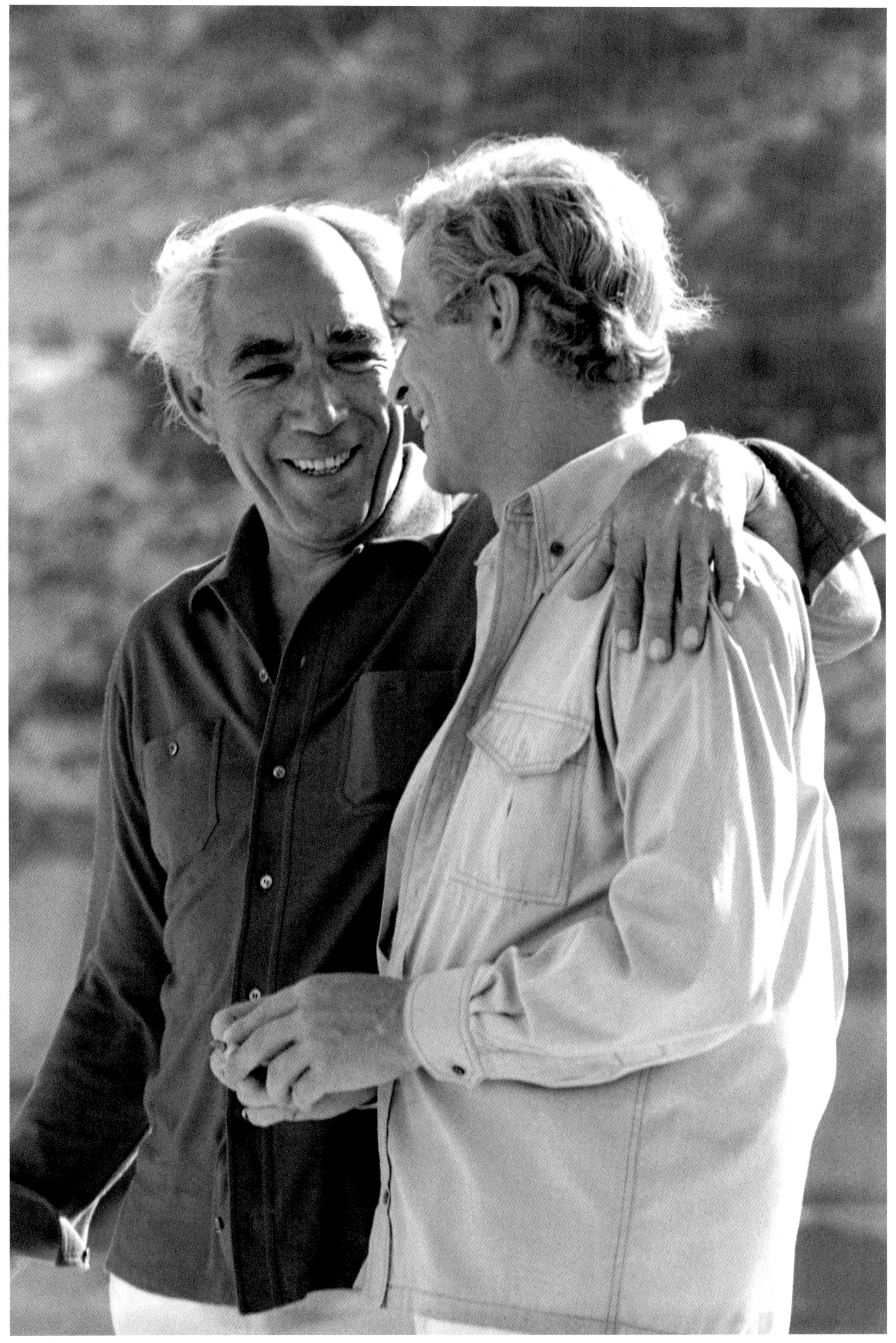

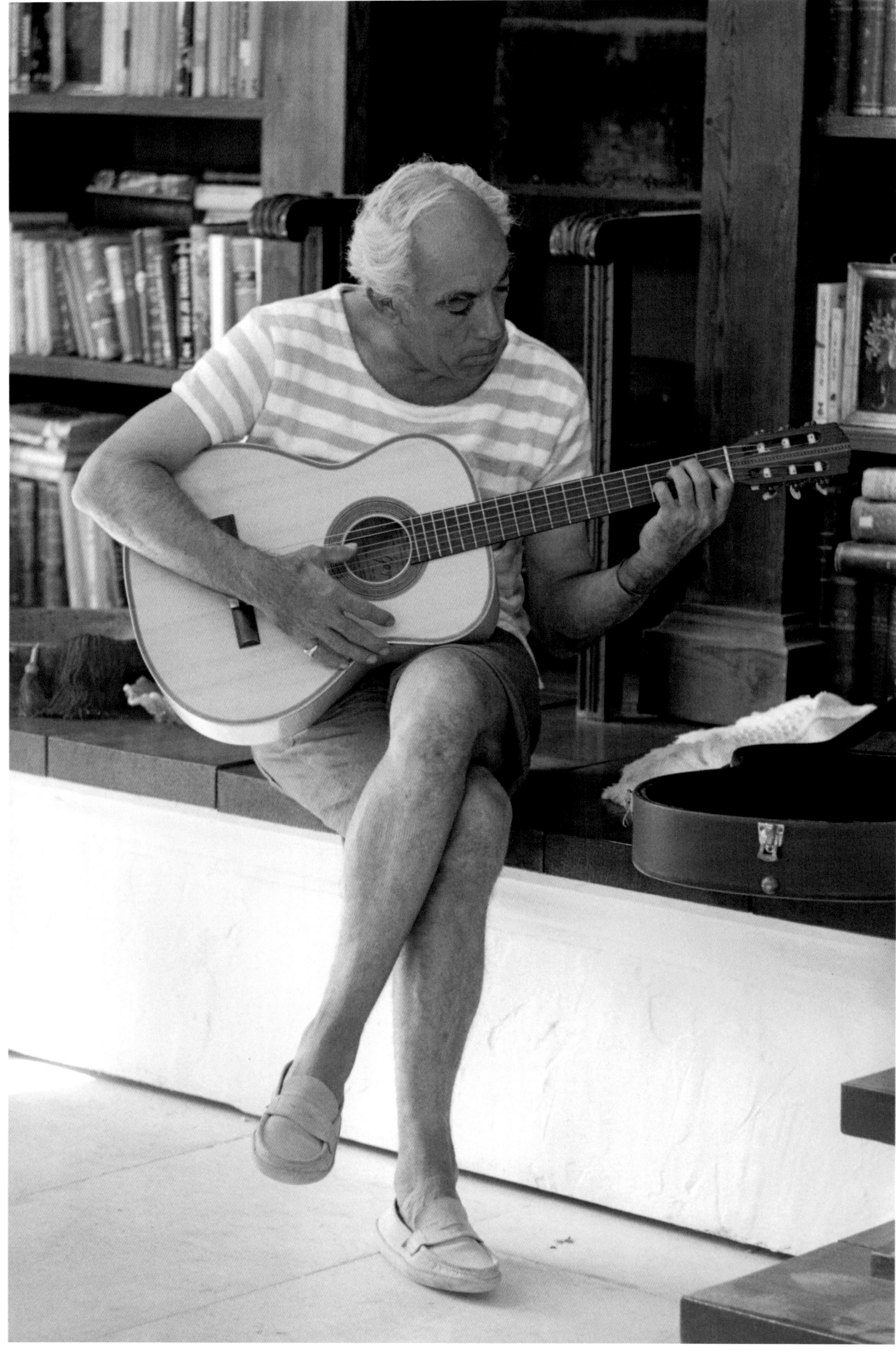

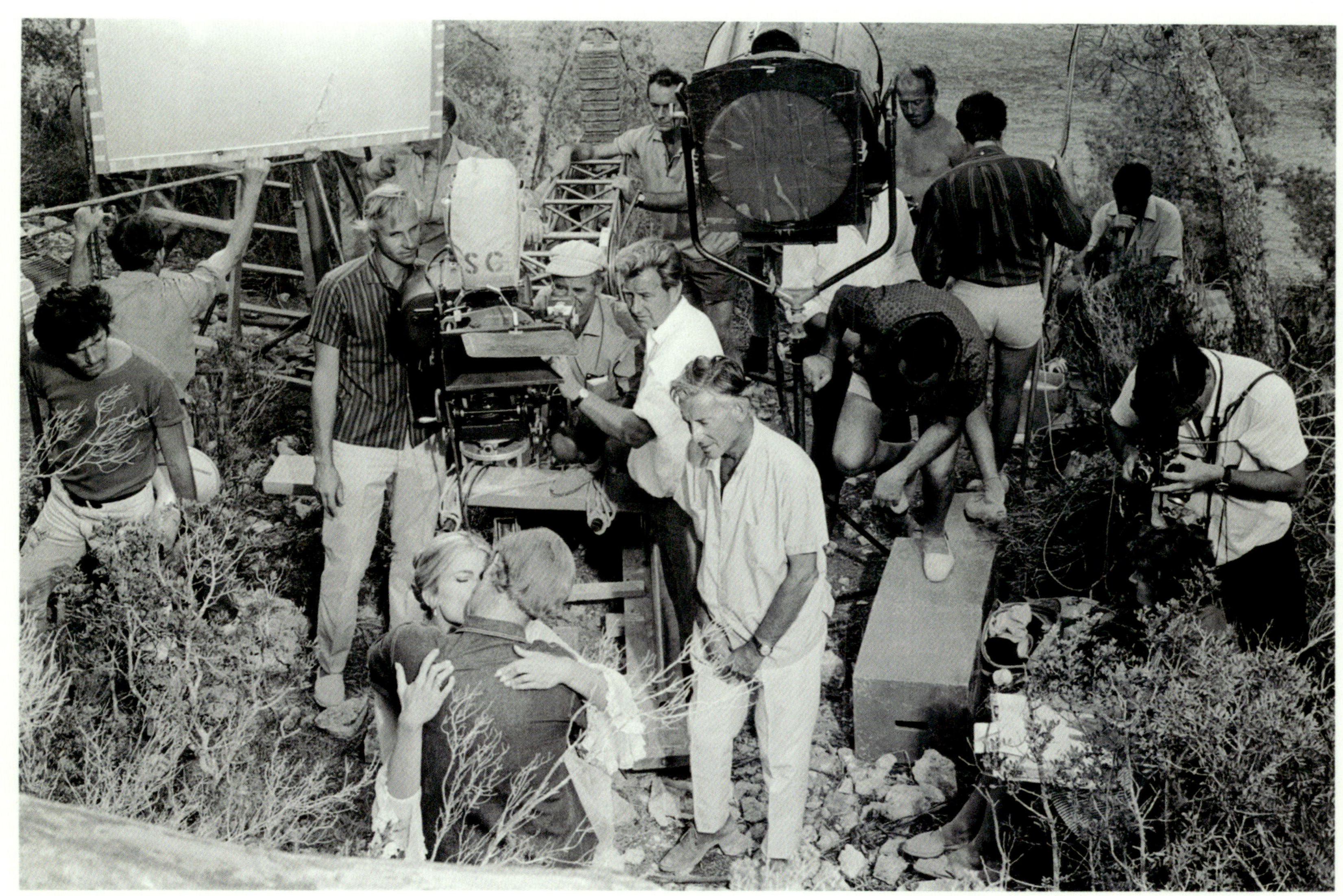

Michael Caine + Candice Bergen

Above: Director Guy Green and his crew focus their attention on Caine and Bergen.
Opposite: Quinn and his guitar.

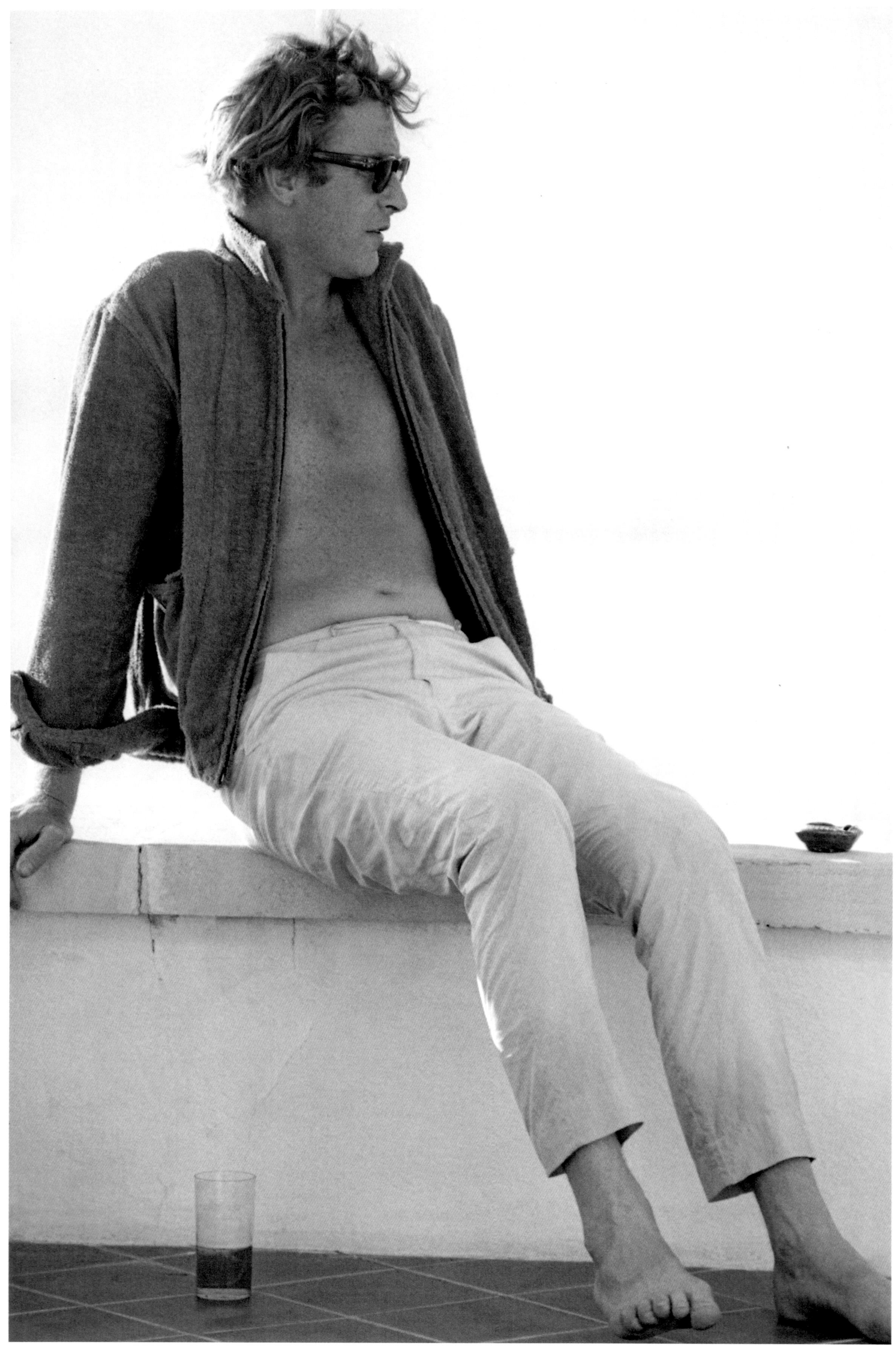

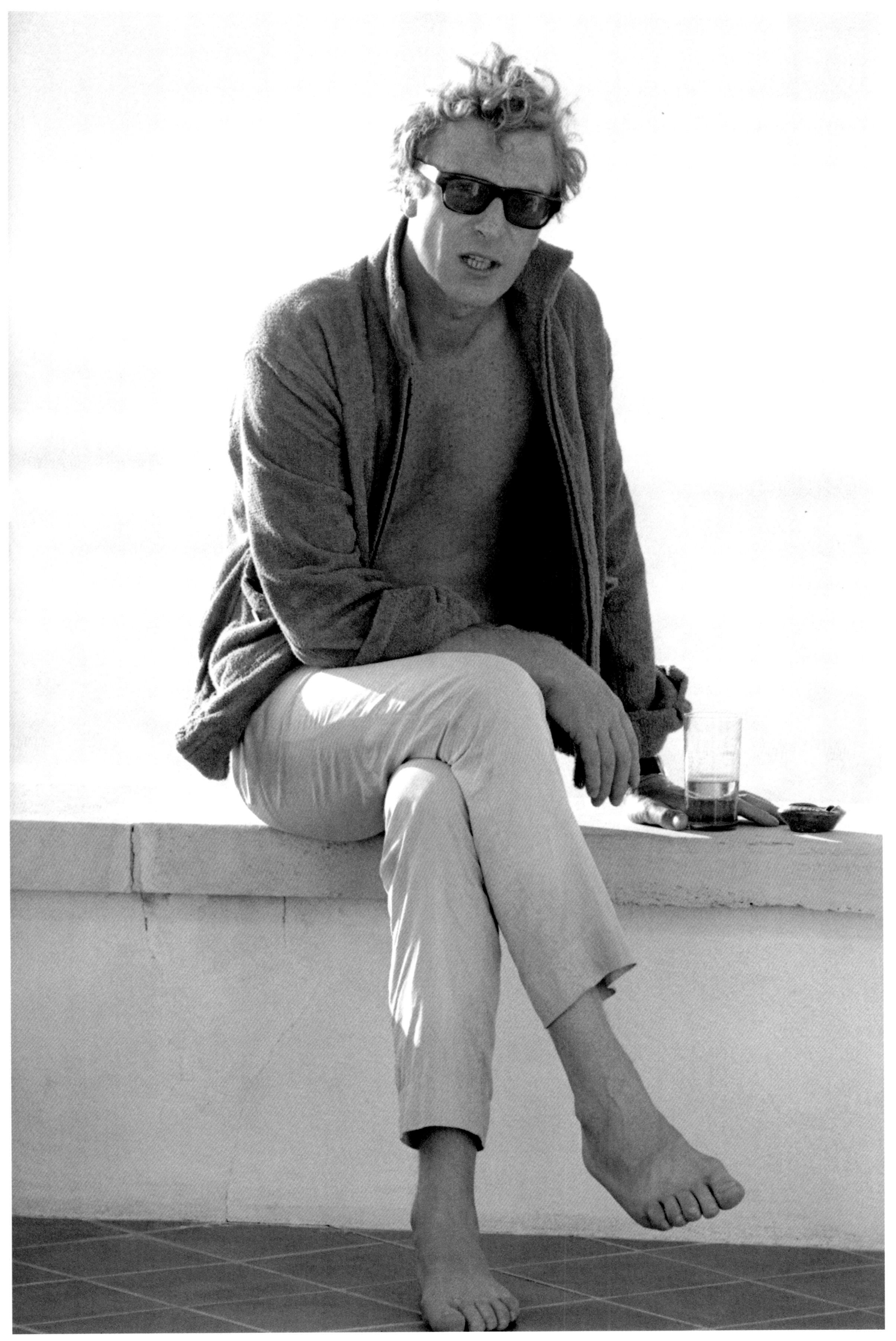

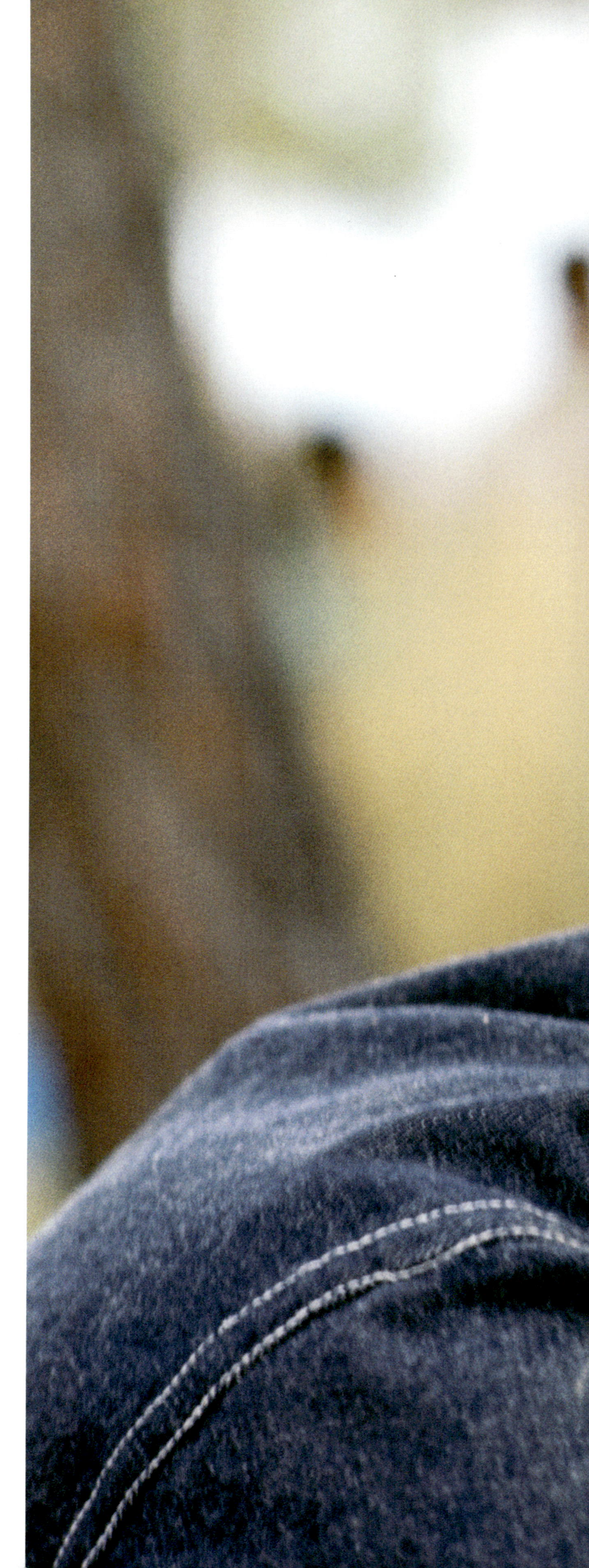

Caine the movie star.

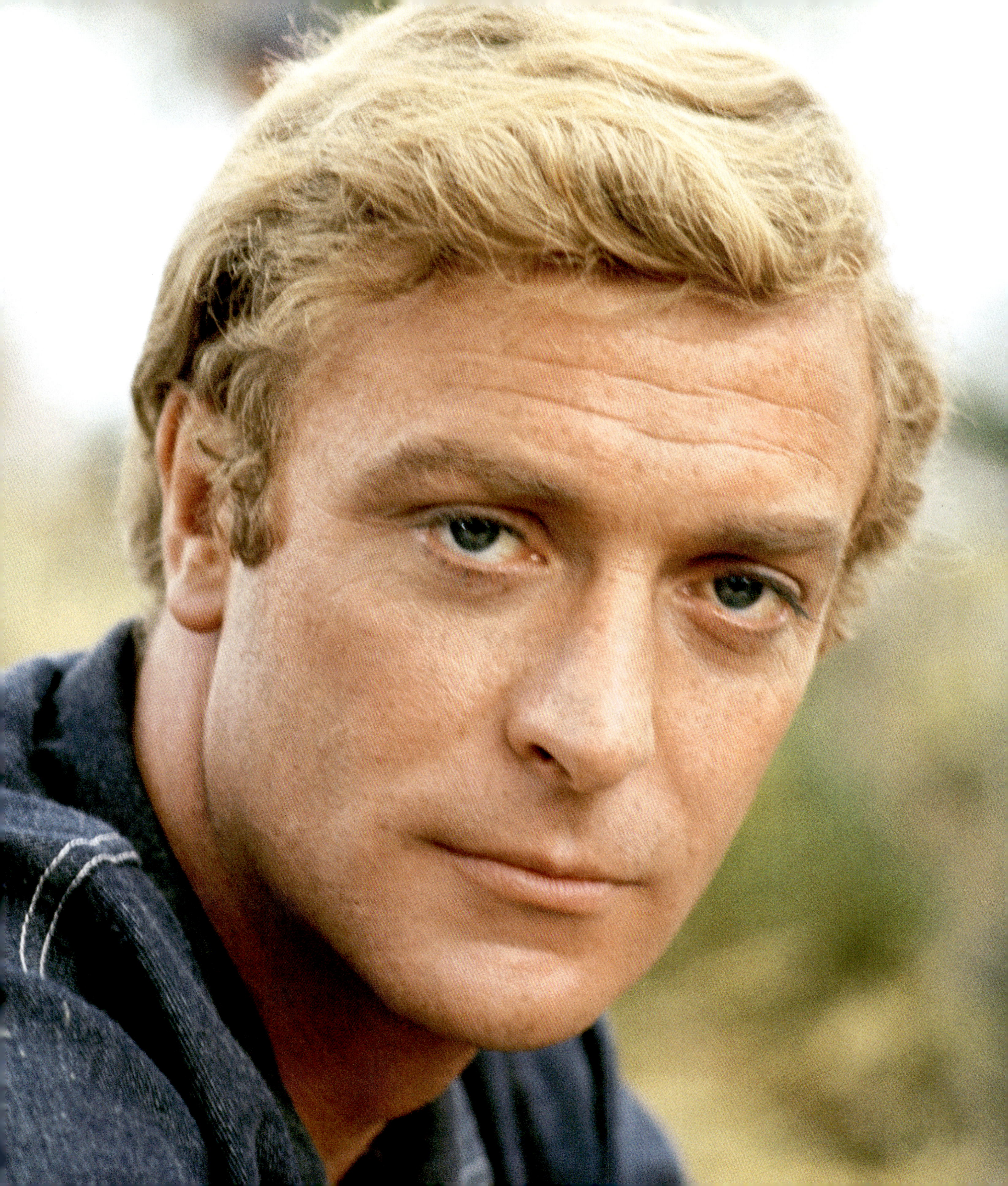

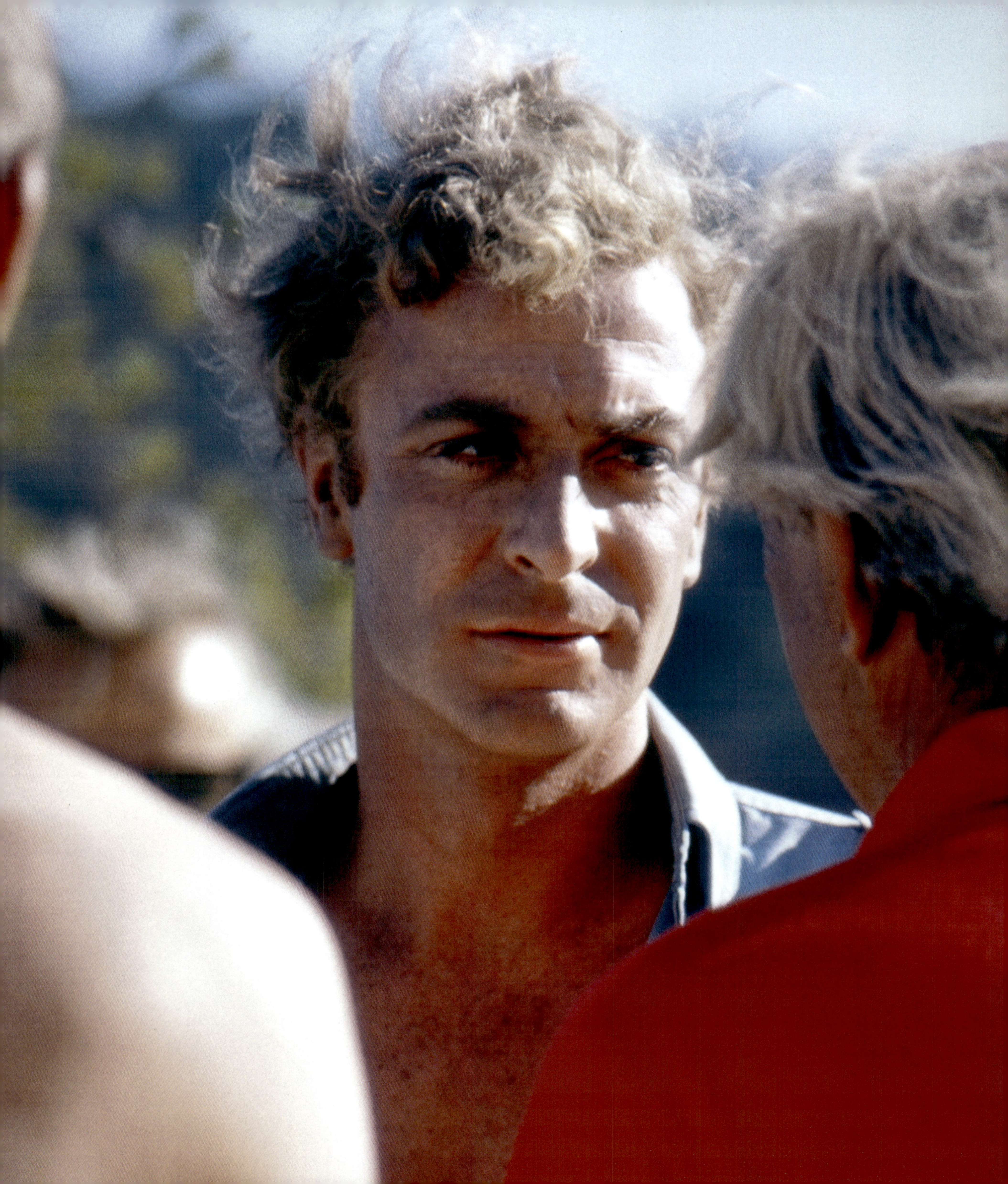

This near-miss is not without many notable virtues. Fowles's script sustains interest in its convolutions; direction is resourceful and sensitive; Caine is far more dynamic than usual and Quinn and the two femme stars register strongly.

Variety

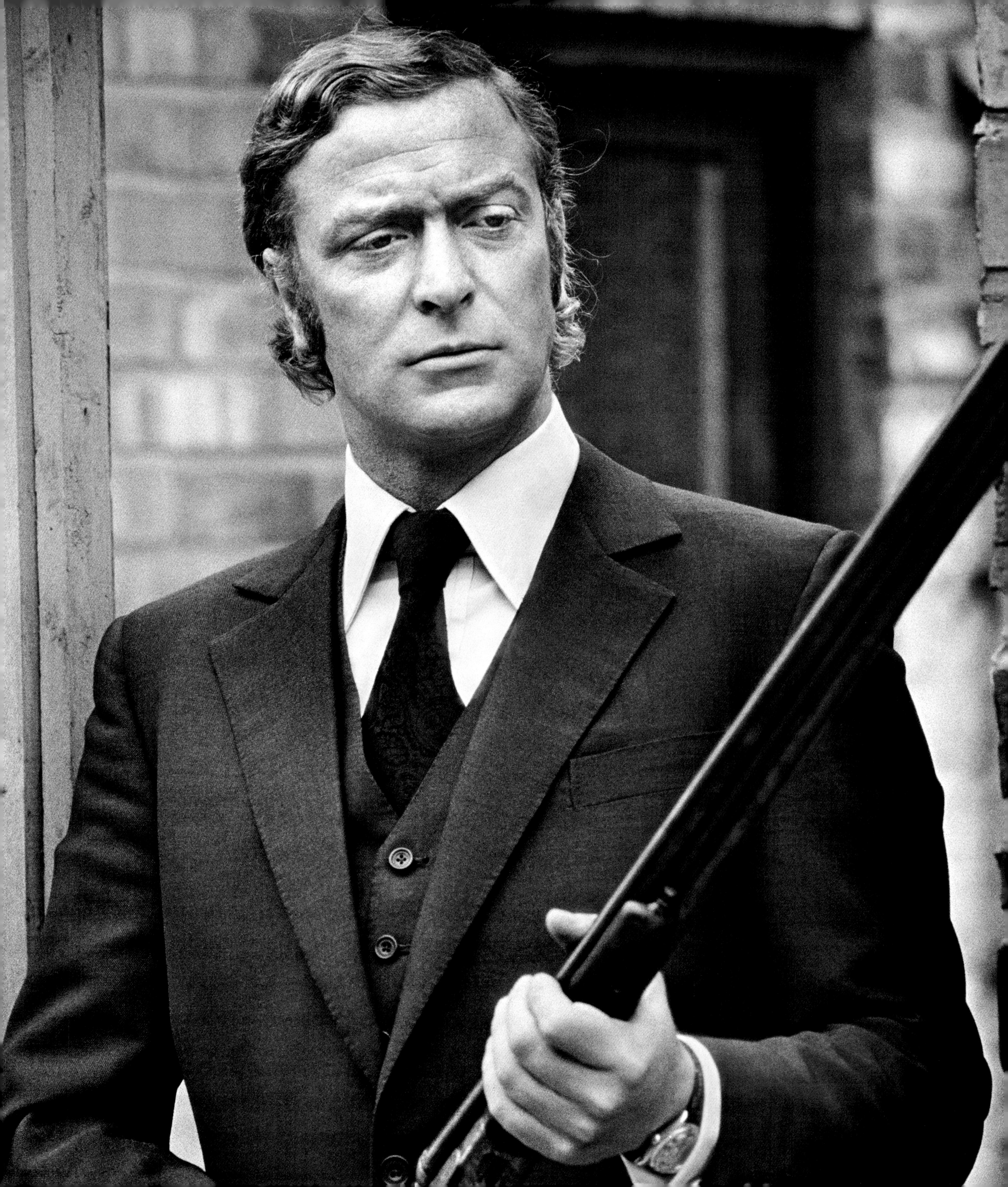

GET CARTER

1971

"Alongside its clear and intensely rendered genre specifics, the film also finds a place for a telling strain of British social realism."

Of his decision to essay the role of the distinctly unlovable Jack Carter, Caine explains, "One of the reasons I wanted to do it was because I had this image on the screen as a Cockney ersatz Errol Flynn. The Cockney bit was alright, but the ersatz suggested I'm artificial and the Errol Flynn tag misses the point. One's appearance distracts people from one's acting. Carter was real."[1] In fact, Carter's life dovetailed with Caine's own background and there's a sense of 'what might have been' if Caine hadn't made good in the movies. "Carter is the dead-end product of my own environment, my childhood. I know him well. He is the ghost of Michael Caine."[2]

A muted, aggressive and flinty thriller, *Get Carter* crystallises a British social realist tradition that focuses on very ordinary, often difficult lives within the thriller genre. At BFI Screenonline we read that "The film evokes a society in the throes of a profound change, capturing a mood of disillusionment that signals the replacement of 1960s idealism by the 'rampant materialism' of the 1970s."[3]

Alongside its clear and intensely rendered genre specifics, the film also finds a place for a telling strain of British social realism. For Director Mike Hodges, the toughness of the characters and the setting worked together quite vividly and Hodges was aware that Caine's casting brought a degree of movie star glamour to a character that was all the tougher in the source material. Speaking to the film's evolving status and the recognition of it as a major British movie, it was re-released by the BFI in 1999.

Previous page: Jack Carter is one of Caine's most significant performances in a long-running filmography.

Opposite page: Caine's performance is an essential part of the British crime film tradition. Here he is photographed on location in Benwell, Newcastle with its distinctive rows of terraced houses and with Dunston Power Station in the distance.

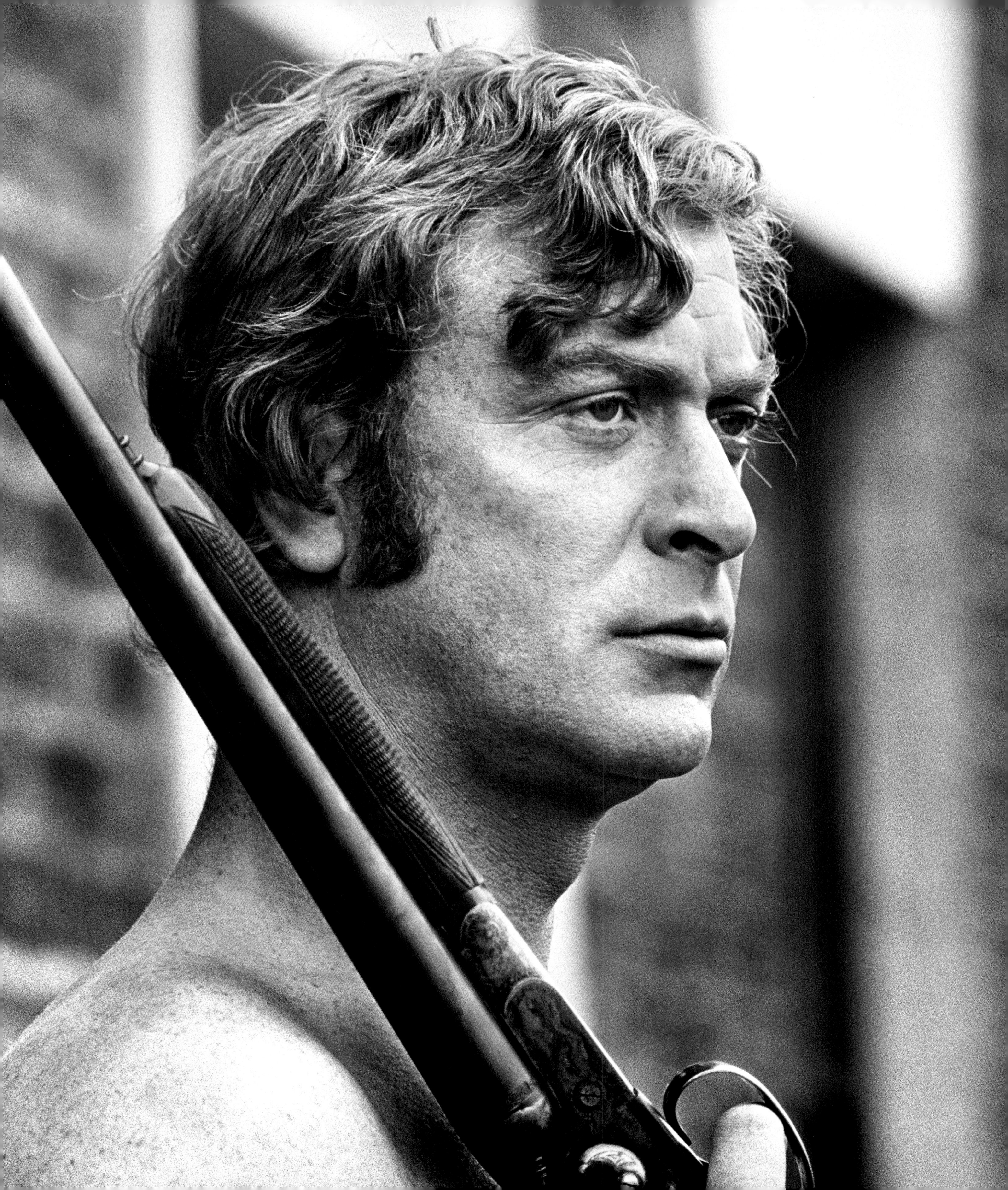

Based on the 1970 novel *Jack's Return Home* by Ted Lewis, the plot turns on tough guy Jack Carter coming back home to Newcastle to investigate his brother's death. In doing so, he confronts local gangs and the local crime boss. Reflecting on the film in his memoir, Caine makes the astute observation: "People often think that *Get Carter* is a film about vengeance, but it's not: it's about honour."[4]

The point's been made earlier in this book that Caine and fashion and style went rather hand-in-hand and with that in mind, it's worth a note about Caine's threads in the film. He dons a three-piece suit of Dormeuil's Tonik® – a blend of mohair and wool that made for a crisp, wrinkle-free fabric favoured in the '50s and '60s by Mods. In the early '70s, Caine – along with *everyone* else, including Terry O'Neill – was frequenting showbiz tailor Douglas Hayward of Mount Street, Mayfair. One of the notable aspects of Hayward's work was that he brought to the British tailored look an acknowledged Italian influence and Caine was the beneficiary of this distinctive cut; perfect for wielding a double-barrelled shotgun.

And just like the understated blue suit, there's always been a coolness, a kind of restraint on too much emoting in Caine's performances and this is especially acute in *Get Carter*; the restraint and the quietness draw you in. American critic Roger Ebert's review at the time was effusive: "'Get Carter' is a tense, hard-boiled crime movie that uses Michael Caine, for once, as the sure possessor of all his unconscious authority. ... 'Get Carter' shows him as sure, fine and vicious – a good hero for an action movie."[5]

A little later in his career, Caine would revisit a similarly bleak 'underworld' in the film *Mona Lisa*. Caine has written with sensitivity about *Get Carter* and that relationship between actor and the roles that they inhabit: "There's a danger, when making films, of romanticising violence. I know only too well what the other side of violence looks like and I wanted to show that other side and I wanted to show that other side in *Get Carter*."[6]

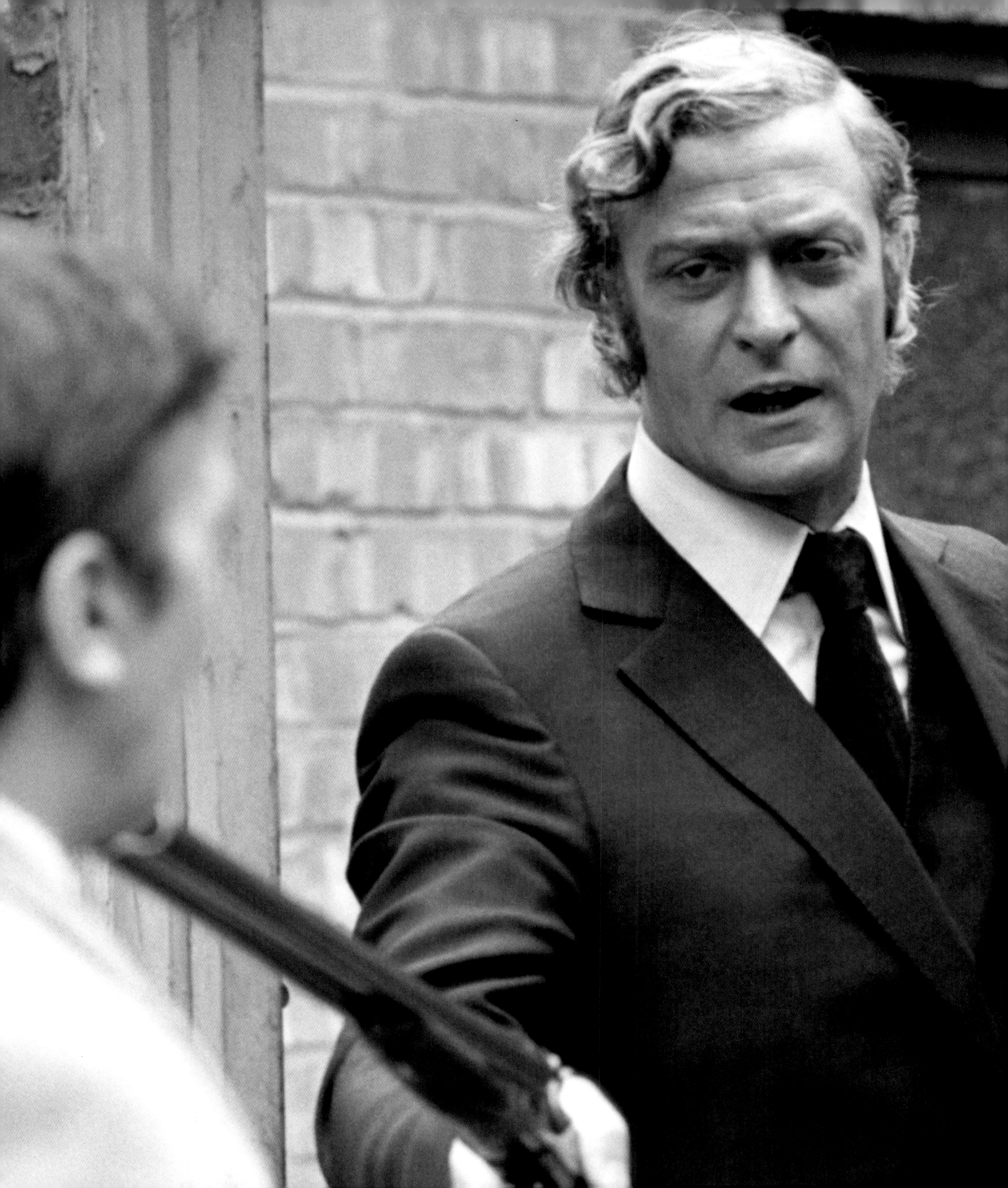

The film's production designer was Assheton Gorton, who had worked with Michelangelo Antonioni on *Blow Up* (1966). In their book *British Film Culture in the 1970s*, film historians, Sue Harper and Justin Smith set the scene: "... the incongruously named La Dolce Vita pub and a betting shop in Hebburn....everything was shot on location...*Get Carter* made straight presentation of some stark modern settings ...Such godless places performed an essentially sociological function for a key film of the post-New Wave era, hinting at the environmental influences on ugly human behaviour."[7]

With a background in broadcast TV documentary, director Mike Hodges brings that sensibility to the movie and O'Neill's photographs tap into and riff on this.

Terry O'Neill's images from the production of the film capture and place Caine so vividly within the north-eastern landscape, a place that Caine has described as "a wild frontier". The black-and-white photographs possess a certain starkness that befits the genre and yet they also depict a creative intensity on set and, at times, a playfulness, too.

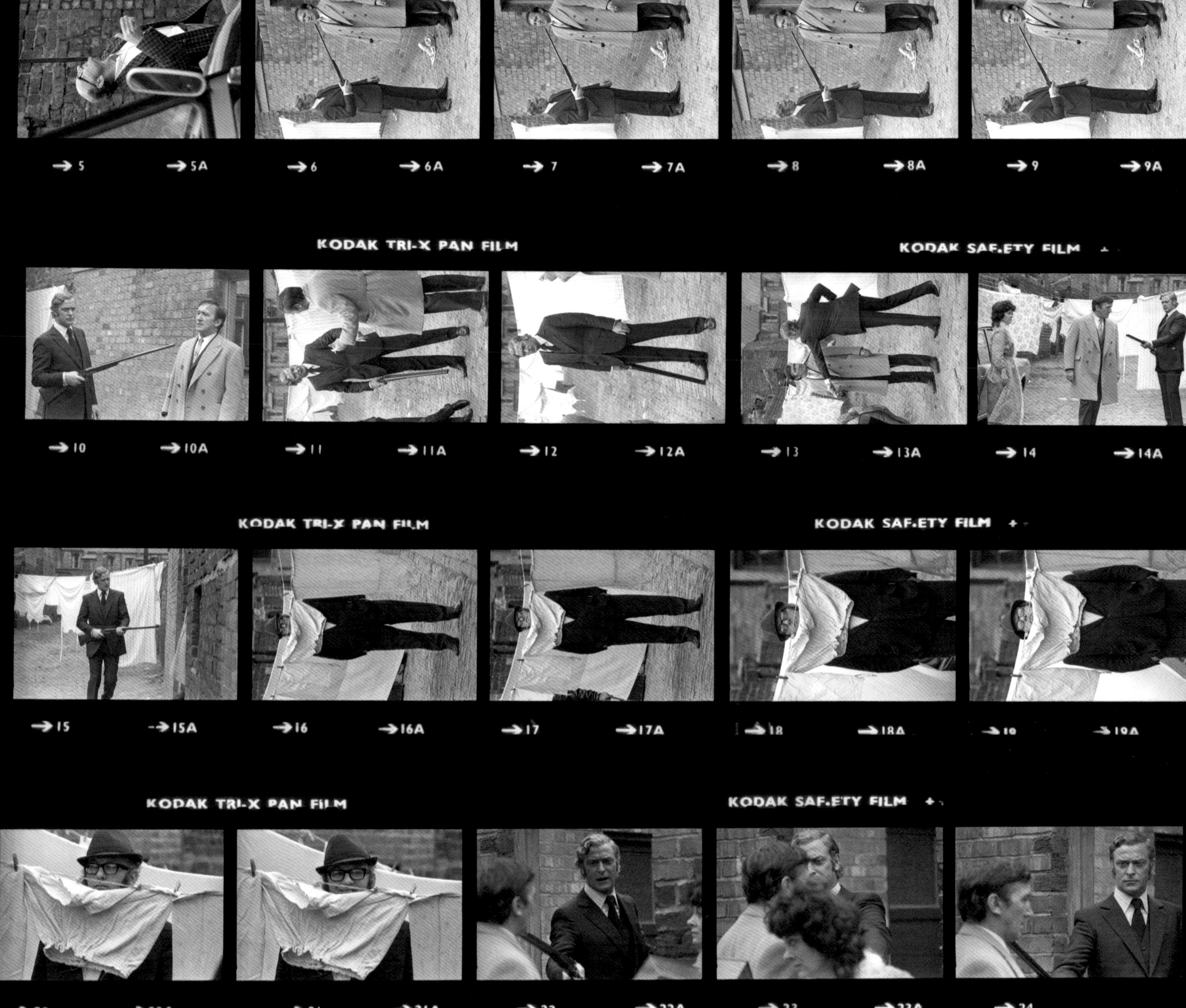
KODAK TRI-X PAN FILM
KODAK SAF.ETY FILM

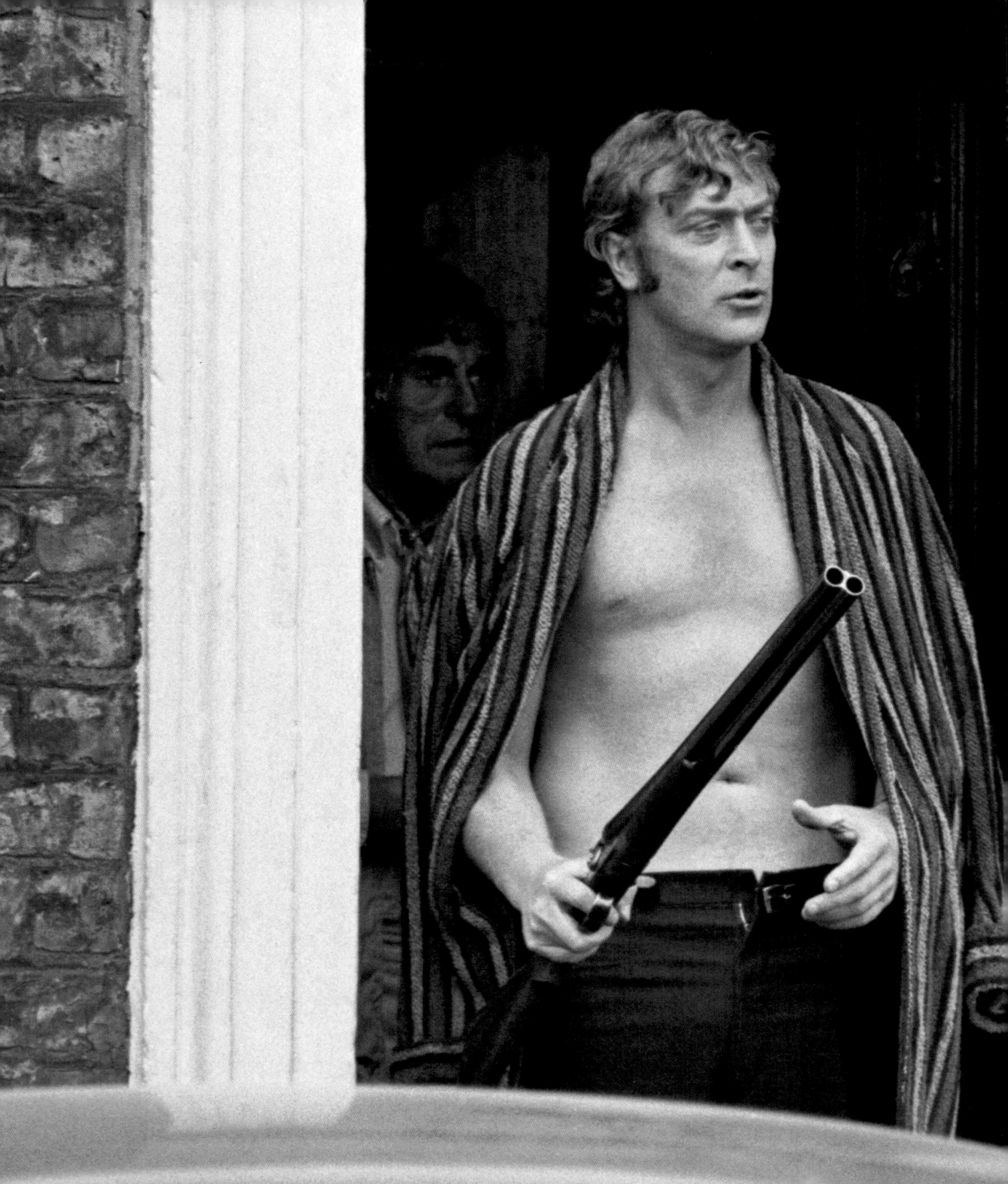

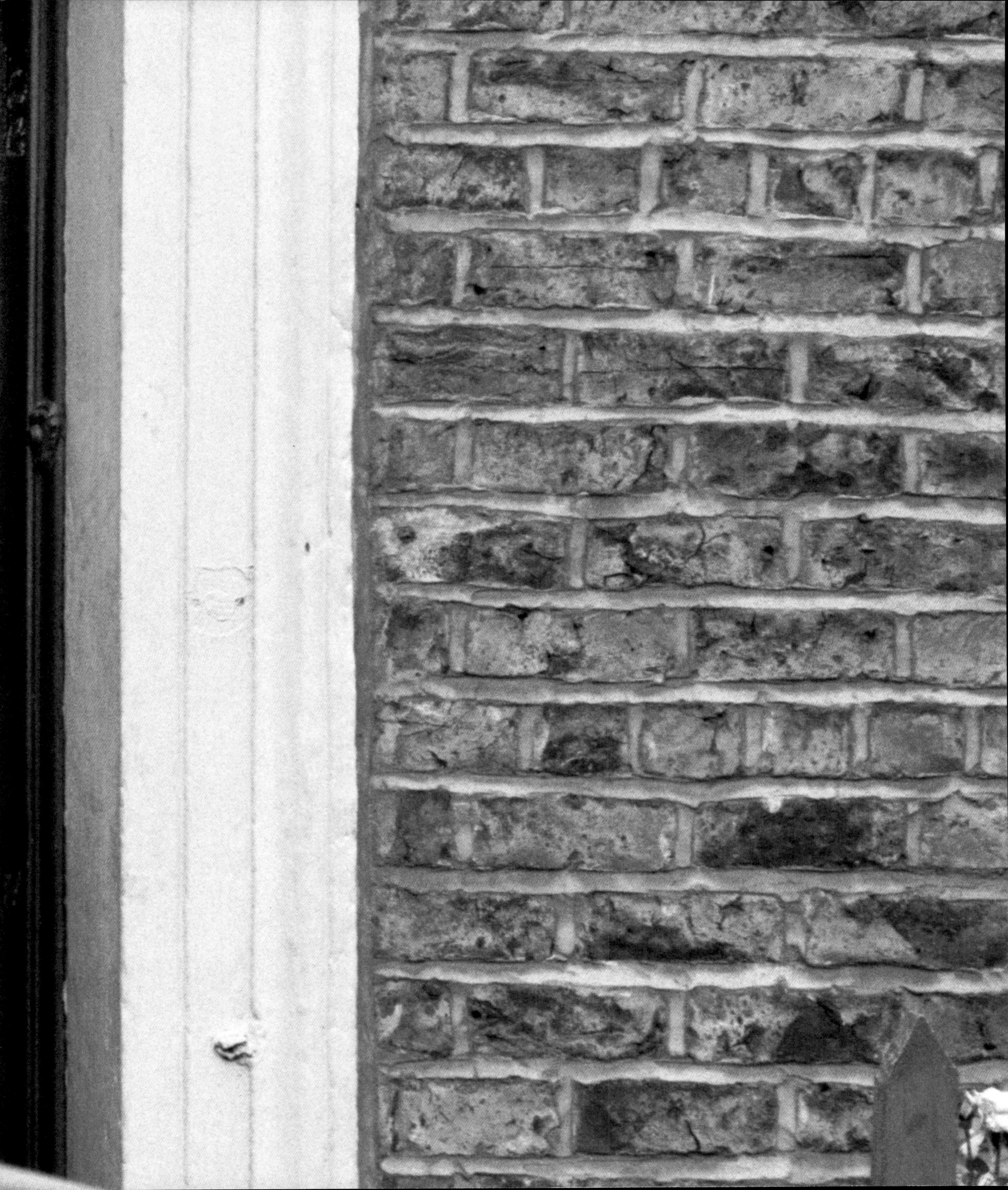

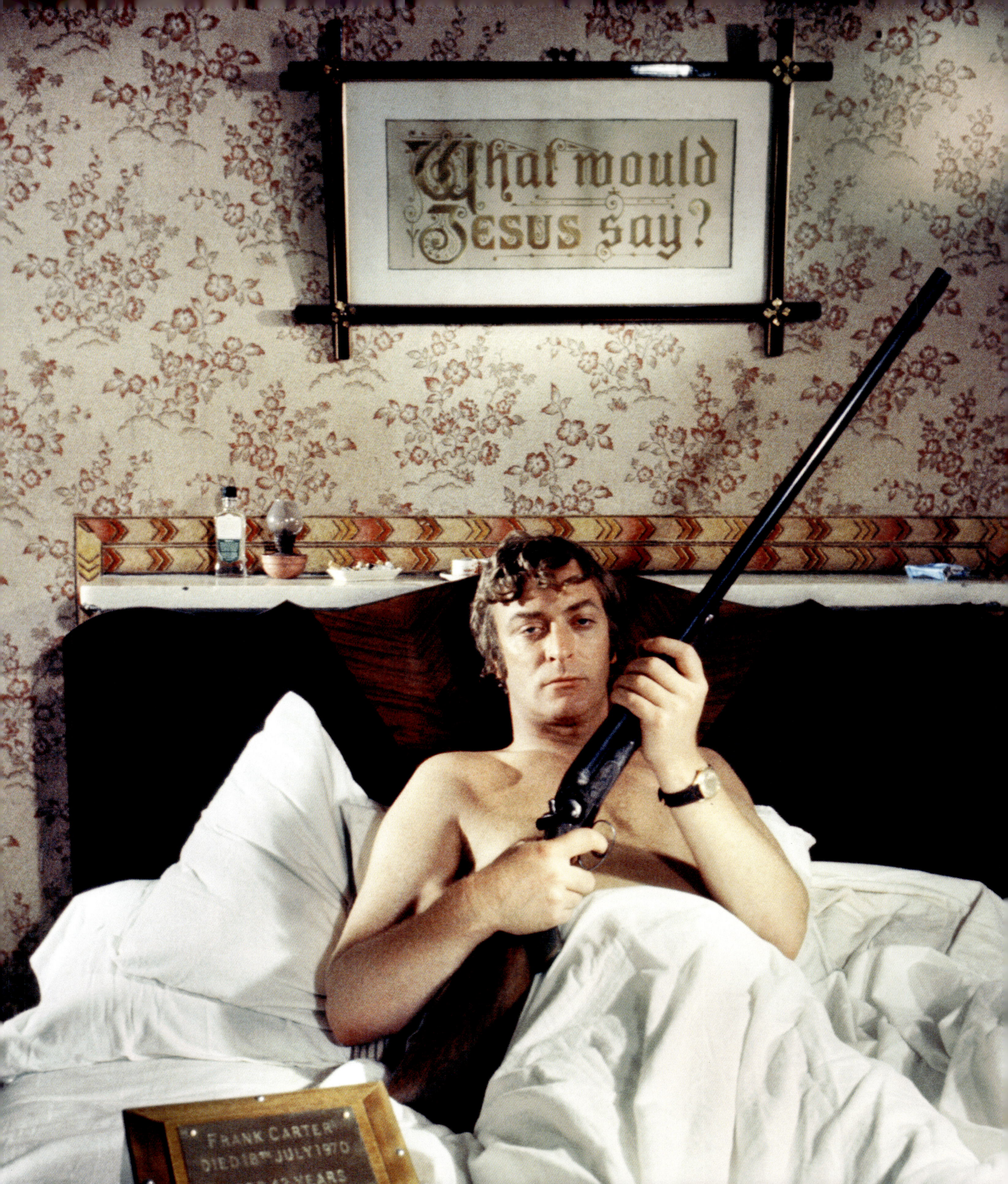
What would Jesus say?
FRANK CARTER
DIED 18th JULY 1970

People often think that *Get Carter* is a film about vengeance, but it's not: it's about honour.

Michael Caine

Caine was always a terrific subject, I loved being on set of a new Caine film.

Terry O'Neill

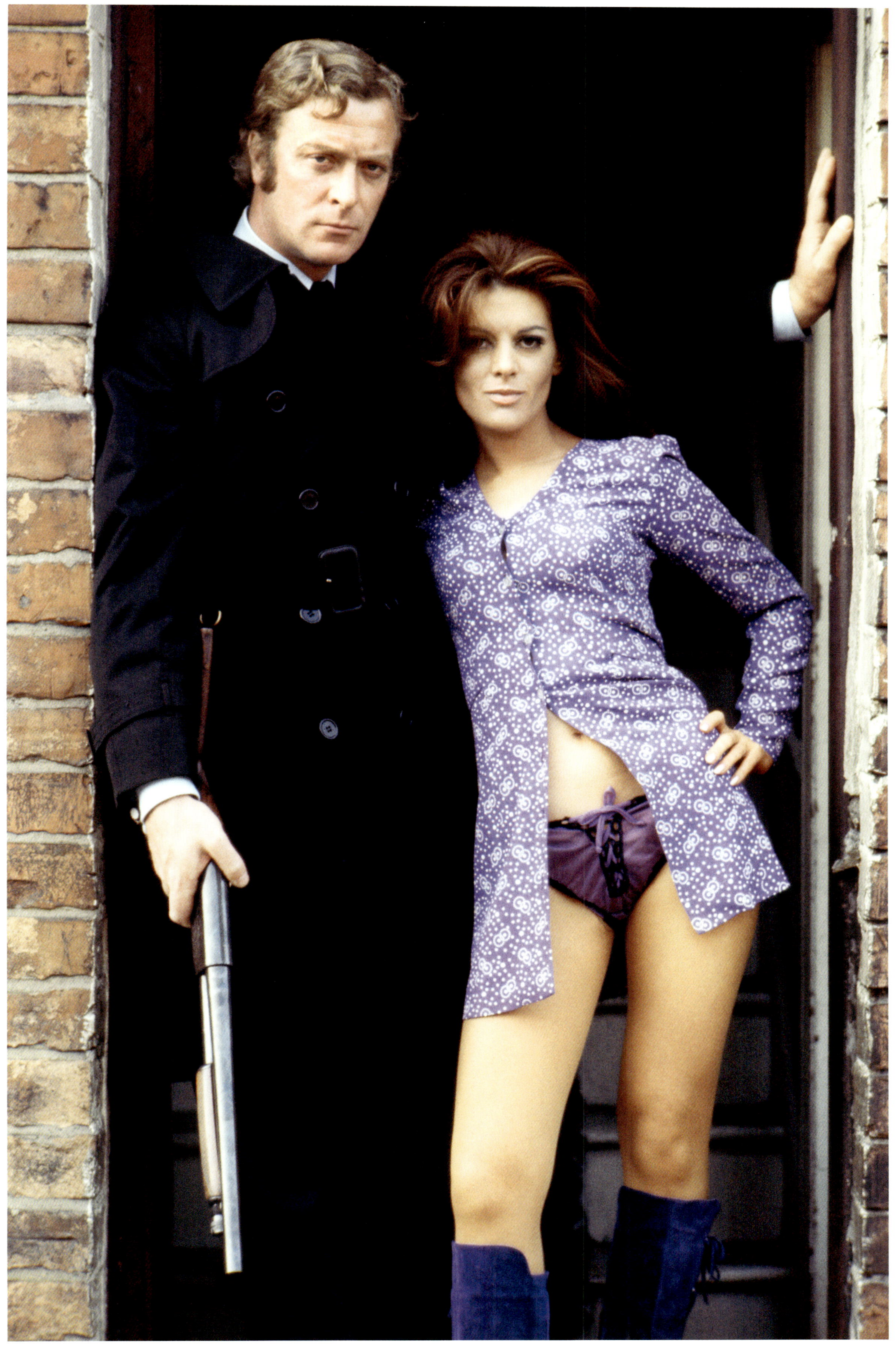

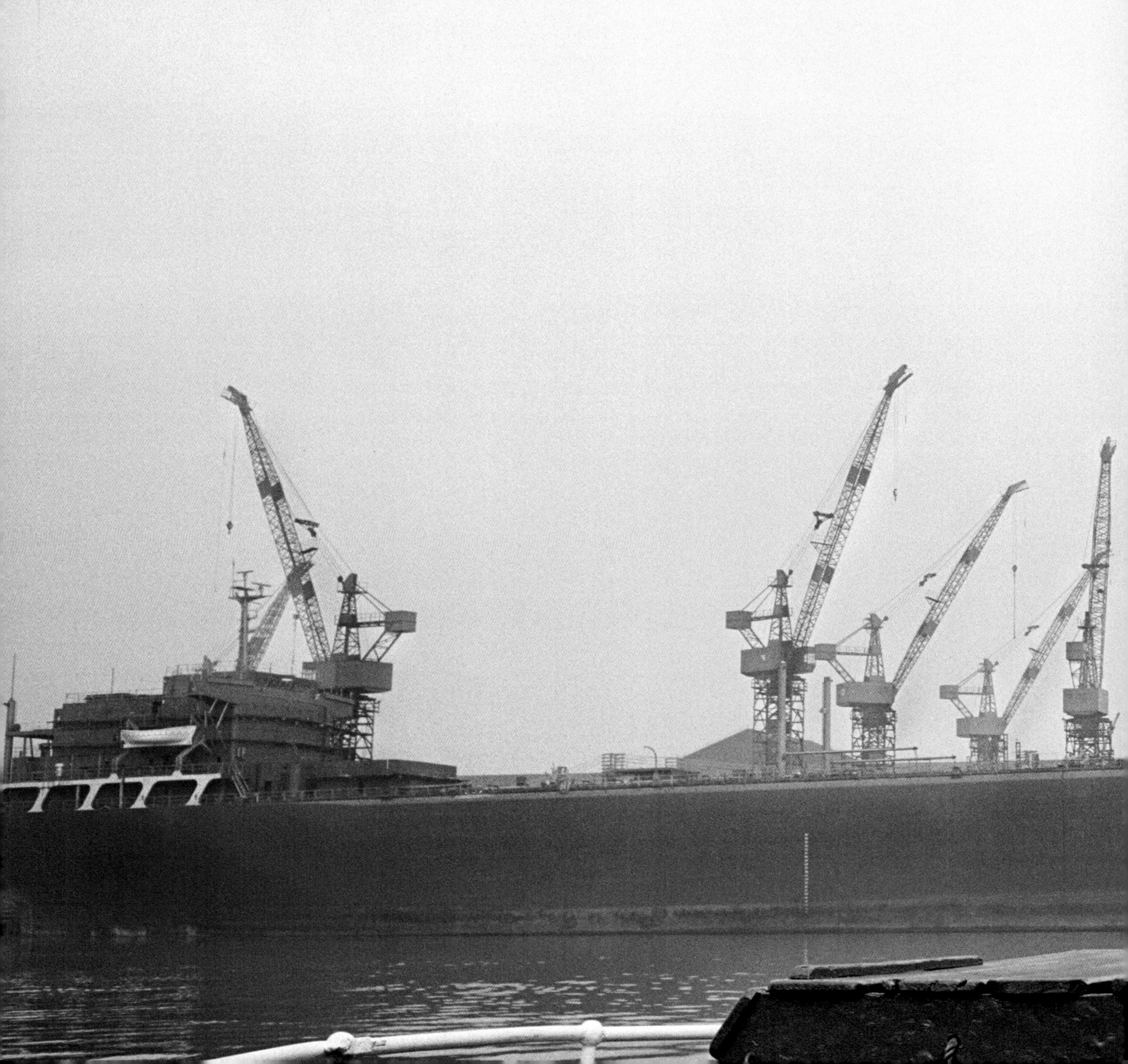

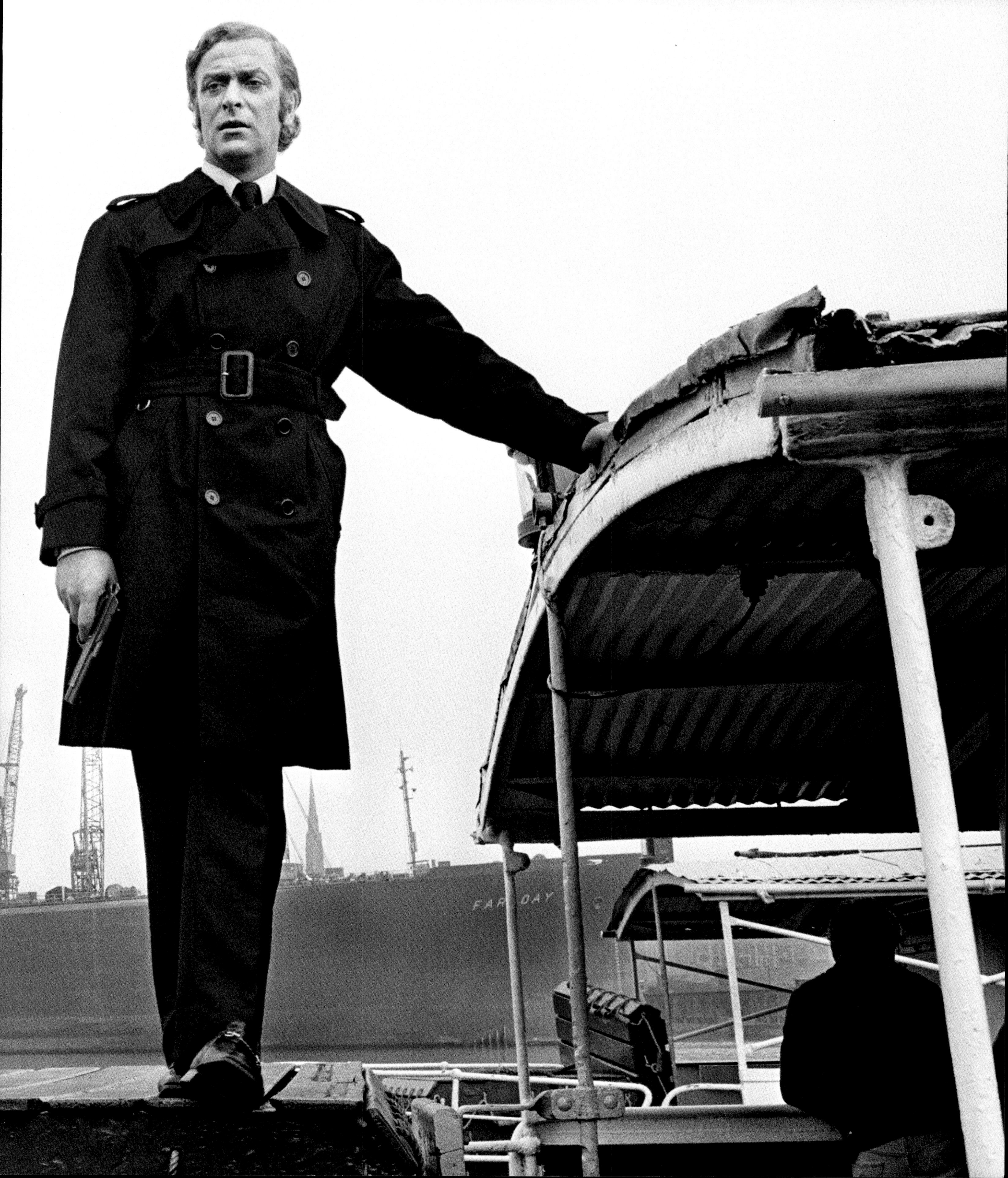
FAR DAY

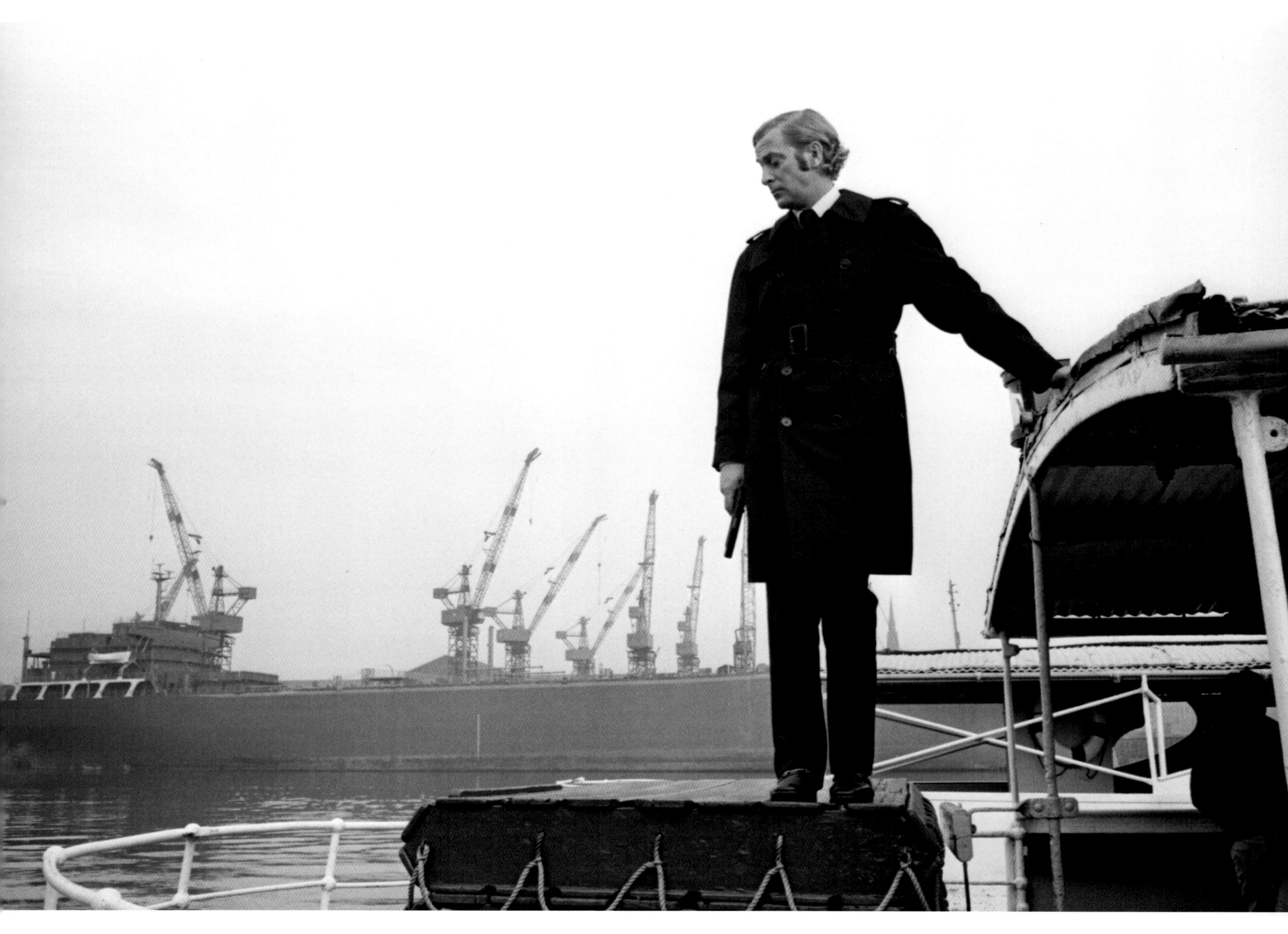

Page 125: Caine and Geraldine Moffat on location and in character in Newcastle upon Tyne for *Get Carter*. Moffat portrays Glenda who is involved with the crimeworld that Jack Carter (Caine) is out to destroy.

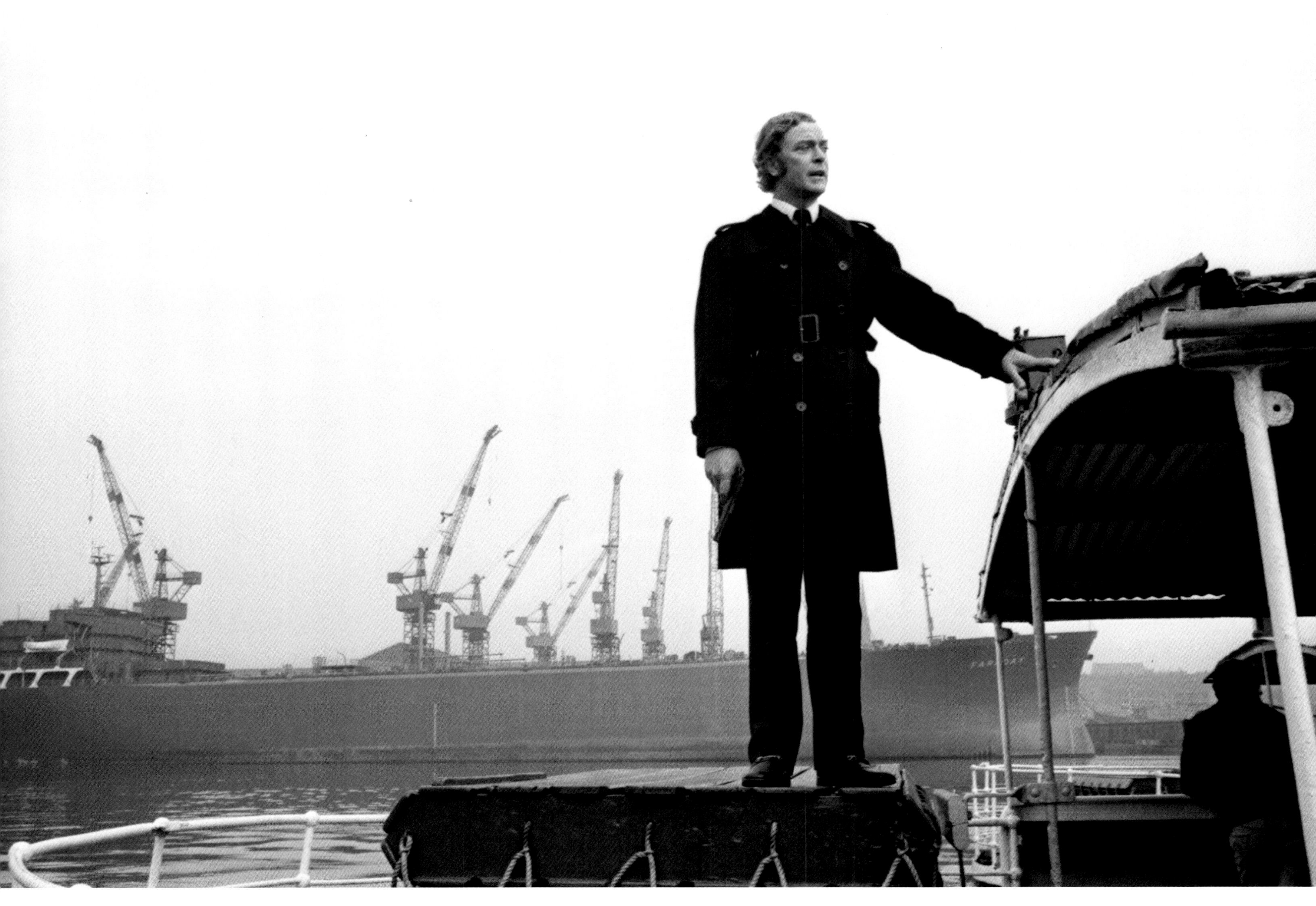

Caine against the dockyard background as he rides the ferry.
Filmed largely on location in and around Newcastle Upon Tyne, O'Neill's photographs ably capture the area's shipping and industrial heritage.

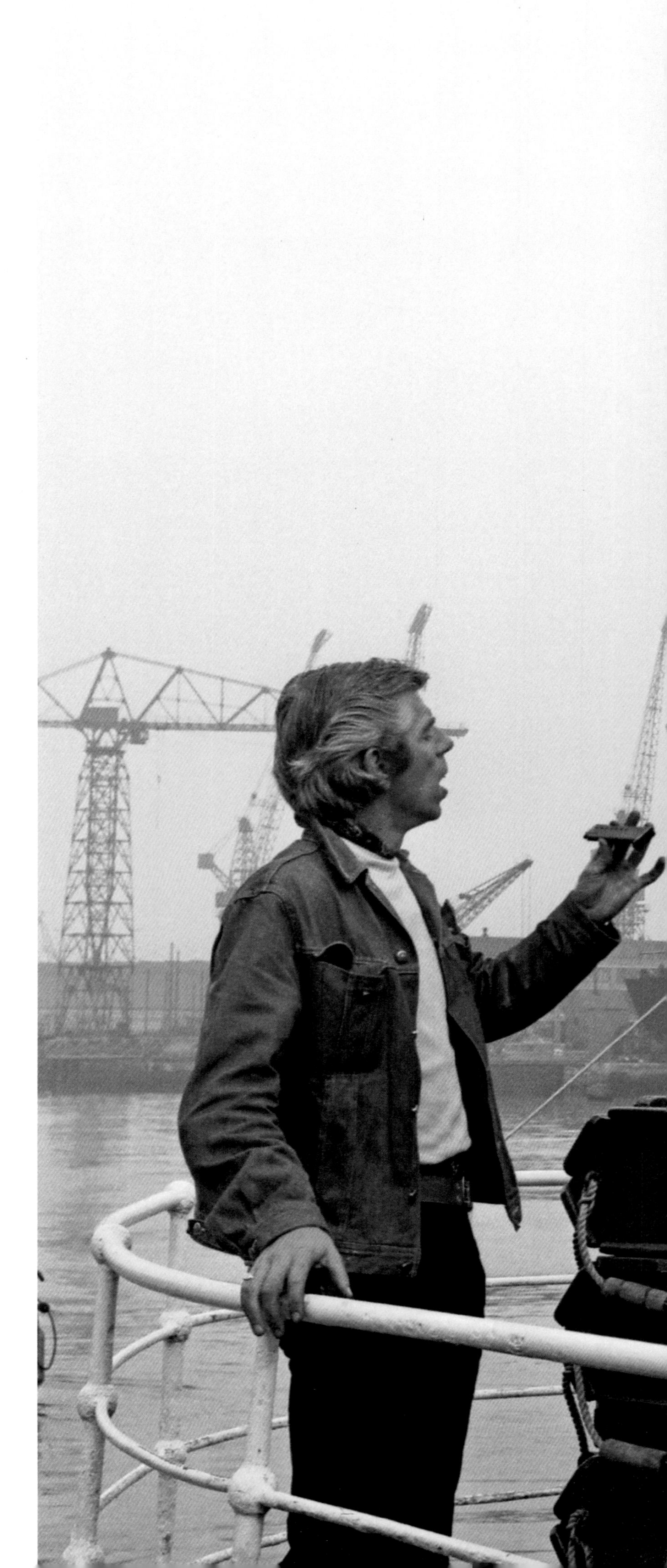

Caine and film crew prepare for a shot.

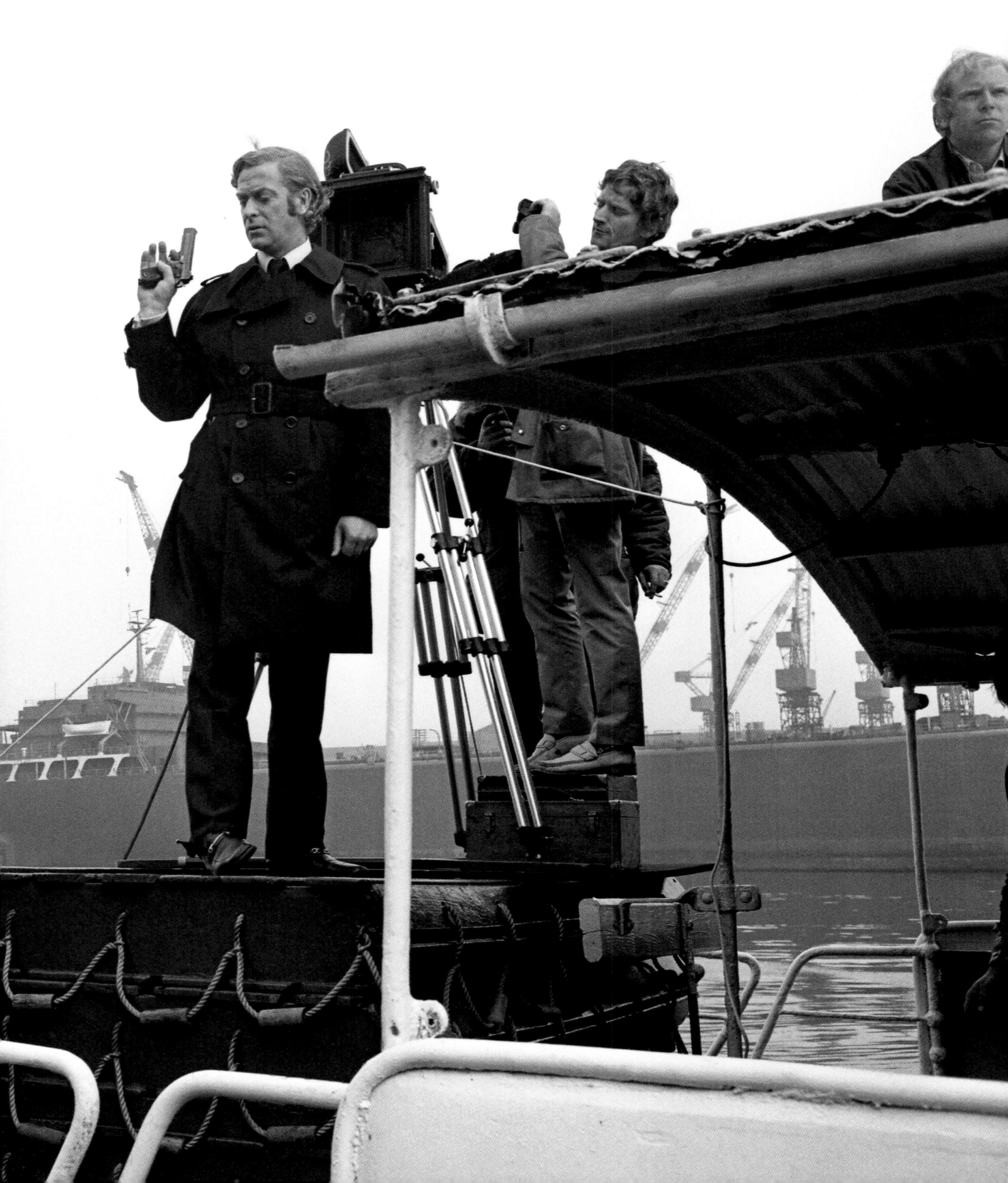

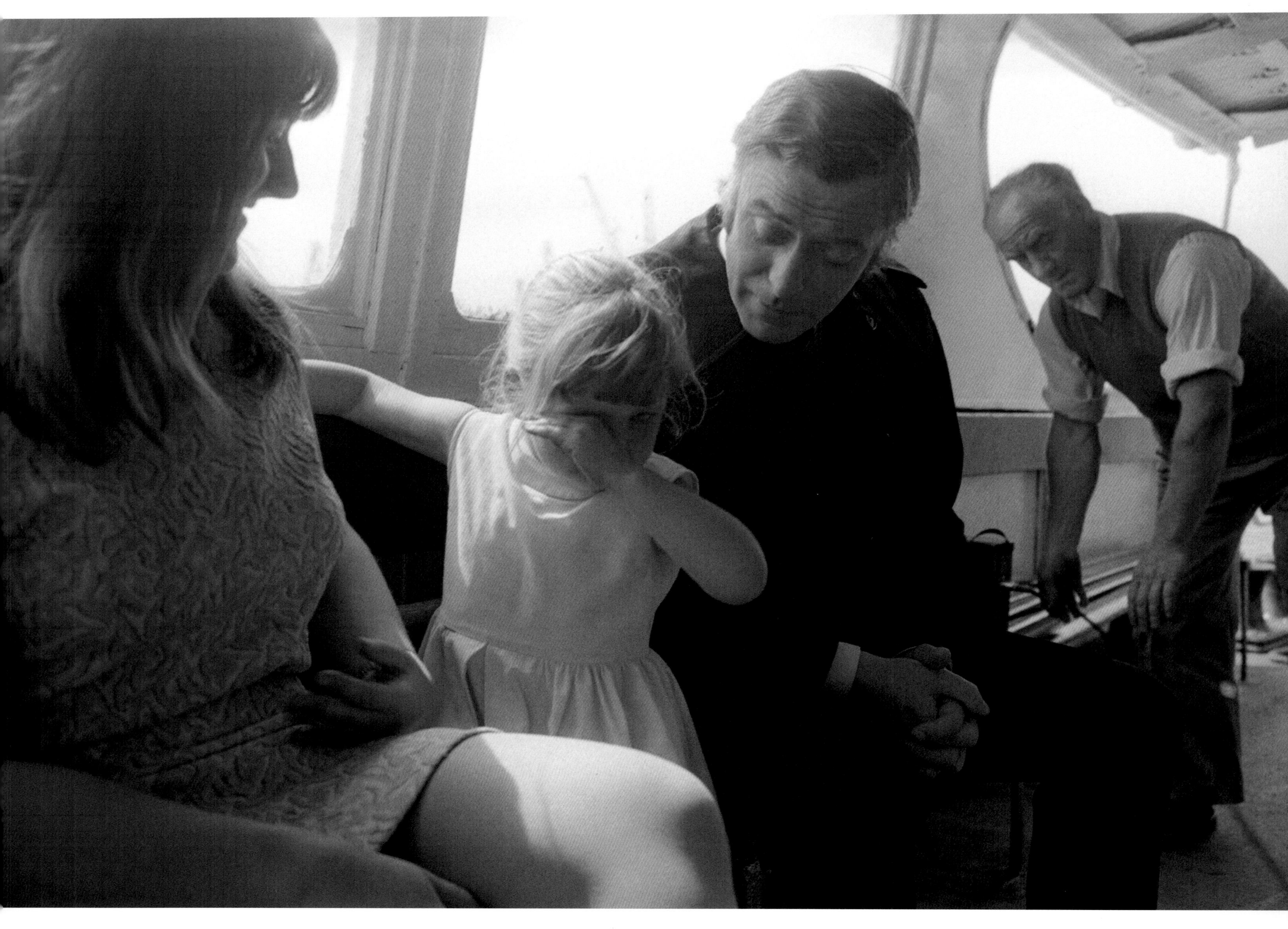

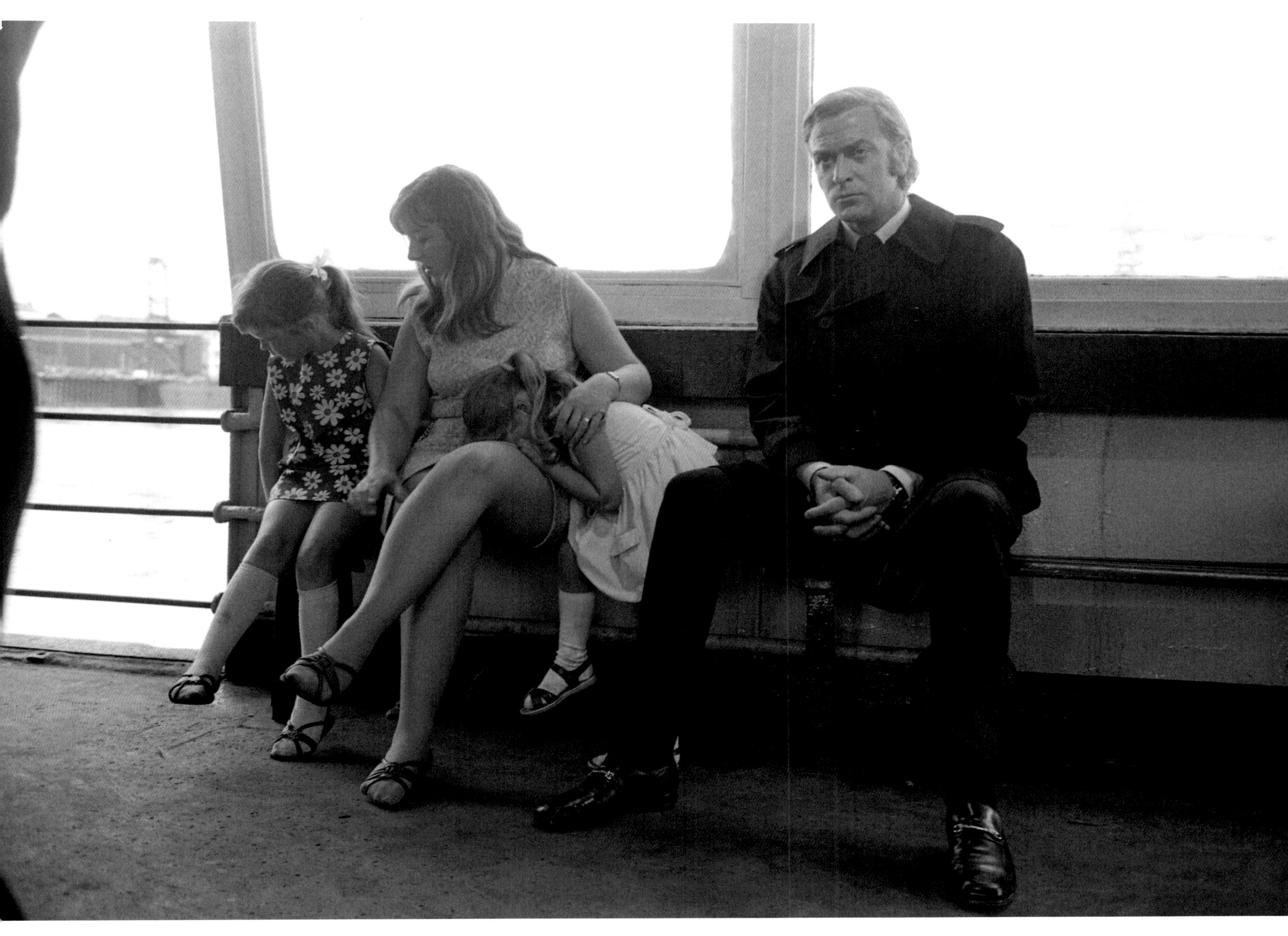

Caine aboard the Wallsend–Hebburn ferry.

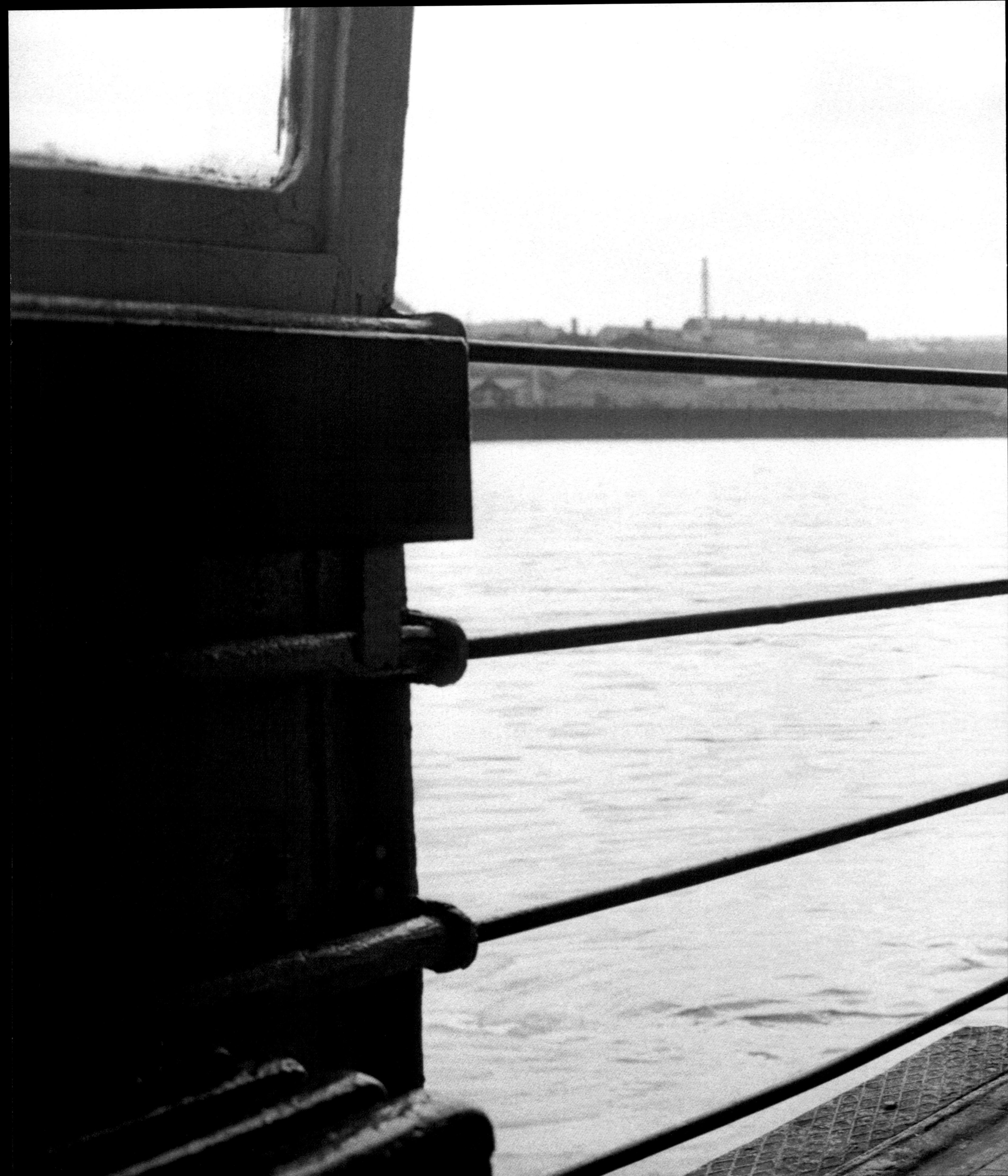

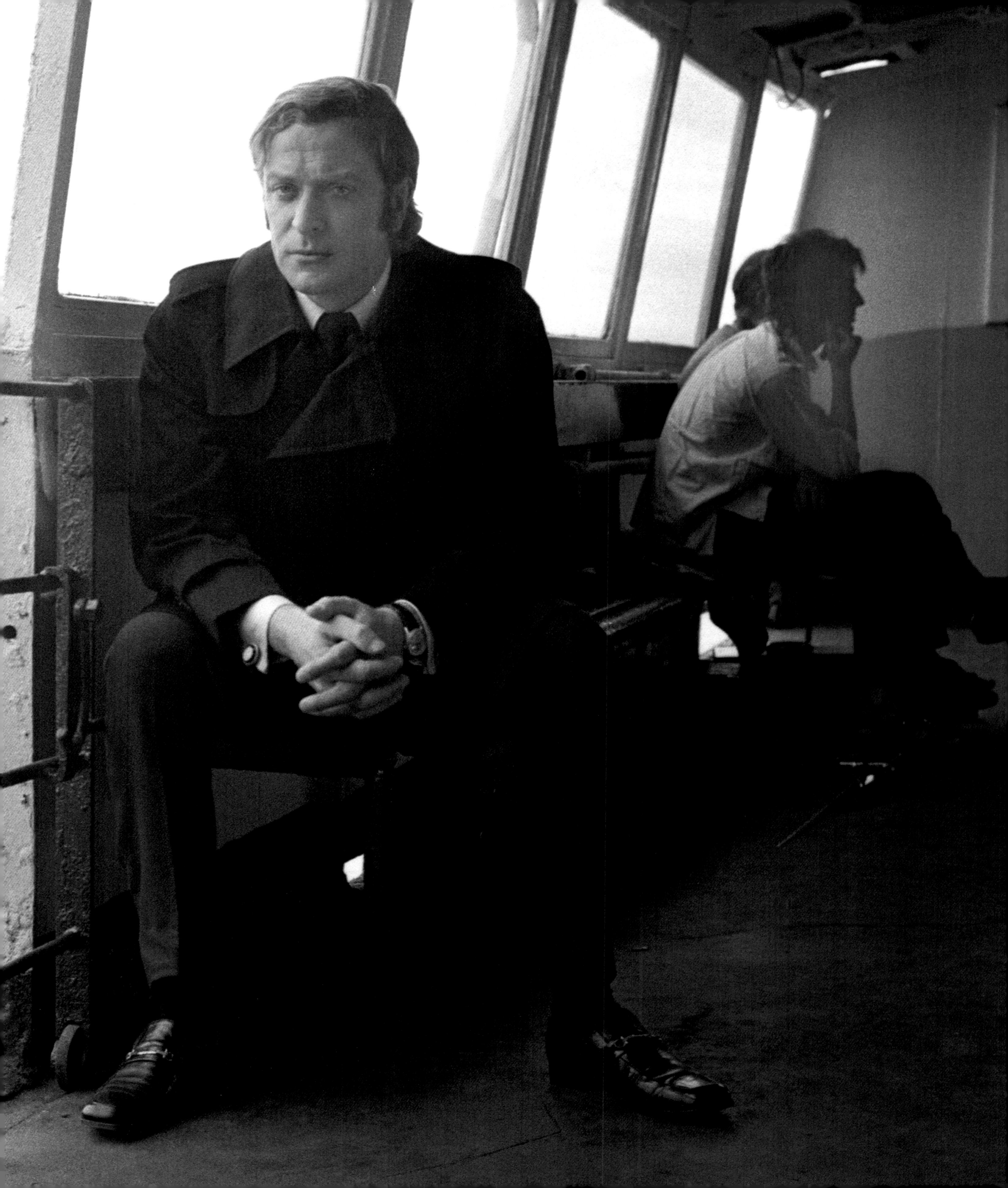

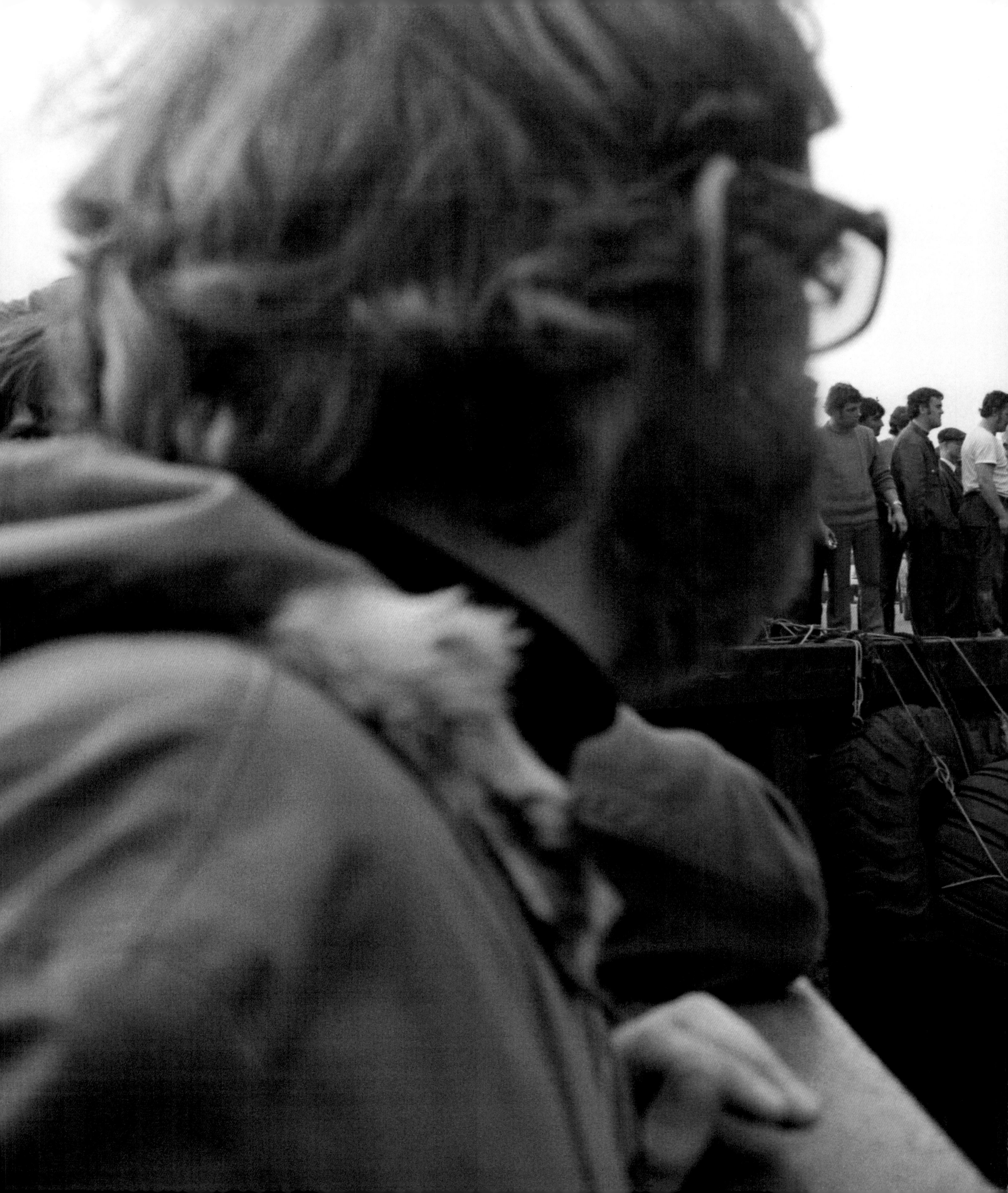

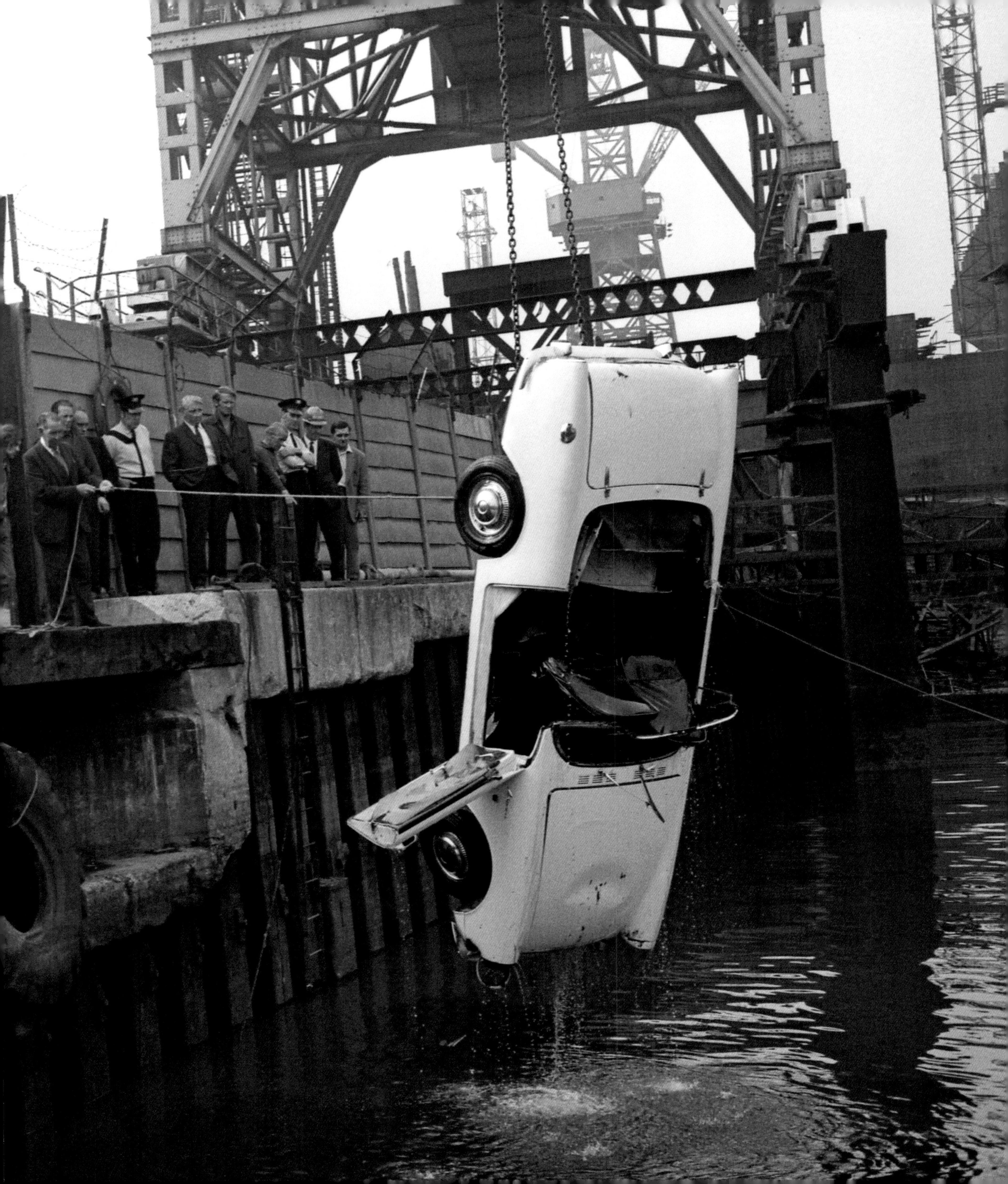

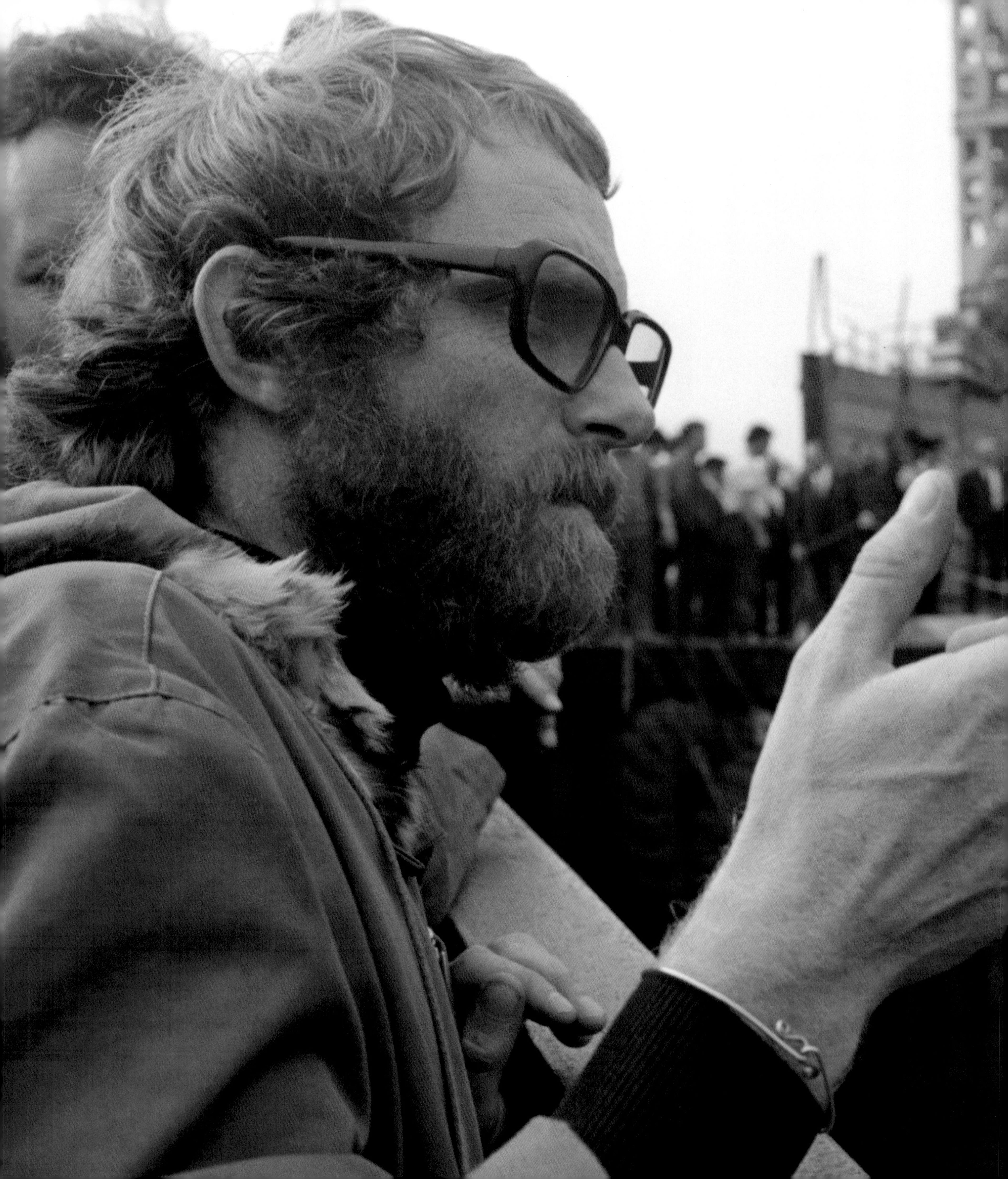

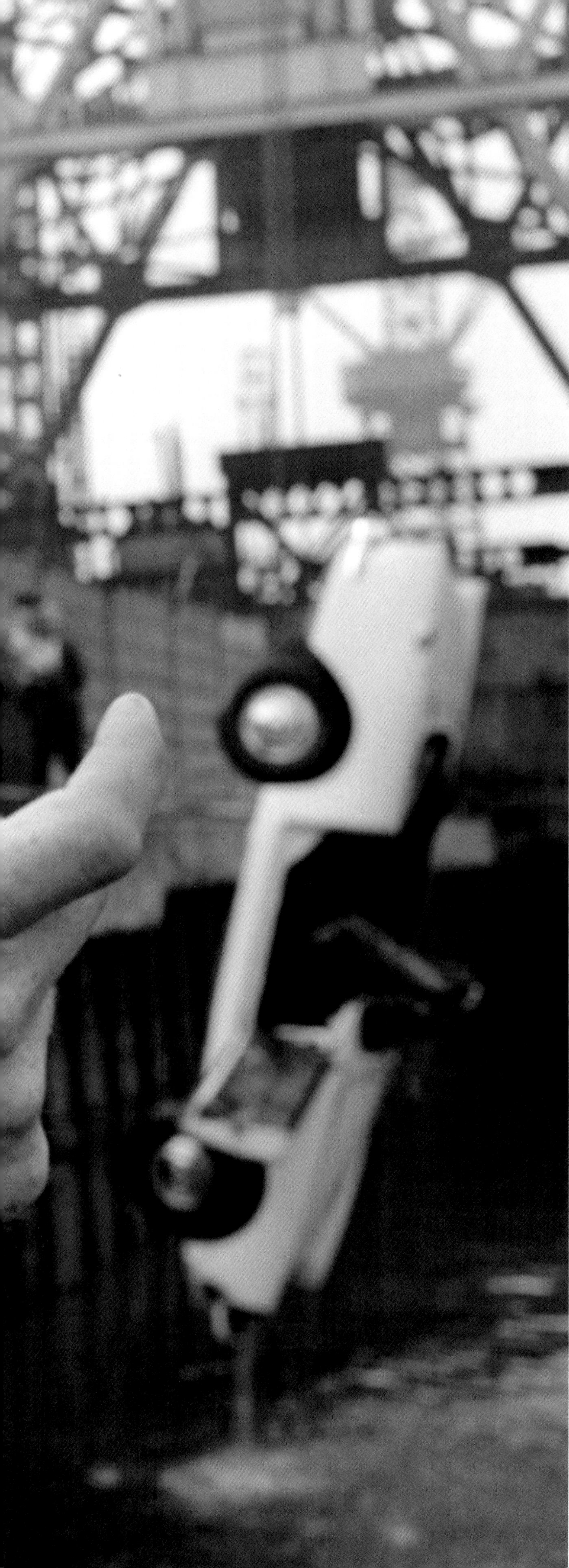

Director Mike Hodges oversees quayside action.

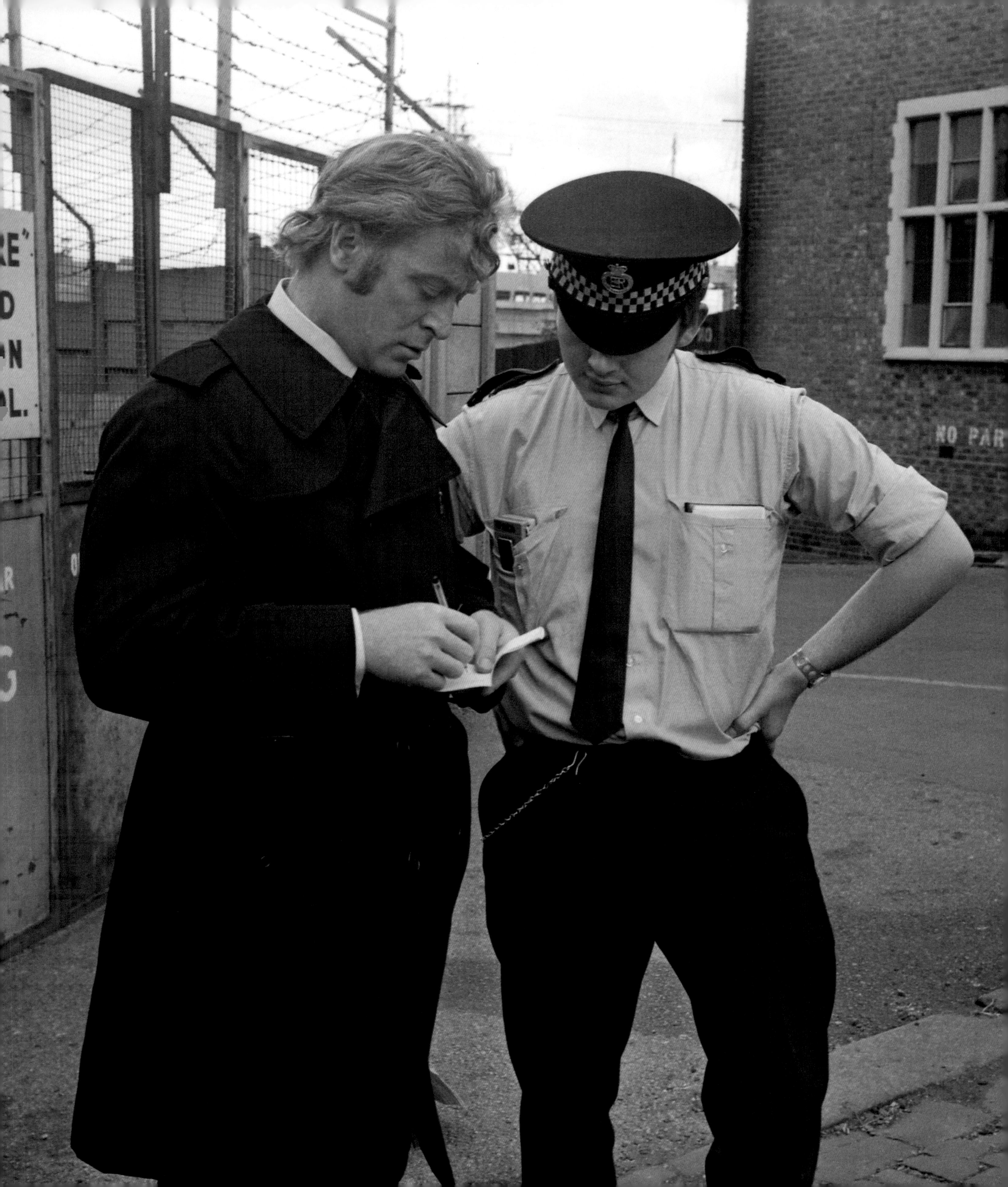
NO PAR

There's a danger, when making films, of romanticising violence. I know only too well what the other side of violence looks like and I wanted to show that other side and I wanted to show that other side in *Get Carter*.

Michael Caine

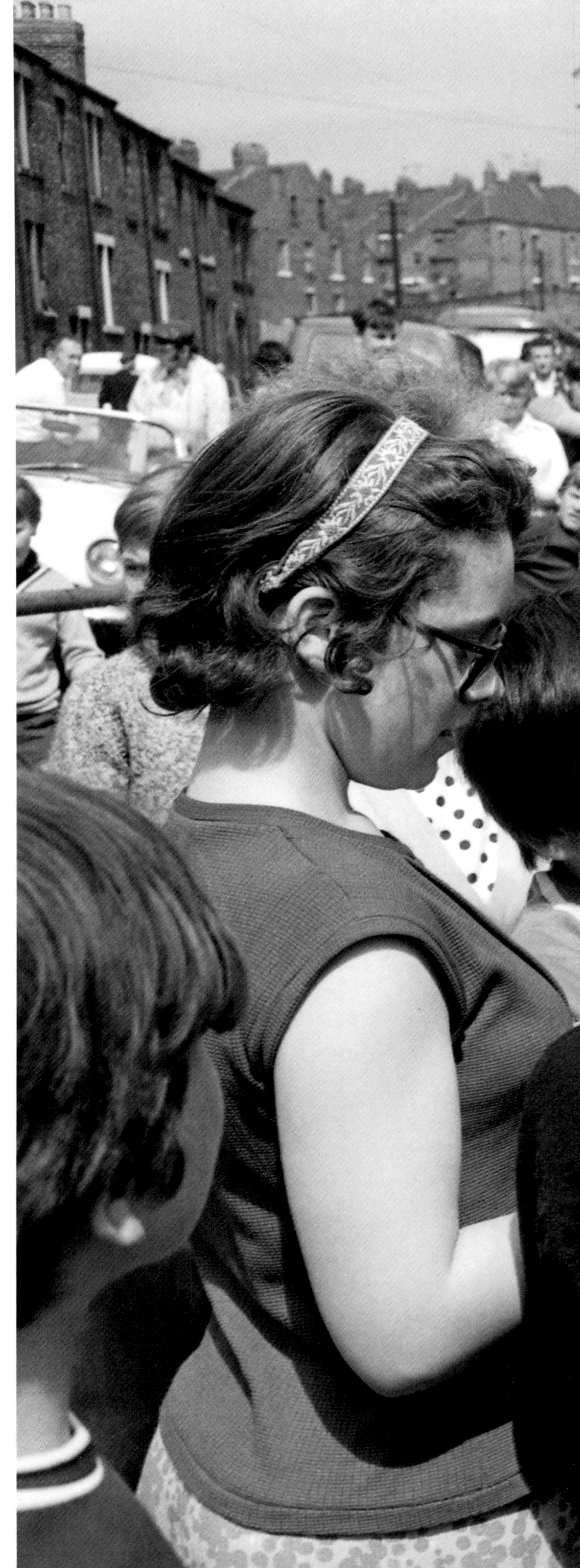

Caine signs autographs: a film fan since childhood who grew up to become a film star.

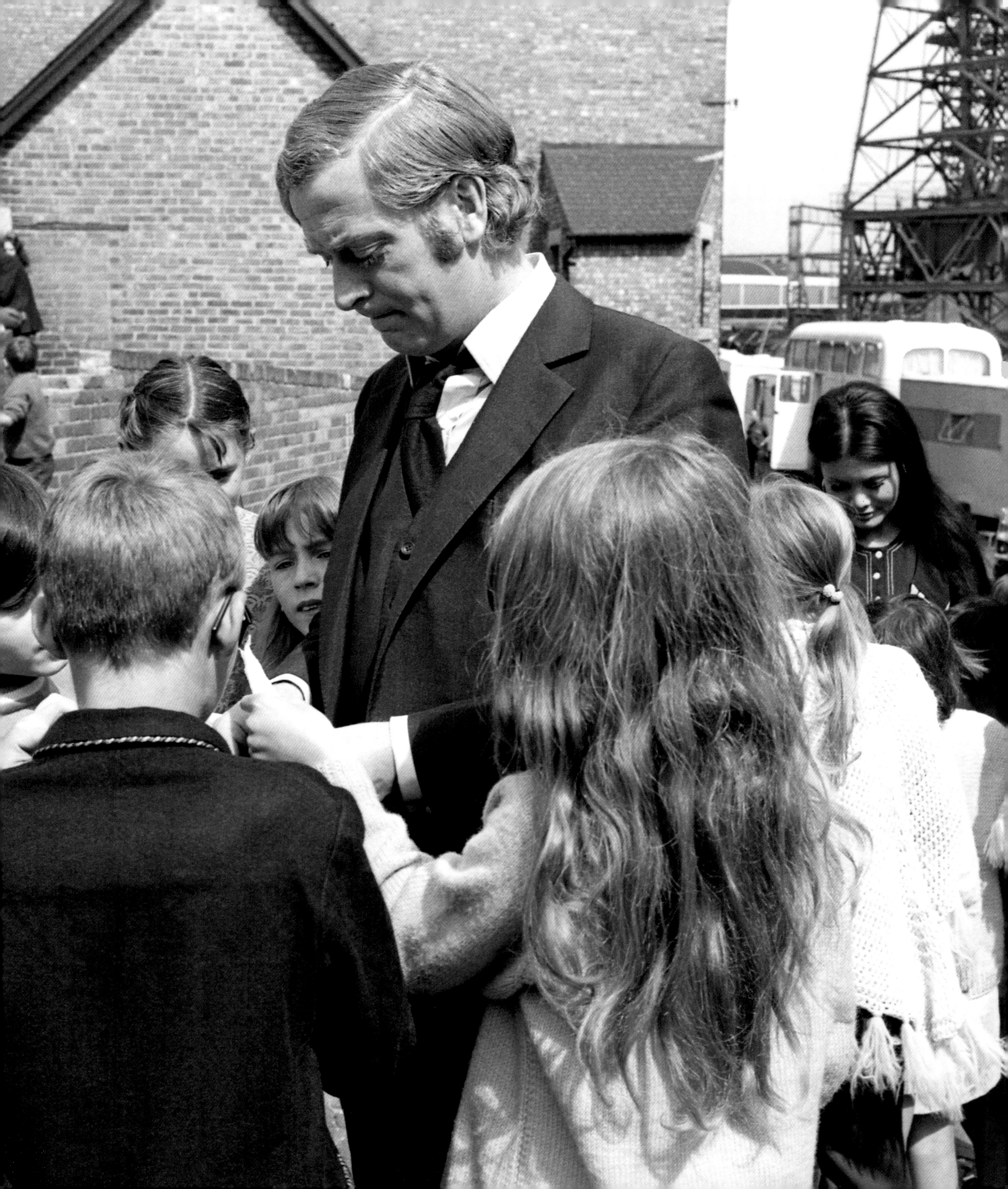

By this time, Michael was a household name – and word would always get out when they were filming on location. Michael always made the time to meet his fans and sign a few autographs.

Terry O'Neill

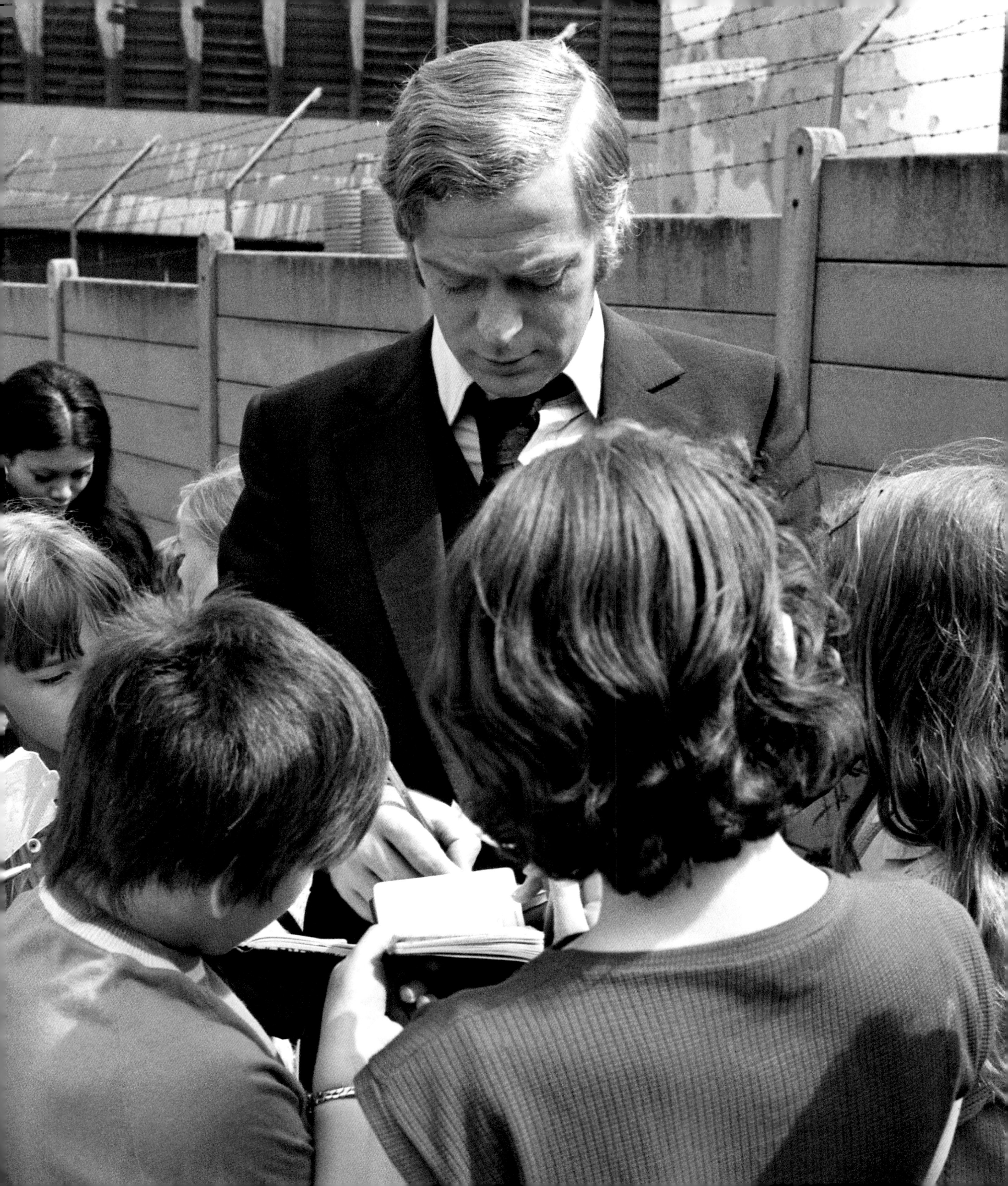

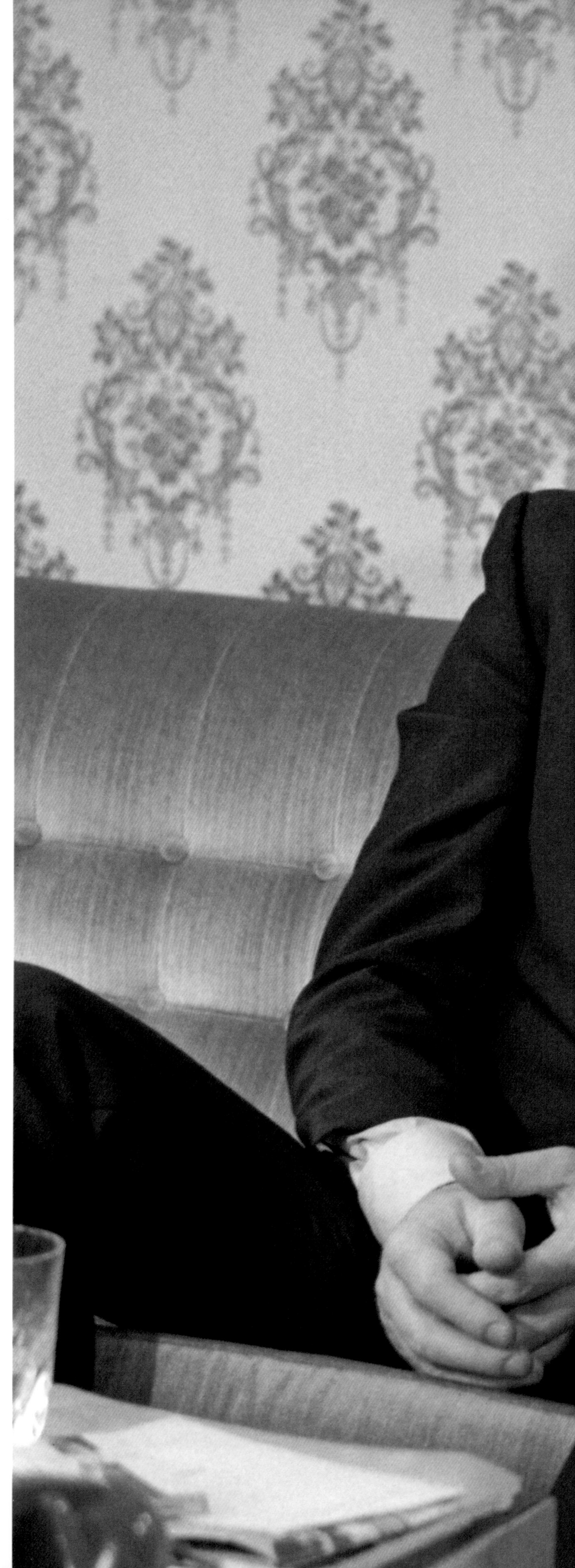

Mike Hodges chooses his shot and framing.

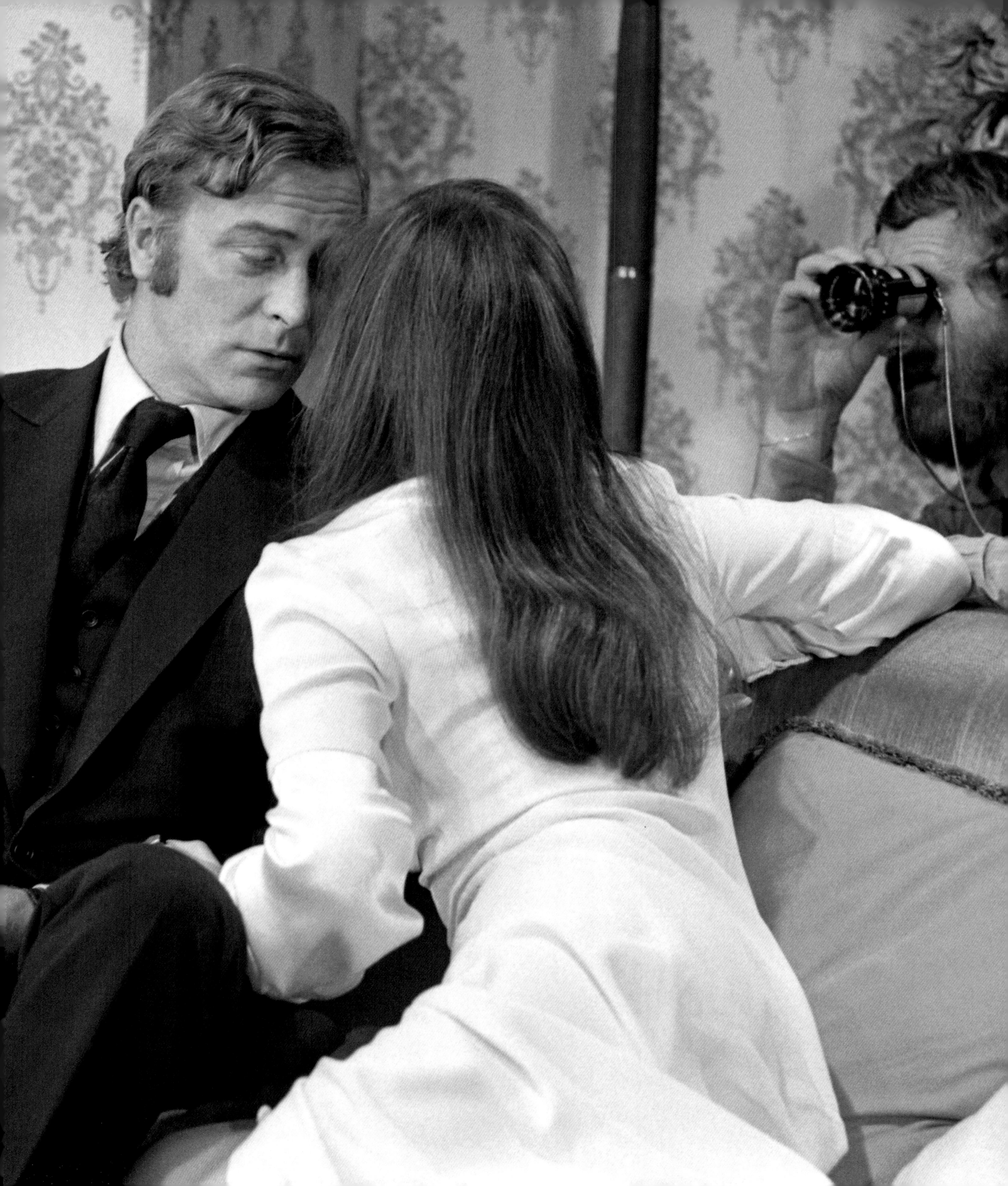

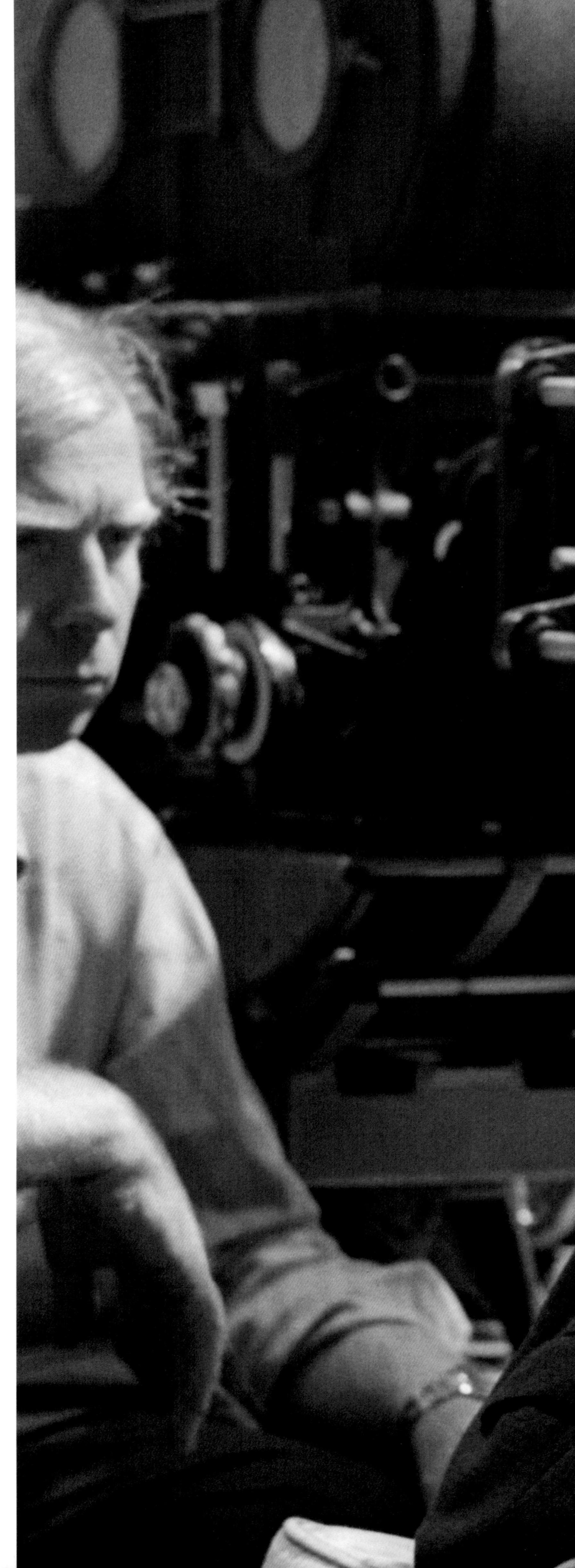

Playwright John Osborne took a role in *Get Carter* as crime-boss Cyril Kinnear.
Following page: Caine at rest as a scene with John Osborne and crime kingpins is prepared on location at Dryerdale Hall.

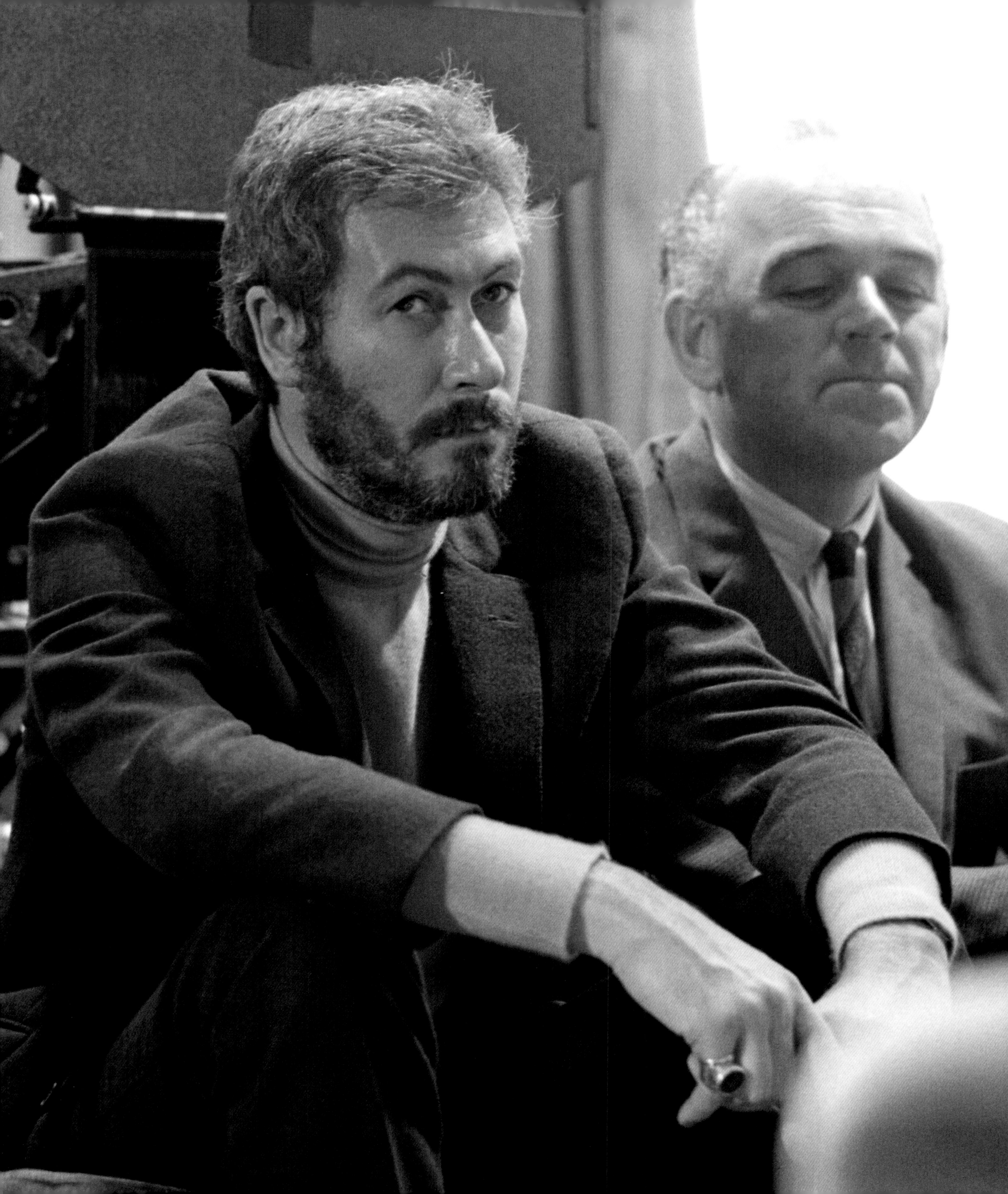

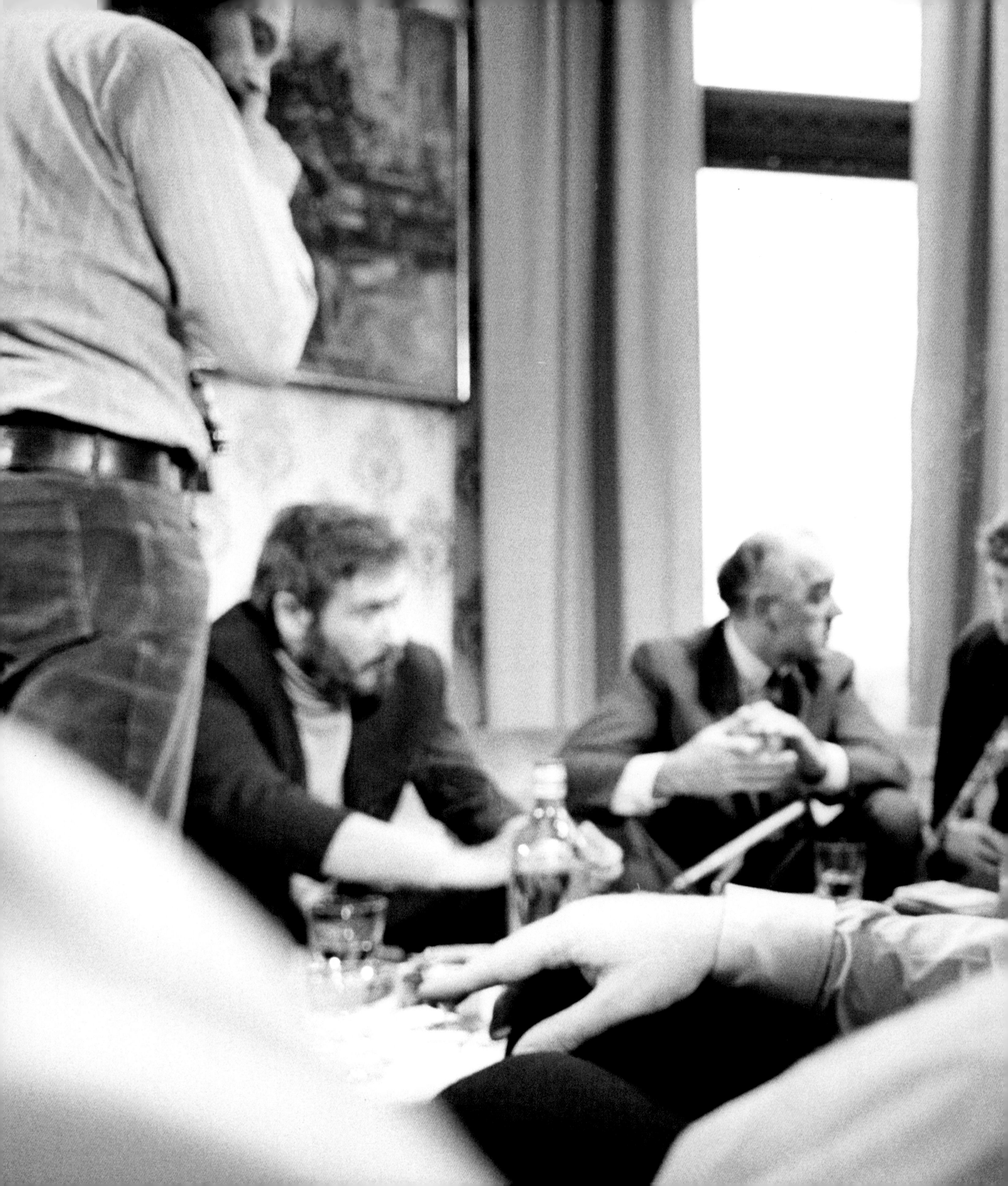

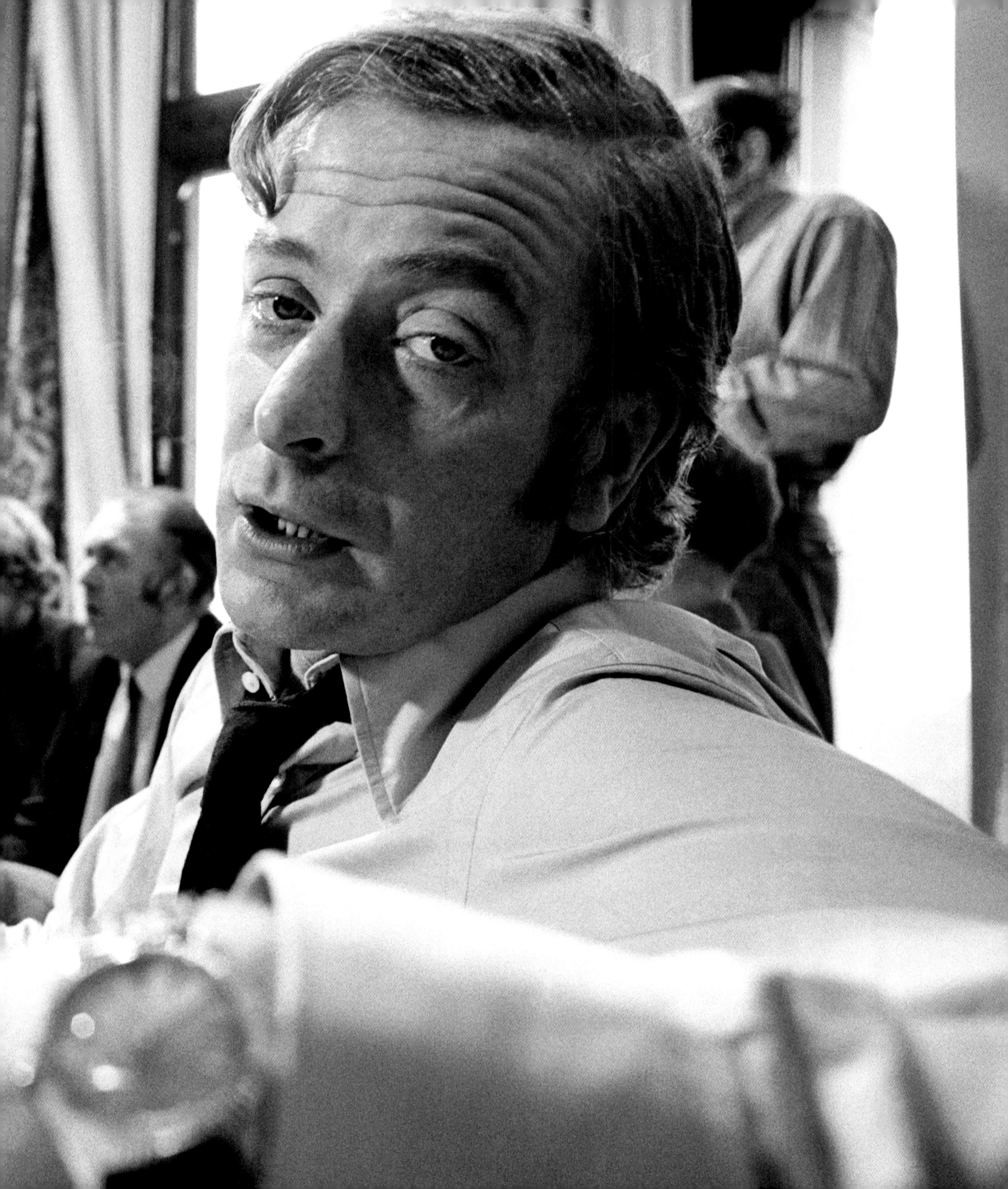

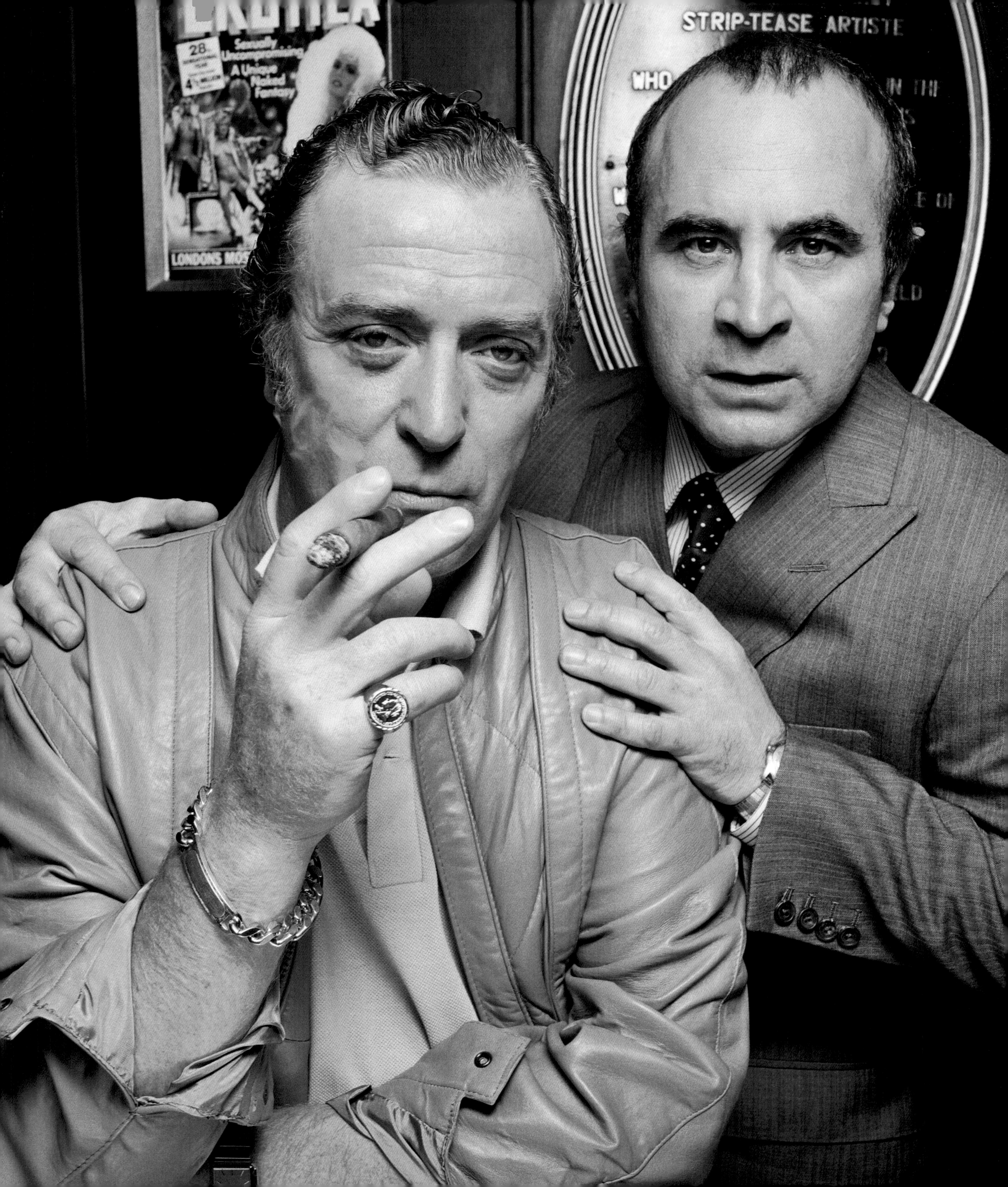

STRIP-TEASE ARTISTE
WHO
28.
Sexually Uncompromising
A Unique Naked Fantasy

MONA LISA

1986

"A number of O'Neill's images on set offer a sense of Mortwell's unforgiving character. They also capture Caine at a particular high point of his career (not the first or the last) but right there in the middle of it as his work was in the resurgence."

Film historian David Parkinson has said of Caine's standing as a movie star that "You don't get to be one of only three actors to be Oscar-nominated in three different decades, or rank number eleven on the all-time box office chart, unless you're good."[1] In part, this idea of 'good' speaks to Caine's facility as both leading man and as character actor. Whilst he might be synonymous with characters like Harry Palmer, Alfie, and the supporting characters in more recent Christopher Nolan films, during the 1980s Caine produced a number of vivid and contrasting performances. Key to this run was his role in *Mona Lisa*, which works well as a companion piece to *Get Carter*.

The movie's plot focuses on a taxi-driver just out of prison named George (Bob Hoskins). George's job is to taxi call-girl Simone around London. In turn, George becomes embroiled in Simone's world including an involvement with crime boss, Mortwell (Caine). Caine's supporting performance in the film pervades its entirety.

Conceived by writer/director Neil Jordan – who had established himself with *Angel* (1982) and *The Company of Wolves* (1984) – *Mona Lisa* was co-written with David Leland. In conversation with me for this book, Jordan explains that it is about "how men totally misunderstand women".[2] Indeed, for all of its crime film genre elements, "It opened it out into an exploration of character."

The film was shot at a number of locations in London, notably around Kings Cross railway station, which capture a "lost sense of British industrialism". Jordan's work with cinematographer Roger Pratt tends to a British social realism aesthetic that dovetails to great effect with the more heightened and overly stylised images of London. Jordan also notes that in contrast to this aspect of the film's visual palette, there is another visual style at work based around "making London look like

---

Previous page: Caine and Bob Hoskins in character as Mortwell and George.
Opposite page: Caine and Hoskins on location in London, in portrait mode.

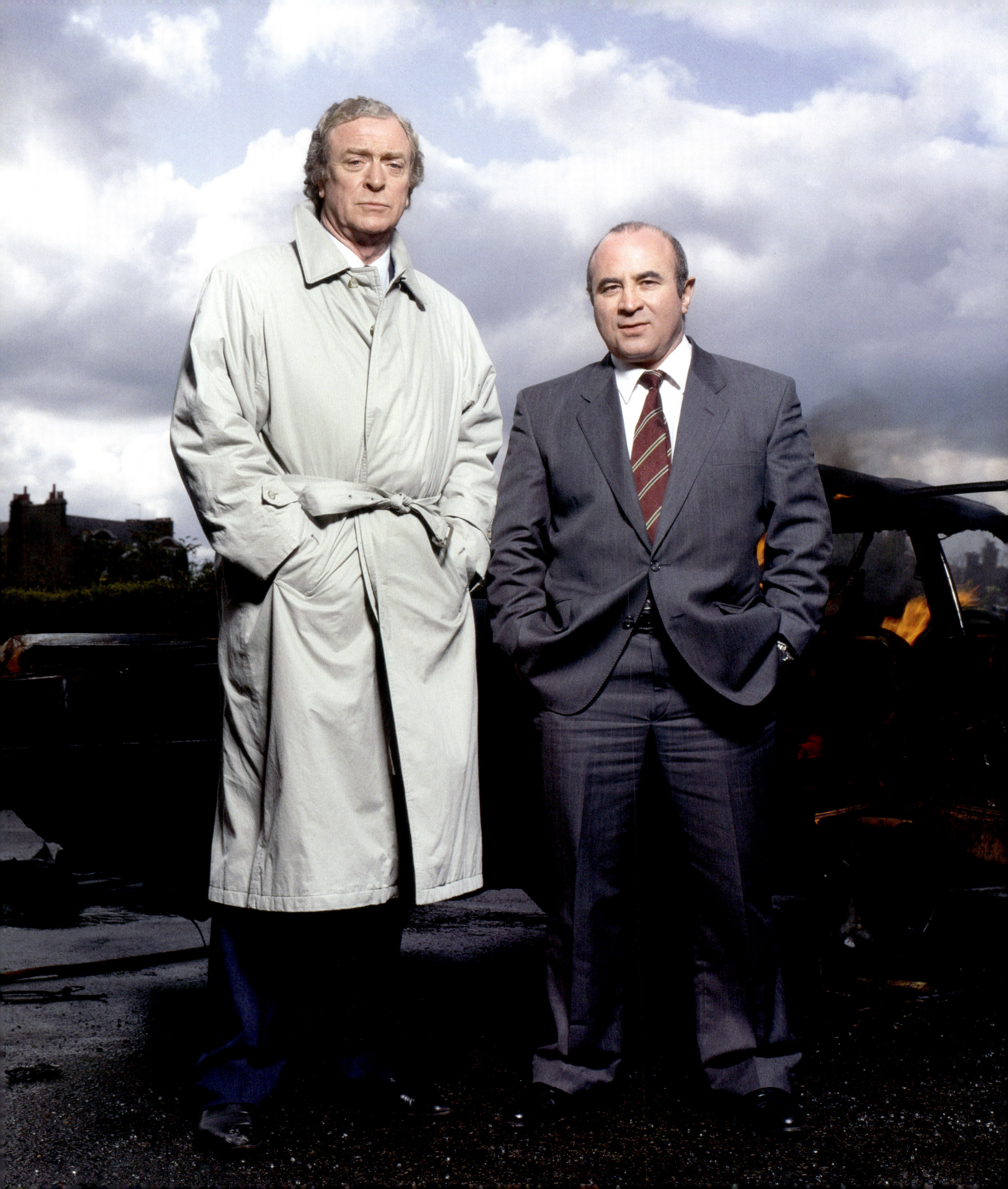

this Danteseque kind of place; dreamlike and surrealist touches that you wouldn't normally find in a crime drama."

Mona Lisa filmed in the autumn of 1985 and it was Bob Hoskins who had approached Caine to appear in the film. Jordan comments: "*Hannah and Her Sisters* brought Michael to a different place" as a performer. Of Hoskins and Caine's on-screen rapport, Jordan recalls how "they began to bounce off each other. They had a great time playing-off each other: really made the dialogue sing."

Jordan notes with some amusement that there was difficulty "in getting him to do more than three takes. We were very lucky to have Michael Caine because we were small producers. He was playing the nastiest possible version of himself." Jordan goes on to explain how the placement of the camera beneath Caine's chin conjured the sense of Mortwell as a 'terrifying' figure. Jordan emphasises: "Caine was extraordinary. In the climax of the movie, he had to be shot in the foot: it's difficult to go between comedy and grotesquerie. He relished playing a monster."

The *Time Out* review considered *Mona Lisa* "A wonderful achievement, a dark film with a generous heart... Plotting a slow descent towards hell, the film deliberately invites comparison to *Taxi Driver*..."[3] In her book, Pauline Kael writes: "So calculatedly cool and soulless and nastily erotic that it seems to belong to a new genre of virtuoso viciousness."[4]

A number of O'Neill's images on set for Jordan's landmark movie capture the essence of Mortwell's character. They also capture Caine at a particular high point of his career when his work was enjoying an undeniable resurgence.

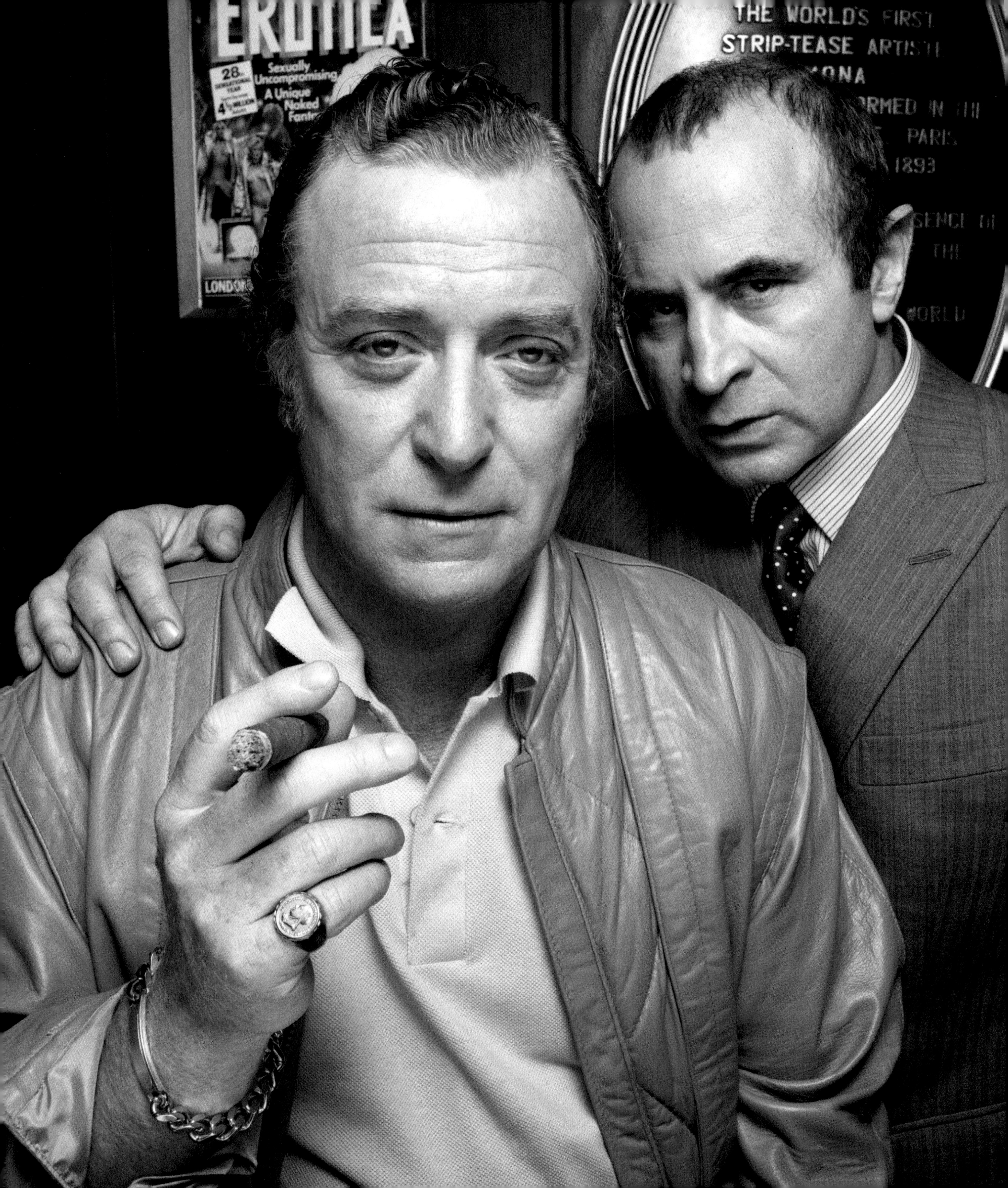
EROTICA
Sexually
Uncompromising
A Unique
Naked
THE WORLD'S FIRST
STRIP-TEASE
PARIS
1893

We were very lucky to have Michael Caine because we were small producers. He was playing the nastiest possible version of himself.

Neil Jordan

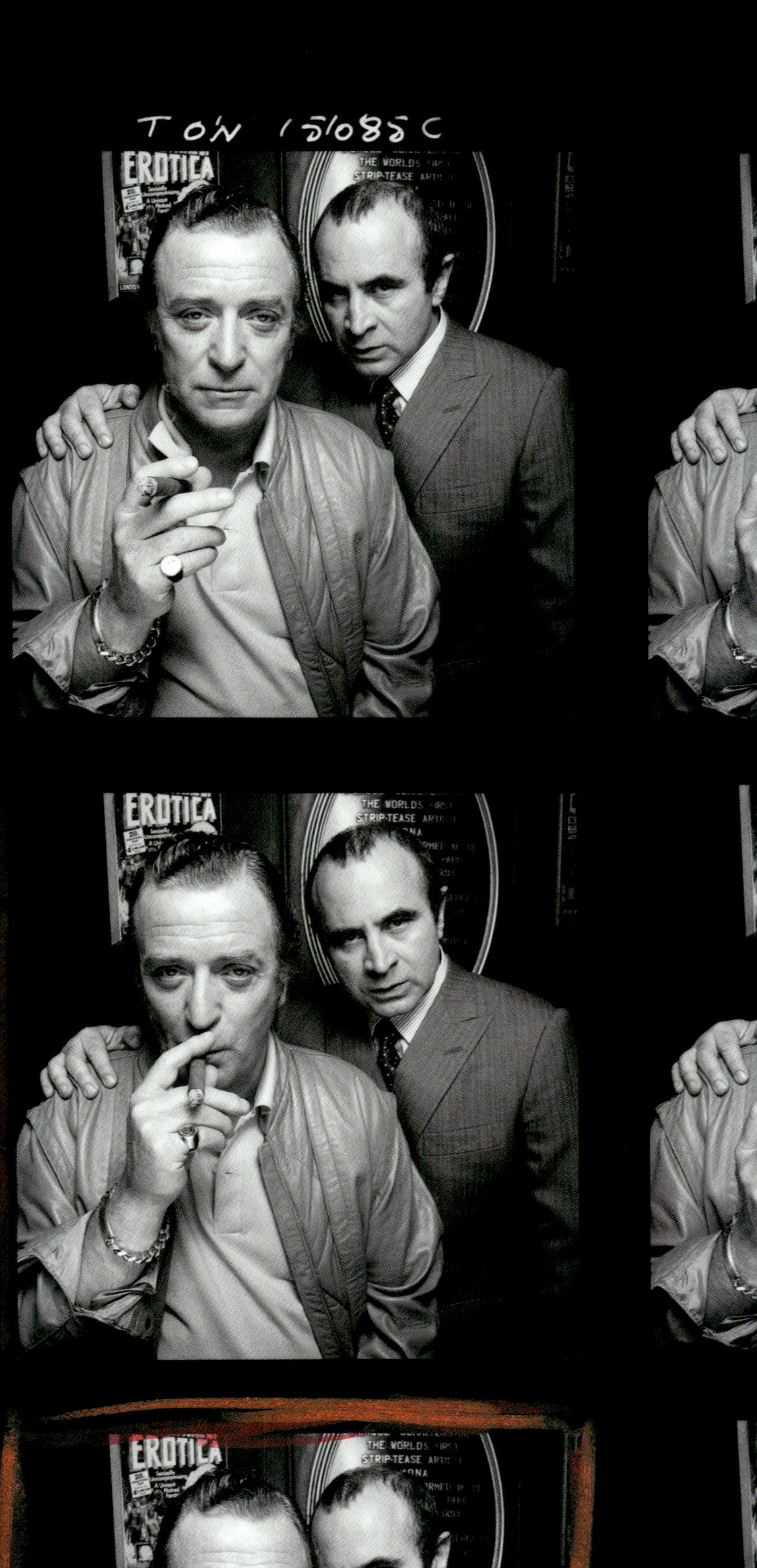
TO'N 151085C
EROTICA
THE WORLDS FIRST
STRIP-TEASE ARTIST

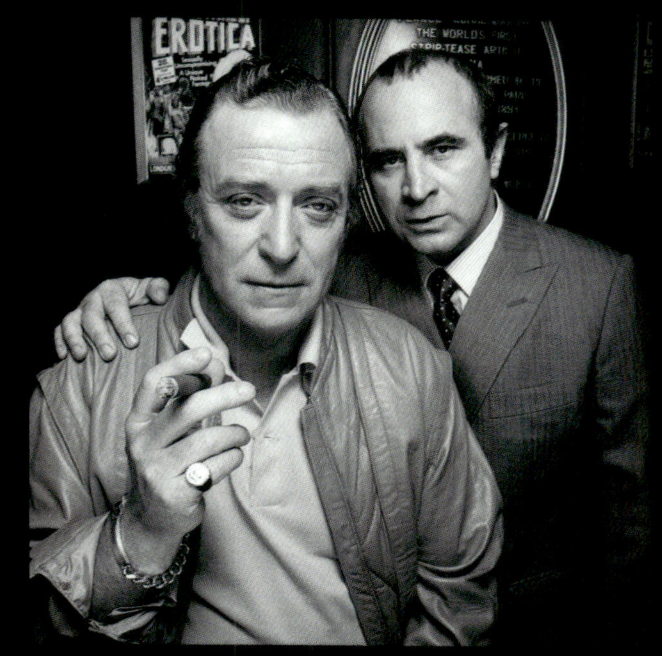

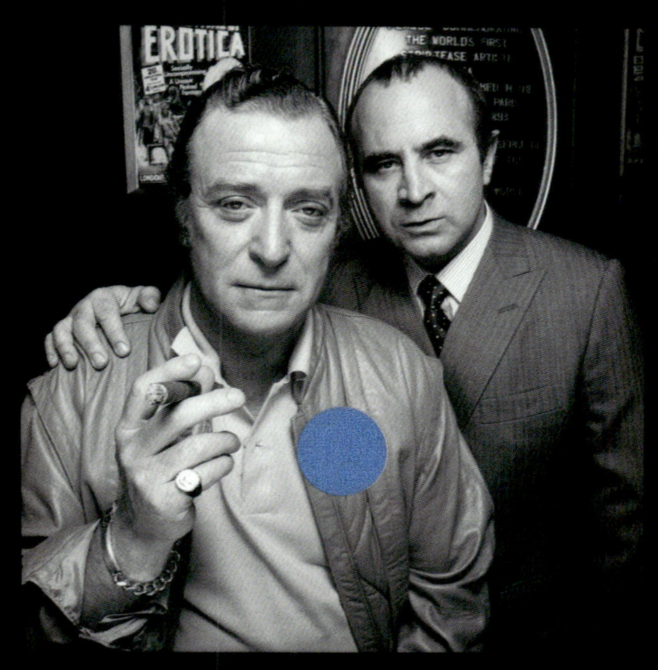

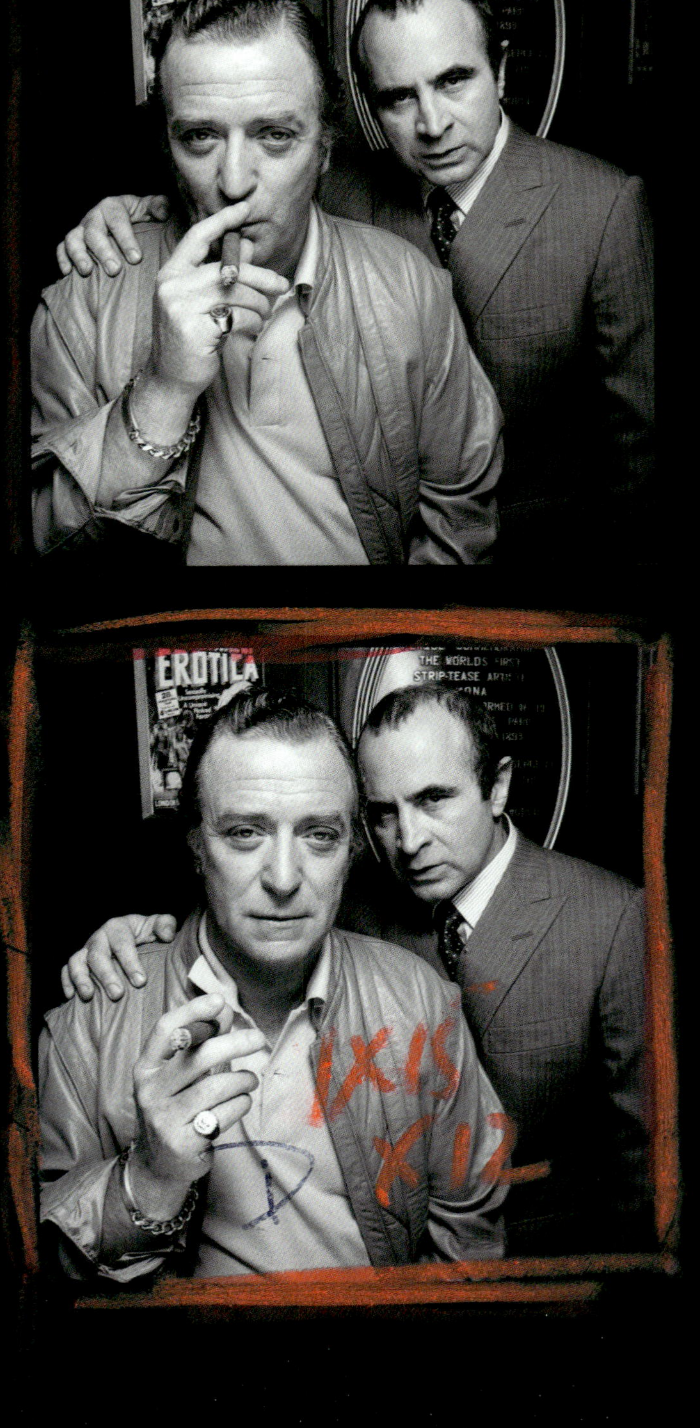
1X15
X12

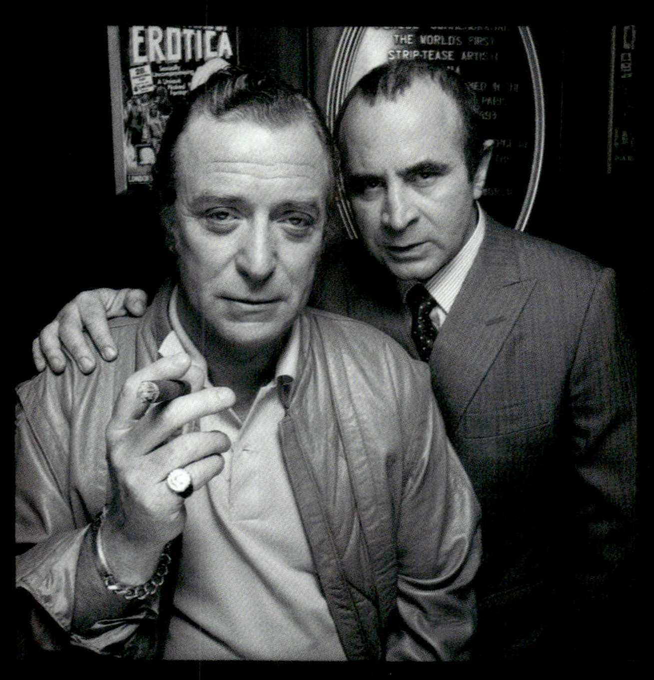

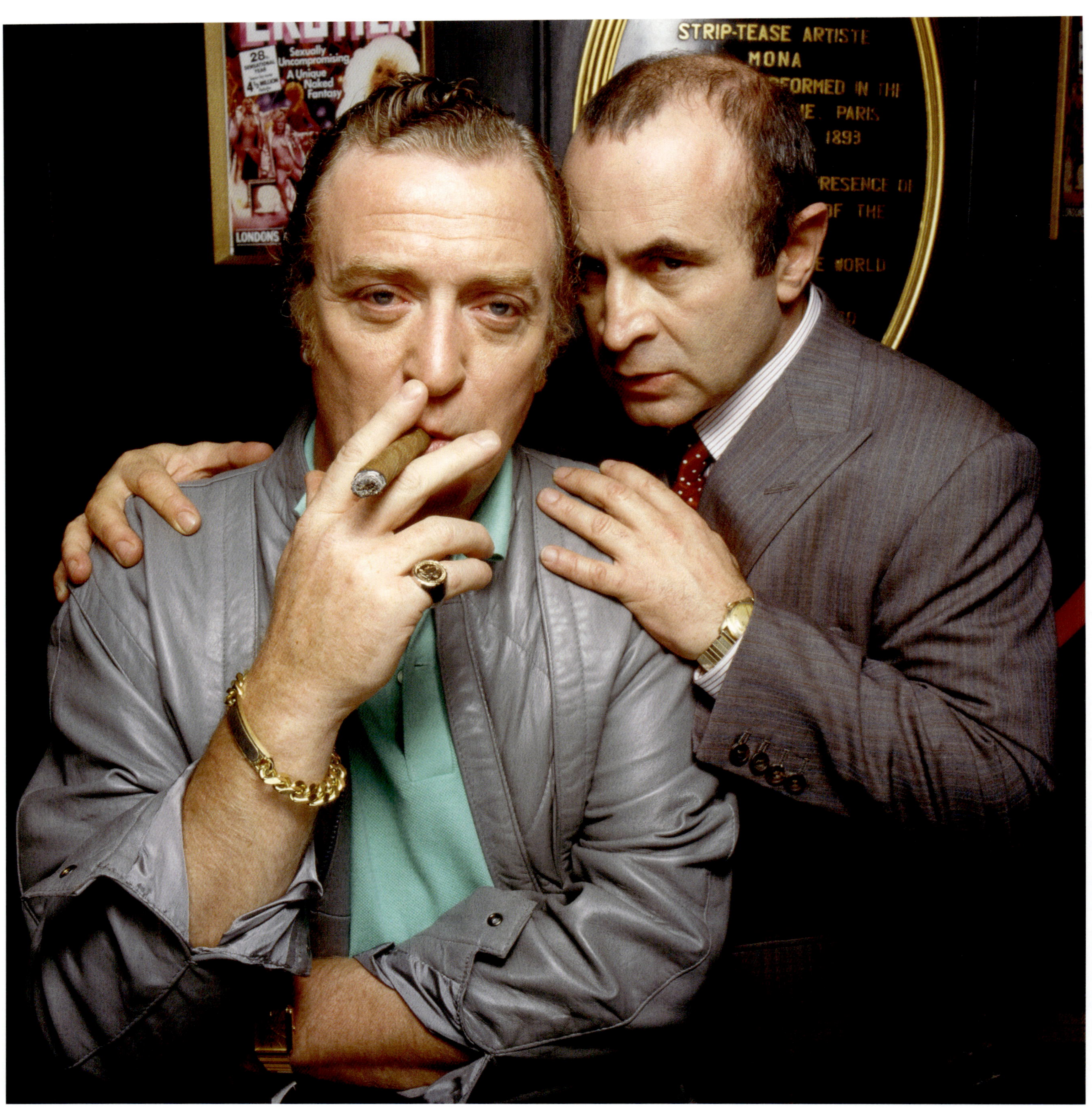

It was Bob Hoskins who had approached Caine to appear in the film as crime boss, Mortwell.

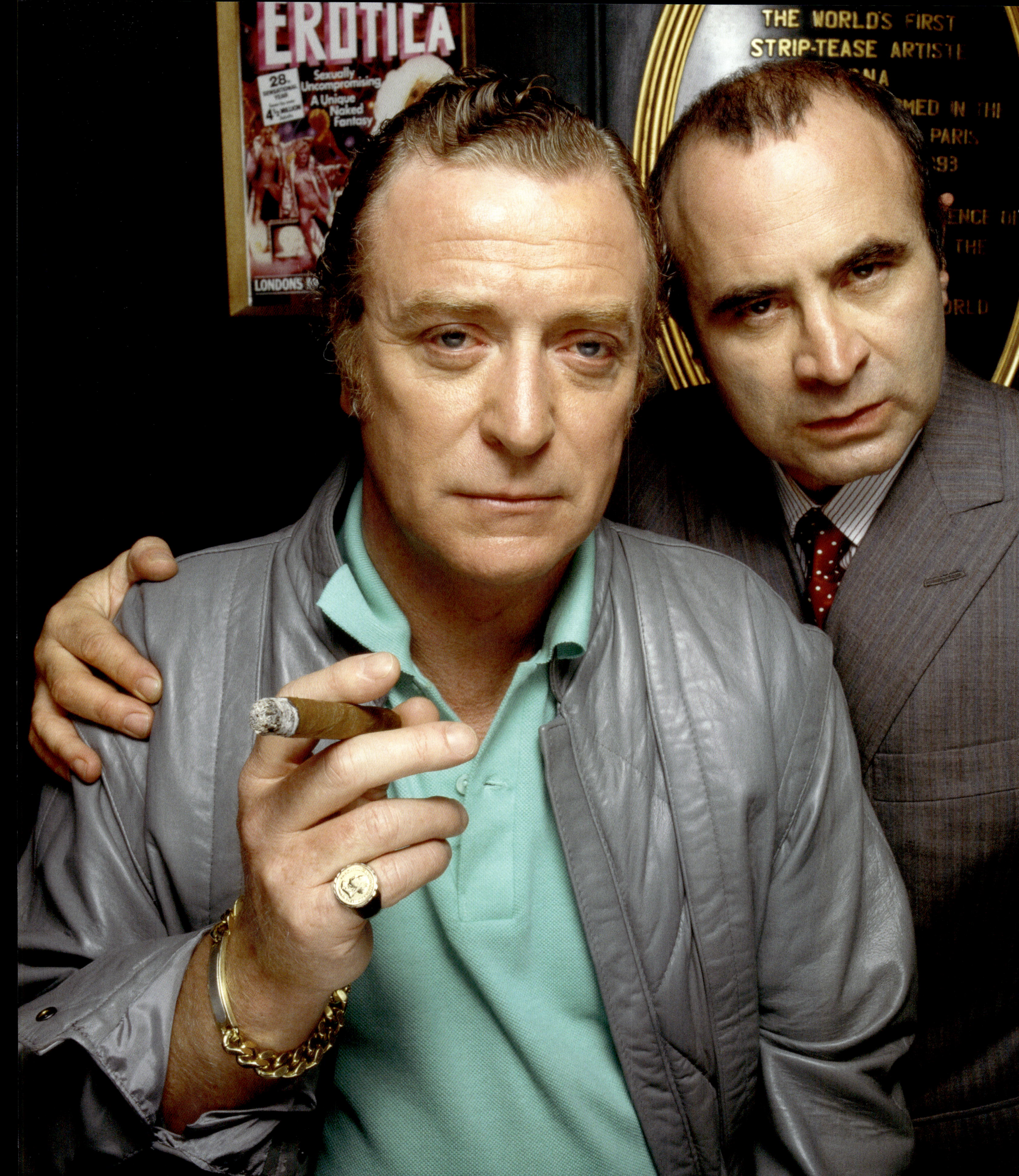
EROTICA
Sexually Uncompromising
A Unique Naked Fantasy
THE WORLD'S FIRST
STRIP-TEASE ARTISTE

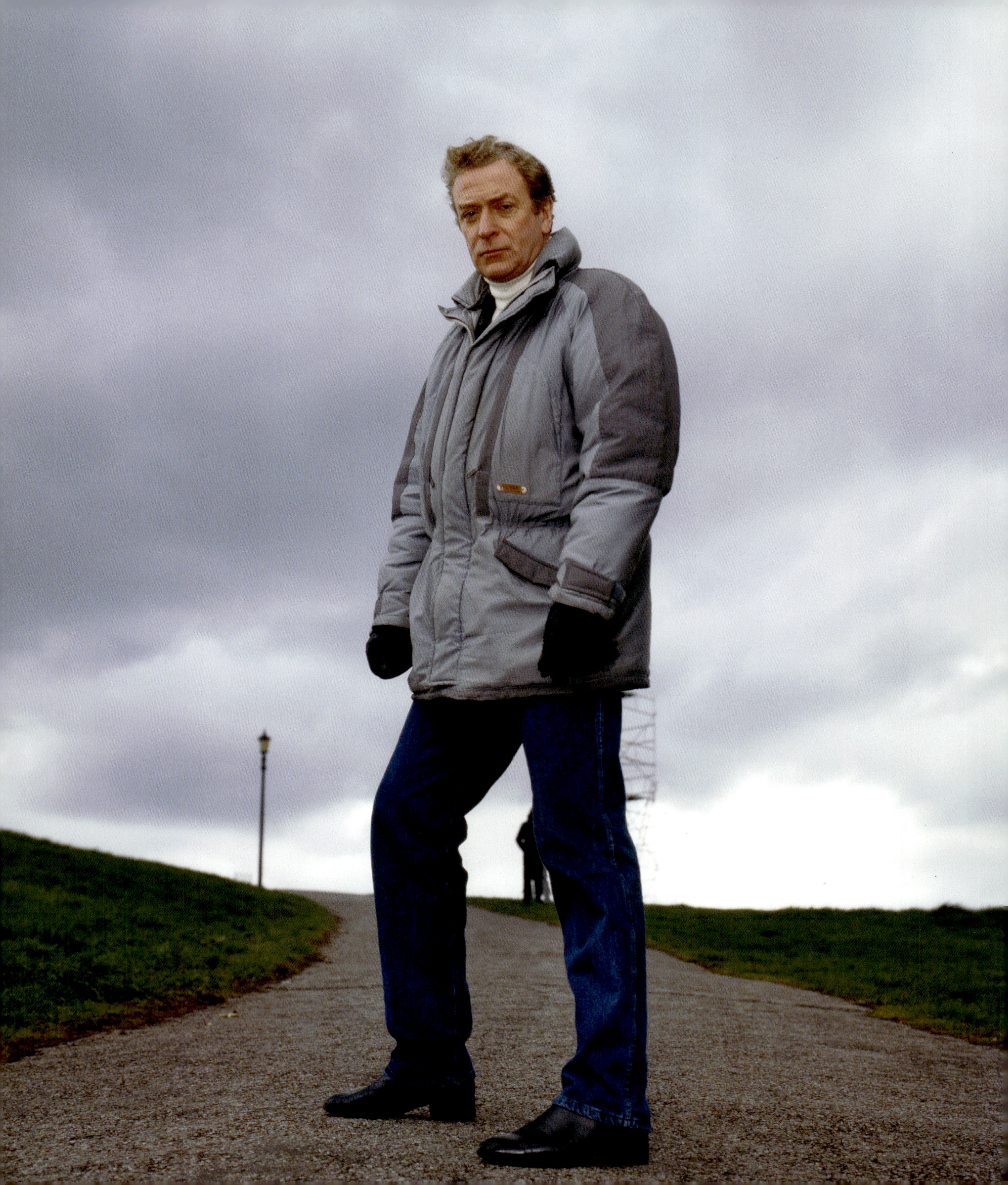

THE FOURTH PROTOCOL

1987

"As he often did, O'Neill was able to commit to camera moments of ease and candour and we can very much see that in the images of Forsyth with Caine."

It might be fair to say that by the mid-1980s, Caine was in the full throes of superstardom; moving readily from the comedy drama of *Educating Rita* ("The most difficult performance I ever did, in my own mind."[1]) to the Oscar-winning success of *Hannah and Her Sisters* and the urban underworld of *Mona Lisa*. Amidst these projects, he also returned to very familiar and productive territory with a starring role in a spy thriller.

An adaptation of Frederick Forsyth's novel (1984), *The Fourth Protocol* tapped into the 1980s preoccupation with the very real nuclear tensions between Russia and the USA during the Cold War. The plot revolves around a KGB plan for Soviet agent Petrovsky (Pierce Brosnan) to detonate a nuclear device near a US base in the UK and make it look like an American accident. British intelligence officer John Preston (Caine), with a tendency to do his own thing, races to stop him.

In his review, Roger Ebert notes, "This essentially is the same character Caine played in the second movie role of his career, 'The Ipcress File' (1965). This time, though, he's older, less cocksure and more wily in getting his way."[2]

The film was shot in the UK under the leadership of director John Mackenzie, who had directed *The Long Good Friday* (1980). Terry O'Neill's photographs capture a day of shooting in location at Primrose Hill, north London, for a scene in which Preston meets with Sir Nigel Irvine (Ian Richardson) and they discuss the possibility of an atomic bomb being put together in the UK. As he often did, O'Neill was able to commit to camera moments of ease and candour and we can very much see that in the images of Forsyth with Caine.

Previous page: Caine on location on Primrose Hill, north London.
Opposite page: Frederick Forsyth and Caine on location on Primrose Hill.

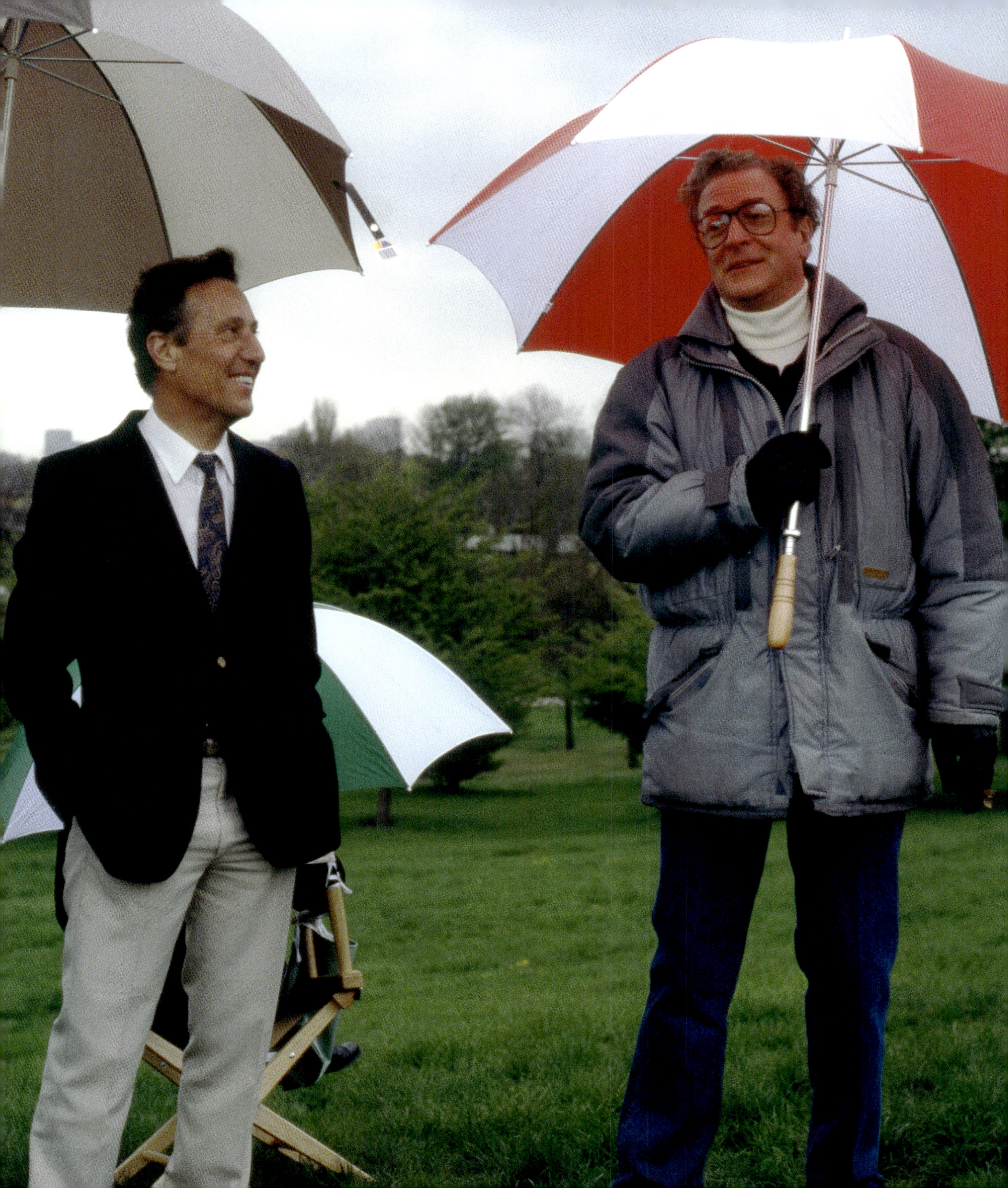

This essentially is the same character Caine played in the second movie role of his career, 'The Ipcress File' (1965). This time, though, he's older, less cocksure and more wily in getting his way.

Roger Ebert

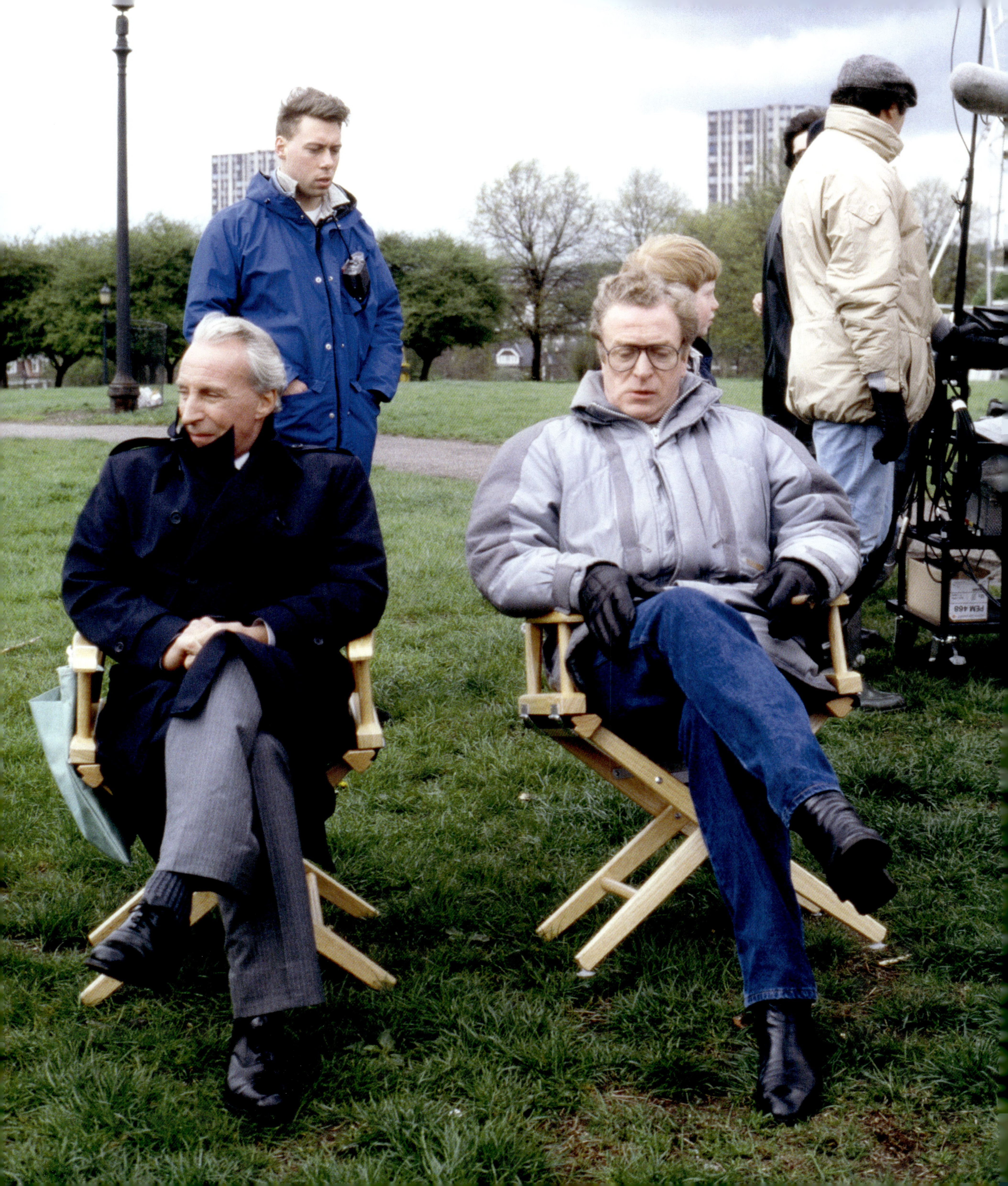

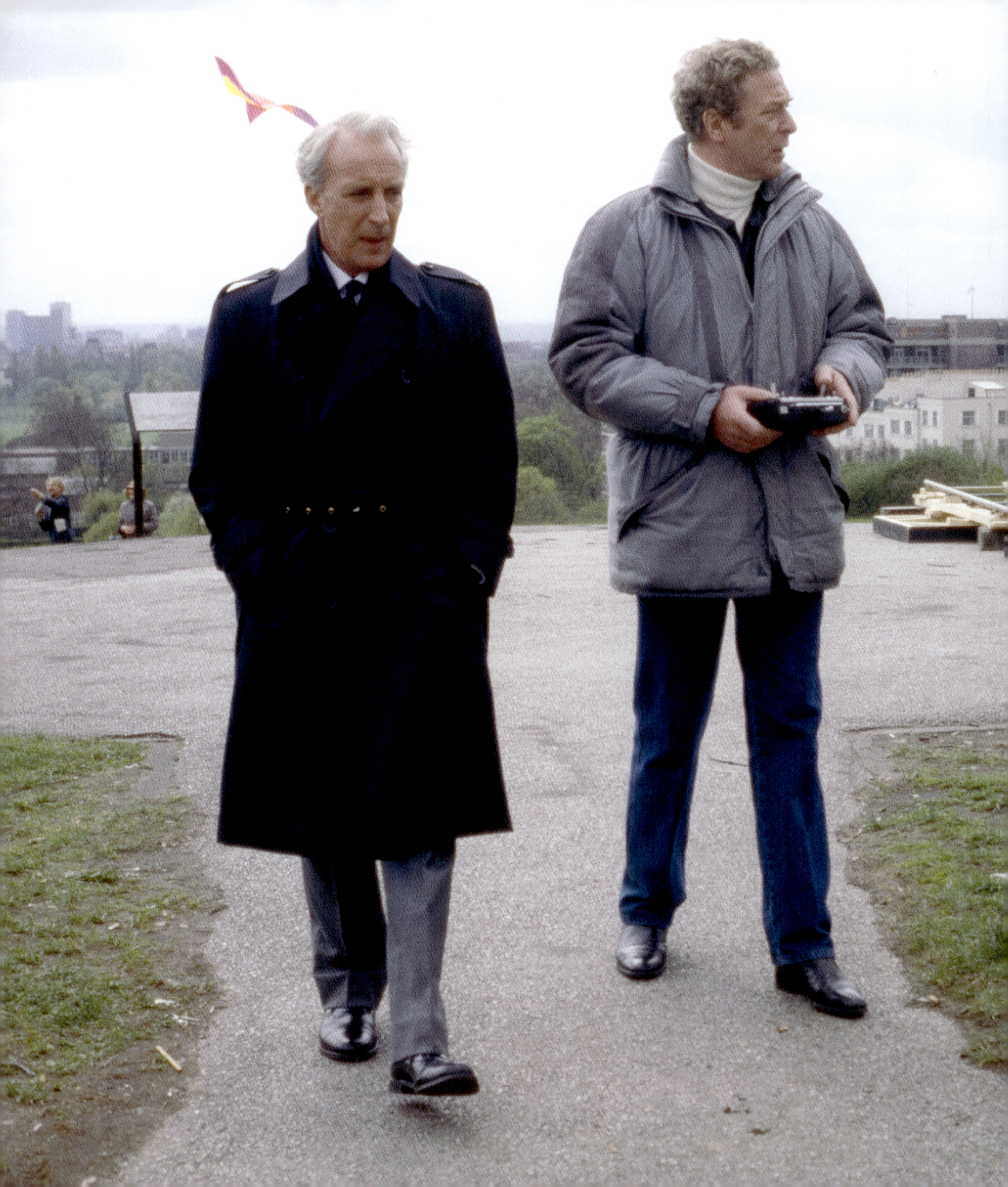

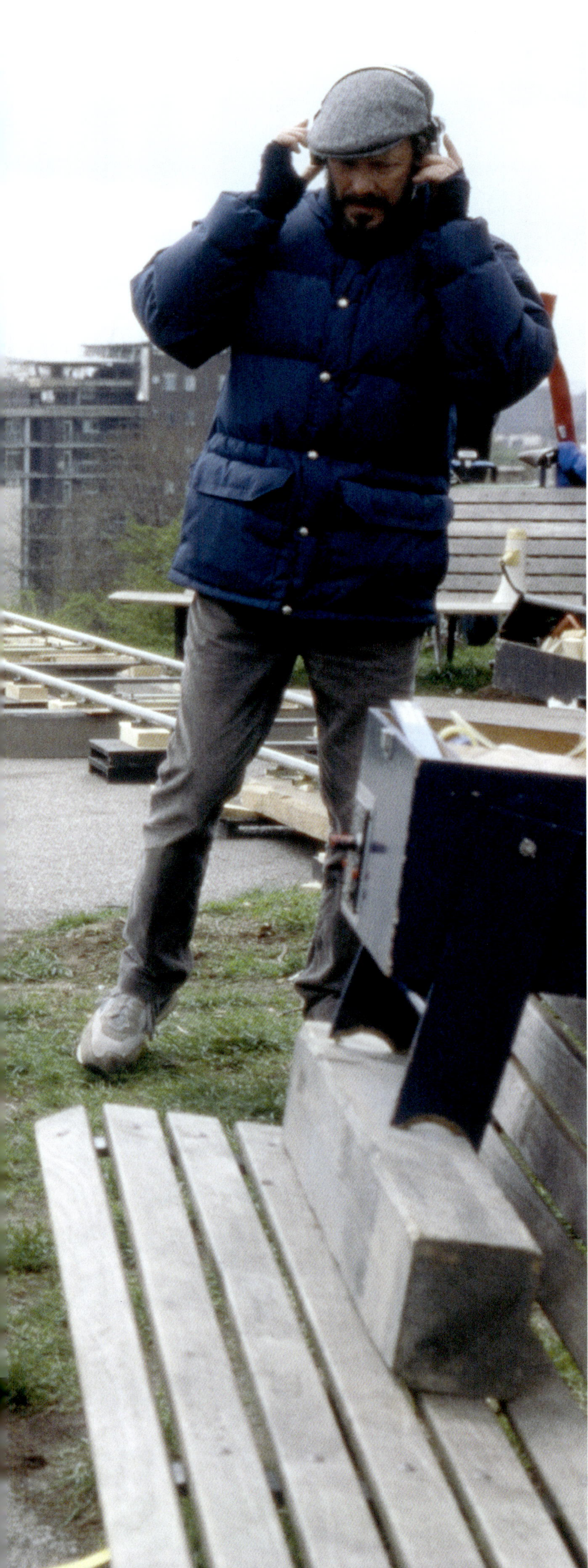

Caine, Ian Richardson and director John Mackenzie on location at Primrose Hill.

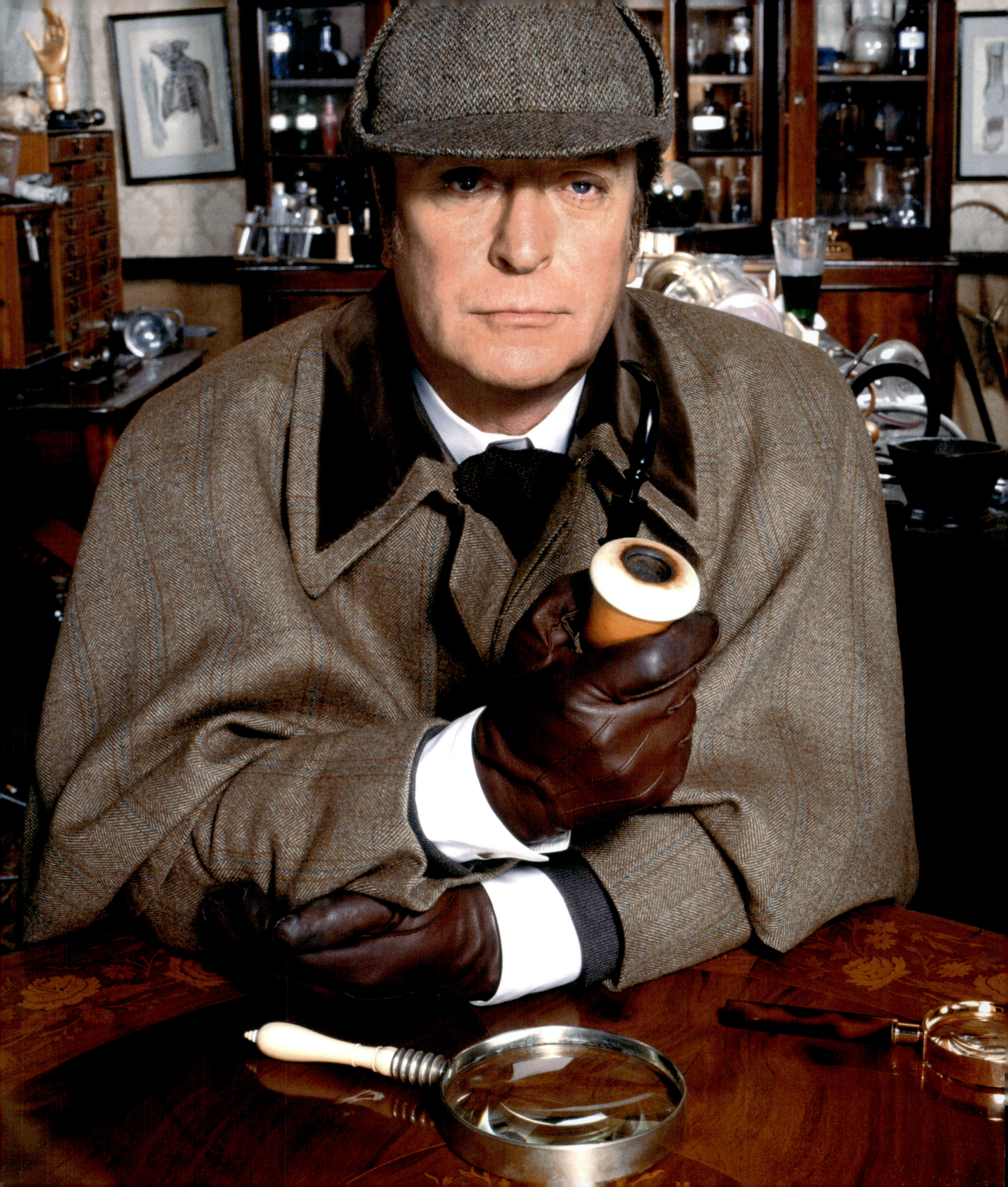

WITHOUT A CLUE

1988

"O'Neill's photographs for Without A Clue *are all portraits that made their way into magazine features, notably a splashy, making-of article in the long-gone, oft-lamented American movie magazine,* Premiere.*"*

Sherlock Holmes is one of the most adapted literary characters for the screen. To date, there have been at least fifty film adaptations, versions, interpretations, riffs on Arthur Conan Doyle's creation, who first appeared on the page in 1887. The first film featuring Holmes was produced as early as 1900 by the American Mutoscope and Biograph Company.

In 1988, Caine – in the midst of a run of commercial and critical success – co-starred with Ben Kingsley in *Without A Clue*. In this playful spin on the Sherlock Holmes mythology, Holmes does not truly 'exist'; instead, he is an actor named Reginald Kincaid whom Dr John Watson has hired to perform the role of 'Holmes'. For Ben Kingsley, this part in a comedy is in sharp contrast to playing *Gandhi* (1982), which made his name in the 1980s. That said, Kingsley has brought a comic touch to a number of movies.

Produced as *Sherlock and Me*, before being retitled, the film was shot in London. During production, Roger Ebert visited the set; producer Marc Stirdivant explained to him, "Michael is very instinctive, Ben is very intellectual. They work marvellously well together. During the read-through of the script, we'd call out 'scene 90' or something, and Ben would instantly be checking to see what had happened to his character before, and what would happen after, so he could fashion the correct frame of mind. Meanwhile, Michael would be slumped on the couch, picking balls of fluff off of his sweater."[1]

Previous page: *Without A Clue* offered Caine an opportunity to showcase his affinity for comic acting.
Opposite page: Terry O'Neill took a range of playful portraits of Caine and Ben Kingsley as Holmes and Watson.

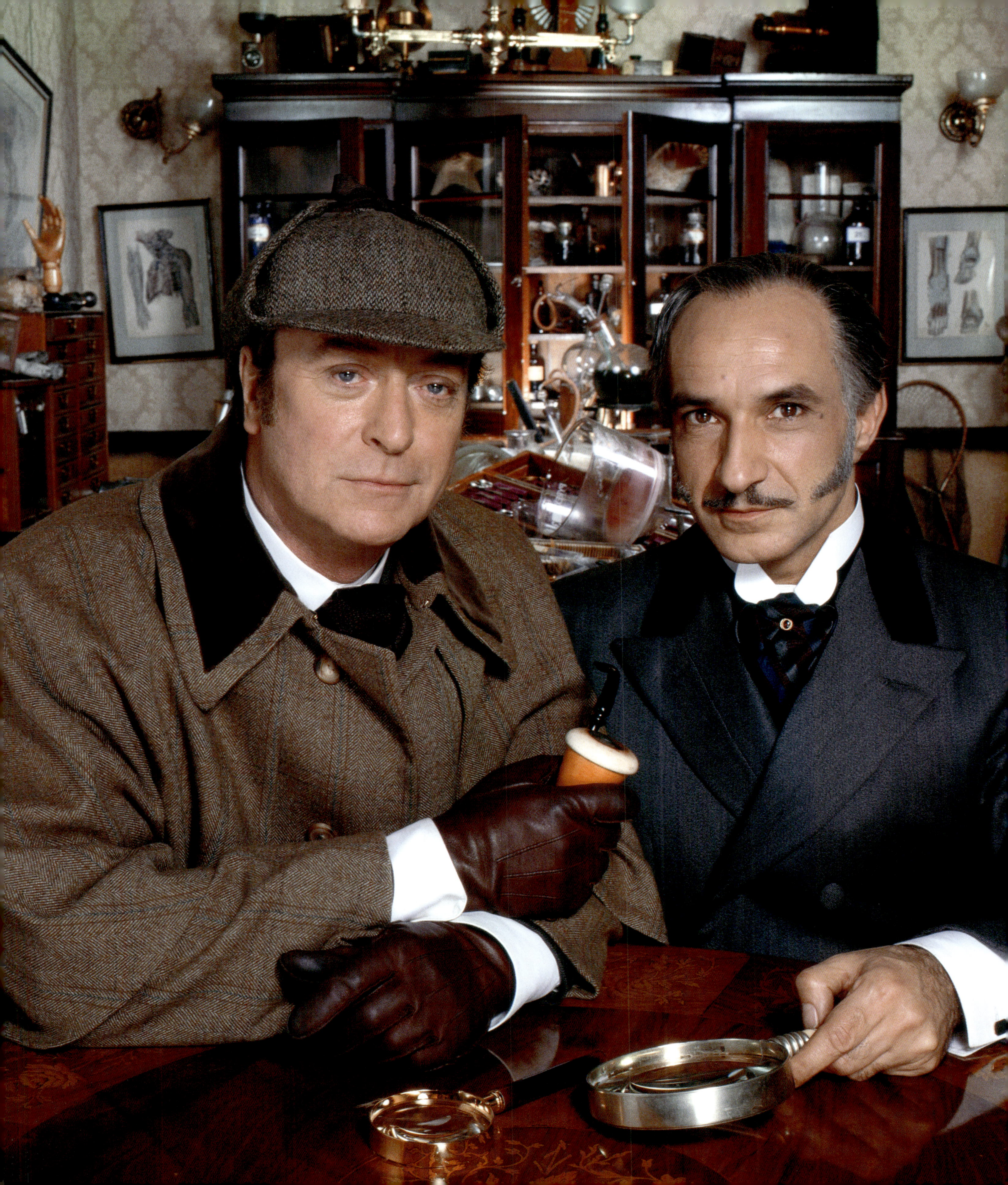

The film's screenwriters, Gary Murphy and Larry Strawther, always envisioned Caine as Holmes. Roger Ebert's review notes: "Both actors have been cleverly typecast. Caine is not playing Holmes, but an actor playing Holmes, and no one is better at playing frauds who become accidental heroes. And Kingsley, who can be the wittiest of men (as he demonstrated in *Gandhi*), is also able to project the complete lack of wit. This is necessary for any actor playing Watson, a man for whom the slightest shred of self-knowledge would have been disastrous."[2]

In *Premiere* magazine's coverage of the film in 1988, film journalist Louise Berkinow writes "*Without A Clue* turns all elements of the archetype (of Holmes) upside down...*Without A Clue* brings Watson's character into the limelight and transforms Holmes into the shabby sidekick. It is a buddy movie about rivalry and dependence between men." Speaking to Berkinow, Caine notes, "I would never think of playing Holmes seriously...I guess this is Mahatma meets Alfie." He goes on to explain, "As you get older people take you less seriously as a romantic lead. Reading the stories as a man, it's such a cozy thing, those two (Holmes and Watson)."[3]

O'Neill's photographs for *Without A Clue* are all portraits that made their way into magazine features, notably a splashy, making-of article in the long-gone, oft-lamented American movie magazine, *Premiere*.[4]

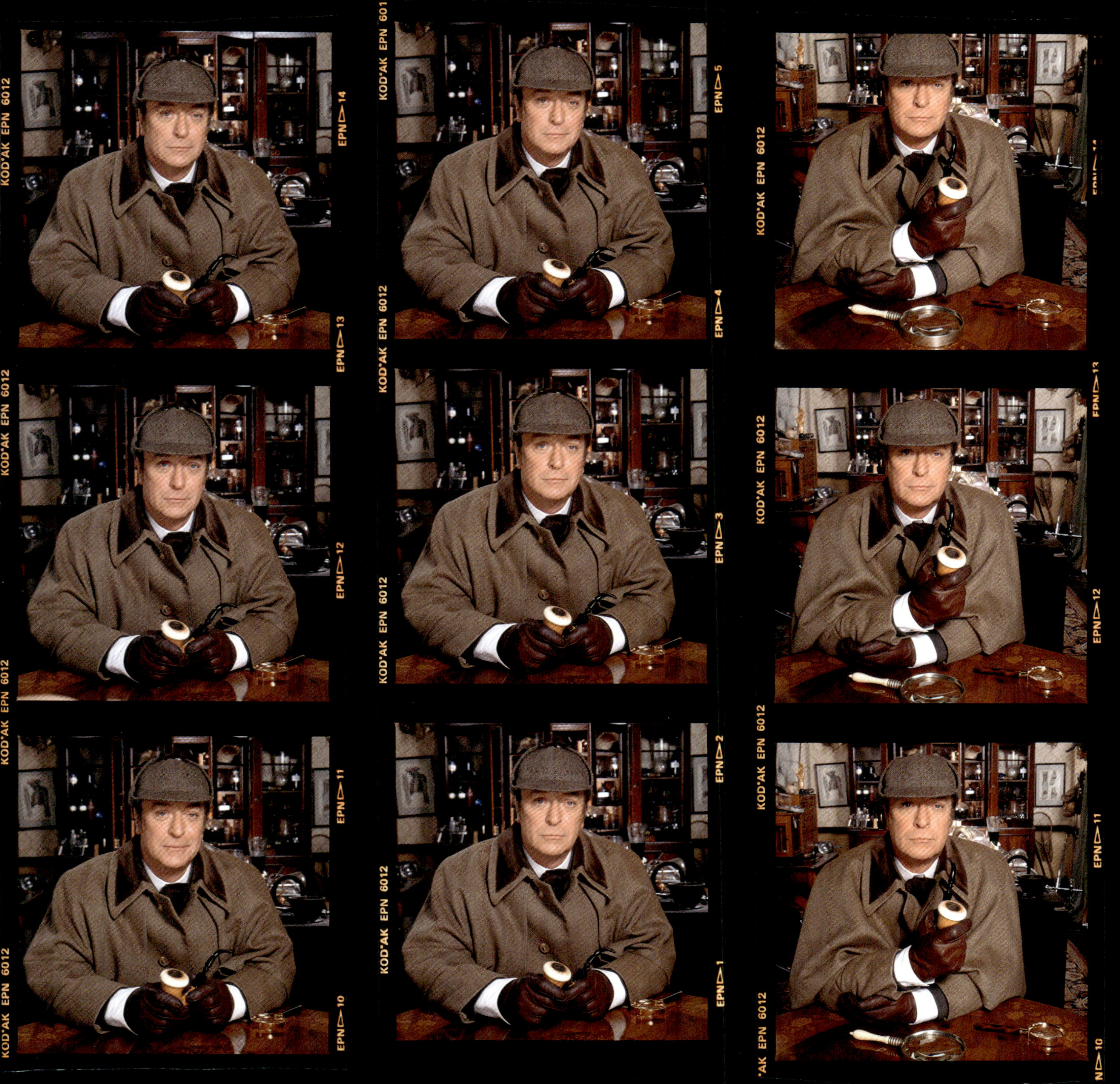

As you get older people take you less seriously as a romantic lead. Reading the stories as a man, it's such a cozy thing, those two (Holmes and Watson).

Michael Caine

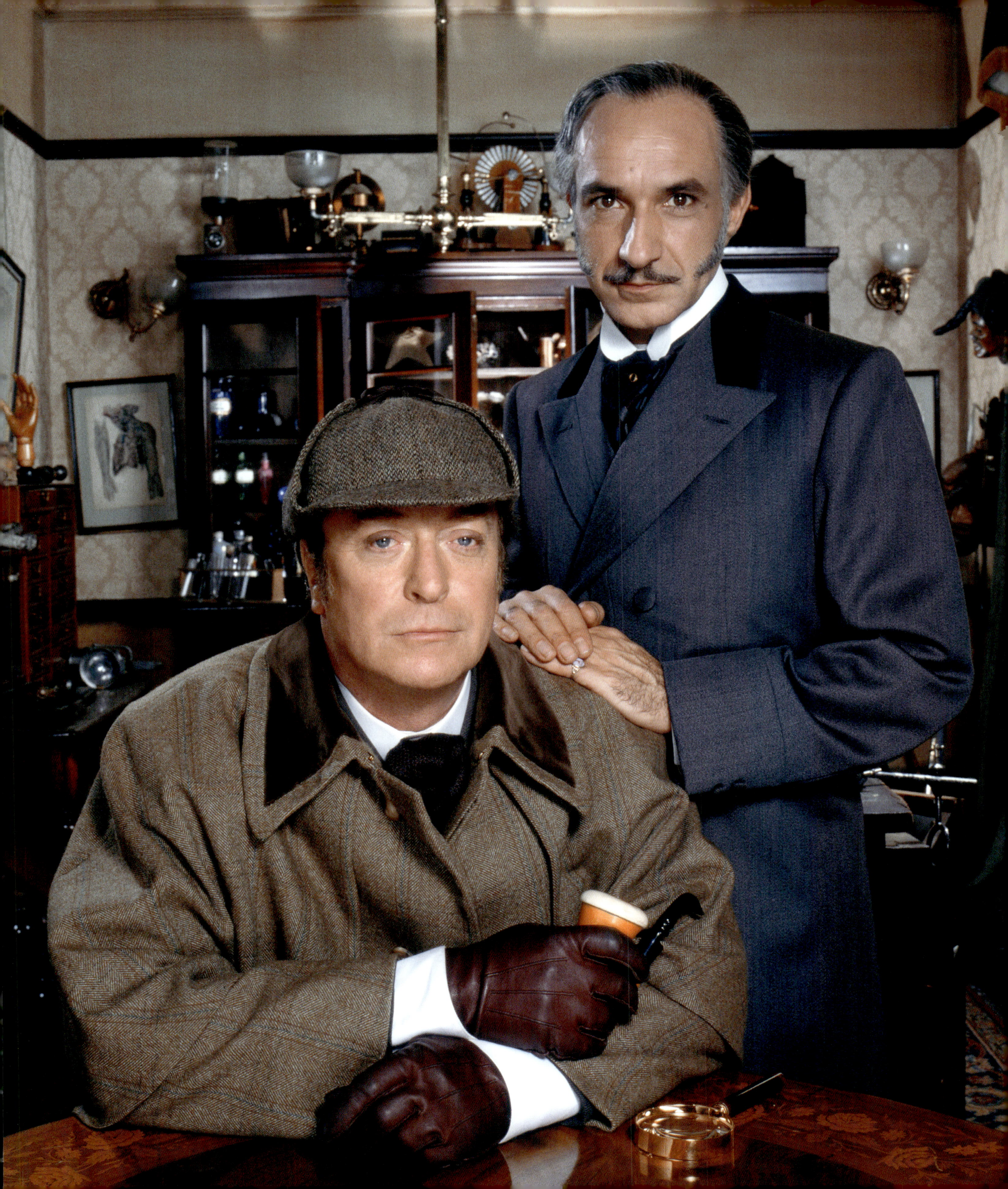

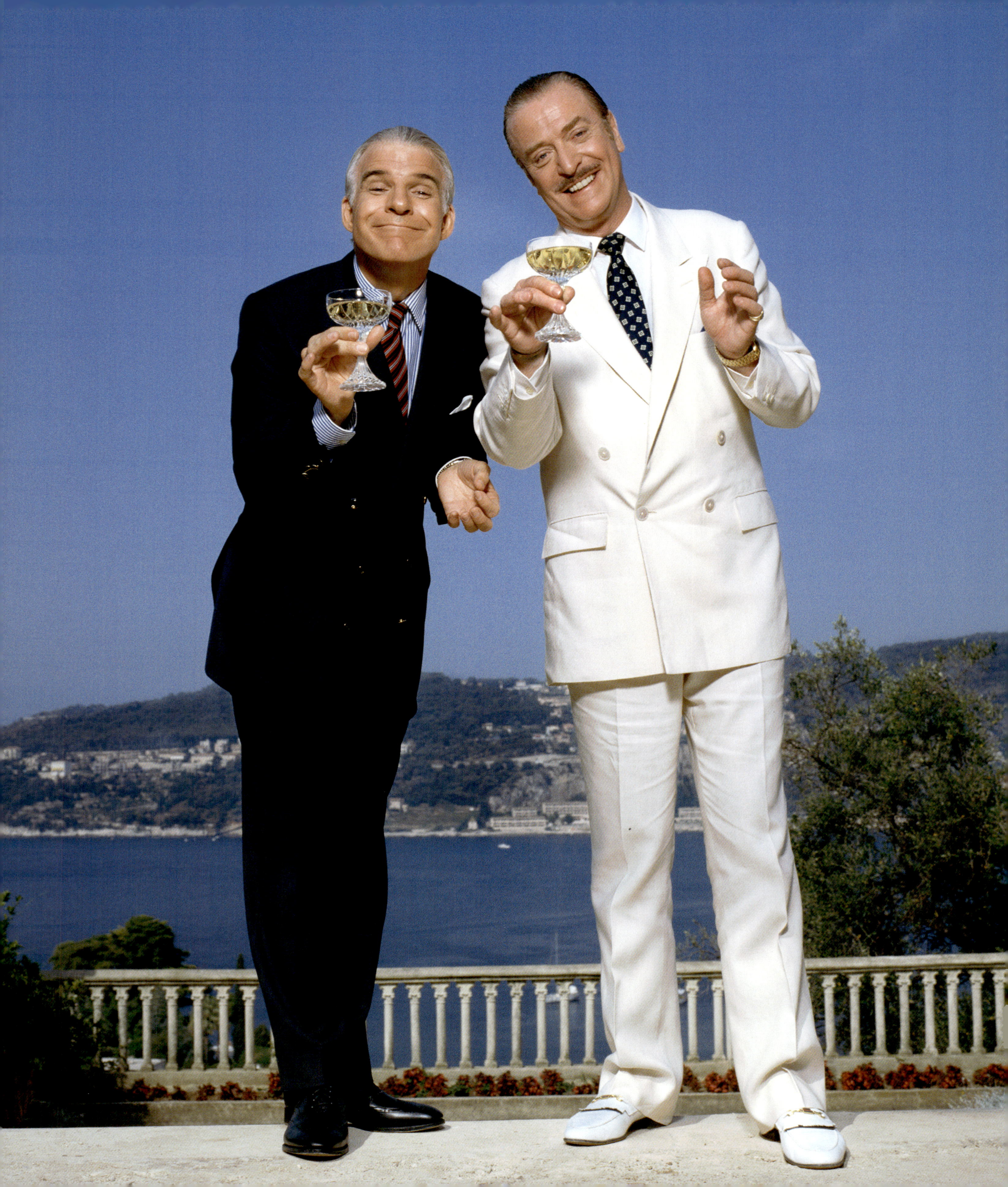

DIRTY ROTTEN SCOUNDRELS

1988

"Terry O'Neill's extensive archive of images from the location shoot, provide countless portrait images and also a feeling of the energy on the set."

Whilst it's fair to say that by the 1980s Caine was particularly synonymous with thrillers and crime stories, he also displayed an affinity for comedy and humour (reaching back to Alfie). Certainly, one of Caine's best known and most beloved movies is the American comedy, *Dirty Rotten Scoundrels*. It is directed by movie comedy expert Frank Oz, who had made his name with The Muppets and then as co-director with Jim Henson on *The Dark Crystal* (1982) and *The Muppets Take Manhattan* (1984). He subsequently enjoyed success with a number of comedies through the 1990s.

A remake of the 1964 film *Bedtime Story* (starring David Niven and Marlon Brando), the plot centres on British con-man, Lawrence Jamieson (Caine) who competes for territory with American con-man Freddy Benson (Steve Martin) – it's a twisty tale of who's conning who. Caine takes evident pride in the film: "*Dirty Rotten Scoundrels* is one of my favourite films – for me it's the funniest movie I ever made. I think its appeal lies in the fact that my character and Steve Martin's are rogues who only ever hurt the pompous and the rich – and they always get away with it."[1]

Steve Martin was already a major American screen comedian by this time, known for his starring roles in films such as *The Jerk* (1979), *Pennies from Heaven* (1981), *All of Me* (1984) and *Three Amigos* (1986). One detail that may surprise: the performers originally considered for the film were David Bowie and Mick Jagger! Luckily casting had a rethink and Caine and Martin turned in some classic comedy timing. In his review for *The New York Times*, Vincent Canby notes: "Playing to (and for) his co-star (Caine), Mr Martin gives a performance of inspired goofiness."[2]

Previous page: By the late 1980s, Caine was a well-established international movie star and *Dirty Rotten Scoundrels* was a highpoint in his Hollywood film career. Here he is with co-star, Steve Martin.
Opposite page: Caine has always expressed his affection for *Dirty Rotten Scoundrels*.

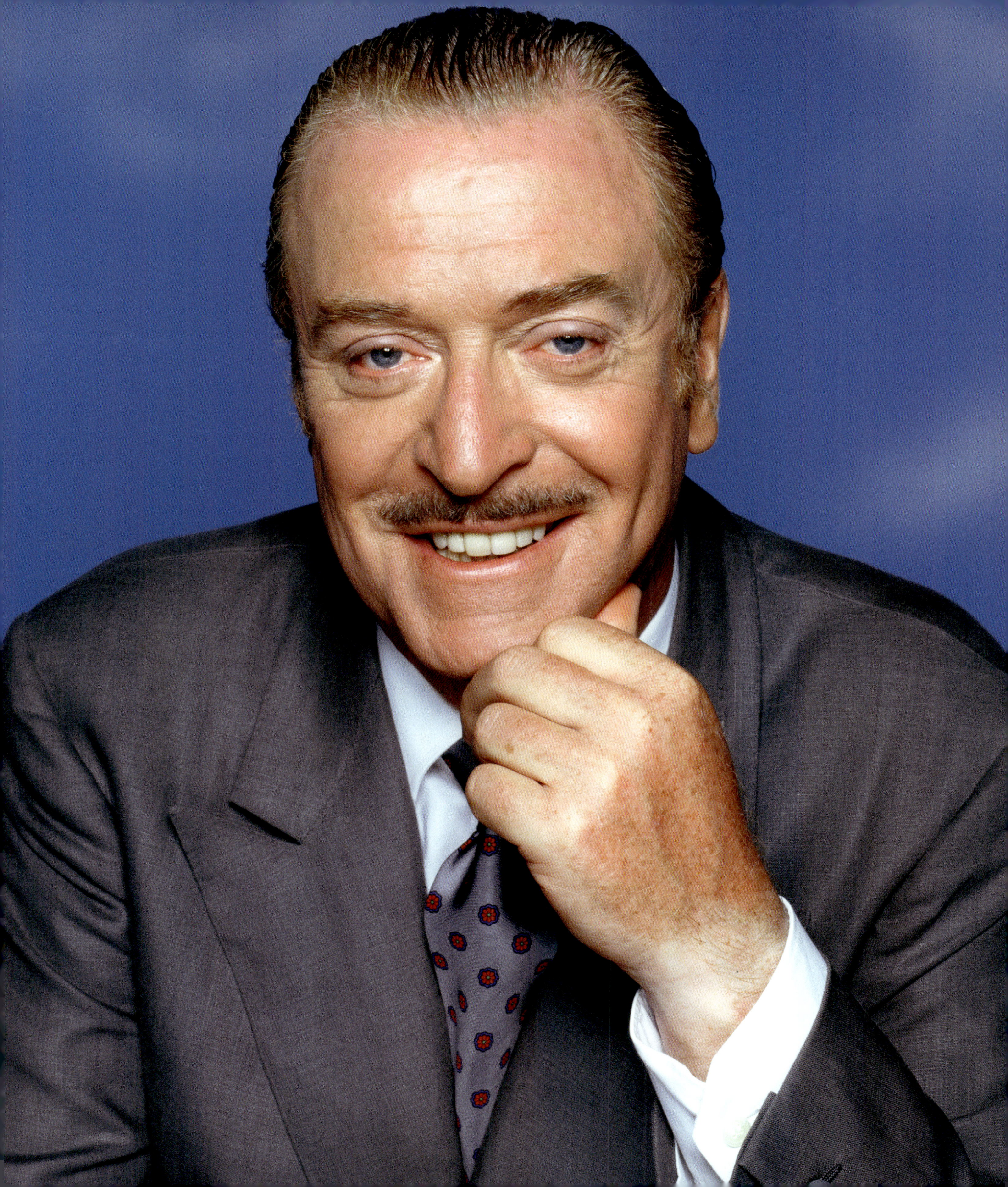

Reviews of the film appreciate the material's light touch; Roger Ebert wrote in his review "...*Dirty Rotten Scoundrels* evokes a more innocent time in the movies...."[3]

Discussing the film with *The New York Times*, director Frank Oz explains, "What I liked about the script was that the actual words weren't so important. I saw an opportunity for the actors to have juice between the lines...there was room for a lot of fun when we got to the floor, the pit, the actual cooking moment."[4] Of Caine, Oz recalls, "After one take, he says, 'Take it; I like it.' He will do more, if asked, but his modus operandi is that he does his best in the first or second take. And he's usually right."[5]

Terry O'Neill's extensive archive of images from the location shoot, provide countless portrait images and also a feeling of the energy on the set. The portraits of Caine and Martin capture quieter moments and perhaps something closer to the 'real' them. We're so used to Martin's goofy screen persona in the films of the 1970s and '80s, that to see his face in repose somehow reveals something entirely different.

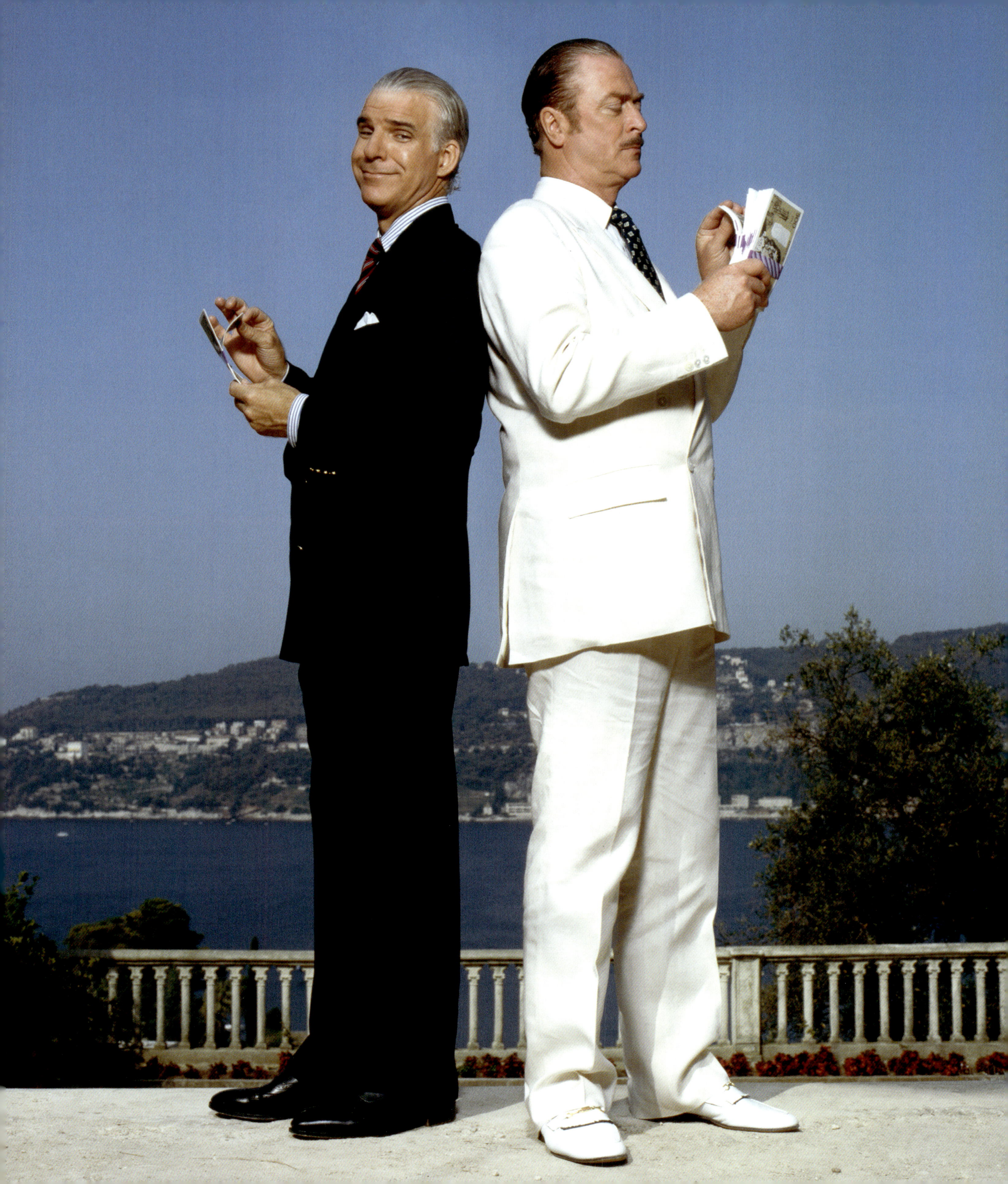

Dirty Rotten Scoundrels is one of my favourite films – for me it's the funniest movie I ever made.

Michael Caine

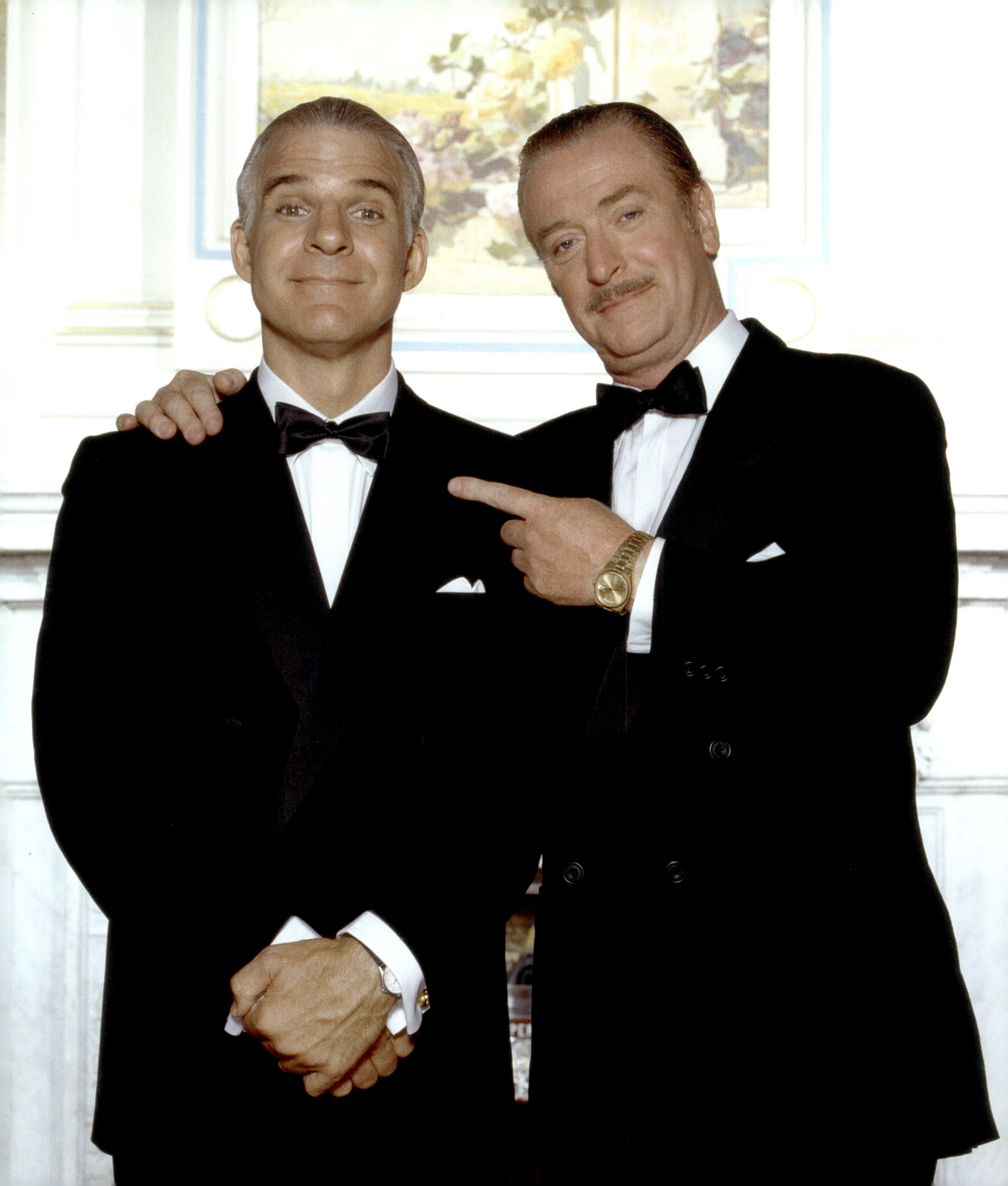

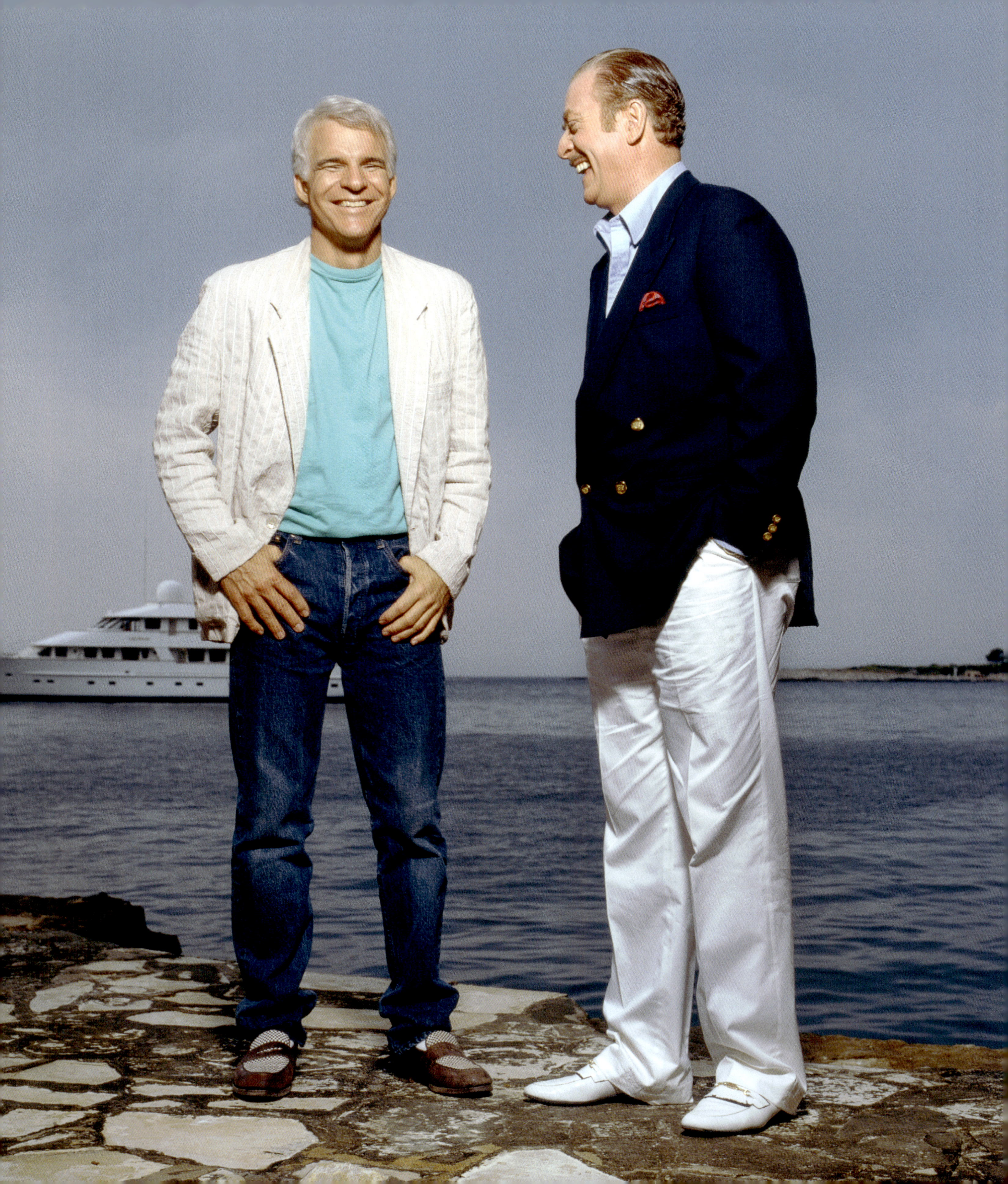

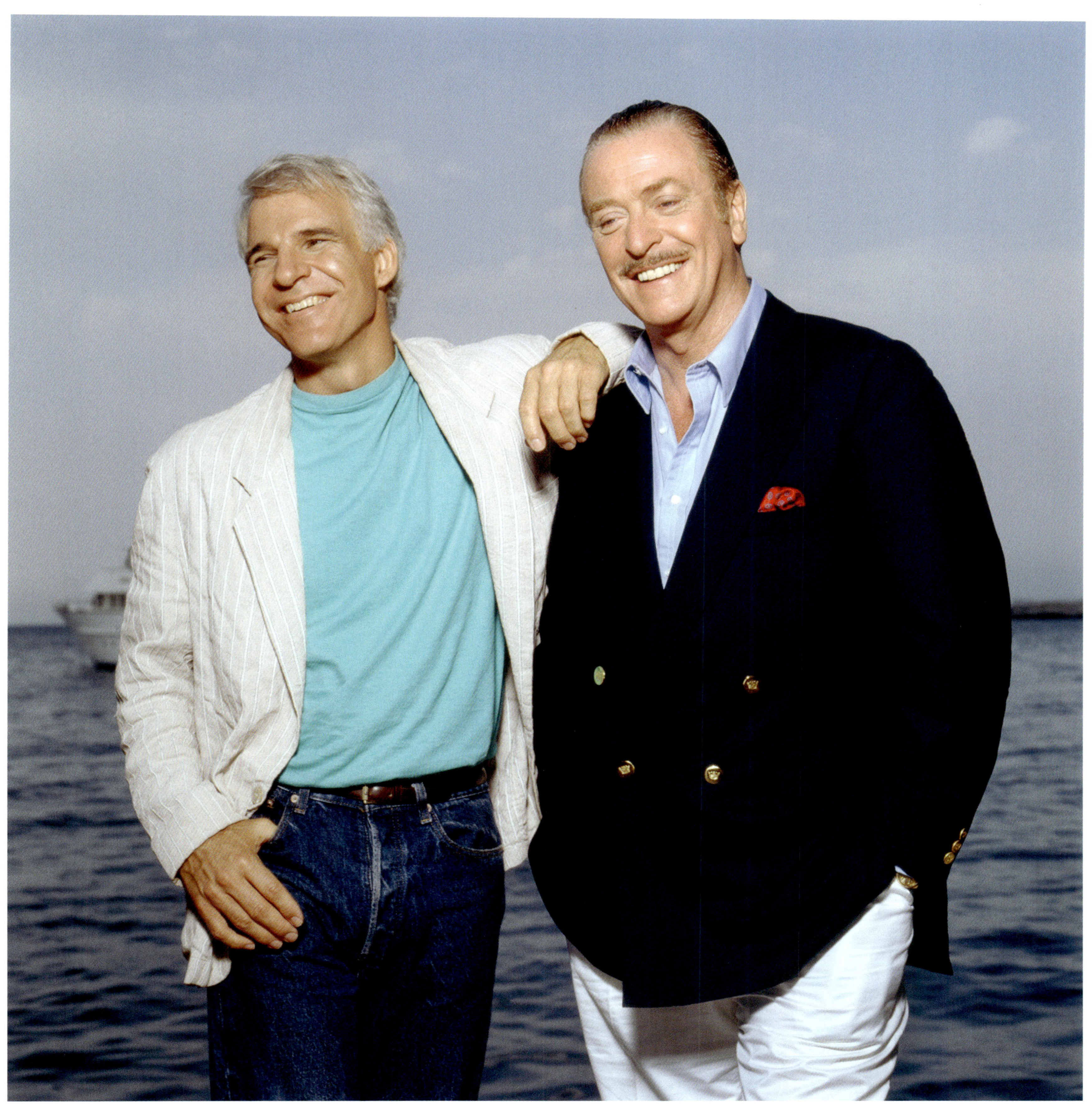

Caine and Martin out of character.

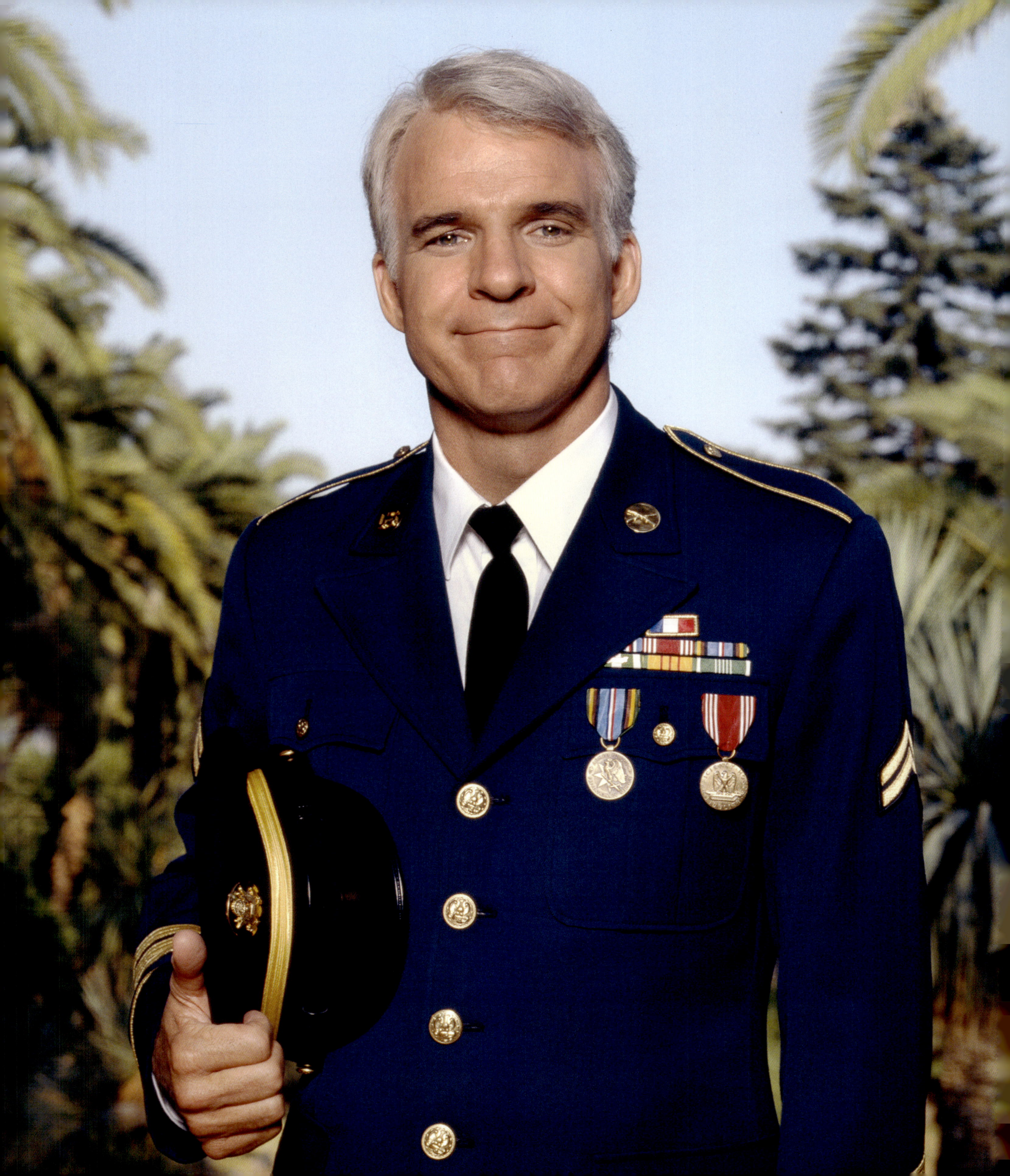

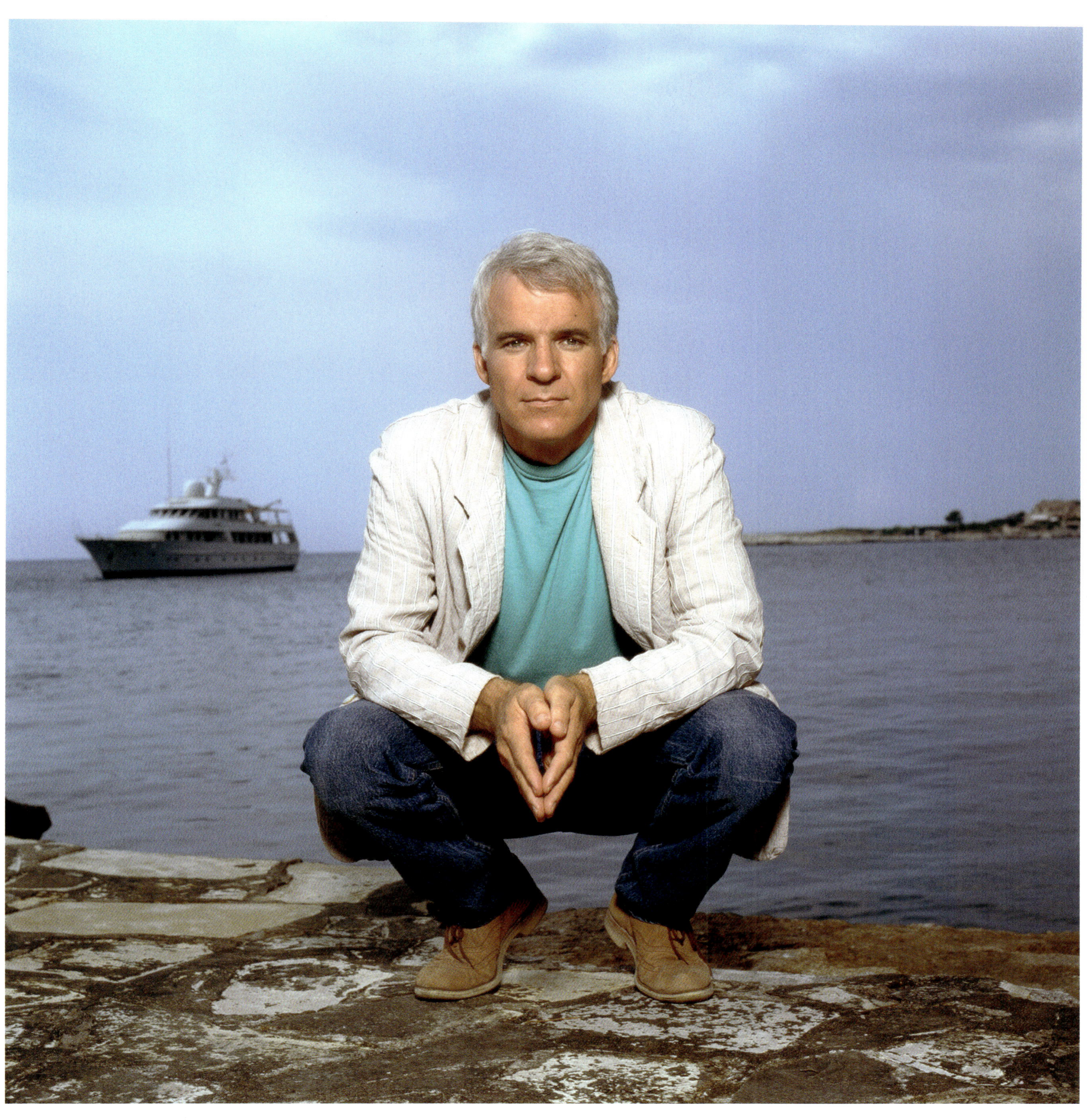

Left: Steve Martin in character as Freddy Benson, a hustler who teams up with Caine's con-man, Lawrence Jamieson.
Above: Steve Martin on set.

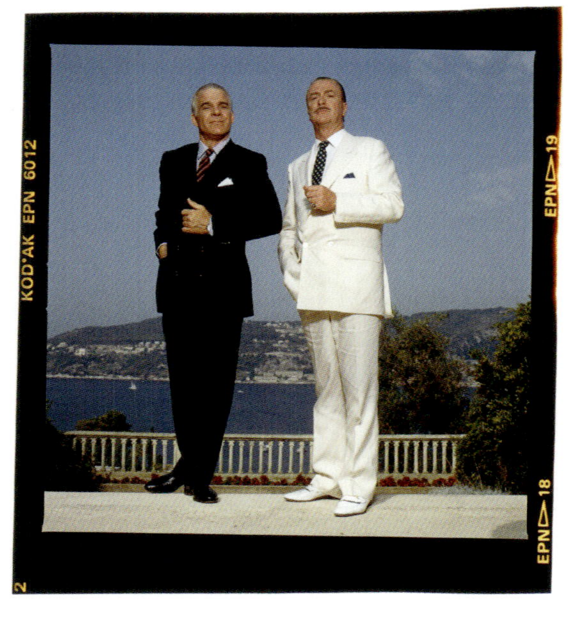
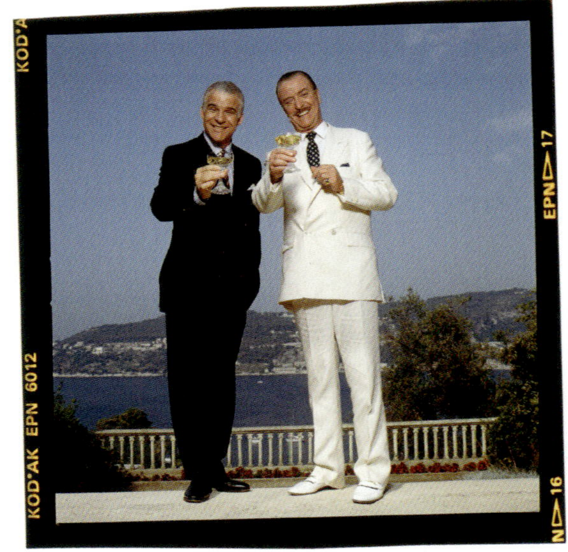
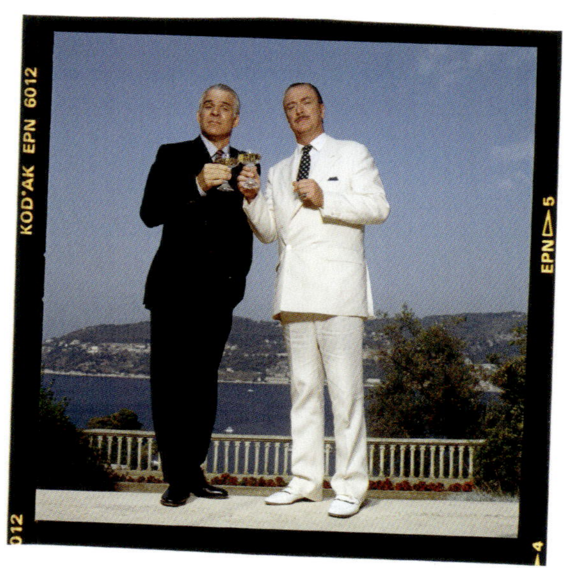
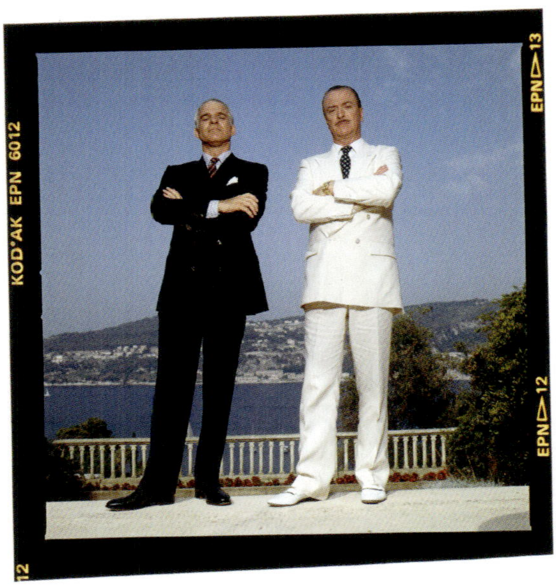
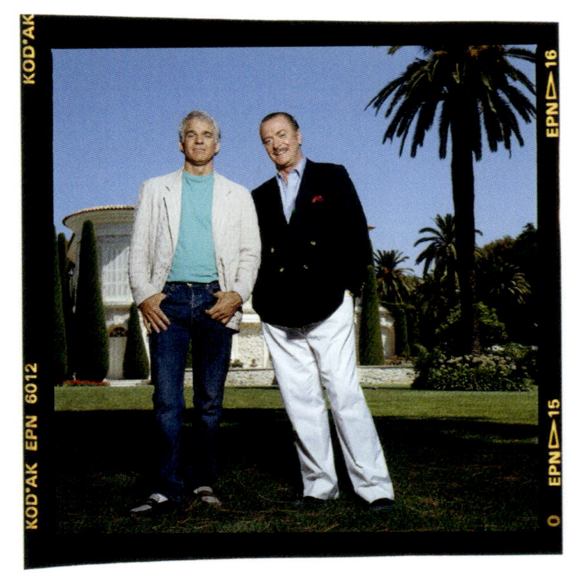
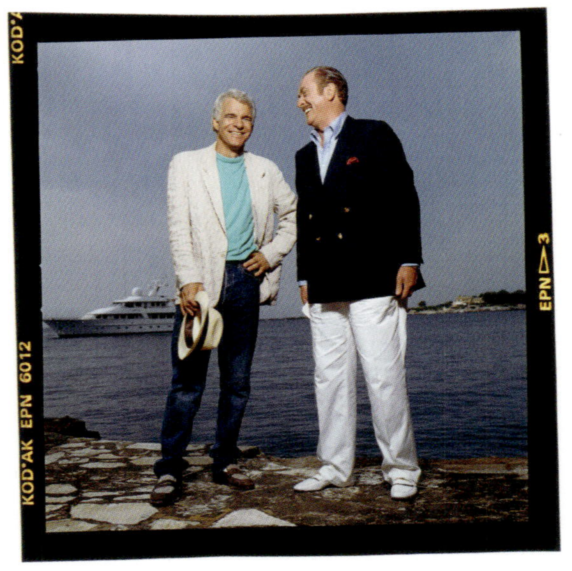
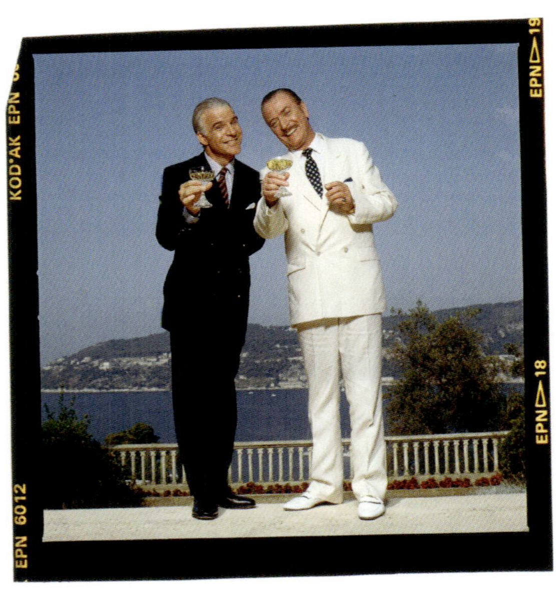
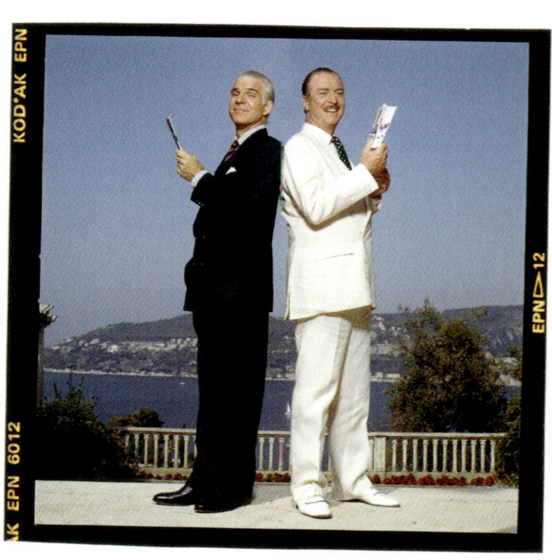
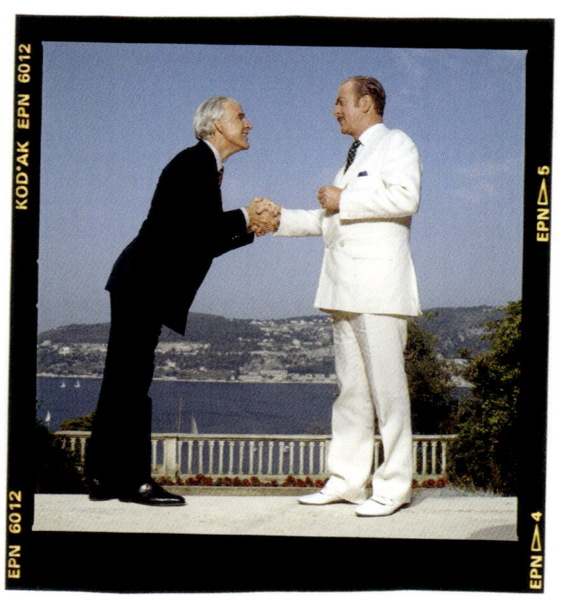

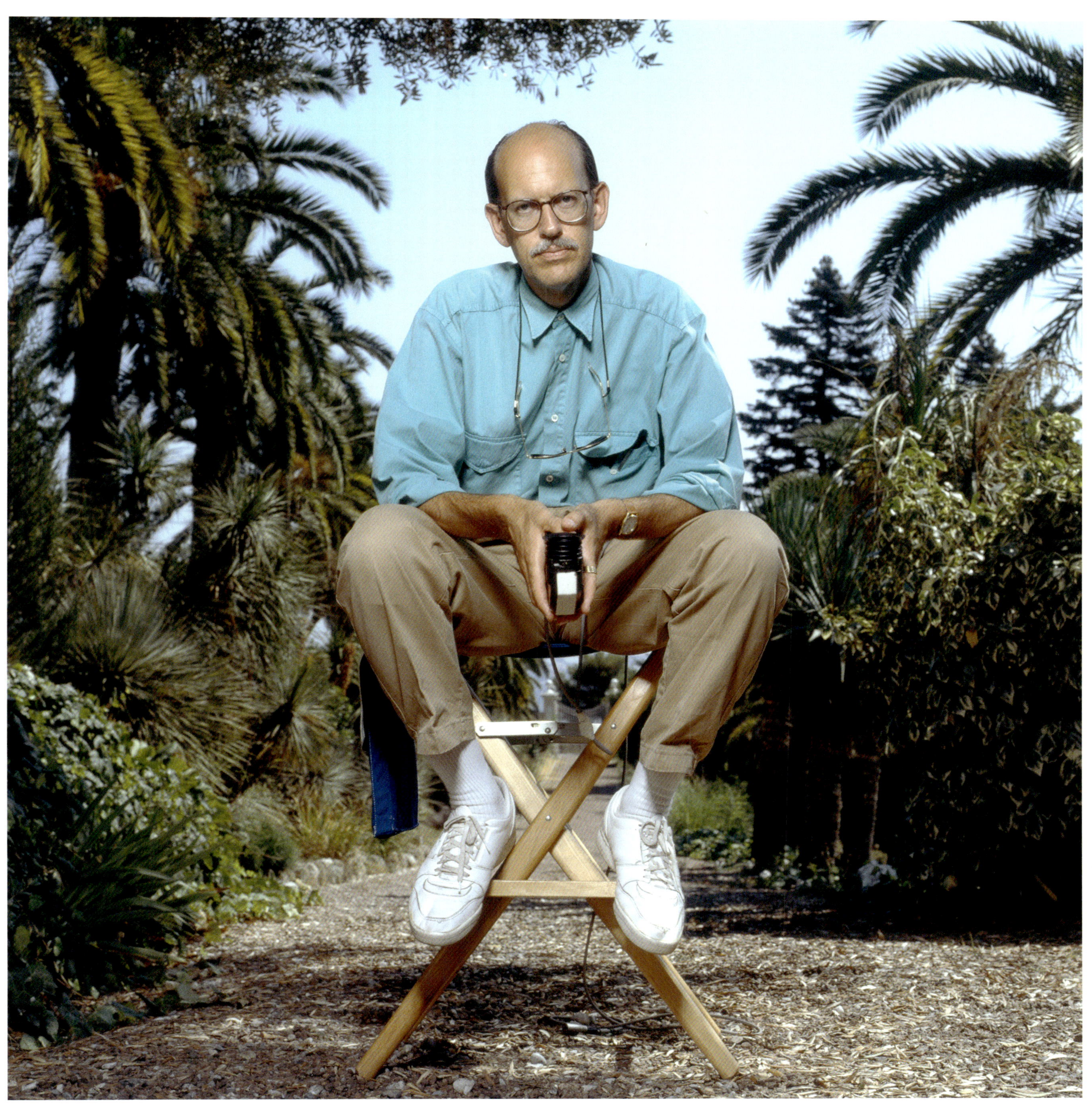

Above: Frank Oz, director of *Dirty Rotten Scoundrels.*

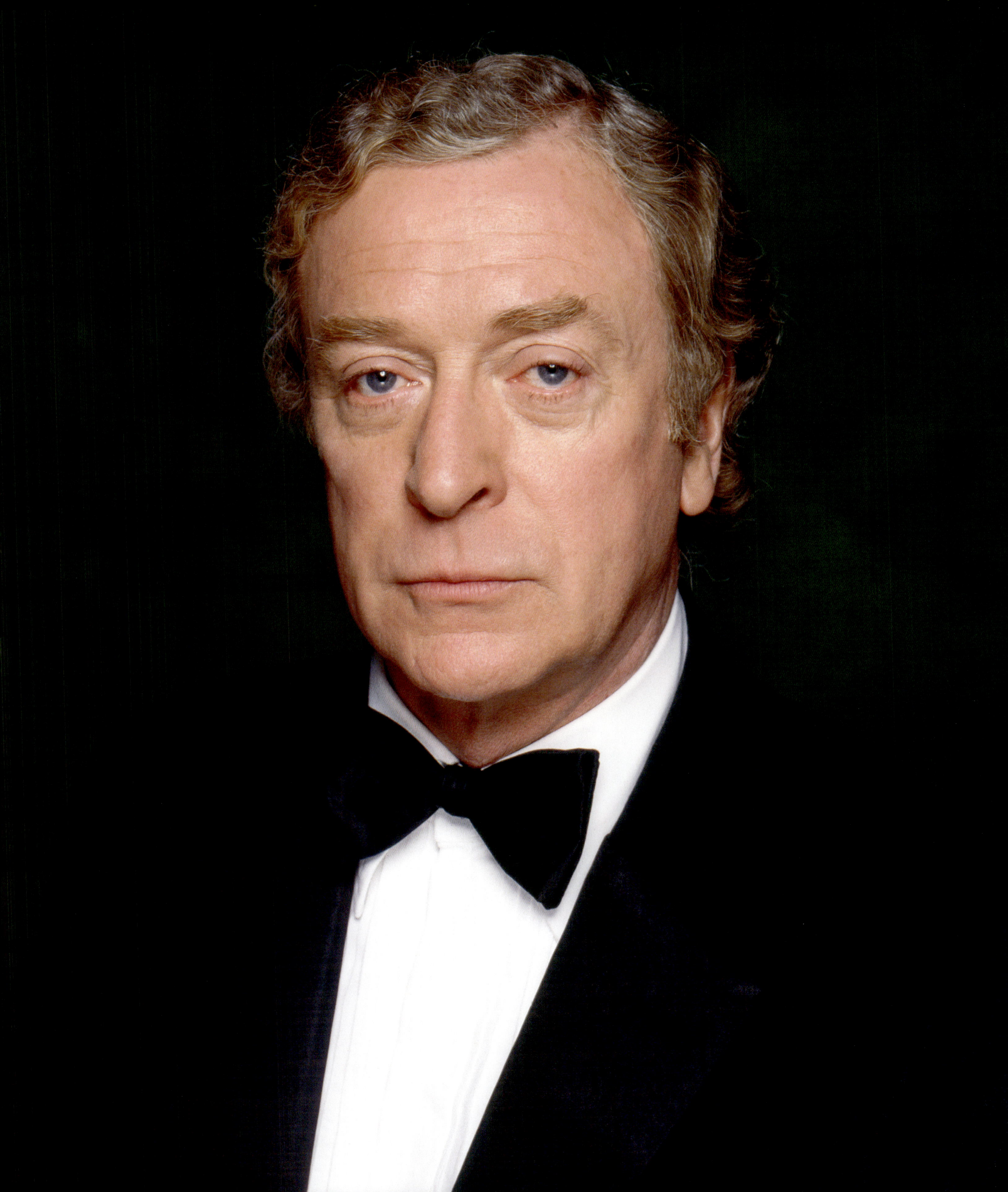

BLUE ICE

1992

"Terry O'Neill's portraits emphasise both in-character moments and candid out-of-character connection between Caine and Young and there's a playfulness to them..."

Thrillers have been a constant throughout Caine's filmography. In *Blue Ice*, Caine plays a riff on Harry Palmer, this time being named Harry Anders: a former MI6 agent who now runs a jazz bar in London. Anders finds himself returning to a world of subterfuge when an Ambassador's wife named Stacy (Sean Young) engages Anders to help her find a former lover. The intention was to produce further Harry Anders movies.

The *Blue Ice* cast includes Ian Holm, Alun Armstrong, Jack Shepherd, Patricia Hayes, Bob Hoskins and, perhaps most notably, Sean Young. Young had made her big screen breakthrough in the Ridley Scott classic *Blade Runner* (1982), going on to star in David Lynch's sci-fi epic *Dune* (1984) and the Roger Donaldson political thriller *No Way Out* (1987).

Director Russell Mulcahy was very aware of how much the template of a Harry Palmer scenario was in the DNA of *Blue Ice*. The *Variety* review at the time noted: "Russell Mulcahy settles on a straightforward narrative with occasional touches of noirish atmosphere...Caine skirts close to an aging Harry Palmer without directly evoking the earlier character."[1] On working with Caine, Mulcahy has recalled how Caine always asked for three takes of a given scene: one for himself, one for the director and one for the camera.[2]

Terry O'Neill's portraits emphasise both in-character moments and candid out-of-character connection between Caine and Young and there's a playfulness to them that rather speaks to an observation made by journalist Chris Willman in an interview with Young in spring 1992 for *The Los Angeles Times* in which he notes: "Young has... an engaging , goofy quality..." Willman reveals that Young evidently enjoyed working with Caine "...she had one of her happiest shooting experiences recently filming the yet-to-be-released 'Blue Ice' with Michael Caine, 'who is a giggler like I am'."[3]

Previous page: For *Blue Ice*, Terry O'Neill photographed a series of promotional portraits.
Opposite page: Caine and his co-star, Sean Young.

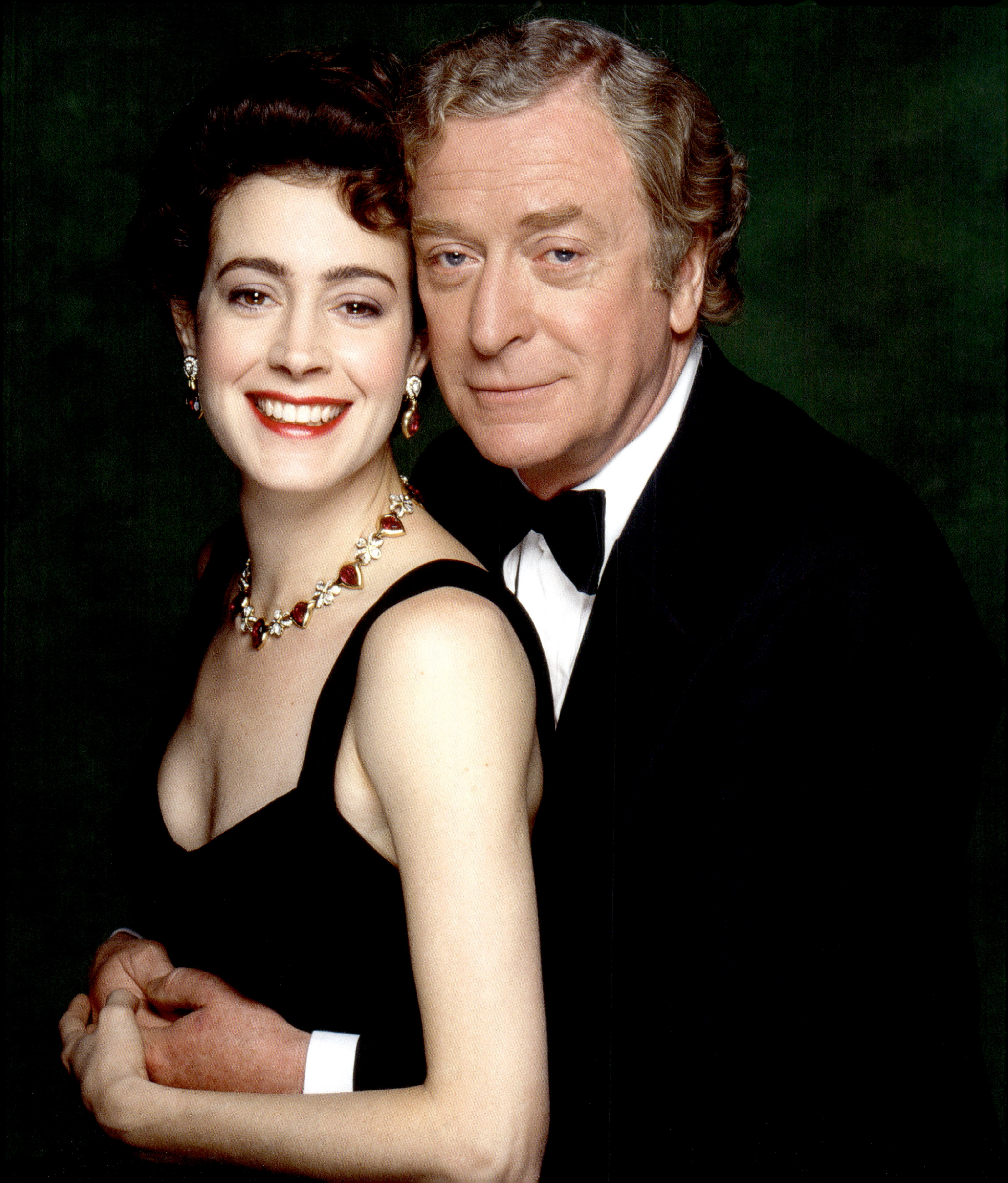

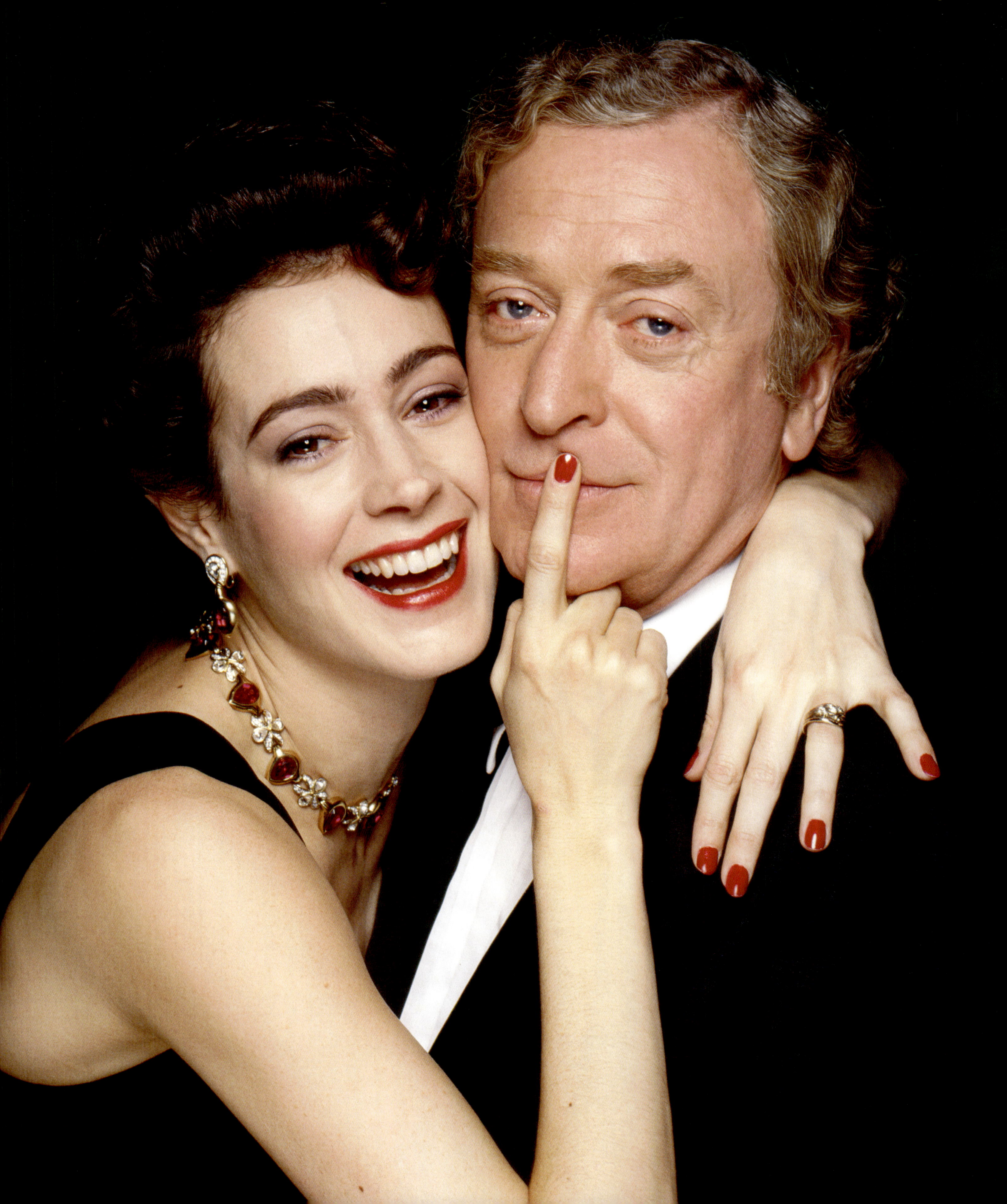

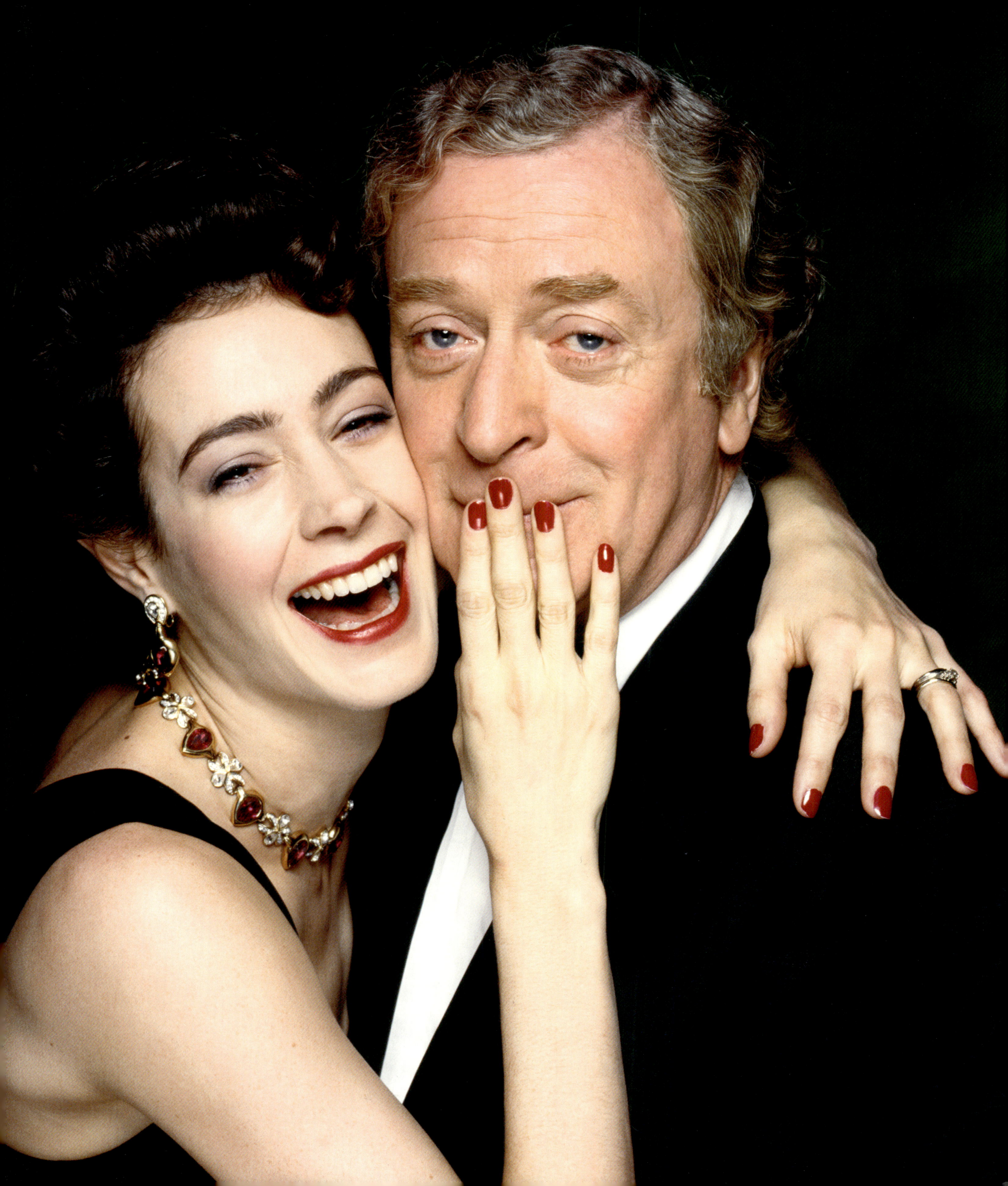

Russell Mulcahy settles on a straightforward narrative with occasional touches of noirish atmosphere… Caine skirts close to an aging Harry Palmer without directly evoking the earlier character.

Variety

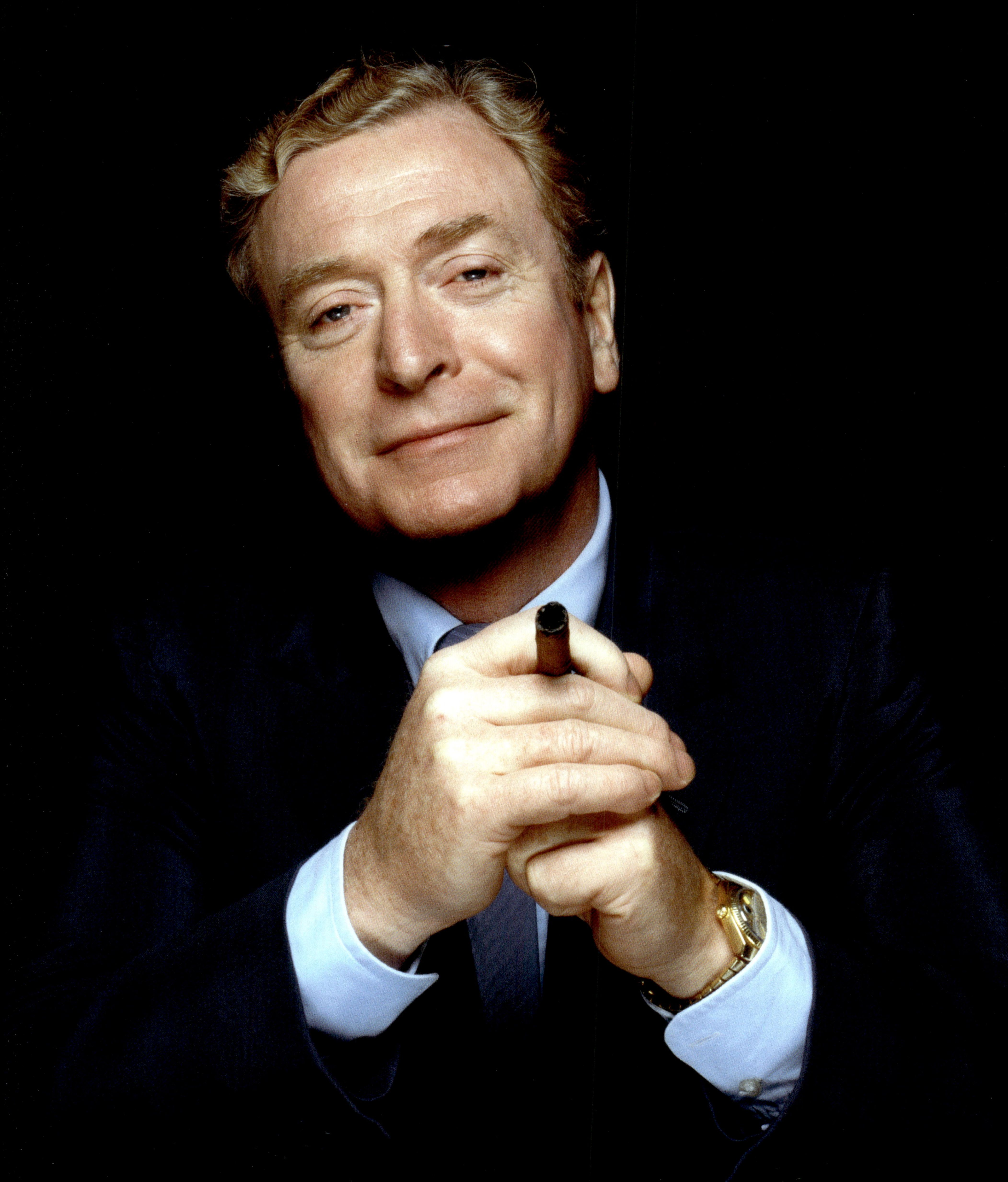

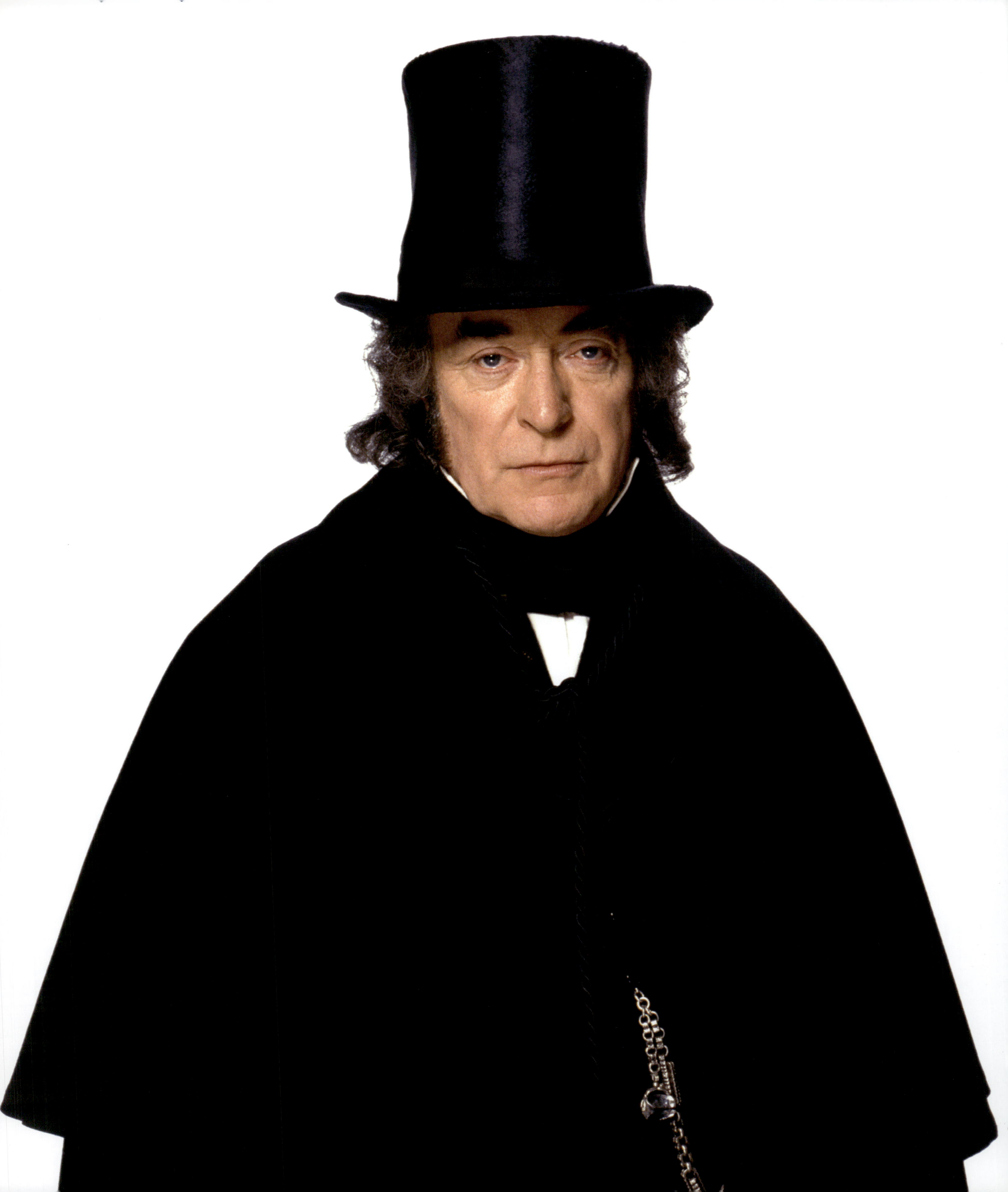

THE MUPPET CHRISTMAS CAROL

1992

"Scrooge's tough carapace fits well with familiar Caine characters and so it's all the more touching when that breaks."

The Muppets truly attained TV and film star status in the '70s and it's never really ebbed since. Created by Jim Henson in 1955, *The Muppet Show* placed film and pop culture stars in the company of character-led puppets. That combination is key to the charm of *The Muppet Christmas Carol*, which was Brian Henson's film directorial debut, having inherited the mantle from his late father, Jim Henson.

Henson recalls Caine telling him: "I'm going to play this like I'm working in the Royal Shakespeare Company. I will never wink, I will never do anything Muppety. I am going to play Scrooge as if it is an utterly dramatic role and there are no puppets around me." Henson replied: "Yes, bang on!"[1] Caine recalls "I had a wonderful time doing it, although I found it a very long process because the continuity is a nightmare. I loved working with the Muppeteers who are all very gentle souls and really do inhabit their characters and I found that I didn't have to change my style as an actor at all..."[2]

The film follows Dickens's story quite closely with Caine playing Scrooge and other roles portrayed by Muppet regulars: The Great Gonzo narrates as Charles Dickens, Miss Piggy (performed by *Dirty Rotten Scoundrels* director, Frank Oz) is Emily Cratchit and Kermit the Frog is Bob Cratchit; Statler makes a memorable Jacob Marley.

Scrooge's tough carapace fits well with familiar Caine characters and so it's all the more touching when that breaks. Ethan Warren notes: "...the outlandish presence of the Muppets enables him (Caine) to underplay Scrooge to subtle effects no other actor has been allowed, yielding the first instance of Scrooge's graveside repentance reading as genuine human tragedy rather than allegorical turning point."[3]

Previous page: Caine has a lifelong affection for Christmas and his performance as Scrooge is informed by this.
Opposite page: Stars of film and TV since the early 1970s, The Muppets were the creation of Jim Henson and his collaborators; *The Muppet Christmas Carol* now stands as one the greatest of all Muppet endeavours.

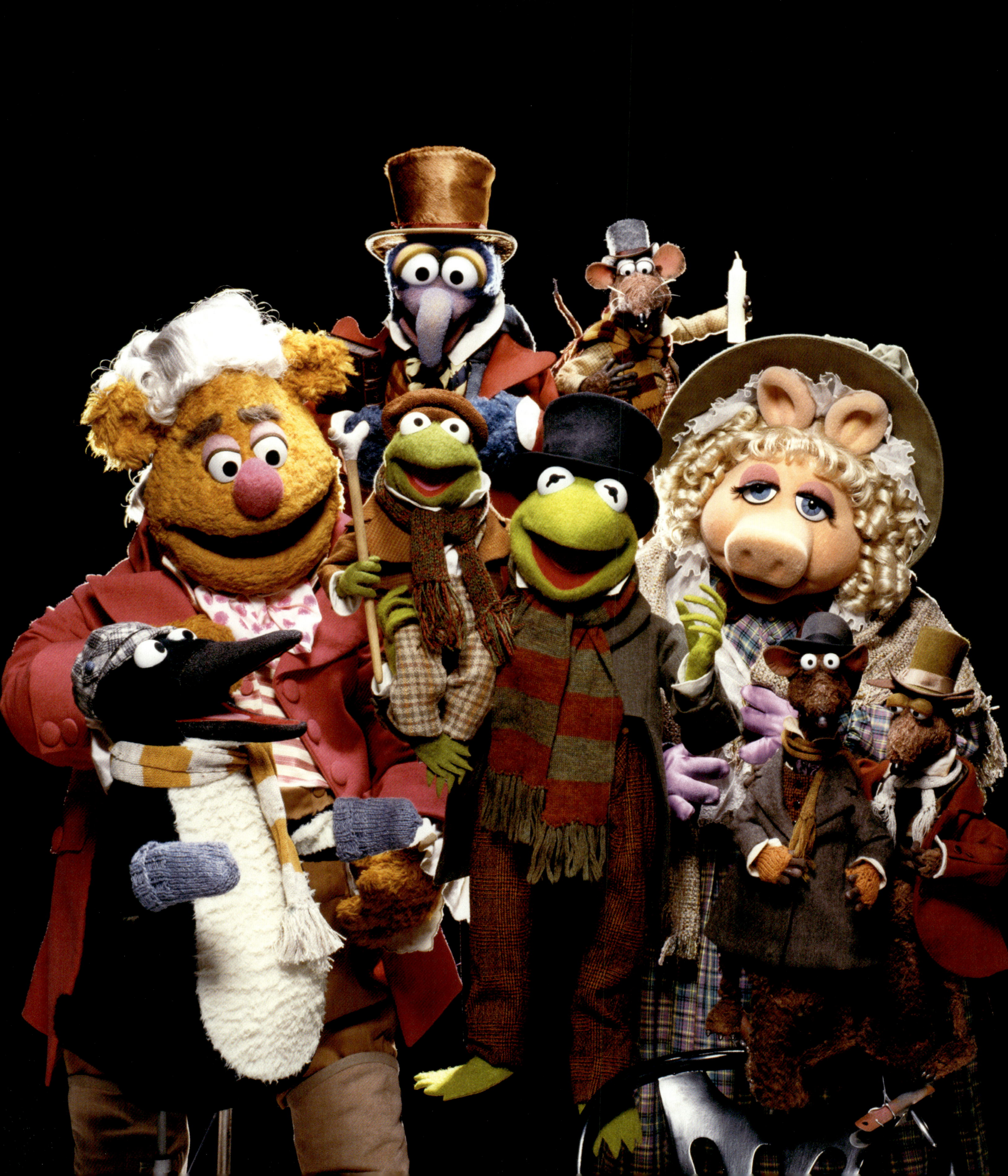

I'm going to play this like I'm working in the Royal Shakespeare Company. I will never wink, I will never do anything Muppety. I am going to play Scrooge as if it is an utterly dramatic role and there are no puppets around me.

Michael Caine

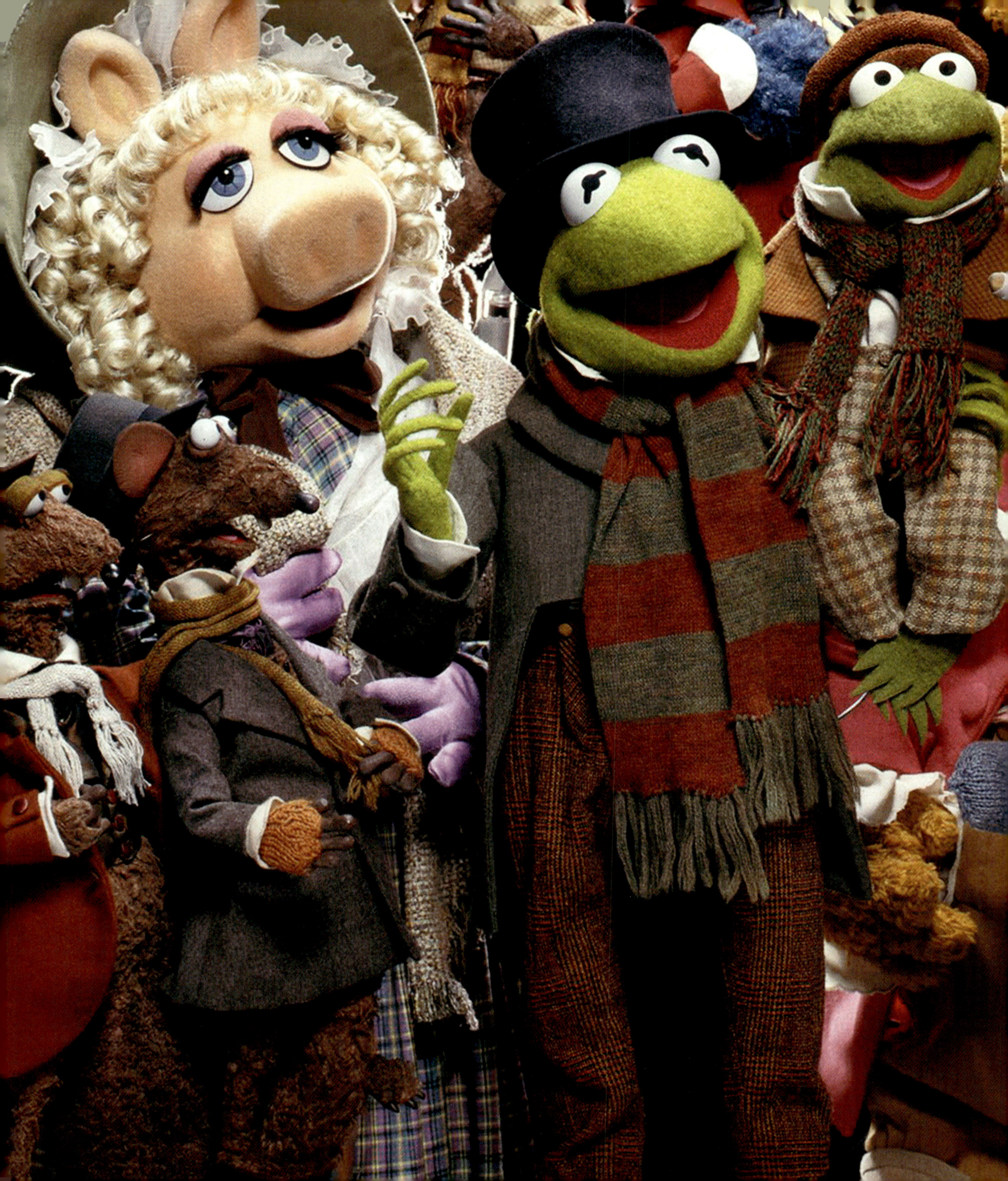

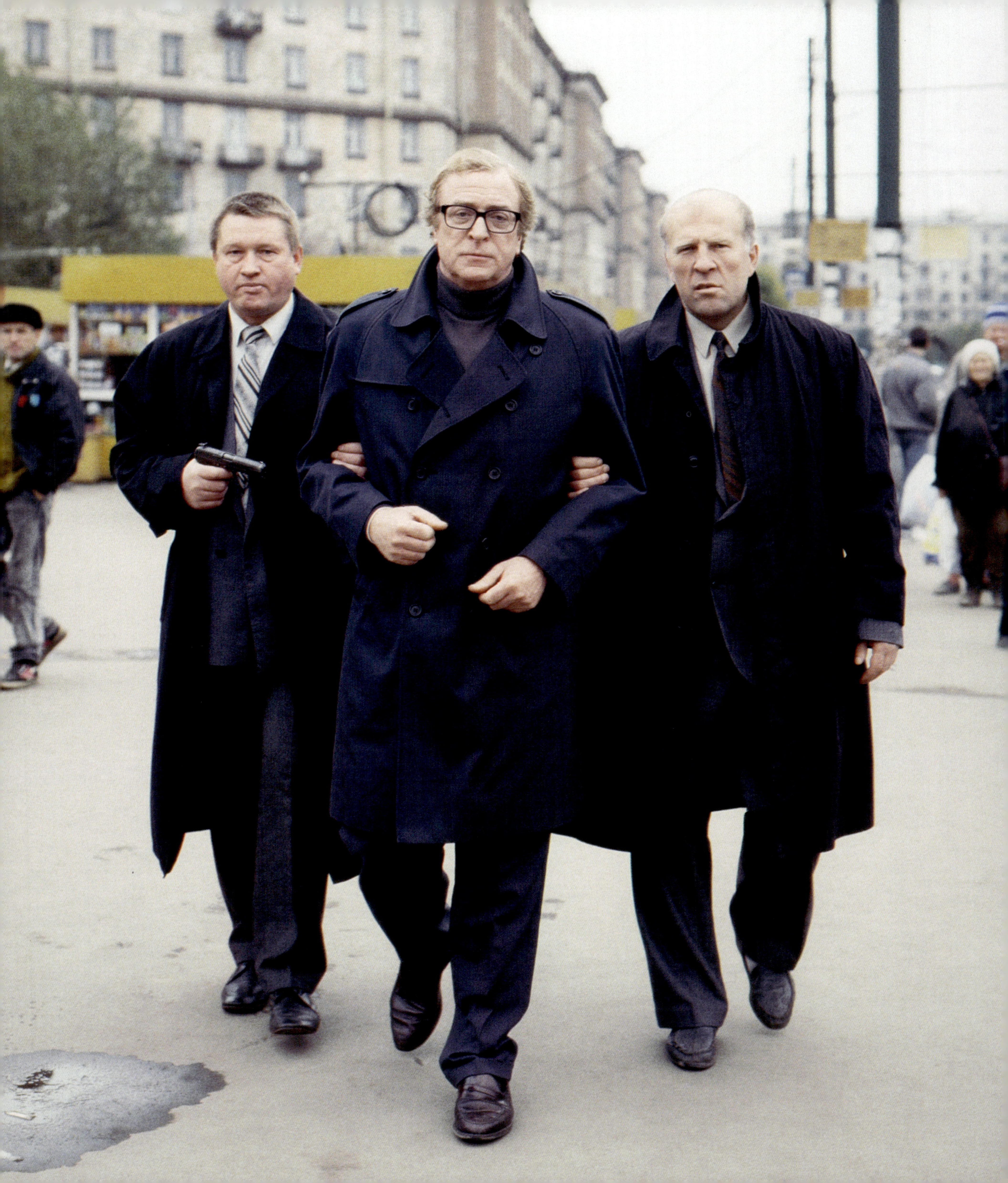

MIDNIGHT IN ST. PETERSBURG

1996

"For Caine, the difficult experience of these two 'late' entries into the Harry Palmer series proved to be a turning point in his career."

Certain characters become synonymous with actors and the working-class spy Harry Palmer certainly fulfilled that relationship for Caine. During the '60s Caine portrayed Harry Palmer in *The Ipcress File, Billion Dollar Brain* and *Funeral in Berlin*; he reprised the role in the mid-1990s in *Bullet to Beijing* and *Midnight in St. Petersburg*, which were shot back to back on a modest scale.

By Harry Palmer's final outing, in *Midnight in St. Petersburg*, he has retired from MI5 and heads up a private investigation team, including "Nick" (Jason Connery), on the hunt for stolen plutonium. Palmer's mission inevitably gets him into trouble as he comes up against the Russian mafia (Michael Gambon).

O'Neill's images of filming on location give a glimpse of the history and sights of St. Petersburg from the pre-Soviet golden-winged griffons guarding Bank Bridge over the Griboyedov canal, to the austere Stalinist-style House of Soviets and Lenin, pointing the way.

For Caine, the difficult experience of these two 'late' entries into the Harry Palmer series proved to be a turning point in his career: during filming Caine decided enough was enough. But, as is so often the case, the darkest hour comes before the dawn and Caine was persuaded out of retirement for a role opposite Jack Nicholson in Bob Rafelson's *Blood and Wine* (1997), winning him 'Best Actor' at the San Sebastián International Film Festival. This far more rewarding filming experience immediately 'resuscitated' and renewed Caine's energies for the subsequent twenty years. Indisputably the consummate screen actor, sometimes in character mode, sometimes as leading man, Caine has identified the secret to his longevity: "A film actor must be able to dream another person's dreams before he can call that character his own."[1]

Previous page: Caine returns to the character of Harry Palmer.
Opposite page: In a fitting connection to the spy and thriller traditions, Caine co-starred with Sean Connery's son, Jason Connery.

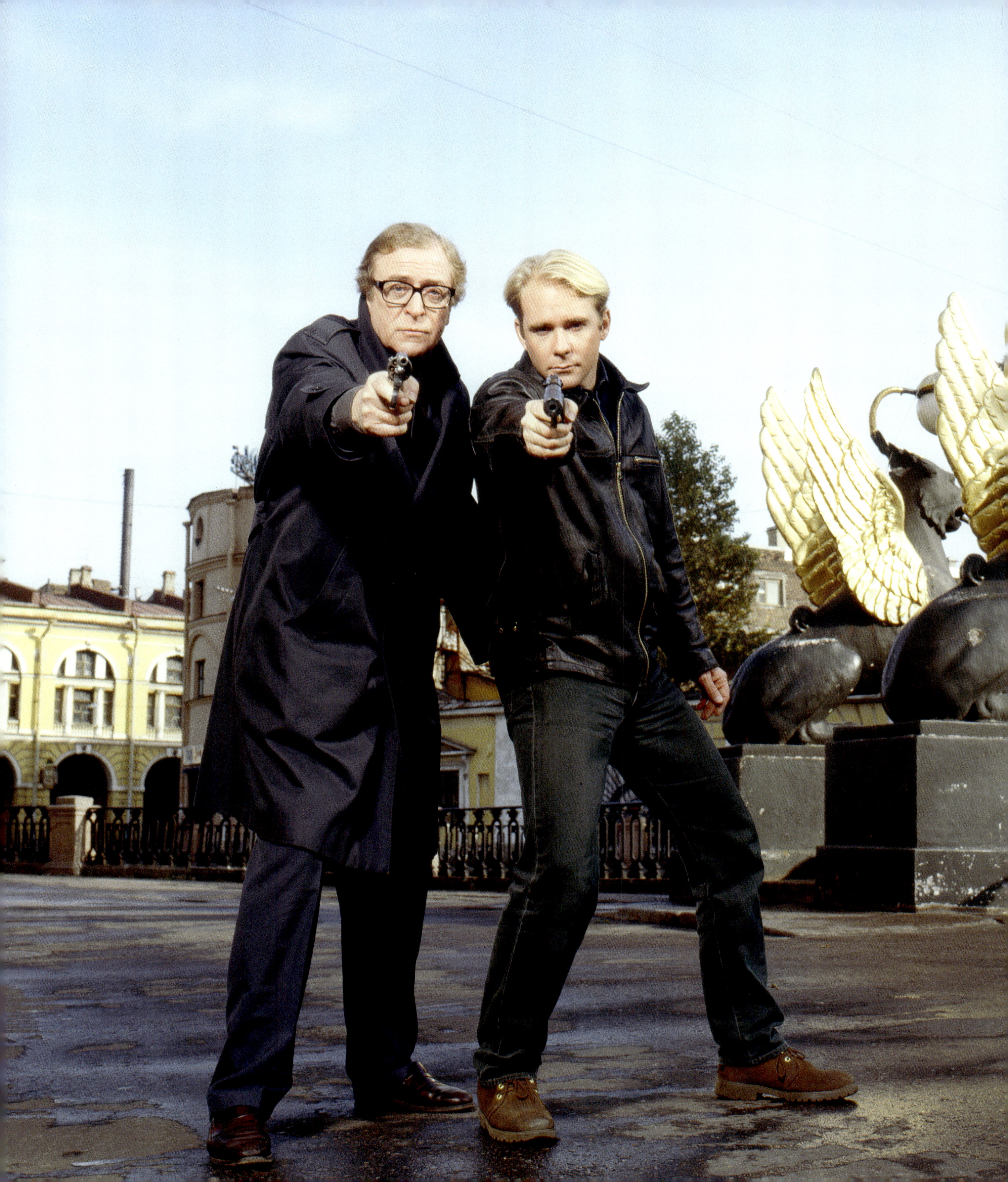

A film actor must be able to dream another person's dreams before he can call that character his own.

Michael Caine

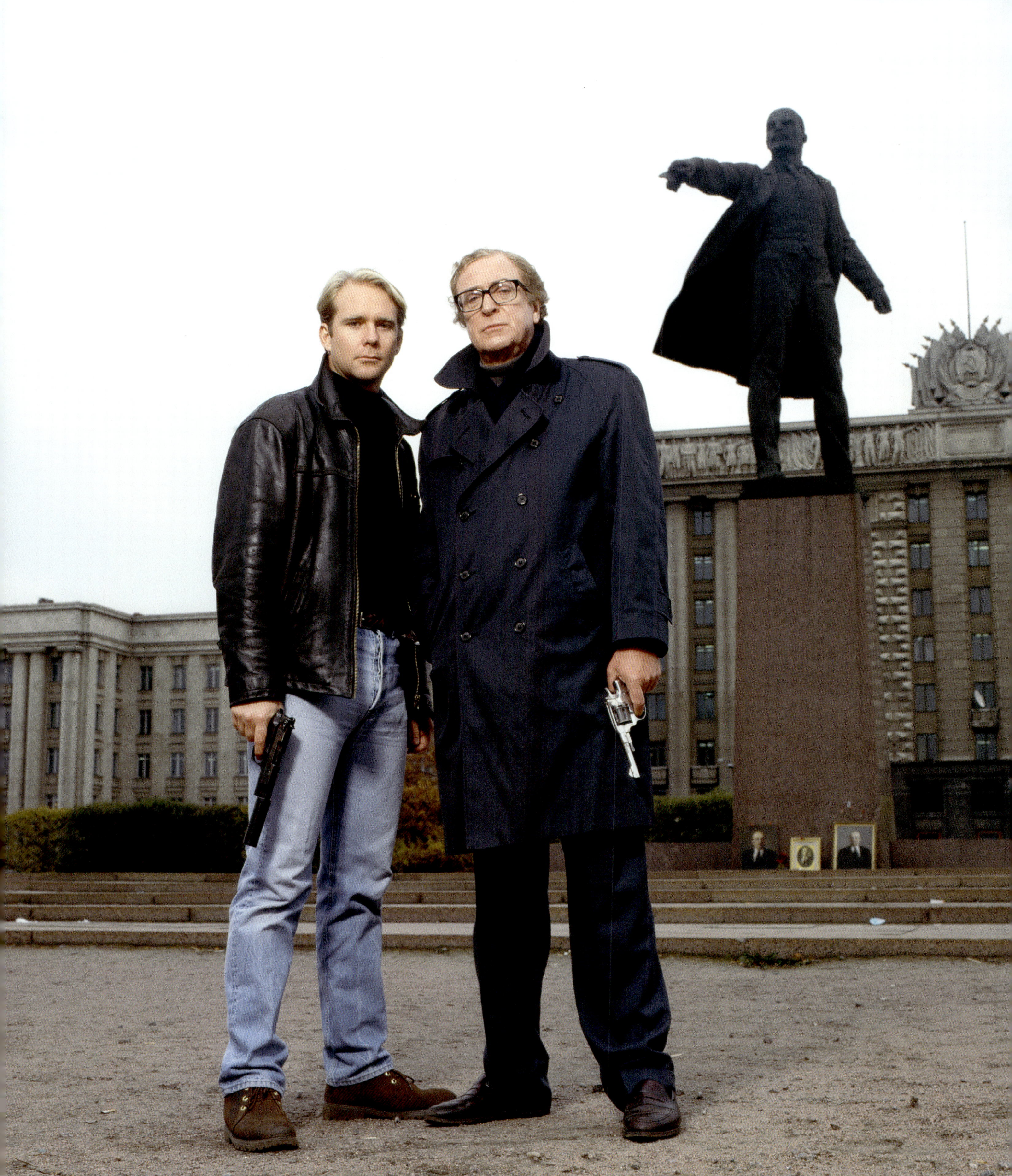

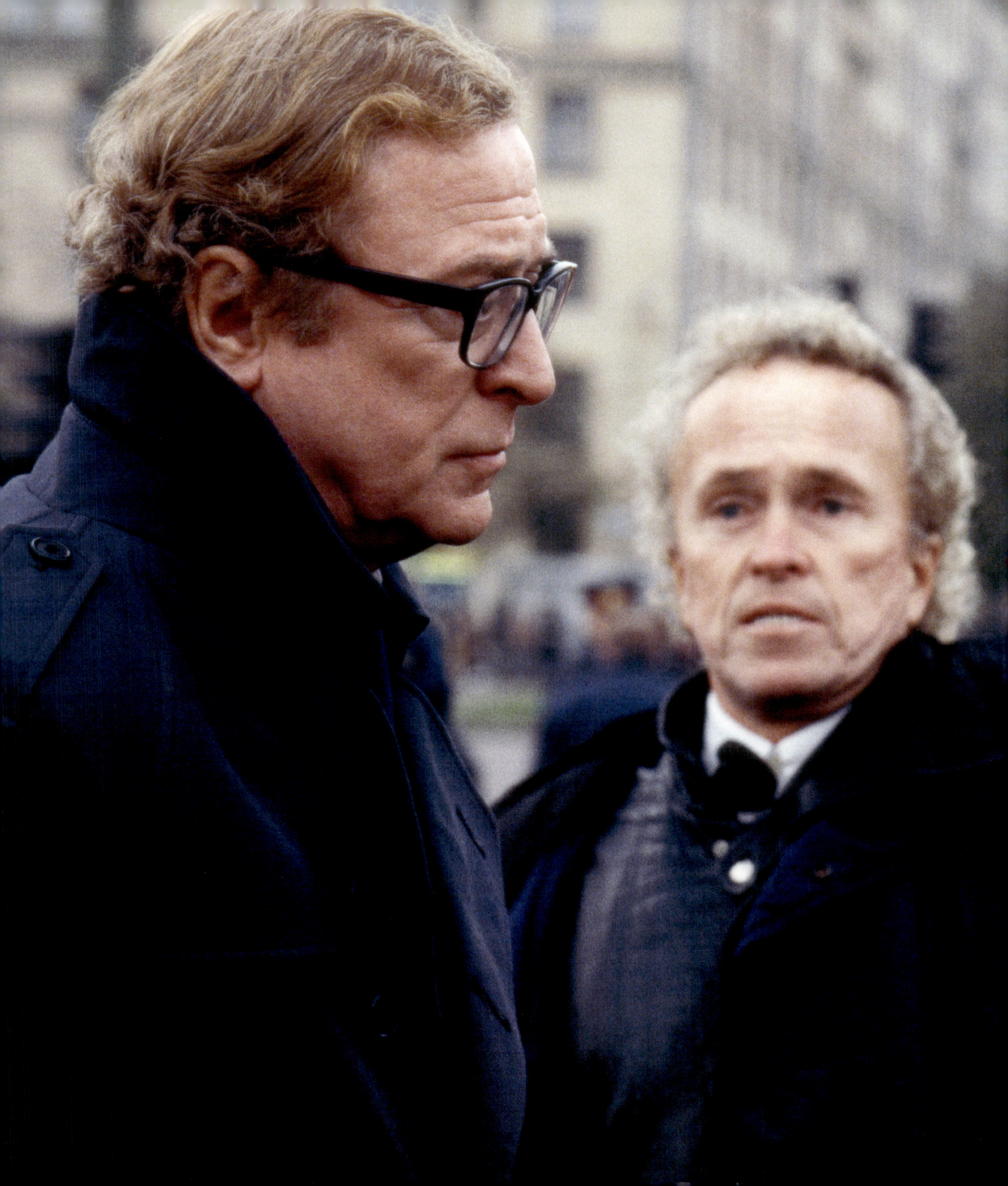

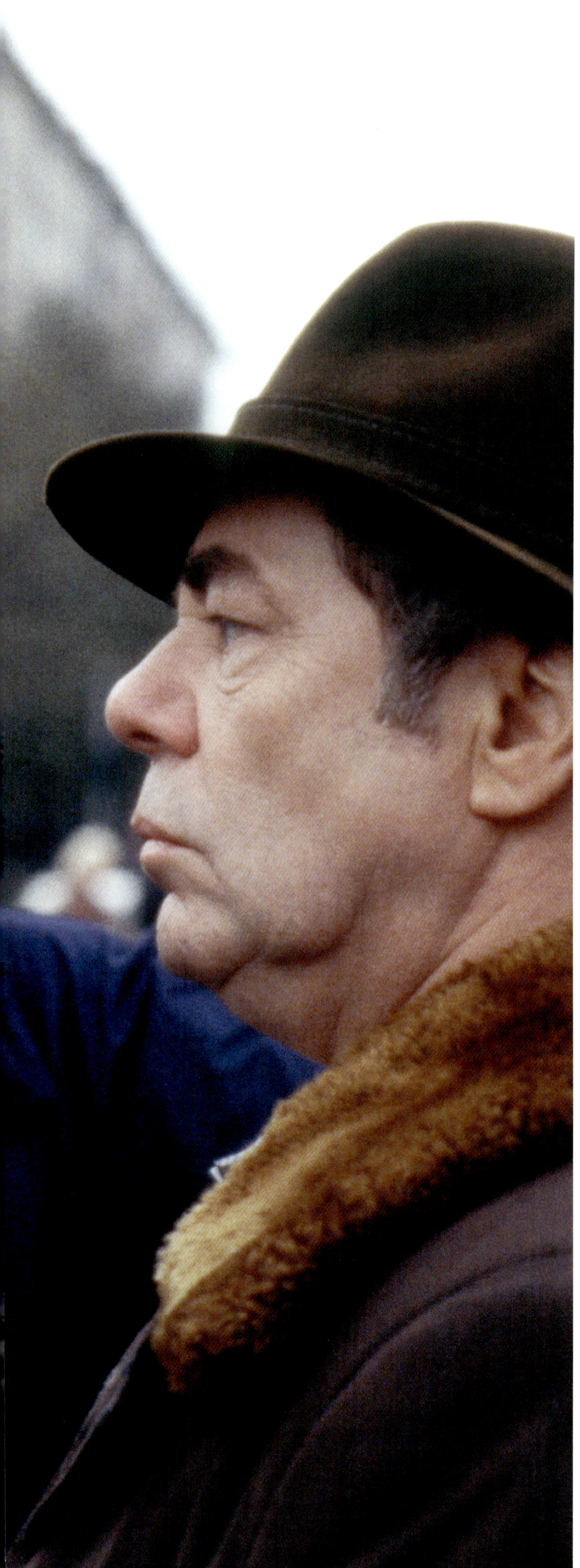

Previous page: Caine and Connery in front of the House of Soviets.
Left: The two 'Harry Palmer' films *Bullet to Beijing* and *Midnight in St. Petersburg* were shot back-to-back on location in St. Petersburg.

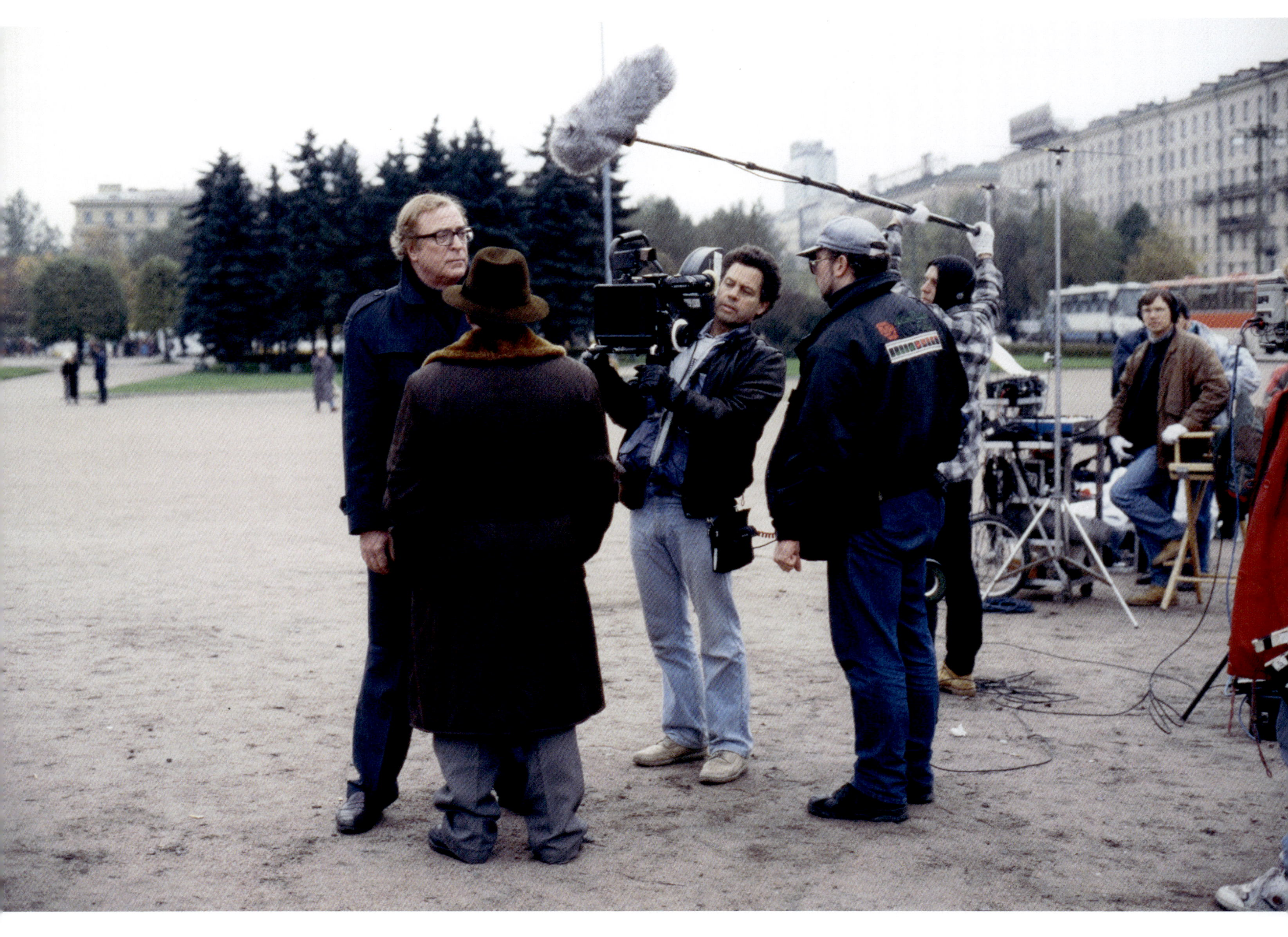

Above: Caine filming on location in St. Petersburg.

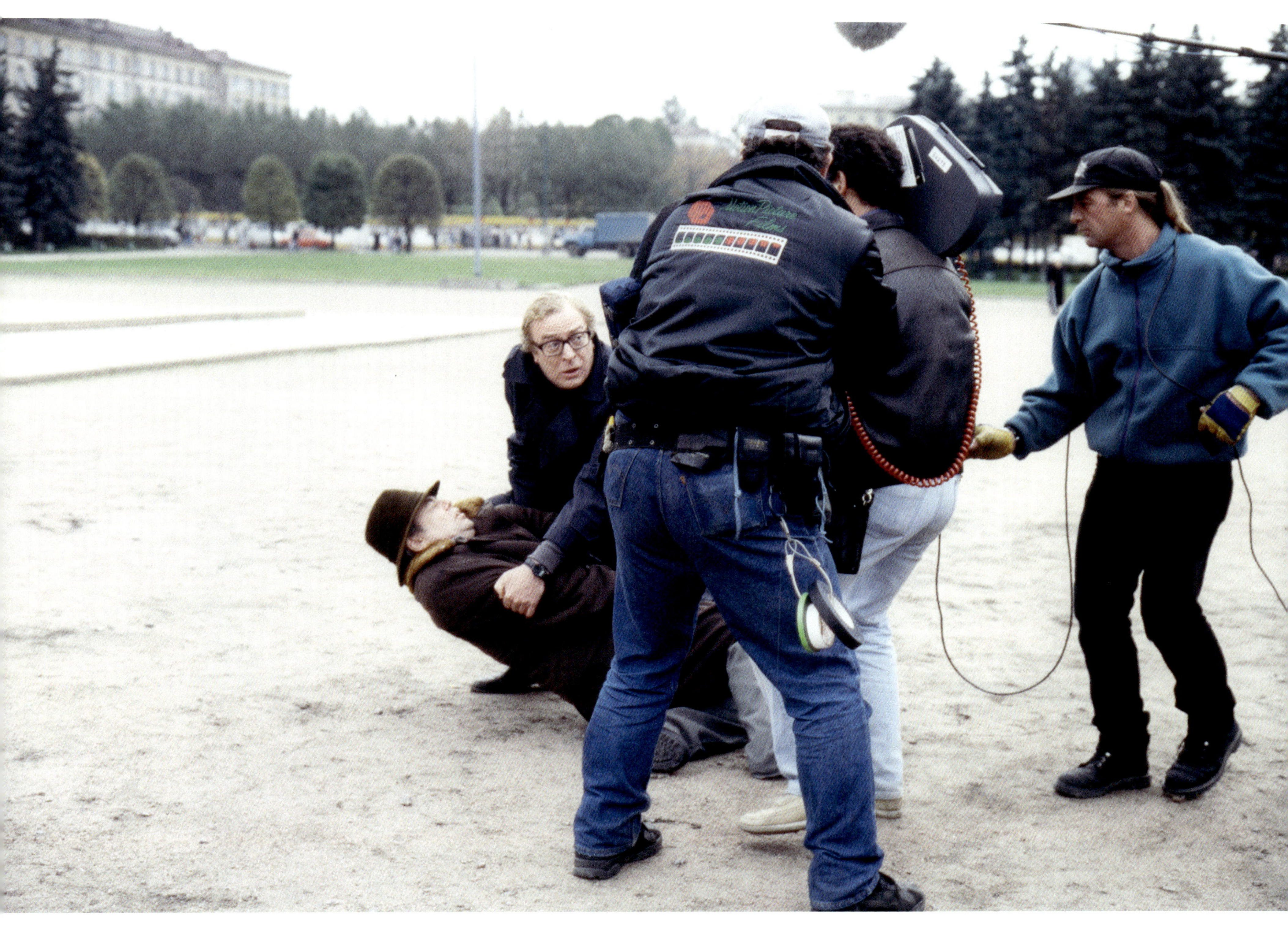

Following page: Caine has always found character moments within action scenes.

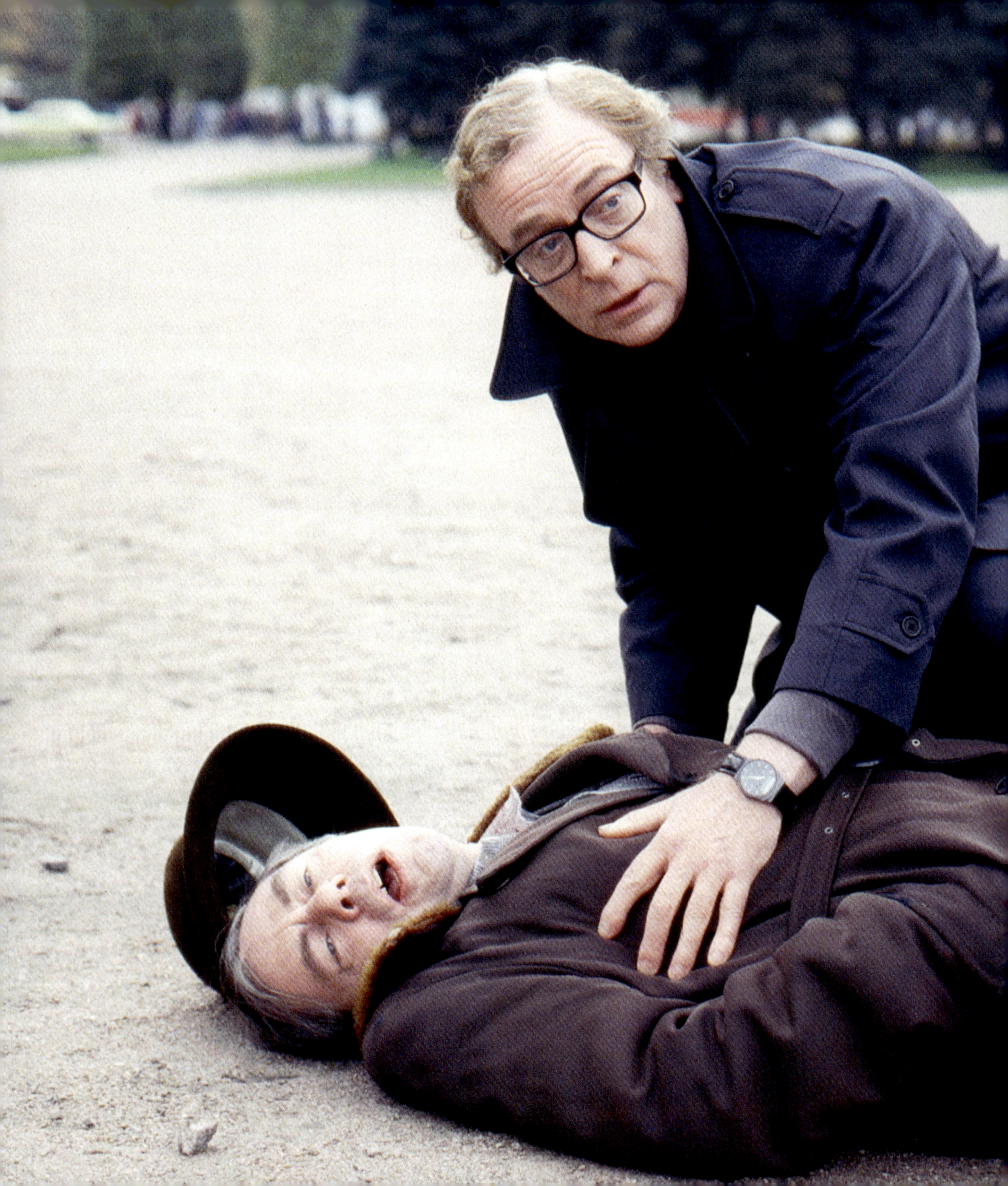

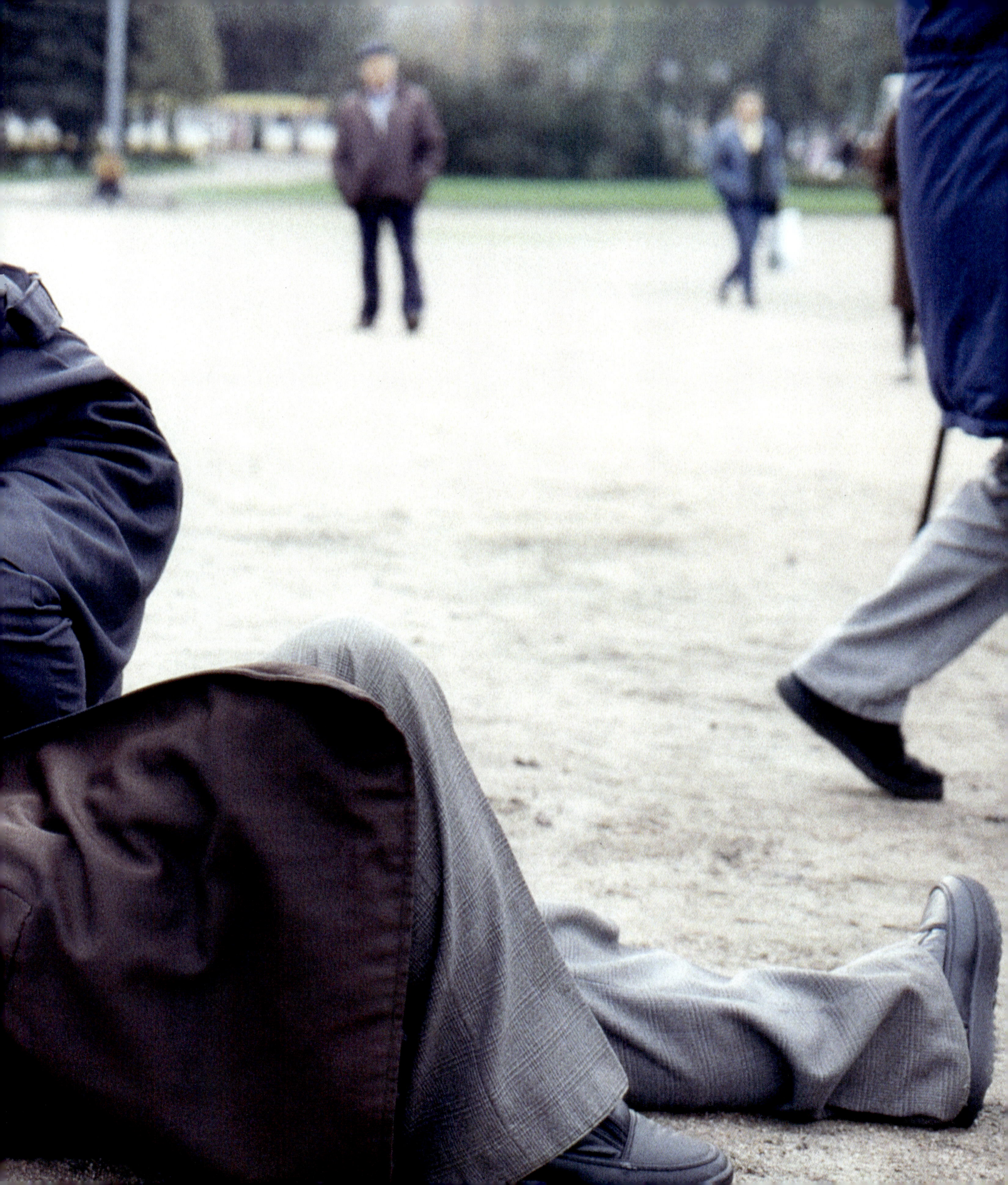

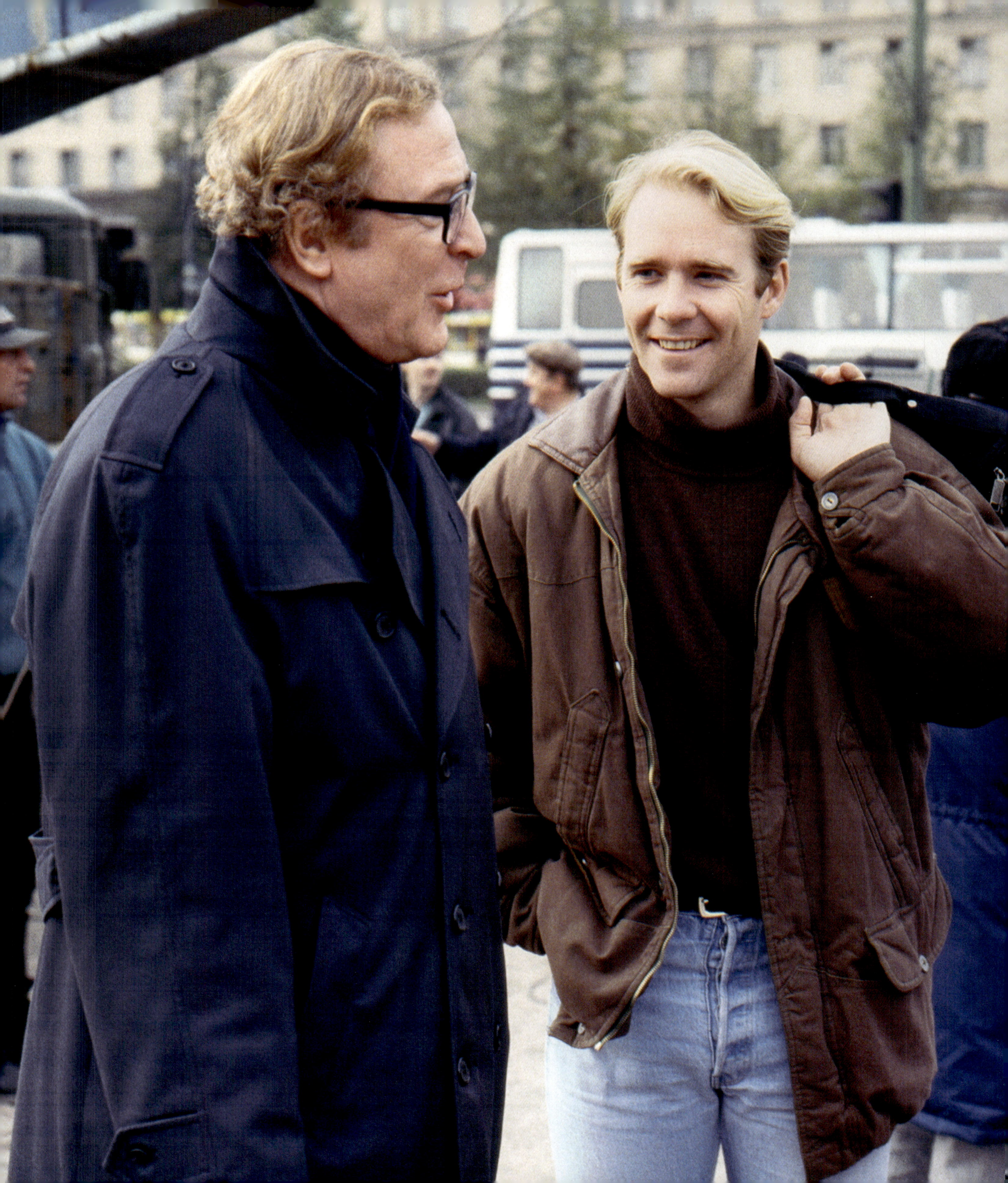

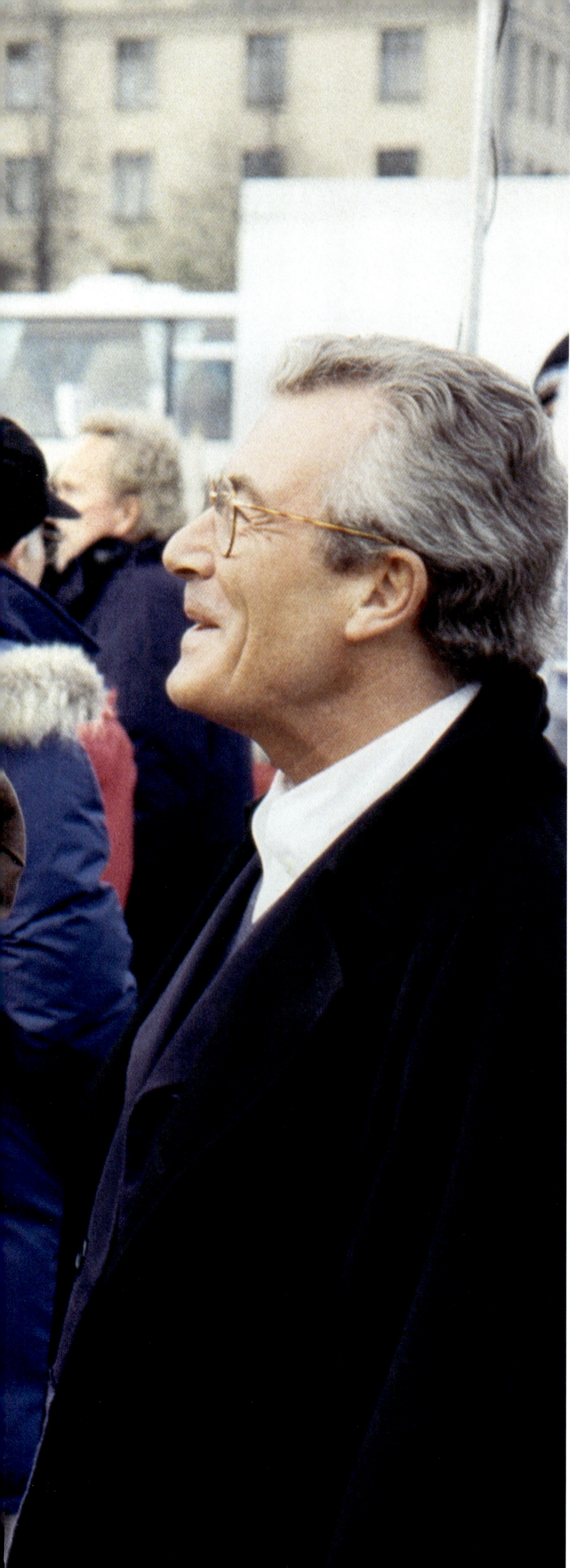

Caine, Jason Connery and Terry O'Neill on location in St. Petersburg.
Following page: O'Neill and Caine: lifelong pals.

ENDNOTES

MICHAEL CAINE: AS ICON

1. Ari Shapiro interviews Sir Michael Caine, *All Things Considered* radio programme, NPR, USA, 1 November 2018. Interview available at this link: (https://www.npr.org/2018/11/01/662710016/actor-michael-caine-85-on-his-long-career-the-alternative-was-a-factory?ft=nprml&f=)
2. Michael Caine, *Acting in Film, An Actor's Take on Movie Making*, Revised Expanded Edition, Applause Theatre Book Publishers New York, London, 1997, p.xiii.
3. Michael Caine, *Acting in Film, An Actor's Take on Movie Making*, Revised Expanded Edition, Applause Theatre Book Publishers New York, London, 1997, p.xiv.
4. Michael Hogan, 'Interview. Michael Caine: 'What ruined the 60s was drugs', *The Guardian*, 10 March 2018.
5. Michael Caine, *Acting in Film, An Actor's Take on Movie Making*, Revised Expanded Edition, Applause Theatre Book Publishers New York, London, 1997, p.4.
6. Jonathon Ross interviews Michael Caine, 'Michael Caine: "I was a loser until I started playing losers" ', *Radio Times*, 20 October 2018.
7. David Parkinson, 'Michael Caine: 10 Essential Films', BFI online, 14 March 2018. (https://www2.bfi.org.uk/news-opinion/news-bfi/lists/michael-caine-10-essential-films)
8. Robin Stummer, 'Len Deighton's Observer cookstrips, Michael Caine and the 1960s', *The Guardian*, 14 December 2014.
9. Faye Fearon, 'Five Essential items to steal from Michael Caine's 1960s wardrobe', GQ magazine, 16 March 2020.
10. Michael Caine, *Acting in Film, An Actor's Take on Movie Making*, Revised Expanded Edition, Applause Theatre Book Publishers New York, London, 1997, p.xx.
11. Michael Caine, *The Elephant to Hollywood*, Hodder & Stoughton, 2010, p245.
12. Michael Parkinson interviews Sir Michael Caine, BBC, 2002.
13. Michael Caine page, imbd.com.

TERRY O'NEILL: POP CULTURE IMAGE MAKER

1. Ruth Huntman, interview for 'This Much I Know', *The Guardian*, 23 June 2018.
2. Terry O'Neill quoted by Ellen Millard, 'Terry O'Neill on a Life Behind the Lens', 27 November 2018, Luxury London online. (https://luxurylondon.co.uk/culture/art/terry-oneill-photographer-interview)
3. Terry O'Neill quoted by Ellen Millard, 'Terry O'Neill on a Life Behind the Lens', Luxury London online, 27 November 2018. (https://luxurylondon.co.uk/culture/art/terry-oneill-photographer-interview)
4. Terry O'Neill quoted in his obituary, 'Swinging Sixties Photograph Terry O'Neill dies of prostate cancer, aged 81', *The Daily Telegraph*, 17 November 2019.
5. Terry O'Neill in conversation with Iconic Images, for 'Iconic Spotlight' online, 15 November 2018. (https://iconicimages.net/news/iconic-spotlight-ursula-andress-terry-oneill/)
6. Lucy Davies, 'Interview with Terry O'Neill', *The Telegraph*, 14 January 2014.
7. Magazine cutting, Iconic Images archive, publication unknown.
8. Terry O'Neill in conversation with Christies in 2016, quoted in 'Studio Visit', Christies online, 18 November 2019. (www.christies.com/features/Terry-O-Neill-My-life-in-pictures-7647-3.aspx)
9. Terry O'Neill in conversation with Iconic Images, for 'Iconic Spotlight' online.
10. Terry O'Neill quoted in 'Terry O'Neill: 'A Life in Pictures', *The Guardian*, 17 November 2019.

MICHAEL AND TERRY: COLLABORATORS AND FRIENDS

1. Michael Caine, *The Elephant to Hollywood*, Hodder & Stoughton, 2010, p287.
2. Terry O'Neill in conversation with Iconic Images, for 'Iconic Spotlight' online, 2 March 2017. (https://iconicimages.net/news/iconic-spotlight-terry-oneill-funeral-berlin/)
3. Terry O'Neill in conversation with Iconic Images, for 'Iconic Spotlight' online, 2 March 2017. (https://iconicimages.net/news/iconic-spotlight-terry-oneill-funeral-berlin/)

FUNERAL IN BERLIN (1966)

1. Michael Caine, *The Elephant to Hollywood*, Hodder & Stoughton, 2010, p.39.
2. Caine voice over on *Man at the Wall*, a short promotional film about the making of *Funeral in Berlin*.
3. 'Interview with Michael Caine', *Uncut* magazine, 18 January 2006.
4. Alan Burton, 'Jumping on the Bandwagon: The Spy Cycle in British Cinema in the 1960s', *The Journal of British Cinema and Television*, July 2018, vol. 15, No 3: pp. 328-356.
5. 'Review of *Funeral in Berlin*', *Variety*, 31 December 1966.
6. Michael Caine, *The Elephant to Hollywood*, Hodder & Stoughton, 2010, p.130.

WOMAN TIMES SEVEN (1967)

1. Michael Caine, *The Elephant to Hollywood*, Hodder & Stoughton, 2010, p.136.
2. Michael Caine, *The Elephant to Hollywood*, Hodder & Stoughton, 2010, p.6.

DEADFALL (1968)

1. Michael Caine, *The Elephant to Hollywood*, Hodder & Stoughton, 2010, p.136.

THE MAGUS (1968)

1. *The Elephant to Hollywood*, Hodder & Stoughton, 2010, p.292.
2. 'Review of *The Magus*', *Variety*, 31 December 1968.
3. Renata Adler, 'Screen: "The Magus", with Michael Caine, Opens', *The New York Times*, 11 December 1968.
4. Nick Dybek, '"The Magus": A Thrilling, Chilling Guilty Pleasure', 30 April 2012, npr.org (https://www.npr.org/2012/08/27/150727161/the-magus-a-thrilling-chilling-guilty-pleasure?t=1611247499264)

GET CARTER (1971)

1. William Hall, *Sir Michael Caine: The Biography*, John Blake Publishing, 2006, p.151.
2. David Parkinson, 'Michael Caine: 10 Essential Films', BFI online. (https://www2.bfi.org.uk/news-opinion/news-bfi/lists/michael-caine-10-essential-films)
3. Andrew Spicer, 'Profile of Mike Hodges', BFI Screenonline. (http://www.screenonline.org.uk/people/id/479789/index.html)
4. *The Elephant to Hollywood*, Hodder & Stoughton, 2010, p.148.
5. Roger Ebert, 'Reviews *Get Carter*', rogerebert.com, 15 March 1971. (https://www.rogerebert.com/reviews/get-carter-1971)
6. Michael Caine, *The Elephant to Hollywood*, Hodder & Stoughton, 2010, p324.
7. Sue Harper and Justin Smith, *British Film Culture in the 1970s: The Boundaries of Pleasure*, Edinburgh University Press, 2012.

MONA LISA (1986)

1. David Parkinson, 'Michael Caine: 10 essential films', BFI online, 14 March 2018. (https://www2.bfi.org.uk/news-opinion/news-bfi/lists/michael-caine-10-essential-films)
2. All Neil Jordan quotes in this chapter: James Clarke, telephone conversation with Neil Jordan, September 2020.
3. Review of *Mona Lisa*, *Time Out*, August 1986, now available online: (https://www.timeout.com/movies/mona-lisa)
4. Pauline Kael, review of *Get Carter* in *5001 Nights at the Movies: A Guide from A to Z*, Holt, Rhinehart and Winston, First Edition, 1985, quoted by Sven Mikulec in 'Get Carter: Why Mike Hodges' Uncompromising Gangster Film Gained Cult Following', Cinephilia & Beyond. (https://cinephiliabeyond.org/get-carter-why-mike-hodges-uncompromising-gangster-film-gained-cult-following/)

THE FOURTH PROTOCOL (1987)

1. Bobby Wygant interviews Michael Caine about "The Fourth Protocol", The Bobbie Wygant Archive, 1987. (https://www.youtube.com/watch?v=-4Fif-XPq_I)
2. Roger Ebert, 'Reviews *The Fourth Protocol*', rogerebert.com, 28 August 1987. (https://www.rogerebert.com/reviews/the-fourth-protocol-1987)

WITHOUT A CLUE (1988)

1. Roger Ebert, 'Interviews: Michael Caine on the trail of Holmes', rogerebert.com, 21 February 1988. (https://www.rogerebert.com/interviews/michael-caine-on-the-trail-of-holmes)
2. Roger Ebert, 'Reviews *Without a Clue*', rogerebert.com, 21 October 1988. (https://www.rogerebert.com/reviews/without-a-clue-1988)
3. Louise Bernikow, 'Sherlock Who?' *Premiere* magazine, November 1988.
4. Louise Bernikow, 'Sherlock Who?' *Premiere* magazine, November 1988.

DIRTY ROTTEN SCOUNDRELS (1988)

1. Michael Caine, *The Elephant to Hollywood*, Hodder & Stoughton, 2010, p.223.
2. Vincent Canby, 'Review/Film; A Way With Wealthy Women', *The New York Times*, 14 December 1988.
3. Roger Ebert, 'Reviews *Dirty Rotten Scoundrels*', rogerebert.com, 14 December 1988. (https://www.rogerebert.com/reviews/dirty-rotten-scoundrels-1988)
4. Sonia Taitz, 'FILM; In the Land of This Oz, Character Is King', *The New York Times*, 25 December 1988.
5. Sonia Taitz, 'FILM; In the Land of This Oz, Character Is King', *The New York Times*, 25 December 1988.

BLUE ICE (1992)

1. Derek Elley, 'Blue Ice', *Variety*, 14 October 1992. (https://variety.com/1992/film/reviews/blue-ice-1200430811/)
2. Paul Rowlands, 'An Interview with Russell Mulcahy', money-into-light.com, 2016. (http://www.money-into-light.com/2016/07/an-interview-with-russell-mulcahy-part_30.html)
3. Chris Willman, 'Profile: Sean Young', *The Los Angeles Times*, 17 May 1992. (https://www.latimes.com/archives/la-xpm-1992-05-17-ca-173-story.html)

THE MUPPET CHRISTMAS CAROL (1992)

1. Brian Henson, quoted by Ben Beaumont-Thomas in 'How we made: The Muppet Christmas Carol', *The Guardian*, 21 December 2015.
2. Michael Caine, *The Elephant to Hollywood*, Hodder & Stoughton, 2010, p.243.
3. Ethan Warren, 'A Grand Yuletide Theory: *The Muppet Christmas Carol* is the Best Adaptation of *A Christmas Carol*', brightwalldarkroom.com, 20 December 2019. (https://www.brightwalldarkroom.com/2019/12/20/a-grand-yuletide-theory-the-muppet-christmas-carol-is-the-best-adaptation-of-a-christmas-carol/)

MIDNIGHT IN ST. PETERSBURG (1996)

1. Michael Caine, *Acting in Film, An Actor's Take on Movie Making*, Revised Expanded Edition, Applause Theatre Book Publishers New York, London, 1997, p.3.

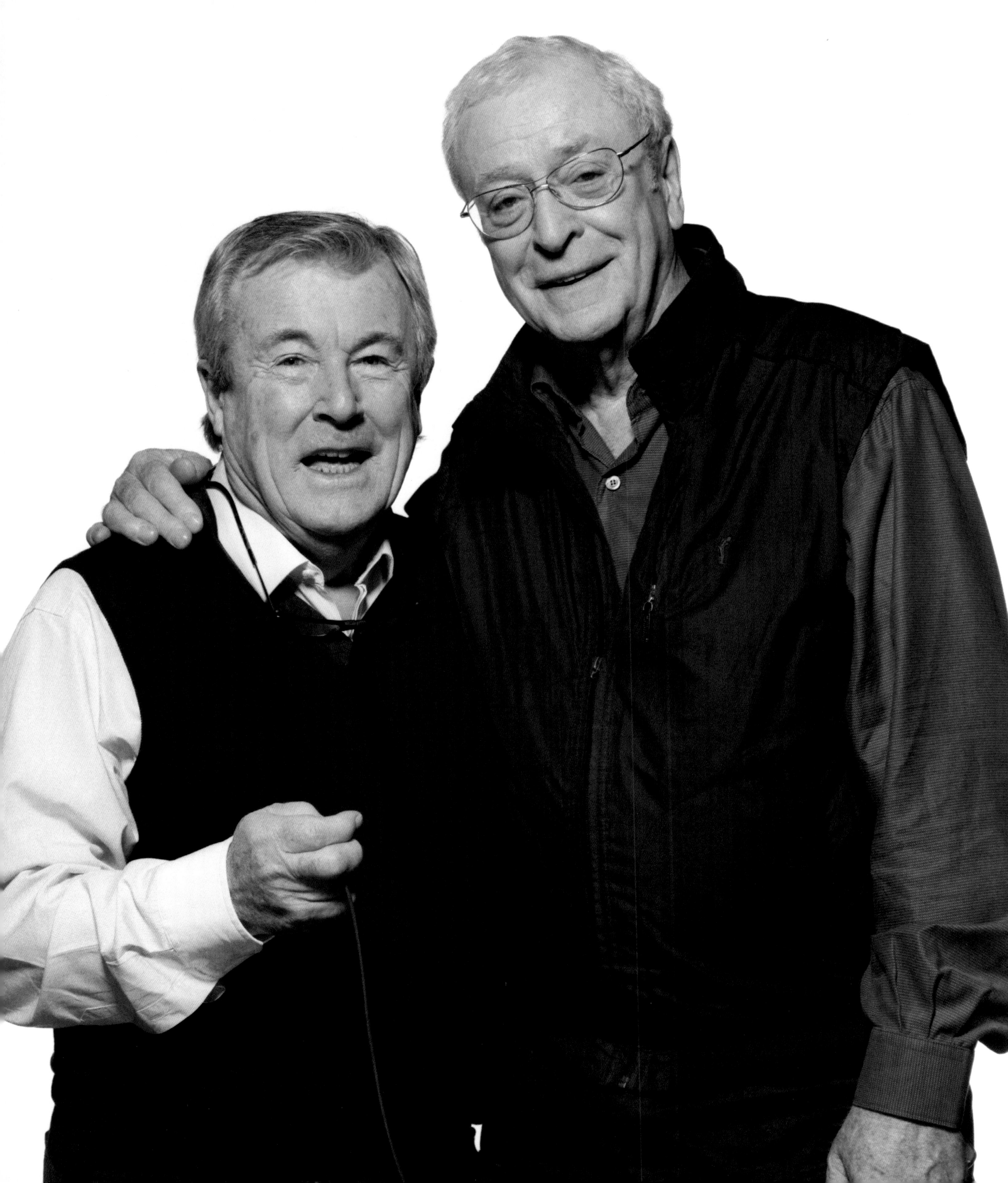

This book is dedicated to the late John Sheppard; he was a schoolteacher of mine and died in autumn 2020. John loved acting and theatre and, a very long time ago, he encouraged a bunch of us to get out there and play our part.

ACKNOWLEDGEMENTS

Big thanks and a virtual hug during these pandemic times to Carrie Kania for the opportunity for another adventure in writing about movies and photography. Thanks, too, to Adam Powell at Iconic Images and Susannah Hecht and Craig Holden at ACC Art Books, it has been so very good to work with you all. And, of course, thanks to James Smith for the chance to write for ACC Art Books again.

James Clarke

JAMES CLARKE

James Clarke is the author of numerous books on and about the world of film, including *The Year of The Geek; The Virgin Film Guide: War Films; The Virgin Film Guide: Coppola; Bodies in Heroic Motion: The Cinema of James Cameron*; and as a contributor to *Through Her Lens: The Stories Behind the Photography of Eva Sereny*. Clarke writes for *Little White Lies* and has been published in *Empire, Moviescope, Sci Fi Now, 3D World* and *3D Artist* magazines. Clarke currently teaches on the MA Screenwriting course at the London Film School.

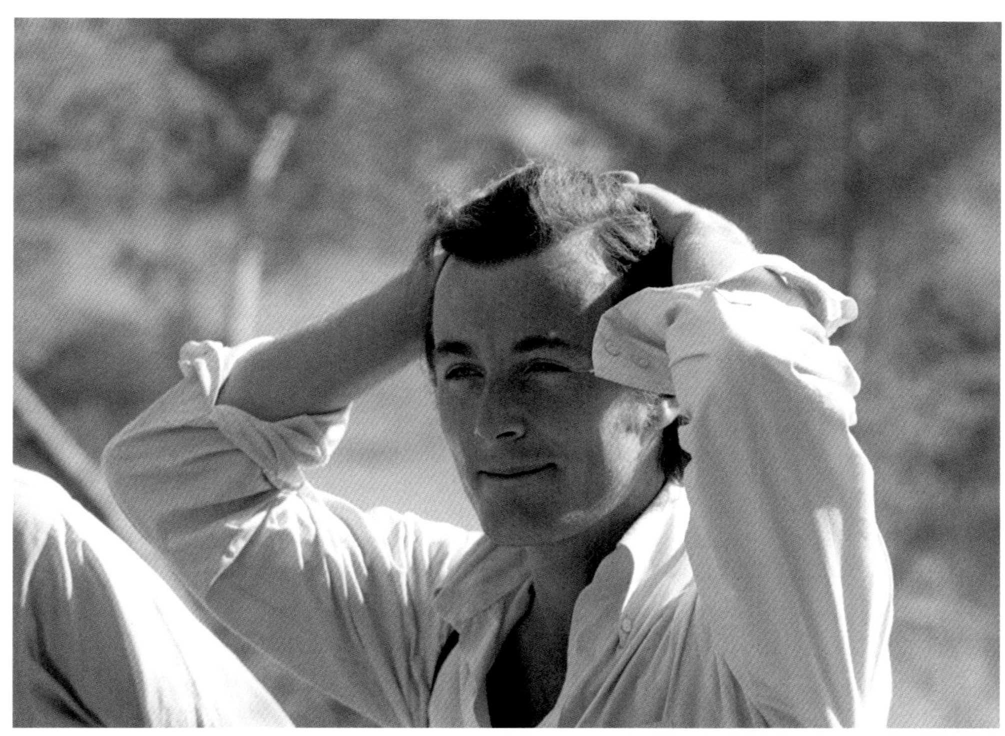

TERRY O'NEILL

Terry O'Neill CBE is one of the world's most collected photographers, with work hanging in national art galleries and private collections worldwide. From presidents to pop stars, he photographed the frontline of fame for over six decades. O'Neill began his career at the birth of the 1960s. While other photographers concentrated on earthquakes, wars and politics, O'Neill realised that youth culture was a breaking news story on a global scale and began chronicling the emerging faces of film, fashion and music who would go on to define the Swinging Sixties. By 1965 he was being commissioned by the biggest magazines and newspapers in the world. Few photographers have embraced the span of fame like O'Neill, capturing the icons of an era, from Winston Churchill to Nelson Mandela, and Frank Sinatra and Elvis to Amy Winehouse, Audrey Hepburn and Brigitte Bardot. He photographed The Beatles and The Rolling Stones when they were still struggling young bands in 1963, and pioneered backstage reportage photography with David Bowie, Elton John, The Who, Eric Clapton and Chuck Berry. His images adorned historic rock albums, movie posters and international magazine covers. In amongst the rock stars and politicians, he also turned his lens on James Bond, shooting onset and behind the scenes on several landmark films in the 007 series.

In 2012 Terry O'Neill was awarded the Royal Society of Arts' highest honour, the Centenary Medal. He received a CBE just a few months before he passed away in November 2019.

ISBN: 978 178884 117 7

British Library Cataloguing-in-Publication Data
A catalogue record for this book is available from the British Library

—

Front cover: Michael Caine in *Funeral in Berlin*, 1966.
Back cover: Michael Caine in *Get Carter*, 1971.
Frontispiece: Caine in his iconic role as Jack Carter in *Get Carter*.
Page 5: Present by his absence: the accoutrements of stardom glasses and a cigar on a chair on-set.

—

Design: Craig Holden

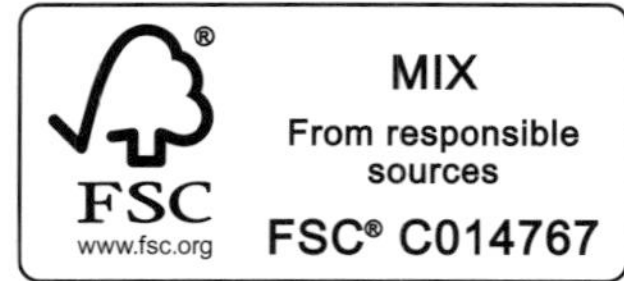

Printed in Belgium
for ACC Art Books Ltd., Woodbridge, Suffolk, England

www.accartbooks.com

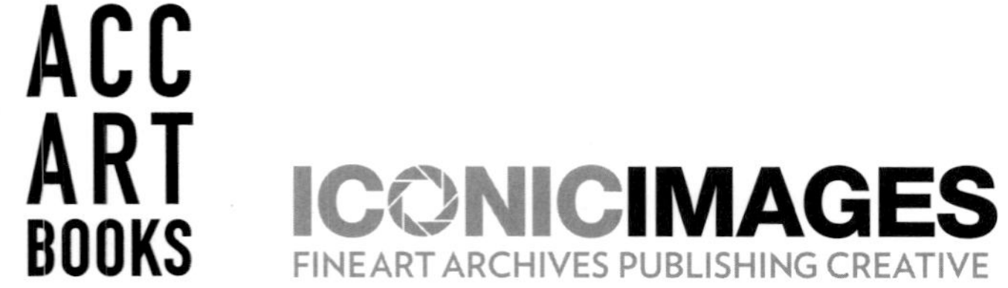